The New Global Brands

Managing Non-Government Organizations in the 21st Century

The New Global Brands

Managing Non-Government Organizations in the 21st Century

John A. Quelch

Senior Associate Dean, Harvard Business School

Nathalie Laidler-Kylander

Fletcher School of Law and Diplomacy, Tufts University

THOMSON

SOUTH-WESTERN

Australia · Canada · Mexico · Singapore · Spain · United Kingdom · United States

THOMSON

SOUTH-WESTERN

The New Global Brands: Managing Non-Government Organizations in the 21st Century, 1e
John A. Quelch and Nathalie Laidler-Kylander

VP/Editorial Director:
Jack W. Calhoun

VP/Editor-in-Chief:
Dave Shaut

Sr. Publisher:
Melissa Acuña

Executive Editor:
Neil Marquardt

Sr. Developmental Editor:
Trish Taylor

Marketing Manager:
Nicole C. Moore

Production Editor:
Emily S. Gross

Sr. Manufacturing Coordinator:
Diane Lohman

Art Director:
Stacy Jenkins Shirley

Production House:
GEX Publishing Services

Cover Designer:
Mike Stratton,
stratton(design)

Cover Image:
©EyeWire

Internal Designer:
Mike Stratton,
stratton(design)

Printer:
Quebecor World Taunton

Table of Contents

About the Authors

John A. Quelch

The Senior Associate Dean for International Development at Harvard Business School, Professor John Quelch is an expert on global marketing and branding. He graduated from Oxford University, Harvard Business School, and the Harvard School of Public Health. Professor Quelch serves as a director of Accion International, a leading microfinance lender.

Nathalie Laidler-Kylander

A PhD candidate at The Fletcher School–Tufts University, Nathalie Laidler-Kylander graduated from University College–London and Harvard Business School. She worked previously for Médecins Sans Frontières.

INTRODUCTION

Nongovernmental organizations (NGOs) are among the best-known and most trusted brands in the world. A recent study concluded, "NGOs are no longer perceived as small bands of activists but rather as the new super brands."[1]

Global NGOs include both not-for-profit associations providing humanitarian and social services across national boundaries and other not-for-profit associations focused on achieving international, social, and economic change through influencing governments and corporations.[2] Some commentators refer to these two types of NGOs as operational NGOs and advocacy NGOs, with hybrid NGOs attempting to straddle both roles.[3]

The number of NGOs with international programs exceeds 2,500. However, their collective budgets are hard to determine. Dichter has estimated private and public support for all NGOs working internationally at $20 billion.[4] These funds are, of course, inadequate to solve the world's social problems, but because of the public trust they enjoy, global NGOs can and do exert influence well beyond what their monetary resources might imply.

As we enter the twenty-first century, hardly any of the major problems we confront can be considered purely domestic. The world's challenges are daunting:

- According to the World Bank's 2003 World Development Report, the world's population stands at 6.3 billion. Twenty-four percent of these (including 650 million children) live on less than $1 per day and a further quarter on less than $2 per day. By 2300, assuming a fertility rate of two children per woman, the United Nations forecasts that world population could rise to 9 billion, with Africa's share almost doubling from 13 percent to 24 percent.

- Almost 1 billion people suffer from malnutrition. More than 1 billion lack potable water, and 2.4 billion lack access to proper sanitation. Around 10 million children die annually from completely preventable diseases.

- The World Health Organization estimates that 40 million people are infected with the AIDS virus: 6 million are in immediate need of anti-retroviral treatment, but only one-twelfth of them are receiving it.

- A 2003 UNICEF report on The State of the World's Children shows that 65 million girls and 56 million boys of primary-school age receive no education, and that only eight of 148 developing nations are committing at least 20 percent of government spending to education.

The global NGOs cannot address these challenges alone. But they have the ability, perhaps the responsibility, to lead the debate that sets the agenda for change. The goal of this book is to highlight—through twelve in-depth case studies—the managerial challenges confronting global not-for-profit organizations. We include NGOs with their origins in Europe, such as the World Wildlife Fund and Médecins Sans Frontières, and other NGOs, such as Acción International and CARE, which were launched in the United States. We include NGOs with an operational focus such as Habitat for Humanity, and advocacy NGOs such as Amnesty International.

In addition to covering the well-established "northern" NGOs from Europe and the United States, we include two case studies on the Bangladesh Rural Advancement Committee (BRAC), a "southern" NGO headquartered in an emerging economy, which is beginning to venture overseas. We also present a case study on Peace Winds, a young Japanese NGO committed to humanitarian relief and sustainable development. Finally, for the sake of comparison, we include case studies on the International Red Cross and UNICEF. Neither are NGOs in the sense that they are largely enabled by government funding. But they are both important global not-for-profit brands whose organizations are dedicated to delivering relief and, in UNICEF's case, advocating specifically on behalf of children.

All of these organizations face a similar set of challenging questions as they enter the twenty-first century.[5] How should they respond to the increasing number of complex emergencies? To what extent should they cooperate with national governments and the private sector if doing so will advance their missions? How should they balance operational activities and advocacy efforts? How can they better measure performance against their missions and improve accountability to stakeholders?

Many of these organizations face a midlife crisis. They have achieved global reach and recognition and have done good, yet they have neither solved, nor are they capable of solving, single-handedly the world's problems. In many cases, they must reevaluate their missions, reaffirm their commitments, and rejuvenate their organizations to respond to the challenges of a new century.

COMING OF AGE.

Although the International Red Cross dates back to 1859, most of the global NGOs reviewed in this book developed during the second half of the twentieth century. International trade flowing from the global empires of the nineteenth-century European powers, two world wars in the twentieth century, the telephone, and, later, television and the Internet have all brought the world progressively closer together. The U.S. government's Marshall Plan to facilitate the reconstruction of Europe after World War II spawned the concept of foreign aid transfers from rich to poor countries. A sense of obligation emerged, initially in elite circles, that the rich should aid the poor, not merely in their local communities but around the world. Well-publicized international emergencies fueled the public interest in donating to relief funds. For several decades, the new NGOs operated at the periphery of foreign aid. Many development economists working for national governments or international organizations such as the World Bank looked down on the NGOs as unimportant, under-resourced, utopian, and often obstructionist. Largely as a result, the funds flowing through these fledgling NGOs remained modest compared with overall government aid.

However, over time, the tables began to turn. The ability of donor governments to deliver taxpayers' dollars effectively to those in need rather than into the pockets of third-world dictators was repeatedly called into question during the 1950s and 1960s. Foreign aid was often used during the cold war by national governments as a tool of diplomacy to reward friendly regimes. To an increasingly skeptical public, the motives of the global NGOs seemed considerably more pure. Thanks to television coverage of famines and other disasters, donor and volunteer interest increased and the best of the NGOs developed into global networks, spawning loosely affiliated chapters in countries around the world.

The importance of global NGOs accelerated during the 1990s. By 2000, there were more than 400 international humanitarian relief organizations, with the lion's share of resources flowing through the largest twenty of the group. Nobel Peace Prizes were awarded in 1998 to the International Campaign to Ban Landmines, a consortium of 1,200 agencies, and to Médecins Sans Frontières in 1999. Two years earlier, representatives of CARE, the International Federation of Red Cross Societies, Médecins Sans Frontières, and Oxfam participated in the first NGO testimony ever given before the United Nations Security Council. Global NGOs were no longer marginal players; by the 1990s, they were in the mainstream of civil society.

Global NGOs that focused on humanitarian relief came of age in the 1990s for three main reasons:

- Prompted by the fall of the Berlin Wall in 1989, the worldwide collapse of communism exposed poverty, removed whatever social safety nets had been in place, and opened up countries that had previously been off-limits to international relief organizations. At the same time, the fall of communism created a power vacuum in many geographies, resulting in failed states, ethnic and tribal hostilities, famines, and massive displacements of populations. Add this to an estimated 400 natural disasters around the world, and one in every 133 people was in flight in 1999.[6]

- Improved communications via satellite television and the Internet brought the plight of millions into the living rooms of increasingly well-off Westerners. More individuals than ever before began bringing an international perspective to their philanthropic decisions. The percentage of the total giving in the USA accounted for by international NGOs more than doubled during the 1990s. E-mail and the Internet also enabled small international NGOs to coordinate operations more effectively. Many governments in the developing world diverted too high a percentage of national resources into arms and defense at the expense of education and public health. Although globalization gave the West the strongest-ever-sustained period of economic growth during the 1990s, the poor simply became poorer, with population growth outpacing growth in gross domestic product in many developing countries, especially in Africa and the Muslim world. In many cases, governments proved willing to let "northern" NGOs compensate for their declining capacity or interest in providing public services.

- Many "northern" donor governments reduced their commitments to foreign aid as a percentage of gross domestic products after the end of the cold war. At the same time, foreign direct investment in emerging economies increased significantly during the 1990s, reducing, in the minds of policy makers, the need to continue government overseas aid at previous levels. This policy shift placed an extra burden on the global NGOs. But there was a silver lining, for as state aid declined, an increasing percentage was outsourced to or channeled through the large NGOs that had achieved the scale necessary to absorb and implement substantial state-funded programs. They were often rightly considered more nimble, committed, and cost effective than state development agencies. The Dutch government led the way in requiring that at least 10 percent of its official overseas development assistance be channeled through NGOs. By 2003, almost 20 percent of World Bank and U.S. Agency for International Development assistance was disbursed through NGOs.

DEFINING MISSION: FROM RELIEF TO ADVOCACY.

Mission is critical to any NGO. Private corporations have as their core mission the creation of shareholder value. NGOs have no such obvious and easily compared bottom line. The mission statement, therefore, assumes a special importance. It offers a definition of purpose, an assertion of distinctive competence, a motivation to stakeholders, and a basis for performance measurement.[7]

A good mission statement has three components. It states what the mission is, how it will be achieved, and whom the mission serves. For example, UNICEF's mission is to "protect children's rights, help meet children's basic needs, and establish opportunities for children to reach their full potential." It aims to help children in these ways by leveraging the mandate and support provided by the United National General Assembly. The World Wildlife Fund's mission is "to build a future in which humans live in harmony with nature" (the "what"), by "stopping and eventually reversing the degradation of the earth's natural environment" (the 'how'), "for the benefit of all humanity" (the "whom"). Unlike the WWF, many not-for-profits have mission statements that are too broad and abstract. A broadly defined mission allows for flexibility and growth but can often tempt an NGO to bid for institutional grants that do not fit with its capabilities. In an increasingly cluttered NGO marketplace, the importance of a precisely stated mission that is up-to-date in its appeal and relevance cannot be underestimated.

The end of the cold war allowed the world's opinion leaders to focus on new issues, particularly the challenges emanating from an increasingly integrated global economy that national governments and multinational corporations were not addressing adequately. Environmental fallouts from economic growth such as global warming spanned national boundaries and spawned policy recommendations from Greenpeace, the World Wildlife Fund, and other new global NGOs focused on environmental advocacy.

NGOs advocating fair trade also came to the fore during the 1990s in response to the surge in foreign direct investment and international trade. The latter quadrupled from $5 trillion in 1990 to $21 trillion in 2001. But as the 1990s progressed, there was an increasing belief that the benefits of globalization had not been shared evenly between the rich and poor nations.[8] Indeed, some fifty countries saw their per capita incomes decline during the 1990s. Meanwhile, the revenues of the five largest global corporations exceeded the combined gross domestic product of the 100 poorest countries.[9] In many cases, irresponsible governments had saddled their citizens with inordinate levels of debt service that condemned them to an unbreakable cycle of poverty. New NGOs such as Jubilee 2000 emerged to campaign for third-world debt relief.

Single-issue NGOs were hardly new. In the late 1700s, for example, societies formed in America and Britain to campaign for the abolition of slavery. By the 1990s, activist NGOs were cleverly campaigning not only against governments but against multinational corporations with high-profile brands that often have the power to pressure national governments for the changes the NGOs desire.[10]

Established global NGOs focused on humanitarian relief began to wrestle with whether they should redefine their missions with greater emphasis on either sustainable development and/or advocacy. To answer this question required a detailed consideration of the meaning of the word "development." It could mean development through the delivery of social services, perhaps in collaboration with local government agencies. Or it could mean development through the mobilization of communities to demand their rights from their national governments. Korten identified three stages of development for the global NGO: an initial focus on relief and welfare delivery, followed by the organization of local resources to facilitate community self-help, followed by advocacy of government policy changes.[11]

There were five reasons why many established NGOs redefined their missions toward a greater emphasis on sustainable development and advocacy during the 1990s:

- Relief-oriented NGOs may achieve some short-term success, but the beneficial effect of their activities is rarely sustained. Relief organizations that have shifted to increased emphasis on disaster preparedness and prevention, often through technical assistance, have also found it hard to achieve a sustainable effect as a result of deliberate or unwitting government interference. As a result of the fact that they are barely scratching the surface in solving the world's problems, many NGOs have increasingly embraced advocacy in their mission statements. Their purpose is to change the underlying structure (on fair trade and fair pay, for example) and to persuade governments and the private sector to put more resources behind solving world poverty.

- Emergency relief work requires an ability to deploy resources anywhere in the world at short notice. Though there is no shortage of emergencies, this mission requires the ability to maintain—at considerable cost—relief capability during down periods. Increasingly, it became apparent to many NGOs that, to have a sustained effect, they must focus on development in selected countries rather than "ambulance chasing" after every new emergency. The leap from development work to policy advocacy flowed as a natural consequence of this evolution of mission.

- Relief work depends first and foremost on the effectiveness of local operations at the point of delivery. The headquarters leadership of an NGO is important but not critical to implementation. Advocacy, on the other hand, is a role much better suited to headquarters, which has the global "big picture" and often the inclination to take a high-profile stand. In some cases, the shift to advocacy reflects a reassertion of "northern" headquarters control over a far-flung federation of mainly "southern" NGO affiliates.

- The end of the cold war permitted more attention to be paid to international human rights. Despite decades of effort by NGOs, the scope of human suffering and deprivation of basic rights seemed greater than ever. Hence, perhaps partly out of frustration, there was an increasing desire among NGO leaders to address the causes of poverty and conflicts that governments were often willing to tolerate, rather than merely aid their victims.

- Globalization has connected young people around the world as never before. Sometimes idealistic and naïve, young people nevertheless have a healthy appreciation for what is wrong and what to do about it. Established NGOs need to continually refresh their supporter bases with young people who will challenge their established missions, even at the risk of creating tension with older, wealthier donors. A mission with a strong commitment to advocacy is helpful in attracting young people who might otherwise join upstart advocacy-centered NGOs that, in the age of the Internet, don't require worldwide networks of field offices to achieve their missions.

Advocacy organizations such as Greenpeace and Amnesty International often refer to themselves as movements and rely more heavily than humanitarian relief organizations on members' subscriptions. It is typically more difficult to raise funds from government and private-sector donors as an advocacy organization than as a provider of humanitarian relief services. Some of the contrasts between pure relief and pure advocacy NGOs are summarized in **Exhibit 1**.

Accordingly, many well-established global NGOs remain very careful about engaging in advocacy. Médecins Sans Frontières, for example, does comment on social exclusion issues but does not campaign against human rights abuses; its staff is required to remain strictly neutral, bear witness, and give testimony ("temoinage") rather than take sides in any conflict environment. Similarly, the Red Cross cannot jeopardize its relief work by advocacy activity that might offend a government controlling an area where relief is required. Other NGOs worry that their donors or

---

Exhibit 1   Relief and Advocacy NGOs Compared

Relief	Advocacy
Charity	Movement
Donors	Members
Save People Today	Change the System for Tomorrow
Field Operations Focus	HQ Strategy Focus
Easier to Manage	Harder to Manage
Reactive	Proactive
Uncontroversial	Adversarial
Emotional	Cerebral
Worthy	Edgy
Older members	Younger members

members would not welcome a shift to advocacy and that more revenues would be lost than would be gained, or that a muddled mission might disenchant dedicated relief workers in field operations. In some cases, local affiliates of an NGO have successfully objected to mission creep toward more of an advocacy role for headquarters, arguing that this might risk their safety and effectiveness in crisis areas.

Any humanitarian relief organization should be wary of a wholesale and precipitous shift in mission toward pure advocacy. A balance is required, as Oxfam is currently seeking to discover. Cumulative expertise stemming from decades of front-line relief work, often buttressed by research, have afforded many established global NGOs an understanding of suffering and its causes that can legitimize their policy advice. But their mission statements must reflect accurately the relative weight that they place on front-line work and advocacy. Furthermore, these mission statements must delineate whether advocacy means behind-the-scenes efforts to influence policy makers or direct action for social transformation. They may also have to delineate the NGO's policy philosophy; for example, some human rights organizations advocate for poverty reduction, whereas others emphasize improving opportunity and empowerment.

CARE is an established NGO that has adjusted its mission over time from pure relief—the delivery of care packages—to incorporate a degree of advocacy. CARE headquarters has around a dozen staff on its payroll researching and developing policy positions. CARE believes that its policies must flow from the knowledge of its field operations around the world. It is, therefore, not much involved in advocacy for debt relief and fair trade. On the other hand, it was a major supporter of the International Campaign to Ban Land Mines, an effort that brought together 1,100 organizations from sixty countries. Indeed, CARE's work on this project gave it cover to develop its advocacy capability.

Far from being nongovernment, NGOs are increasingly involved with governments.[12] They are either lobbying governments, competing for government grants, partnering in the delivery of donor government aid, or collaborating with local government agencies to deliver it. Though not a global NGO, BRAC, for example, collaborates with the Bangladesh government on curriculum development in its 30,000 schools and acts as a government contractor for the implementation of health programs through BRAC's network of village health workers. Despite, or perhaps because of, these interactions with government, BRAC manages to maintain a level of independence that does not compromise the moral authority that the public associates with its work and brand name.

Nevertheless, the ambitions of NGOs to enter policy debates and engage in policy advocacy have prompted third parties to question their legitimacy. David Henderson, former chief economist at the Organization for Economic Cooperation and Development, argues that "NGOs have the right to be consulted but they have no right to be involved in substantive decisions."[13] And George Soros says, "They (NGOs) cannot be entrusted with making the rules any more than the business sector."[14] Why, it may be asked, should the World Trade Organization be answerable to Greenpeace when Greenpeace is barely accountable to its own membership?[15] Why should the World Bank include seventy NGO experts on its payroll? The answer lies in the public trust that the global NGO brands have earned over the years and the power that this trust gives them.

BRANDS, TRUST, AND NGOs.

Brands offer the convenience of early identification. For centuries, livestock have been branded on the open range to enable their owners to differentiate among them. Today, a brand is also a signal, not just of the brand owner but of the consistency of quality that we can expect from the product or service in question. When we reach for a brand from the supermarket shelf, we trust that the contents of the package will be the same this week as they were last time we purchased the same item. Marketing communications in the form of advertising, the price that we pay, and the type of store where we make the purchase all contribute to the expectations we have of the brand. If, in use, our expectations are fulfilled, our trust in the brand, our willingness to purchase it again, our inclination to recommend it to a friend, all increase. The best brands act as clubs, providing a sense of affiliation and sometimes status to those involved with them.

To succeed, any brand must have a consistent meaning among those who know about it. The richer the brand meaning, the more those who believe in it will care about it. In the case of an NGO brand, the more its supporters care, the more time, money, and positive word of mouth they will commit. In other words, they will develop a relationship with the brand. It will become an important part of their lives. But for such brand relationships to succeed, the NGO must have as much respect for its stakeholders as they have for it. This means engaging the NGO's supporters, understanding that they (rather than the full-time management at NGO headquarters) own the brand, and asking not just what they think of the brand but what they think the brand thinks of them.

NGO brands depend mightily on trust. This trust is hard to earn for two reasons. First, the benefits of most NGOs are intangible rather than tangible. Habitat for Humanity is an exception in being able to point to the number of houses built. Most NGOs deliver services, not tangible products. Second, donors and volunteers essentially make the purchases but do not consume the products of the NGOs. Indeed, contributors to global NGOs may never see the beneficiaries of their help. They have to trust that their contributions will be husbanded properly. Just as you trust FTD or Interflora to deliver a high-quality bouquet of fresh flowers to some distant relative on an important anniversary, so a donor contributes to a global NGO to reach people in need in some foreign land. In the case of the flowers, you might hear back from the recipient. In the case of donations to NGOs, that's much less likely.

Donors—individuals and governments alike—are more likely to trust an NGO when a high percentage of the value of donations is passed on to the intended beneficiaries and these monies are disbursed in a way that maximizes their effect. The support of celebrities can also be invaluable in building trust: the commitment of former U.S. President Jimmy Carter has greatly enhanced public awareness of and support for Habitat for Humanity. Princess Diana did the same for the International Campaign to Ban Land Mines.

Strong NGO brands that have built a reservoir of trust over many years can get through a time of crisis. In the United States, the reputations of both the Red Cross and the United Way suffered as a result of the questionable behavior of recent leaders, but the negative effects were temporary as the public realized that the overall integrity of the organizations had not been compromised. To this day, when a new humanitarian crisis surfaces, many citizens instinctively send donations to the Red Cross without even being solicited by the charity: that is brand strength.

Greenpeace presents a different example. It is often highly critical of corporations and governments and engages in sometimes-questionable stunts to attract media publicity to a cause. Yet the public tolerates the occasional transgression because it values Greenpeace's role as a gadfly. The public knows that those who are criticized have plenty of resources to make their cases, and it knows that Greenpeace itself can't really cause any harm. Hence, Greenpeace still commands a high degree of public confidence.

The increasing globalization of philanthropy—giving by individuals, foundations, and corporations beyond their domestic borders—depends heavily on global NGO brands that can be trusted to put donations to good use halfway around the world. Evidence indicates that these global NGO brands command impressive levels of trust relative to corporate brands. Edelman Public Relations annually assesses consumer trust in a selected mix of corporate and NGO brands. The most recent results for the USA and for Europe are shown in **Exhibit 2** and **3.** The four most trusted brands in Europe are NGOs. In the USA, they are farther down the list but have been gaining ground in the past three years.

What can explain these high levels of public trust in NGOs? First, consumers—perhaps naïvely—are less suspicious of the motives of the NGO sector than they are of business. Frequent examples of corporate malfeasance and the collapse of the Internet bubble, all at the expense of the small investor, have added to the comparative distrust of business.

Second, the global NGOs are noble forces for good; their missions are highly worthy. The people associated with them are thought to be dedicated and not that well compensated for their efforts. A certain guilt that we are not doing much ourselves underpins our approval of NGOs.

Third, global NGO brands have—perhaps unthinkingly—benefited from simply using a single brand umbrella for all their activities worldwide, rather than spreading themselves thin by using sub-brands. Indeed, in many far-flung, decentralized NGOs, the common global brand may be the only glue holding the organization together, offering continuity across generations of volunteers and enabling local affiliates to more easily raise funds.

Fourth, the best-known global NGO brands state clearly what their organizations are about and do so consistently in all their communications. There is little ambiguity around the core purpose of, say, Human Rights Watch or Save the Children.

Fifth, while doing very little advertising compared with their corporate counterparts, global NGO brands have, by focusing on emotional, newsworthy issues (such as famine, suffering children, etc.), been able to generate substantial free media publicity for their causes and their brand names. In fact, the work of many global NGOs speaks for itself and permits an easy emotional appeal that many corporate brands rightly envy.

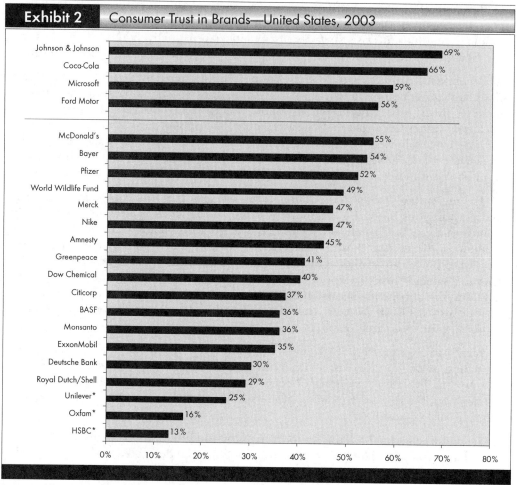

Exhibit 2   Consumer Trust in Brands—United States, 2003

Brand	Percentage
Johnson & Johnson	69%
Coca-Cola	66%
Microsoft	59%
Ford Motor	56%
McDonald's	55%
Bayer	54%
Pfizer	52%
World Wildlife Fund	49%
Merck	47%
Nike	47%
Amnesty	45%
Greenpeace	41%
Dow Chemical	40%
Citicorp	37%
BASF	36%
Monsanto	36%
ExxonMobil	35%
Deutsche Bank	30%
Royal Dutch/Shell	29%
Unilever*	25%
Oxfam*	16%
HSBC*	13%

Source: Edelman Public Relations.
*"% Who have never heard of"—over 15.

In several respects, however, brand building is more challenging for a global NGO than for a multinational corporation:

- In the absence of the profit motive, NGOs are mission driven. Mission effect is the surrogate for profits. Mission aligns the organization with its stakeholders, sets the boundaries for the organization, and provides the foundation on which trust is developed. Strong NGO brands succinctly articulate their missions in terms of what, how, and for whom; these missions are equivalent in many ways to brand-positioning statements. Successful NGOs also stay true to their missions, are vigilant against "mission creep," and are regarded by their stakeholders as uniquely able to deliver against them.

- NGO brands must often cater to a more diverse mix of stakeholders. Not only are donors and beneficiaries usually distinct, but donors may include corporations and governments as well as individuals; many NGOs are therefore B2B (business-to-business) as well as B2C (business-to-consumer) marketers. In addition, volunteers around the world who can easily shift

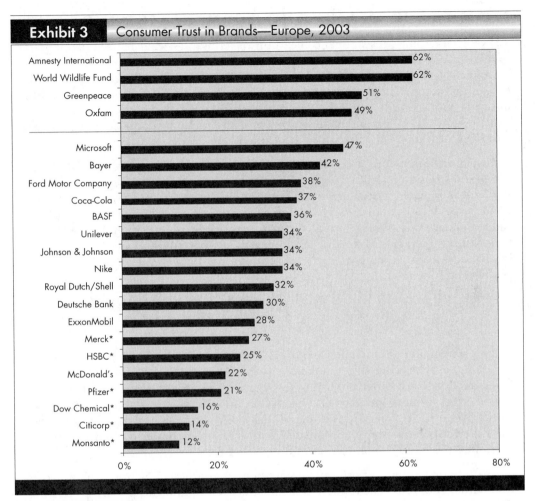

| Exhibit 3 | Consumer Trust in Brands—Europe, 2003 |

- Amnesty International — 62%
- World Wildlife Fund — 62%
- Greenpeace — 51%
- Oxfam — 49%
- Microsoft — 47%
- Bayer — 42%
- Ford Motor Company — 38%
- Coca-Cola — 37%
- BASF — 36%
- Unilever — 34%
- Johnson & Johnson — 34%
- Nike — 34%
- Royal Dutch/Shell — 32%
- Deutsche Bank — 30%
- ExxonMobil — 28%
- Merck* — 27%
- HSBC* — 25%
- McDonald's — 22%
- Pfizer* — 21%
- Dow Chemical* — 16%
- Citicorp* — 14%
- Monsanto* — 12%

Source: Edelman Public Relations.
*"% Who have never heard of"—over 15.

allegiances must be constantly reinforced, and at Médecins Sans Frontières, for example, the supply of doctor volunteers must be constantly replenished. For them, money is not an issue; what is important is the psychic attachment to the MSF brand and what it stands for. In addition, relations with government agencies and local NGOs in the countries where help is being directed are often as important as those with donor governments. The brand essence of the global NGO may be different for each stakeholder group, but these different brand meanings must be complementary rather than contradictory, and must be equally powerful and motivating to all.

- NGO brands are competing for the same donor dollar, but norms preclude aggressive competition for funds. Comparative advertising and competitive positioning are not common. This makes sense since the size of even the largest NGOs is so inadequate relative to the scale of the problems to be tackled that collaboration among NGOs is often essential to achieving the greatest effect per dollar.

FROM BRAND MEANING TO BRAND MARKETING.

Every NGO must research the meaning of its brand—what its brand uniquely stands for—to all stakeholder groups. The results are not always gratifying. The brand may lack clarity or distinctiveness, or different stakeholder groups may perceive it differently. The brand's image may reflect its past rather than current reality, implying an important corrective role for marketing communications. Or, as in the case of UNICEF, the brand image may be dependent in part upon the image of the parent organization (in this case of the United Nations).

Clarity and precision in defining a brand's meaning will help an NGO arrive at the brand's positioning. The positioning statement is the marketing expression of the NGO's mission. There are three components to any brand positioning statement: a specification of the target audience, a claim of superiority (what the brand can do better than others), and a powerful reason why the target audience should believe the superiority claim. In an increasingly cluttered NGO marketplace with low barriers to entry, standing out is more important than ever. Consider UNICEF's positioning statement:

> *For people who want to make a difference, UNICEF is the champion of rights for all the world's children, with the knowledge, certainty and resources to get things done.*

This statement does include each of the three required components. However, a critic might say that the target audience is not well defined and could just as easily be claimed by many other not-for-profit organizations; that the superiority claim is not asserted strongly (perhaps because NGOs are reluctant to publicly claim superiority over other organizations doing similar work); and that the reasons to believe the superiority claim are not delineated that precisely, perhaps to avoid an explicit reminder of UNICEF's connection to the United Nations.

To develop a unique positioning statement is not easy, but trying to do so is invaluable. Different stakeholder views are uncovered, and the process of striving for consensus around a single positioning deepens the mutual understanding among all who participate. If handled patiently and inclusively, the process can reenergize an organization and its supporters. If, on the other hand, an NGO does not develop a clear positioning statement, it risks a fuzzy image that will leave stakeholders confused and suspicious about the organization's effectiveness.

Once an NGO's positioning is clarified, decisions about its communications program—which audiences to target, what messages to send them, and through which media—will fall into place more easily. Many NGOs have to communicate with a diverse range of audiences from national governments to individual small donors. Different types of messages are appropriate for each. For example, messages about the size and reach of an NGO may appeal to donor governments but discourage small individual donors who want their contributions to count. Effective appeals to small donors typically highlight success stories of individuals who are benefiting from the NGO's work. Such positive messages, which humanize the NGO's work, appear to engage more prospective donors than shock tactic advertisements depicting, for example, starving children.

The same is true of media: different vehicles are appropriate for different stakeholders. Those NGOs whose business models depend heavily on donations and membership revenues will spend proportionately more on advertising and direct mail than those that act primarily as conduits for government and aid-agency funds. Either way, brand raising and fund-raising are intertwined. Global NGOs also need to understand how to leverage the World Wide Web to attract and engage a new generation of younger, tech-savvy supporters. The anti-globalization protesters at the World Trade Organization meeting in Seattle and the World Economic Forum in Davos demonstrated the convening power of the Web and its ability to mobilize like-minded supporters of a particular viewpoint from around the world in the late 1990s.

No one can question the value to the Red Cross of the near-universal recognition of its logo—a red cross (or red crescent) on a white field. However, logos—the visible representations of brands—receive perhaps more emphasis than they deserve. They should be descriptive, unique, memorable, enduring, inviting, and international in appeal. Attempting to change a tagline or a logo—or to rein in independent affiliates to follow a common approach—can cause considerable consternation. The result is equivalent to opening Pandora's box; all the pent-up emotions that employees and volunteers harbor about the brand's mission and values are up for an often healthy and long-overdue debate that, once initiated, may take a year or two to resolve. The tension between headquarters control and affiliate autonomy may also surface—with affiliates in developing countries often claiming that, with high rates of illiteracy, maintaining an existing logo is essential to continuing easy identification of the NGO's employees, vehicles, and offices, and therefore, to their security. Others argue that logo consistency (supported by a consistent look and feel in all the NGO's publications) is important to the confidence of international donors. But a well-recognized local logo that is at odds with the standard global logo should not necessarily be brought into line without careful thought and research. After all, does it really matter to the beneficiaries of an NGO's efforts if its logo is different in Botswana and Bolivia?

Every NGO seems to have a tagline. Here are three. Can you match the correct NGO to each?

Where the end of poverty begins

More than hope—success

The power of humanity

In order, these are the taglines of CARE, Acción International, and the International Red Cross. These taglines are not especially distinctive, but a close reading indicates how they aim to embody the mission and meaning of each brand. CARE is repositioning itself as an organization interested not just in relieving poverty but in tackling its underlying causes. Acción's tagline captures the belief that its microfinance loans will enable many beneficiaries to become self-sufficient entrepreneurs. Meanwhile, the Red Cross remains focused on humanitarian relief.

What are the characteristics of the strongest global NGO brands?

- They are strong in their domestic markets and known worldwide.
- They are focused and positioned consistently around the globe.
- They incorporate a human, emotional appeal to universally shared values.
- They are led by professionals who understand their roles as temporary brand stewards.

- They set standards of integrity for themselves and, in so doing, raise stake-holder expectations for all NGOs.

- They each operate under a single brand name worldwide, a name that embodies the mission, never the name of the founder.

As Paul Temporal has said, "Great brands are like great people: respected for humility, compassion, leading-edge thinking and the trust they place in consumers."[16]

The strongest global NGO brands are those that have spent the most on marketing. Many have achieved high recognition by letting their work speak for them. As one senior Amnesty International executive commented, "We don't actively manage our brand. Perhaps we have a strong reputation as a result."

Some argue that it is not important that an NGO brand be famous but rather that it be respected among critical stakeholder groups. Acción International, for example, is not a household name. It is an expert in microfinance lending in Latin America and now Africa. It lends not directly to end consumers but through local financial institutions, many of which grow in stature over time and become freestanding. Most beneficiaries never know that Acción funds help them. Does this matter? Acción's work is well known to all in the microfinance arena. Relevant government agencies and any financial institution interested in microfinance quickly learn of Acción and its work. Should Acción complement its behind-the-scenes push marketing with an effort to build brand recognition among donors and beneficiaries—as Grameen Bank, a Bangladeshi microfinance organization, succeeded in doing? The answer is "yes." Because its brand profile is low, Acción may not be raising individual donations (and thereby diversifying its funding base) commensurate with its track record and potential to make a difference in the world. For the same reason, there are few mega-donor celebrities on the Acción board. When competing against other NGOs for contracts from government agencies, international organizations, and foundations, an NGO's brand profile, its number of donors or members, and its level of private funding can be important tiebreakers.

ASSESSING BRAND VALUE.

An increasing percentage of NGOs are seeking to track their brand health. They can do so through periodic stakeholder surveys of aided and unaided awareness, knowledge of the brand, what it stands for and what it does, and brand relevance. Young & Rubican's Brand Asset Valuator assesses both brand strength (a function of perceived differentiation and relevance) and brand stature (based on knowledge of the brand and the esteem in which it is held). Brand health also encompasses brand loyalty. Measures of loyalty should focus on the durability and intensity of commitment to the NGO. When members, donors, and volunteers view a particular NGO as their most important affiliation after home, family, and workplace, that is a sure sign of strength. In contrast, loyalty toward some well-known NGOs is surprisingly shallow; an organization may have many members, but if those members are also affiliated with other NGOs to which they are more committed, its foundations are far from strong.

Most global NGO brands are highly trusted. They are, therefore, highly valuable. But only recently have these NGOs become aware of just how valuable they are. The consultancy Interbrand, which has a long track record of valuing corporate brands, has recently turned its attention to not-for-profits.

The Interbrand methodology, applied to corporate brands, calculates at the discounted value of the future cash flows generated by the brand. Because NGOs do not exist to generate profits, this approach cannot be used. As an alternative, Interbrand focuses on the value of future NGO revenues net of expenses. Next, Interbrand identifies the factors that drive these revenues and the importance of the NGO brand in explaining each driver. This analysis results in a percent score, which is then applied to future revenues net of expenses to calculate that portion attributable to the brand. Third, the NGO brand is rated on seven criteria (market, stability, leadership, geographical coverage, trend, support, and protection) that Interbrand uses when valuing for-profit brands. The resulting score translates into a discount rate that is applied to the future revenues net of expenses attributable to the brand. The result is the brand value.

The United Way brand, the leading charitable fund-raising organization in the United States, was recently valued at $34.7 billion using this Interbrand methodology. Using the same approach, the Habitat for Humanity brand was valued at $1.8 billion. These valuations are not comparable to Interbrand's corporate brand values because of the different baselines used (revenues net of expenses versus profits), but it can be argued that they understate the true values of NGO brands because the value of volunteer time is not included in the calculation of revenues.[17]

The leaders of global NGOs are beginning to understand that a high brand valuation does the following:

- Focuses them on better understanding the drivers of the NGO's "business model" and the relative importance of brand in influencing each driver.
- Highlights the importance of the brand and logo as key assets that should not be tampered with lightly.
- Enables headquarters to require standard presentation of the brand by its affiliates and local chapters around the world.
- Supports investment in marketing communications to reinforce and build upon the brand meaning.
- Justifies a seat at the policy-making table with national governments and international agencies.
- Attracts, motivates, and retains high-quality and committed employees, board members, government and individual donors, and volunteers.
- Allows them to select top-quality, trustworthy corporate partners and negotiate more favorable terms, including higher cash grants and/or gifts in kind, longer duration, and exclusivity.
- Aids corporate partners in justifying NGO relationships to their shareholders and increases the chances of success because more money is on the line.

Brand valuations of NGOs are likely to become commonplace in the next decade as NGOs seek to benchmark each other. Global NGO brands are especially likely to benefit because their very globalness signals expertise, quality, and innovation and attracts supporters around the world who wish to be associated with elite international organizations. A ranking of the ten most valuable NGO brands in the world is probably imminent. Like the ranking of corporate brands, it will be dominated by global NGO brands of American origin—even more so because the not-for-profit sector and the tradition of individual giving are so strongly developed in the United States. But in no case does the name of the NGO brand refer to its American origin, and given the decentralized, consensual decision making in their worldwide organizations and their nonassociation with American lifestyles, it is unlikely that these global NGOs will suffer anti-American opposition that could seriously diminish their brand values.

There are, however, three caveats that we should be aware of if NGO brand valuation becomes a trend:

- Such valuations reinforce the strength of established players and present entry barriers to start-up NGOs.

- Valuations based on cash flows may diminish "southern" NGOs such as BRAC, which have lower revenues yet often deliver a higher impact per dollar of revenue because of variations in purchasing power, frugal use of cash, and more use of volunteer time.

- An NGO's board of directors should not allow attention to brand valuation to distract management from the organization's central mission.

LEVERAGING AND SUSTAINING BRAND VALUE.

A sound and diversified funding base is essential for any NGO to continue its work and sustain its brand value. In addition to relying on government agencies and donations from individuals and corporations, many NGOs are increasingly embracing corporate support. In addition, many are engaging in their own commercial activities. These enterprises now go well beyond UNICEF Christmas cards and WWF-sponsored postage stamps of endangered species. Both Acción and the International Red Cross are offering internally developed assessment exercises along with consulting support to private-sector firms. Most impressively, BRAC has created an entire commercial line of food products under the Aarong brand name, the profits from which support BRAC's social mission in Bangladesh and help ensure its financial independence from the government.

Recognition of the value of global NGO brands and their increasing importance is raising the interest of multinational corporations in exploring partnership opportunities with them. To what extent should global NGOs work in partnership with business? Some NGOs believe that mission integrity—and the views of their members (in advocacy-oriented NGOs in particular)—requires that they accept no corporate funds; to do so would be to sell out the brand and the trust it has built for a short-term injection of cash. Certainly, an NGO such as Greenpeace that makes a virtue out of criticizing high-profile corporations is well advised to follow this policy.

Other NGOs believe that corporate funds are no more tainted than government funds and are often granted with fewer strings attached, and that progress toward solving the world's problems can be advanced faster by leveraging market forces and collaborating with the private sector. Like Greenpeace, the World Wildlife Fund is focused on environmental issues, but it is willing to partner with corporations that commit to changing their behavior, for example by reducing their environmental pollutants and having the WWF monitor their progress in doing so. A typical long-term corporate partnership brings WWF cash contributions and communications impact through joint publicity, but, most important of all, it also brings actual improvements in conservation.

Many companies are seeking to partner with NGOs. At one level, this behavior is motivated by short-term image building with customers and employees through simple philanthropy or a cause-related marketing scheme. At a second level, it is motivated by risk management, the desire to co-opt the critic, and the self-interest implicit in the notion that "if you can't beat them, join them." At a third level, it is motivated by a genuine belief that poverty and related environmental and social problems that impede market growth are so profound that an all-hands-to-the-deck spirit of partnership across sectors is essential; a sustained relationship, involving joint project teams, third-party certification and audits of performance, and even interlocking boards may result. Organizations such as the Prince of Wales International Business Leaders Forum help bridge the divide between NGOs and corporations to encourage this third approach.

What assets do global NGOs have to offer potential corporate partners?[18] First, there is the opportunity to associate the corporation with the moral authority and highly trusted brand name of the global NGO. The corporation's credibility and consumer appeal may be enhanced. Second, they can offer an opportunity for corporate employees to take pride in the association and to become involved as volunteers for the NGO or to take on short-term assignments with the NGO to improve the capabilities of its staff (in information technology skills, for example). Third, a corporation seeking to understand the needs of poor consumers at the bottom of the social pyramid and knowledge of how to deliver products and services to them and change their behaviors may find that an NGO with experience addressing this target audience can provide much insight. Fourth, a global NGO with a network of local affiliates offers multinational corporations, most of which bias their charitable contributions toward their domestic markets, the potential convenience of a worldwide partnership in strategic philanthropy.[19]

The requirements for effective strategic collaboration between NGOs and corporations have been delineated by Austin.[20] His seven conditions are summarized in **Exhibit 4**. In short, any strategic alliance, to be effective, has to be equally important to both parties. Both sides have to feel that the "give" and the "get" are in balance. Of course, there is reputation risk in these as in any other alliances, but perhaps more so to the NGO than the corporation. First, there is the risk that the corporation will not live up to its part of the bargain, and that other corporate activities outside the scope of the alliance will embarrass the NGO and jeopardize the loyalty of its members or donors. Alternatively, there is the risk that the "fit" between the alliance partners will prove so successful that the NGO risks being seen as co-opted by the corporation—though this would not be in the corporation's interests either.

Exhibit 4	Strategic Collaboration

Clarity of Purpose
Connection between Purpose and People
Congruency of Mission, Strategy, and Values
Creation of Value
Communication between Partners
Continual Learning
Commitment to Partnership

Source: James E. Austin, *The Collaboration Challenge* (San Francisco: Jossey-Bass, 2000)

Third, there are the opportunity costs of choosing the wrong partner and the administrative costs of managing a type of relationship with which the NGO is not familiar. Given these risks, it is essential that both parties include in the initial agreement an understanding of when and how performance reviews should be conducted and how disputes are to be resolved.

Nothing succeeds like success. The global NGO brands enjoy many privileges and benefits. They are often in the news, sustaining their visibility and top-of-mind presence. But they cannot afford to rest on their laurels. They must work hard every day to sustain their leadership positions. This requires that they continuously search for new ways to improve the efficiency with which they approach their missions and overall impact. The services that once distinguished an NGO can, as in the private sector, become commoditized over time. Demand for the services that NGOs can offer is high and barriers to entry are low. New organizations can emerge—such as Rising Tide or Peace Winds in Japan—that can capture the imagination of internationally minded young people who may see the established global NGOs as traditional, bureaucratic, and lacking in edge.

As in the corporate world, NGO brand images may grow stale over time. To use the terminology of Balmer and Greyser, the NGO's actual identity may become inconsistent with its conceived identity, desired identity, communicated identity, or ideal identity.[21] Any brand requires periodic refreshment to attract a new wave of young enthusiasts without, it is hoped, alienating long-standing supporters. And success should give any brand permission to explore moving beyond its original core competence. For these two reasons, Amnesty International is seeking to broaden its identity beyond aiding prisoners of conscience to "preventing and ending grave abuses of [human] rights to physical and medical integrity." But even though the largest NGO global brands enjoy a mass-market appeal, as in the corporate world, they must coexist alongside numerous emerging global niche brands that may be more aggressive or specialized in mission or target audience. Amnesty International's repositioning might not have happened had it not been for the emergence of Human Rights Watch.

How essential is continued growth to sustaining the success of the global NGO brand? Corporations strive to increase shareholder value through organic growth and/or through mergers and acquisitions. The same motive does not exist in the not-for-profit sector, and there is certainly little merger and acquisition activity as a result. But, for at least three reasons, many NGOs are interested in growth. First, the missions of most NGOs imply that the more people who benefit from the NGO's work, the better; there is, therefore, a drive to expand the number of beneficiaries. Second, founders, leaders, and managers within the NGO sector are not without pride and tend to compare themselves on the basis of annual revenues. Moreover, with many private-sector—and therefore growth-oriented—individuals sitting on their boards, they are often accountable for achieving annual growth objectives. Third, so pervasive are the problems that NGOs seek to address that they become useful to large donor agencies only if they have the scale and capacity to absorb and deploy substantial funds. Fourth, NGOs whose brand names have become well known can leverage those brands by attracting new donors and volunteers by opening new affiliates around the world, and by retaining high-quality managers who can be promoted into positions offering greater responsibilities in a growing organization.

Yet, as in the corporate sector, there are risks to organizational growth. Decision making may become either more bureaucratic or less consensual. Flexibility and responsiveness may diminish. A new generation of professional managers hired to support the path to growth may lack—or be perceived as lacking—the passion of the founders. In conclusion, although continuous attention to revitalization is essential to sustaining the global NGO brand, it must be balanced by a strong appreciation of the NGO's historic mission.

ORGANIZING THE NETWORK.

Most global NGOs have evolved, like international corporations, from a base in North America or Europe, gradually adding overseas affiliates, often without too much attention, at least initially, to structure and process. Yet, as in the private sector, strategy should drive structure, not vice versa. For example, a humanitarian relief NGO, dependent on the operational effectiveness of local affiliates, may require a more decentralized structure than an advocacy-oriented NGO whose success depends on the research competency and government relations' clout of its headquarters staff.

In most global NGOs, national affiliates enjoy considerable autonomy—more so than in global corporations. There are three principal reasons for this. First, these affiliates are usually launched by social entrepreneurs rather than by teams from world headquarters. (However, in some cases, affiliates have been set up by headquarters to channel the funds of large government donors into particular countries.) Second, they typically grow and evolve thanks to local volunteers without much aid or encouragement from headquarters—resulting in an understandable pride and independence that resists heavy-handed patronizing direction from a handsomely paid headquarters staff halfway around the world. Third, headquarters management often does not control the funds flow into the affiliate, particularly when membership dues and individual donations are important revenue streams. Fourth, few NGOs have paid much attention in the past to global brand building, a task that has prompted more central control in many global corporations.

A further complication in the management of global NGOs is that some affiliates are net suppliers of funds, whereas others are net users. True, in the corporate world there may be some business units or country organizations that do not make a profit, but that is understood to be every manager's objective. The NGO world is more complicated. Affiliates that are net suppliers of funds may resist having to remit to world headquarters their surpluses or some percentage of funds raised; they may prefer to disburse their funds to whichever net user affiliates or pet projects they choose to support. In the absence of headquarters leverage (for example, by replacing or withholding funds from the directors of an affiliate), coordination mechanisms are nevertheless essential to optimize the deployment of the funds raised across the network. The result may be a more federal type of organization as opposed to a collection of autonomous affiliates where the whole is rarely greater than the sum of the parts.

Arguments for placing relatively more decision-making influence at headquarters include the following:

- The need to maintain performance standards throughout all affiliates.
- The need to assure major donors that the brand is presented consistently and delivers the same level of quality worldwide.

- The need for an NGO to speak with a single voice if it is engaging in advocacy work.
- The need to integrate back-office systems and make them as efficient as possible.

On the other hand, the effectiveness with which humanitarian relief NGOs deploy their resources depends ultimately on service delivery at the local level.[22] The brand recognition and stature of a global NGO invariably differs from one country to another. An NGO that is too centralized will not adapt sufficiently to local circumstances. It will not attract or retain high-quality field operations staff who must be trusted to make flexible, on-the-spot judgments in response to local circumstances that no one at headquarters can foresee. Nor will an affiliate that is overly reliant on subsidies from headquarters be motivated to develop its own sources of funds and thereby become more autonomous.

There is no right answer, no single organization model that is best for all global NGOs. As Grossman and Rangan have pointed out, each NGO has a different history, and there are different forces for autonomy (more decentralization) and for affiliation (more centralization) that bear on effective mission delivery for each NGO.[23] Nevertheless, decisions on more strategic issues tend to be made centrally, albeit with local input. Headquarters can play an especially valuable role in articulating the NGO mission to all stakeholders, ensuring the transfer of best practices throughout the network, and upholding the integrity of the brand when a local affiliate steps out of line. Any brand is only as strong as its weakest link, so a scandal at one national affiliate can quickly tarnish the brand's image worldwide, particularly in the age of the Internet. To minimize this and other risks, the International Red Cross, seeking to raise standards among its affiliates in a nonthreatening way, recently instituted a worldwide self-assessment exercise to check on its affiliates' governance procedures.

Leading a complex international NGO can be akin to herding cats and typically requires a patient, consensus-building leader willing to take on the role for many years, rather than a traditional, hierarchy-bound manager or a flamboyant entrepreneur. Achieving needed change can be challenging, particularly in membership-based NGOs. The chief executive at NGO headquarters often has the right only to inform and persuade, perhaps to issue guidelines. Long-standing traditions of decentralization and autonomy often limit his or her ability to approve, let alone direct, the worldwide organization.

One approach to improving control by enhancing mutual dependency is to have individual national affiliates become the network specialists or task force leaders in particular areas, responsible for raising standards or developing a strategy for the organization as a whole. Another approach has one "northern" affiliate coordinating the disposition of network funds from all affiliates into a particular recipient country. The coordination challenges associated with these approaches are substantial; the leadership of the NGO must work doubly hard to build trust and ensure that the roles of individual country affiliates are rotated periodically so that they do not become entrenched.

Because the leadership of any global NGO increasingly has a choice of whether to channel its efforts through its own affiliates or through freestanding "southern" NGOs, it is useful to compare the two. In most cases, the "wholly owned" affiliate model seems preferable. First, best practices—in fund-raising, training, market research, and financial controls, to name a few examples—can be shared throughout the NGO's network, not only through manuals but through transfers of personnel across borders and through non-nationals sitting on the boards of national affiliates. And, in a high-quality learning organization, the flow of information will be two-way: aided by the Internet and e-mail, there will be practical insights that the local affiliates will be able to share with each other and with headquarters. Second, and relatedly, the local affiliate and its leadership will have the opportunity to influence the NGO's global policy and potentially have an effect way beyond their national boundaries. Third, the overall effectiveness of each affiliate and the comparative effect of different programs can be benchmarked across the multinational NGO, resulting in improved performance.

For all these reasons, the quality of management and support staff that the global NGOs are able to attract in developing countries is often superior to that found in indigenous NGOs—just as is the case in the corporate sector. A global NGO brand can therefore attract and retain good people as well as preferred local partners. The name may also provide a measure of legitimacy and security for its employees. But the rapidly developing capabilities of freestanding "southern" NGOs should not be underestimated. They are often more understanding of local citizen needs, more capable of responding quickly, and better able to relate to local government agencies. The quality of management can grow to be strong—as in the case of BRAC in Bangladesh—and sustained, with many patriotically-minded managers viewing the development of an indigenous NGO as their life's work. BRAC's leadership commands considerable respect, but its importance to the economic development of Bangladesh is now such that managing relations with the government is a significant organizational challenge. Unlike the global NGOs that focus on a particular issue and address that issue worldwide, BRAC has diversified its outreach within its domestic market, and is only now venturing overseas. Increasingly, "northern" NGOs have to manage relationships in the field with local "southern" NGOs such as BRAC as well as with their own affiliates.[24]

ASSESSING PERFORMANCE AND IMPROVING ACCOUNTABILITY.

The increasing size and influence of NGOs, and their increasing propensity to engage in policy advocacy, have raised concerns about their mandates and accountability.[25] The power of any NGO stems from five factors. First, recognition of its brand name and widespread trust in its motives and actions as a force for good in the world. Second, the number of active volunteers, donors, and members that it can claim. Third, the NGO's ability to attract favorable publicity. Fourth, its actual and perceived expertise on the specific topics that are the subject of its advocacy efforts. And fifth, the transparency of its governance and its willingness to open its books to public inspection and allow its performance to be evaluated.

Pressure for measurement and accountability is increasing for several reasons. Individual donors, especially younger donors, are becoming more demanding.[26] Donor governments and agencies are under more public and watchdog pressure to demonstrate value for money in government expenditures. Corporate accounting scandals and well-publicized problems at charities such as the United Way of America and the American Red Cross have fueled interest in accountability and governance of NGOs. *Forbes* magazine now rates 200 U.S. charities each year on a combination of charitable commitment, fund-raising efficiency, and donor dependency. The U.S. Financial and Accounting Standards Board for not-for-profits prescribes a 25 percent limit on fund-raising and administrative costs as a percent of revenues. The American Enterprise Institute runs an "NGO Watch" Web site.

A donation to an NGO is not the same as an investment in the stock of a public company: the donor expects no monetary return and therefore should not be expected to take a comparable risk when making the donation. The standards to which NGOs are held should arguably be higher than those for corporations. Furthermore, because individual donors are not able to monitor the NGO's performance (since they are the sources but not the beneficiaries of funds), any NGO—indeed the sector as a whole—depends on a huge reservoir of public trust. It is in every NGO's interest to assess, indeed police, itself and to manage prudently the funds with which it is entrusted. A major scandal can quickly undermine public confidence in the sector as a whole and dry up the flow of funds.

Pressure for performance measurement benefits NGOs.[27] First, it brings a necessary discipline to an NGO's financial management and controls and to the allocation of its scarce resources. Second, it encourages the use of well-monitored pilot projects and focuses an organization on results rather than activities. Third, it prompts the NGO to understand better the results that each stakeholder group is seeking from its investments. Fourth, it can lead to a more expansive understanding of the indirect as well as the direct benefits that the NGO delivers to society. Fifth, it can reinforce an understanding of what drives the NGO brand's reputation. Finally, if done well, it can improve donor confidence and support.

In the absence of a standard bottom line, such as profit in business or election results in politics, NGO performance is very much a matter of delivery against mission.[28] But there is often a disconnect between the NGO's mission and how it measures performance. Most NGO mission statements are broad and ambitious. In this vein, Peter Drucker declared that the ultimate objective of not-for-profit organizations is "changed human beings."[29] Measures can cover inputs, outputs, and effect. But few NGOs measure their performance in terms of the effects implied by their mission statements. Most are content to measure inputs and, at best, intermediate output measures.

For example, an emergency relief organization responding to a famine in Africa can count donations in response to an appeal. It can count the number of sacks of grain delivered to those in need and report the percentage of funds collected that were passed on to the intended users (rather than spent on administrative overhead or diverted into the stomachs of local militias). It can monitor malnutrition rates in the affected region over time. Attributing causality to the efforts of the NGO becomes harder the further one moves along the metrics continuum from inputs to effect. And so, as NGOs become more interested in sustainable development rather than short-term relief, the measurement challenge becomes greater. Can we develop common measures for sustainability, empowerment, and capacity building? Or is every community so unique and complex that attempting to benchmark progress across communities can only be superficial at best?

There are risks associated with an excessive emphasis on measurement. First, although investing time and money in measuring effect can be helpful, it should not be at the expense of the core mission. A balance must be struck: the right amount of measurement to prove performance to the satisfaction of stakeholders on whom future funding—and, therefore, the survival of the NGO—depends. Second, too much emphasis on performance measurement can lead NGOs to limit their activities to projects where performance improvements are most likely and most easily measured (often in the short term): ambitious, complex challenges that require long-term investments to effect change may be passed over. In addition, there is always a temptation to game the evaluation system and to exaggerate success to secure further funding. Third, an emphasis on performance measurement as a basis for funds allocation risks disadvantaging "southern" NGOs with less experience and fewer resources. Fourth, the effects from the pressure to perform may discourage NGOs from partnering with other NGOs, governments, or corporations for fear of losing control over outcomes and difficulties in attributing responsibility for program results.

But the pressures on NGOs for more accountability and transparency are inescapable. Here are five principles, which we believe should guide global NGOs:

- Accountability must go beyond mere contract compliance.
- Accountability should focus on effect against mission.
- Accountability should be as much to the beneficiaries as to the donors.
- Accountability should seek to establish the causal linkages between inputs, outputs, and mission success.
- Accountability should result in learning that will drive decisions and improve future organizational performance.

A CHALLENGING FUTURE.

In 2003, in the wake of the Iraq war, guerilla attacks forced the International Red Cross to withdraw from the capital city of Baghdad. Perhaps its well-known brand profile made the Red Cross a prime target for attack? Or was the Red Cross perceived by the guerillas, no doubt unfairly, as a brand co-opted by the Americans? On that same day in 2003, more than 400 international NGOs were tripping over each other in Kabul trying to aid in the reconstruction of Afghanistan. Were they coordinating their efforts, focusing on particular geographies or areas of expertise? Or were some of them in Kabul to maintain their brand profiles because their members and donors expected them to be there on the front line—even at the expense of redirecting resources away from equally challenged, though less publicized trouble spots around the world?

Perhaps the most fundamental challenge for any NGO in the twenty-first century remains the definition of mission. The mission must be ambitious and current enough to excite volunteers, donors, and members across national boundaries. Yet it must also be distinct, enabling the NGO to stand out amidst the increasing clutter of NGO brands. The mission may focus on humanitarian relief—old-fashioned to some, but still much needed around the world. Or it may focus on sustainable development, providing small loans that enable families to break out of poverty, or on the better husbanding of environmental resources. Or, like the Jubilee 2000 campaign for third-world debt relief, it may focus purely on advocacy, pressing governments, international agencies, and multinational corporations for policy changes and new legislation. The message here is that mission clarity is the key to effectiveness. There are simply too many NGO brands for any one to successfully be "all things to all people."

NGOs must mesh their missions with their sources of funds. Some NGOs, including Greenpeace and Oxfam America, refuse all corporate funding. This makes them entirely dependent on membership dues, individual and foundation donations, and government grants. Other NGOs, such as Habitat for Humanity and the World Wildlife Fund, do partner with multinational corporations. These corporations increasingly realize that growth in shareholder value depends on the people of the world being free, educated, and healthy—and they are increasingly willing to commit resources to achieve these goals. The funding that global NGOs receive from corporations or the individual foundations of successful businessmen such as Bill Gates and George Soros can extend the reach of their missions and diversify their funding sources. But to what extent does it compromise their integrity? And to what extent do NGOs that partner with companies risk disenchanting their members and donors, with the result that they become increasingly reliant on corporate gifts to maintain their budgets? Those NGOs that accept corporate donations may be better off in the short term, but they open themselves up to being outflanked by new, "purist" organizations doing similar work but without the burden of corporate support.

Another concern is the degree to which the elite group of established global NGOs—almost all of which are "northern" in origin—should work through their own affiliates in beneficiary countries.[30] Or should they, in the spirit of sustainable development, nurture the emergence of freestanding "southern" NGOs and transnational grassroots movements which, once effective, might prove to be more attractive conduits than their own affiliates for the disbursement of funds by donor governments? For example, Oxfam America's Partnership for Impact program requires that it work only through "southern" NGOs. In this regard, global NGOs are like global corporations—having to prove their local value added wherever they operate, for example, by partnering with and training (rather than draining) the talent of indigenous NGOs. Many "northern" NGOs pay lip service to "southern" NGOs but are reluctant to give them an equal seat at the table until they are financially as strong. Is that fair?

The conclusion of the cold war and the forces of globalization have spawned a vigorous and constructive dialogue on how we can move from an interdependent world to an integrated world community with shared benefits, responsibilities, and values. The global NGOs, with their enormous reservoir of public trust and cumulative experience, have an important role to play in setting the international policy agenda and advocating for change.

However, it is increasingly evident that global NGOs cannot do it all on their own.[31] They must be catalysts for change, testing and evaluating new approaches to solving problems of poverty, rights abuse, and environmental degradation. They must set global (rather than "northern") standards of excellence for NGOs worldwide while selflessly helping fledgling "southern" NGOs develop their own capabilities and strengthen civil society in emerging economics. To ensure that their best practices and proven programs are imitated and scaled up around the world, the global NGOs must become experts in partnerships and strategic alliances, working in leadership or supportive roles as appropriate in conjunction with other NGOs, governments, foundations, and/or the corporate sector. Only if they partner will they ensure that maximum resources are put behind the solutions they uncover. Above all, the chief executives of global NGOs must nurture and steward their brands as valued assets, not for egotistical or competitive reasons, but to maximize the trust and continuing flow of resources on which the fulfillment of their missions depends.

Notes to Introduction

[1] Jonathan Wootliff and Christopher Deri, "NGOs: The New Super Brands," *Corporate Reputation Review* 4, no. 2 (2001): 157–164.

[2] Jone L. Pearce, "Foreword" in *Globalization and NGOs*, ed. Jonathan P. Doh and Hildy Teegen, xi–xii (Westport, CT: Praeger, 2003). .

[3] A. Rani Parker, "Prospects for NGO Collaboration with Multinational Enterprises," in *Globalization and NGOs*, ed. Jonathan P. Doh and Hildy Teegen, 81–106 (Westport, CT: Praeger, 2003).

[4] Thomas W. Dichter, "Globalization and Its Effects on NGOs: Efflorescence or a Blurring of Roles and Relevance?" *Nonprofit and Voluntary Sector Quarterly* 28, no. 4 (1999): 38–58.

[5] Marc Lindenberg and Coralie Bryant, *Going Global: Transforming Relief and Development NGOs* (Bloomfield, CT: Kumarian Press, 2001).

[6] International Federation of Red Cross and Red Crescent Societies, *World Disasters Report: 1999* (Geneva: IFRC, 1999).

[7] Sharon M. Oster, *Strategic Management for Nonprofit Organizations* (New York: Oxford University Press, 1995).

[8] S. Hoffman, "Clash of Globalizations," *Foreign Affairs* 18, no. 4 (July 2002): 104–115.

[9] P. Utting, *Visible Hands: Taking Responsibility for Social Development* (Geneva: U.N. Research Institute for Social Development, 2000).

[10] Debora L. Spar and Lane T. La Mure, "The Power of Activism: Assessing the Impact of NGOs on Global Business," *California Management Review* 45, no. 3 (Spring 2003): 78–101.

[11] David Korten and Rudi Klauss, eds., *People Centered Development* (West Hartford, CT: Kumarian Press, 1984).

[12] Paul Streeten, "Nongovernmental Organizations and Development," *Annals of the Academy of Political and Social Sciences* 554 (1997): 193–210.

[13] David Henderson, *Misguided Virtue: False Notions of Corporate Social Responsibility* (Philadelphia: Coronet Books, 2002).

[14] George Soros, *George Soros On Globalization* (New York: PublicAffairs, 2002).

[15] Philippe Legrain, *Open World: The Truth About Globalization* (London: Abacus, 2002).

[16] Paul Temporal, *Advanced Brand Management: From Vision to Valuation* (Singapore: John Wiley & Sons, 2002).

[17] John A. Quelch, James E. Austin, and N. Laidler-Kylander, "Mining Gold in Not-for-Profit Brands," *Harvard Business Review* 82, no. 4 (April 2004): 15–16.

[18] John A. Quelch and V. Kasturi Rangan, "Profit Globally, Give Globally," *Harvard Business Review* 81, no. 12 (December 2003): 16–17.

[19] Rien Van Gendt, "International Giving," Address to the Chicago Global Donors Network, (Chicago, October 1, 2003).

[20] James E. Austin, *The Collaboration Challenge: How Nonprofits and Business Succeed Through Strategic Alliances* (San Francisco: Jossey-Bass, 2000).

[21] John M. T. Balmer and Stephen A. Greyser, *Revealing The Corporation* (London: Routledge, 2003).

[22] Michael Edwards, David A. Hulme, and T. Wallace, "NGOs in a Global Future: Managing Local Delivery to Worldwide Leverage," *Public Administration and Development* 2 (1999): 117–136.

[23] Allen Grossman and V. Kasturi Rangan, "Managing Multisite Nonprofits," *Nonprofit Management and Leadership* 11, no.3 (Spring 2001): 321–337.

[24] Sara Gibbs et al., *Decentralised NGO Management*, INTRAC Occasional Papers Series Number 19 (February 2000).

[25] Michael Edwards and David Hulme, eds., *Nongovernmental Organizations: Performance and Accountability* (London.: Earthscan Publications Ltd., 1993).

[26] John A. Byrne, "The New Face of Philanthropy," *Businessweek* (December 2, 2002) 82–94.

[27] Mike Hudson, *Managing at the Leading Edge* (London: Directory of Social Change, 2003).

[28] John C. Sawhill and David Williamson, "Mission Impossible? Measuring Success in Nonprofit Organizations," *Nonprofit Management and Leadership* 11, no. 3 (Spring 2001): 371–386.

[29] Peter Drucker, *Managing The Non-Profit Organization: Principles and Practices* (New York: Harper Business, 1990).

[30] Michael Edwards, "International Development NGOs: Agents of Foreign Aid or Vehicles for International Cooperation?" *Nonprofit and Voluntary Sector Quarterly* 28, no. 4 (1999): 25–37.

[31] Hildy Teegen and Jonathan P. Doh, "Conclusion: Globalization and the Future of NGO Influence," in *Globalization and NGOs*, ed. Jonathan P. Doh and Hildy Teegen, 203–222 (Westport, CT: Praeger, 2003).

PART 1

Mission and Strategy

CASE 1
Peace Winds Japan

Field coordinators from the six countries where Peace Winds provided assistance met in Tokyo in December 2002 for their annual budget and strategy review. Despite the constant challenge of raising funds, the tone of the meeting was upbeat. There was considerable pride in the achievements and profile that Peace Winds had achieved, both in Japan and internationally, after just six years in existence. Peace Winds was blazing the trail for an emerging group of nongovernmental organizations (NGOs) in Japan. The challenge was how best to focus and sustain the organization's momentum and ensure its further growth and development.

ORIGINS AND MISSION.

In 1993, Kensuke Onishi was in England writing his master's thesis on humanitarian relief efforts in the Kurdish Autonomous Region of northern Iraq. The following year, he went to Iraq as a volunteer for a small Japanese NGO to provide humanitarian relief in the aftermath of the 1991 Persian Gulf war. In Iraq, Onishi earned the nickname "push man" from the refugees he assisted because of the frequency with which he had to push his old truck to jump-start it. In Iraq, Onishi was impressed by the financial and staff resources of the American and European NGOs. In contrast, the Japanese NGO struggled to obtain donor support and had to withdraw from Iraq after eighteen months for lack of funds. Onishi founded Peace Winds with two university friends in 1996 at the age of twenty-eight. He resolved to establish a Japanese NGO that would eventually rival the American and European NGOs in resources and influence.

This would not be easy. Although Japan topped the charts in per-capita overseas development and relief aid, individual and corporate donations for this purpose were far lower than in the United States and were dampened further by the prolonged Japanese recession. Seventeen percent of overseas development money from the United States in 2001 was transferred to NGOs, compared with less than half of 1 percent in Japan. Certain Japanese politicians who influenced heavily the overseas development budget tended to favor construction projects in which Japanese companies played a prominent role.

Professor John Quelch prepared this case with the help of Masako Egawa, Executive Director of the HBS Japan Research Office. HBS cases are developed solely as the basis for class discussion. Cases are not intended to serve as endorsements, sources of primary data, or illustrations of effective or ineffective management.

In 2000, Onishi established and became chairman of the "Japan Platform," a discussion and policy forum involving leaders of Japanese NGOs, representatives of the Ministry of Foreign Affairs, business leaders, and academics. His opinions on overseas development issues were widely aired. In December 2001, he criticized a decision by the Ministry of Foreign Affairs not to pay the expenses of international NGO invitees to a Tokyo conference on aid to Afghanistan. A leading Japanese politician, Muneo Suzuki, who had wielded tremendous influence over the use of the overseas development assistance funds, tried to ban Onishi from the conference. The minister of foreign affairs spoke out in Onishi's favor and he attended the conference, which took place in January 2002. A subsequent investigation of Suzuki led to his resignation from the Japanese parliament because of his illegal involvement in selecting vendors for overseas development projects. The confrontation between Onishi and Suzuki was widely reported in the Japanese media, and Peace Winds' profile was raised as a result.

Peace Winds was one of many small Japanese NGOs concerned with international aid and development. NGOs had emerged in Japan during the 1960s and 1970s, stimulated by the desire to provide humanitarian assistance to the war-torn areas of Indochina. However, by the 1990s, NGOs were still not seen as part of mainstream civil society. Akiko Matsunobu, chief of Peace Winds' marketing and public relations unit and former head of marketing for Federal Express in the North Pacific region, described the situation this way:

> *Japanese NGOs continued to be viewed as quasi-political, leftist, and self-righteous. This, together with the natural tendency of Japanese to rely on the government for their well-being, has limited the development of the voluntary sector in Japan.*

> *For most Japanese, the plight of needy people around the world is of little interest. They are both geographically and culturally distant. Japanese people might become interested temporarily if the media are highlighting a famine in a particular region, but it's hard to persuade most people to take a sustained interest.*

In addition, charitable donations by individuals were not tax deductible in Japan until 1999. However, under the law passed that year, a Japanese NGO could qualify for tax-deductible donation status—but only if it met several criteria. First, the charity's activities could not be focused solely on the local community. Second, the charity had to report its donor list to the government. Third, and most challenging in a nation with little tradition of charitable giving, income from donors had to be one-third of total income. By February 2003, only twelve out of more than 10,000 NGOs in Japan had qualified for tax-deductible status. This severely constrained fund-raising by Japanese NGOs. Individual donations to Japanese not-for-profits amounted to Y360 billion, or only 0.07 percent of gross domestic product, much less than the 1.9 percent in the United States. According to Matsunobu,

> *Lack of tax exemption system discourages donation both by individuals and corporations. For example, the government survey shows that the donation by average household was Y2,936 or less than $25, in 2002. The amount has declined during the past several years due to the long-lasting recession. Contribution from the corporate sector is next to nothing, too. I think the average amount of Y342 million in the Keidanren survey (see Exhibit 3) is vastly misleading since it is based on the responses from 300–400 large companies,*

which are more committed to philanthropy than most companies in Japan. In fact, we often find that there is no department responsible for such activities when we try to raise funds from corporations.

Peace Winds' vision was stated clearly in its 2001 annual report:

To build a world where each and every person can fully realize his/her potential, without the fear of armed conflict and poverty.

There were three components to the Peace Winds mission statement:

1. To provide humanitarian relief and endeavor in resolving and preventing issues, such as conflict, that create the need for assistance.

2. To work for reconstruction and development that empowers people and communities, such as those threatened by poverty, for an independent and sustainable livelihood.

3. To strive for change in the social structure that creates poverty and conflict, and for improvement of the current assistance system.

According to Onishi,

> *NGOs should be professional organizations that can complement government overseas development activities. To influence policy, we have to do our own research. I want to add a "think tank" component to Peace Winds' mission. The key challenge is funding.*[1]

FINANCES.

Peace Winds' income statement and statement of expenditures for 2001 are presented in **Exhibits 1** and **2**. Like most Japanese NGOs, Peace Winds relied heavily on membership fees and grants rather than individual donations. Peace Winds members

Exhibit 1	Income Statement for FY 2001[1] (in yen)[2]
Membership Fees	282,592,300
General Donations	12,524,772
Designated Donations	107,963,487
In-kind Donations	44,577,463
Subsidies[3]	71,344,020
Grants[4]	375,502,411
Other Income	2,451,702
Miscellaneous Income	18,164,202
Profitable Program Income	89,898,451
Carryover from FY 2000	136,184,195
Total:	1,141,184,195

Source: Peace Winds' Data.

[1]FY 2001 ran from February 1, 2001, to January 31, 2002.

[2]One U.S. dollar equals 110 yen.

[3]Subsidies from Ministry of Foreign Affairs and Tokyo International Exchange Foundation.

[4]Grants from UK Department for International Development, Foundation for International Development and Relief, United Nations High Commission for Refugees, Japan Platform.

Exhibit 2	Expenditures for FY 2001 (in yen)

Kurdistan (Northern Iraq) Program	79,211,725
Mongolia	65,387,834
Indonesia	33,228,090
East Timor	34,137,168
Sierra Leone	114,194,489
Afghanistan	291,379,350
Emergency Relief Program	43,770,691
Yunnan (China) Program	589,598
Program Unit Expenditure	35,799,507
Research	15,491,323
Advocacy	30,438,520
Other Program Expenditures	200,900
Tokyo HQ Running Costs	101,564,457
Others	31,417,363
Profitable Program Expenditures	91,950,256
Carryover to FY 2002	172,422,924
Total:	1,141,184,195

Source: Peace Winds' Data.

came from many demographic and socioeconomic groups, with a slight skew toward older women. There were three levels of annual membership: full membership with the right to vote at the annual meeting cost Y120,000; a "friend" membership with the same benefits but without the right to vote was priced at Y12,000; and a corporate membership was offered for Y30,000.

One-off corporate donations were often made to charities on the occasion of a company's anniversary. Companies received no tax relief for such donations. As indicated in **Exhibits 3** and **4**, corporate donations in Japan were low, reduced further by a stagnant economy, and widely dispersed. The most important among a small number of regular individual donors to Peace Winds were independent sales agents for an Osaka-based cosmetics company, Elseraine, run by Masaru Ishibashi, who was also president of Peace Winds. Many of the company's agents voluntarily donated 1 percent of their sales to Peace Winds and other charities. Mr. Ishibashi

Exhibit 3	Japanese Corporate Philanthropy Expenditures

Year (Companies Reporting)	1995 (367)	1996 (405)	1997 (376)	1998 (360)	1999 (309)	2000 (323)	2001 (342)
Total Donations (BN Yen)	145.4 bn.	162.0 bn.	155.7 bn.	137.6 bn.	124.6 bn.	134.5 bn.	117.0 bn.
Company Average (MM Yen)	396	400	414	382	430	416	342
Year-On-Year growth	3.8%	1.0%	3.5%	−7.7%	5.5%	3.2%	−17.8%

Source: Adapted from a survey conducted by Keidanren (Japanese Business Federation), July 2002.

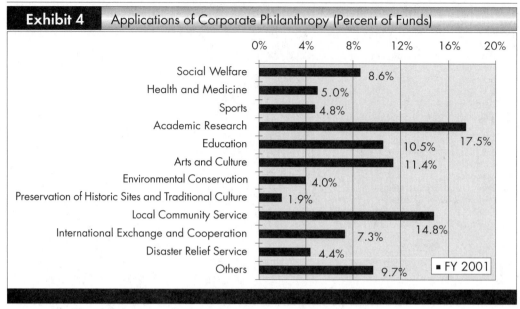

Exhibit 4   Applications of Corporate Philanthropy (Percent of Funds)

- Social Welfare — 8.6%
- Health and Medicine — 5.0%
- Sports — 4.8%
- Academic Research — 17.5%
- Education — 10.5%
- Arts and Culture — 11.4%
- Environmental Conservation — 4.0%
- Preservation of Historic Sites and Traditional Culture — 1.9%
- Local Community Service — 14.8%
- International Exchange and Cooperation — 7.3%
- Disaster Relief Service — 4.4%
- Others — 9.7%

■ FY 2001

Source: Adapted from a survey conducted by Keidanren (Japanese Business Federation), July 2002.

was the father of a close friend of Onishi and had donated funds to help him start Peace Winds when he had returned from Iraq.

FIELD OPERATIONS.

Peace Winds began relief work in the Kurdish area of northern Iraq and in Mongolia in 1996. By 2001, Peace Winds had developed field operations in ten regions. At the end of 2002, it had field operations in six regions. **Exhibit 5** identifies these operations and the numbers of staff and beneficiaries associated with each.

In 2002, Onishi spent half his time in the field in Afghanistan, Indonesia, and Iraq. He spent the rest of the time in Japan speaking in public forums, collaborating with other NGOs on broadening their influence in Japan, and attempting to persuade politicians to change overseas aid and development policies. Looking to the future, Onishi said,

> I am pleased with our progress but there is no end to our work. As long as states keep failing, our emergency aid services transitioning seamlessly to rehabilitation and development will be needed.

> Our biggest challenge is to attract and retain talented people. To work in field operations in difficult regions is a real challenge. Our people have to be knowledgeable and skilled but they also need guts and commitment.

> We have grown rapidly so we have many staff who are both young and new to the organization. In 2003, I'll need to spend more time coaching, training, and inspiring them so they can share a common Peace Winds vision.

Peace Winds was careful to channel as much of its income as possible back into field operations. The challenges Peace Winds staff faced in the field were discussed with the field coordinators for Afghanistan and Iraq.

Exhibit 5	Peace Winds Field Operations: 2002				
	Year Operation Commenced	Number of Offices	International Staff	Local Staff	Number of Beneficiaries
Afghanistan	2001	4	5	40	33,000
China	1999	0	0 (1 in Japan)	0	80
East Timor	1999	1	1	10	24,300
India	2000	(Already Closed)			7,400
Indonesia	1997	1	1	3	49,000
Iraq (Kurdistan)	1996	4	5	120	69,900
Kosovo	1999	(Already Closed)			
Mongolia	1996	1	1	20	9,300
Sierra Leone	2001	3	5	80	6,200

Afghanistan.

Peace Winds decided to become involved in Afghanistan early in 2001. Twenty-three years of conflict and four years of drought had ravaged agricultural production and disrupted irrigation systems and water supplies. Yet the livelihoods of 85 percent of Afghans were still linked to the land. Peace Winds decided to focus on the north of the country, where the drought had been most severe.

The events of September 11, 2001, did not deter Peace Winds from opening a previously planned mission in Afghanistan in November 2001 under the leadership of Kensuke Onishi. Patricia Garcia was an Australian development economist who had twelve years of experience running international NGO field operations for Oxfam and United Nations agencies when she joined Peace Winds. In December 2002, Garcia commented on how September 11 changed Peace Winds' project in Afghanistan:

> Peace Winds originally planned to enter Afghanistan to help Afghan people secure access to water. But the events of September 11 and the subsequent conflict in the country meant that our initial focus was on emergency and humanitarian relief. Peace Winds ran a six-month emergency relief program which provided 6,000 winter tents (purchased in Pakistan) and food to 33,000 displaced persons in the northern province of Sarepul. Peace Winds also repaired two major roads. By delivering on these projects, Peace Winds quickly earned respect and credibility. Now, a year later, the focus has shifted to rehabilitating the infrastructure. Peace Winds is currently helping local communities build four schools and dig one well. To date, we have built twelve schools and dug twenty wells in total. Since 90 percent of the population depends on agriculture, we are lending melon and sesame seeds (recipients returned seeds for recycling after the harvest), training women in poultry and silkworm farming, and advising on pest management.

Garcia worked with two Japanese expatriates and twenty-eight local staff members in eight project sites, clustered around Sarepul. Peace Winds decided to concentrate its efforts in one area despite numerous requests to open offices in other cities. The local office staff represented the ethnic groups in the communities where the projects were being implemented. Several had themselves been displaced by the recent conflict.

Garcia and many of the staff lived and worked in the same building. Garcia spent half her time in the field overseeing the eight Peace Winds projects and working with community leaders to ensure their participation in and ownership of the projects. She spent 30 percent of her time with government and donor agencies. The situation was not without strain:

> *I work close to twenty-four/seven. I have mandated a rest day each weekend for the staff so they feel no pressure to do the same. As a woman in a Muslim country, I cannot go out unaccompanied and have to respect local customs when socializing with the local population.*

Garcia commented on the challenges facing NGOs in Afghanistan:

> *There are more than 150 NGOs operating in Afghanistan. Coordination is a major challenge. The new Afghan government is seeking to control a higher percentage of the overseas aid, pressing for it to be paid directly to the new ministries rather than channeled through NGOs. However, the government does not yet have sufficient, qualified staff to manage these resources. On the other hand, the NGOs pay well and attract some of the brightest locals onto their staffs. A big question is whether the NGOs will help to transfer this talent and capability to the fledgling government.*

> *What keeps me awake at night? First and foremost, continuity of donor funding. Aid dollars, even from the international agencies, depend on the number of TV news stories. Most donor funding is on an annual rather than multiyear basis. Yet the challenges in Afghanistan demand our long-term commitment to rebuilding infrastructure and civil society.*

> *Second, I worry about attracting and retaining quality local staff to ensure that Peace Winds will have the capacity to maximize its impact in Afghanistan. Competition for talented locals among the NGOs is intense. We have to pay good salaries and provide training and promotion opportunities. Sometimes, Tokyo headquarters does not appreciate these pressures. I'd welcome more headquarters staff visiting our field projects and not relying on daily e-mail reports, which I hope will soon be made weekly or monthly, as we have now moved on from emergency relief to reconstruction.*

Iraq.

Many NGOs channeled relief to northern Iraq after the 1991 gulf war. Peace Winds entered in 1996 with a commitment to provide medicines, health care, and social support programs. Miho Kishitani was appointed coordinator of the Peace Winds northern Iraq mission in 2000, overseeing three Japanese expatriates and 110 local staff members in four offices. The mission had an annual budget of Y100 million and targeted 70,000 people for medical, construction, and social care assistance.

The Kurds were the dominant ethnic group in northern Iraq, constituting 15 to 20 percent of Iraq's 24 million people. They had been fighting for self-rule for a separate Kurdistan (an area roughly twice the size of New Jersey), independent of Baghdad, since 1961. In the 1980s, Saddam Hussein razed 90 percent of their villages; more than 200,000 died in chemical weapons attacks or went missing in government roundups. After the 1991 gulf war, U.S. and British aircraft began protecting a new northern no-fly zone. Saddam pulled out and imposed economic sanctions to starve the landlocked Kurds. By 2001, one-third of the population were refugees and average life expectancy had fallen eleven years in a decade. Nevertheless, in 2003, fledgling political parties were competing for popular support and the Kurdish Autonomous Government was extracting $1 million a day from levies on illicit trade.

Peace Winds was effective in northern Iraq for a number of reasons, Kitshitani said:

> First, although northern Iraq currently accounts for the largest United Nations relief program, there are only ten NGOs here, nine European NGOs and us. Second, everyone thinks favorably of Japan through brands like Toyota and Sony. Japan is seen as even-handed and neutral, with no history of involvement in Iraq nor any political interest in its future. Some here are also familiar with Japan's impressive record of reconstruction after World War II. Third, Peace Winds has a six-year track record in northern Iraq, and our attention to communicating thoroughly with community and government leaders sets us apart from some of the European NGOs. As a result, the Kurdish government often asks Peace Winds to represent its views to the Japanese government.

In early 2002, Kishitani summarized the three main challenges she faced as a manager. The first was security and access:

> The Iraqi government has a bounty of $10,000 on my head. I have to be very careful. I have round-the-clock protection. I can only enter Iraq over land from Syria. Since it takes one to two months for me to obtain a Syrian visa, I don't like to leave often.
>
> The Baghdad regime also regards locals who work for NGOs as spies, and they, too, are at risk. Often, staff members will seek my assurance that I will get them out of the country if they are threatened. This stems from the family atmosphere we have built within the Peace Winds organization and the fact that we have over the years promoted four local Kurdish staff to our international staff. In fact, one of these Kurds is now the northern Iraq desk officer at Peace Winds' Tokyo headquarters.
>
> The Kurds have been oppressed for decades. Though there are rays of hope, the future of Iraq is unknown. That's why we are stockpiling food, water, tents, and medicines in anticipation of an invasion to oust Saddam Hussein. The result is a climate of nervousness and negativity. Even the beneficiaries of our projects always seem to be complaining. My guess is that people in Afghanistan are a lot more positive, following the overthrow of the Taliban regime, than they are here.
>
> I spend around 40 percent of my time in the field; 10 percent on staff matters; 20 percent in meetings with UN officials, political leaders from the two rival parties, and community leaders; 20 percent in e-mail and telephone contact with Tokyo and writing my monthly activity and financial reports; and 10 percent listening to the BBC, playing with my cats and rabbits, and learning the local language.

CONCLUSION.

In the eyes of many NGO observers, Peace Winds was already "batting above its weight." It had effective field operations in some of the toughest and most high-profile relief and development environments in the world. As a Japanese NGO working in the international arena, it was practically unique.

As Onishi and the senior staff of Peace Winds contemplated the future during their 2002 meeting, many questions were open for discussion. How should Peace Winds continue to develop? Should it open up offices in more countries, remain in those that it currently served, or concentrate still further to maximize its local impact? Should Peace Winds focus on providing emergency relief, which required substantial manpower, or concentrate on sustainable development, which required less manpower but long-term commitment? If the latter, should the focus be on agriculture, health care, or infrastructure—or should Peace Winds aim to respond to whatever local needs were not being met in the regions it decided to enter? What tradeoffs would Peace Winds have to make to achieve its mission and position itself as a leading international NGO in the twenty-first century?

Notes to Case

[1] Kensuke Onishi, interview, Japan's *Weekly Economist*, July 2, 2002.

CASE 2
Amnesty International

In January 2003, Irene Khan, secretary general of Amnesty International, reflected on the organization's expanding mission, recent organizational changes, and increased competition. "We are starting to take a serious look at brand management," she said. "We need to clearly define who we are and then communicate this through the Amnesty brand."

Amnesty International (AI) was a worldwide campaigning movement that worked to promote internationally recognized human rights. It was impartial and independent of any government, political persuasion, or religious creed and, in 2002, had close to 1.5 million members and supporters in more than 140 countries and a total gross income of more than £90 million.[1] Activities were largely funded through public subscriptions and donations. An International Secretariat was based in London and employed more than 350 staff members and 100 volunteers from more than fifty countries around the world.

History.

AI was founded in 1961 by British lawyer Peter Benenson. Upon learning about a group of students in Portugal who were arrested for raising a toast to "freedom" in a public restaurant, Benenson launched a one-year campaign, called Appeal for Amnesty, in the *London Observer*. The Appeal for Amnesty called for the release of all people imprisoned because of the peaceful expression of their beliefs, politics, race, religion, color, or national origin. Benenson's plan was to encourage people to write letters to government officials in countries that held prisoners of conscience,[2] calling for their release. The campaign grew and spread to other countries, and within a year AI was formed.

AI's mandate was based on the United Nations Universal Declaration of Human Rights established in 1948, which underscored the principle that people have fundamental rights that transcend national, cultural, religious, or ideological boundaries. Early activities by members organized into prisoner-adoption groups focused on letter writing on behalf of specific prisoners of conscience. Members often developed a

Professor John Quelch and Research Associate Nathalie Laidler prepared this case. HBS cases are developed solely as the basis for class discussion. Cases are not intended to serve as endorsements, sources of primary data, or illustrations of effective or ineffective management.

bond with individual prisoners, whose names, cases, and families they grew to know. In this way, AI focused on individuals, not countries or political systems.

During the 1960s, AI members became more active at the local level in publicity, fund-raising, and educational activities. In the late 1960s, to maintain impartiality and protect human rights activists themselves, AI adopted the rule that people in the organization were to work only on cases outside their own countries. In the mid-1980s, a number of musicians and artists adopted AI as a special cause, giving concerts and tours, then donating the profits to the organization. This brought tremendous growth and visibility to AI, whose budget increased dramatically. In 1997, AI was awarded the Nobel Peace Prize.

Throughout the 1970s and 1980s, AI developed its research capability at the International Secretariat and devoted resources to obtaining accurate information about prisoners of conscience. Khan expanded on AI's evolution:

> In the 1960s, AI was just a social movement, but in the 1970s and 1980s, a bureaucracy started to evolve with the International Secretariat at its center, and the organization expanded its capabilities and resources. As it grew, institutions and rules were developed concerning policy, activities, decision making, and funding, with great emphasis being placed on internal democracy. By the early 1990s, AI's internal structure was marked by several large country sections, a centralized International Secretariat, and a large number of smaller sections and structures, primarily in the global South, creating different power dynamics within AI. Several of the larger sections had significant capacity and resources and were eager for greater freedom to carry out their activities. They were getting frustrated with the inability of the International Secretariat to meet their demands as speedily and effectively as they wished. Demands for internal change were matched by enormous changes in the human rights world around AI. Prior to 1990, AI focused on governments and prisoners of conscience, but as the political world changed, AI started to expand its activities both in terms of the kinds of people suffering from human rights abuses and the entities responsible for these human rights transgressions.

Turning 40—AI's Midlife Crisis.[3]

In August 2001, AI drafted an internal document called the State of the Movement 2001 Report that concluded the following:

> On its 40th anniversary, AI finds itself at a critical juncture. The international political, economic, and social landscape has significantly changed. The focus of the global human rights movement has expanded from civil and political rights (CPR) to also encompass violations of economic, social, and cultural rights (ESCR), and whereas AI was among the first human rights organizations in 1961, there has been an explosion in the number, strength, and diversity of NGOs (nongovernmental organizations) addressing human rights issues. While AI's reputation as a leading international human rights organization remains intact, the overall relevance and effectiveness of the organization have become increasingly questioned. AI is going through a critical transition period.

Pierre Sané, AI's then-secretary general, believed that AI's vision and mandate had to be clarified and that the "midlife crisis" the organization was experiencing would enable AI to reassess priorities and develop a more relevant purpose and vision.

A changing global environment. The end of the cold war, the declining role of the nation-state, the increase in conflicts, and the multiple effects of globalization had created a new context for AI. There had been, during the 1990s, an increase in the influence of violent nonstate actors perpetrating human rights violations, and the focus of the human rights community had expanded from political and civil rights to economic, social, and cultural rights.

The number of NGOs focusing on human rights had proliferated, yet in many countries the relationships between NGOs and states had evolved from being confrontational to cooperative. Collaboration among NGOs was also on the rise. Competition for resources, members, and public support had also escalated. The communications revolution and the growth of the Internet had dramatically changed the way human rights activists mobilized support, collected and disseminated information, and launched protests.

AI's key challenges in 2001. A key question was whether AI was still a leading agent of change in the human rights movement. Many people within the organization and outside it thought that, since the 1990s, AI had lost its edge and failed to respond quickly enough.

1. *Shift in mandate* In the early 1990s, the international human rights movement began to embrace economic, social, and cultural rights (ESCR) in addition to the traditional civil and political rights (CPR). AI, however, continued to focus primarily on CPR. Although some members criticized the organization for responding to only one group of rights, arguing that this restricted AI's collaboration with local NGOs and made the organization appear less relevant, other members believed that AI's strength lay in its focus on a core area of rights and that such focus resulted in greater coherence and effectiveness.

2. *Work on own country* By 2001, the restriction against members working on cases within their own countries had become a point of great contention. Some members argued that the restriction was no longer relevant and prevented the organization's being perceived as relevant locally; others believed that it maintained AI's impartiality and international solidarity.

   One of AI's most criticized actions had been to campaign for better conditions for imprisoned members of the Baader-Meinhoff Gang, a left-wing political terrorist group active in Germany in the 1970s. German AI members became deeply involved and pressed the International Secretariat to investigate charges of torture and human rights abuses against members of the Baader-Meinhoff Gang. Jonathan Power, author and journalist, concluded,

   > *Amnesty came dangerously near to being used by a group that had no sympathy for the values Amnesty stood for and which sought to overthrow the kind of Western European democracy that allowed Amnesty to flourish. Looking back, the Baader-Meinhoff effort was not the organization's finest hour. Against the better judgment of some of its members, Amnesty allowed the German national group to involve it more deeply than the case deserved.[4]*

3. *Adapting research and campaigning* During the 1990s, AI had increased its participation in local and regional human rights networking and collective campaigning. Meanwhile, changes in communication had made it easier

to launch global campaigns and promote electronic debate. Some members, however, were concerned that although AI was known for the quality of its information, it did not always disseminate it quickly enough. In addition, some believed AI's centralized campaigning approach limited the flexibility of individual national sections, and the campaigns themselves, always developed through consensus, were thought to be sometimes vague and lacking in effect.

4. ***Streamlining decision making*** Given the democratic nature of AI (described in detail below), the organization recognized that its slow decision-making processes, involving broad participation and consensus building, were costly in terms of organizational effectiveness.

5. ***Membership development*** In 2001, AI's membership was heavily skewed, with almost a million members in Western Europe, a little less than 400,000 in North America, and only a small proportion in the global South and East. Workers at many of the smaller national sections thought they needed additional support, training, and capacity building. Others pointed out that many of the smaller national sections, which were dependent on international funding, were required to submit regular reports, but that the larger self-sufficient sections were not. As a result, no standardized information was available on the entire organization. Yet others worried that the number of national sections depending on funding from the International Secretariat was increasing and that AI had not managed to raise many funds in countries where other NGOs had apparently succeeded. Finally, there was a general concern that AI should strive to promote a more consistent and universal brand, although there was, as yet, no clear definition of what the AI brand represented.

Mission and Objectives.

In August 2001, AI's International Council amended its statute to include a new vision statement, mission statement, and set of core values.

- ***AI's vision*** was of a world in which "every person enjoys all of the human rights enshrined in the Universal Declaration of Human Rights and other international human rights standards."

- ***AI's mission*** was to "undertake research and action focused on preventing and ending grave abuses of the rights to physical and mental integrity, promote freedom of conscience and expression, and uphold freedom from discrimination."

- ***AI's core values*** included the principles of international solidarity, effective action for the individual victim, universality and indivisibility of human rights, impartiality and independence, and democracy and mutual respect.

Khan explained:

> *The essence of the Amnesty brand lies in its core values. The notion of international solidarity stems from the fact that AI is all about people in one part of the world working on behalf of other people in the world. Shining the light on individual cases has been our trademark, and we want to keep it that way. We work hard to maintain impartiality—for example, in the Middle East conflict we report on human rights abuses on both sides—and our organizational structure is highly democratic.*

AI's stated objectives were to address governments, intergovernmental organizations, armed political groups, companies, and other nonstate players. It sought to disclose human rights abuses accurately and quickly, and it systematically and impartially researched the facts of individual cases and patterns of human rights abuses. The findings were publicized, and members, supporters, and staff mobilized public pressure to stop the abuses. AI urged all governments to observe the rule of law and ratify and implement human rights standards, and carried out a wide range of educational activities.

Activities.

AI cooperated with other NGOs, the United Nations, and regional intergovernmental organizations to address human rights abuses. AI had developed a core strength in researching abuses, and in 2002, AI delegates visited dozen of countries to meet victims of human rights violations, observe trials, and interview local human rights activists and officials. The organization then communicated the results of its research, organized human rights education and awareness-raising programs, and sought to mobilize public opinion through specific campaigns.

AI was often cited, by journalists and third parties, as a credible source of information on issues of human rights abuses. In most cases this publicity was beneficial to AI's goal of raising awareness, but in specific situations AI had to ask that a third party not refer to the organization's work. In 1990, for example, during his efforts to build a coalition against Saddam Hussein before the gulf war, President George H. W. Bush quoted AI reports on Iraq. At the same time, U.S. authorities ignored AI's critique of the role of the CIA in torture in Guatemala and the use of capital punishment in the United States. AI members thought its brand name was being used in a one-sided, high-profile diplomatic war that threatened international human rights efforts and requested that U.S. officials stop quoting from the organization's reports.[5]

AI members, supporters, and staff around the world mobilized public opinion to pressure governments and other players with influence to stop human rights abuses. Activities ranged from public demonstrations to letter writing, from human rights education programs to fund-raising concerts, from approaches to local authorities to lobbying intergovernmental organizations, and from targeted appeals on behalf of a single individual to global campaigns on a specific country or issue. "Letter writing has been our core strength in the past," Khan explained, "and our commonest form of action. Over the years, AI members have written millions of letters on behalf of more than 44,000 prisoners of conscience; about 50 percent of the cases were eventually resolved. This is changing now," she added, "and we are shifting to e-campaigning, where text messages are easy to access on our Web site and can be sent on via e-mail." In addition, Khan believed that members were increasingly looking for more visible ways to campaign. "Younger members want to express their views more forcefully," Khan said. "In Poland, for example, Amnesty organized a human chain going from the Israeli Embassy to the Palestine Mission."

Each year, AI members around the world joined forces on one global campaign to achieve change. In 2002, this was the Campaign against Torture, which fought against torture and ill-treatment of women, children, ethnic minorities, and lesbians, gays, bisexual, and transgendered (LGBT) people. During 2002, four countries ratified the U.N. Convention against Torture, and a number of government leaders and officials made commitments to adopt legislation to prevent torture in their countries. (See **Exhibit 1** for an excerpt from AI's "Justice for Torture Victims" briefing, a publication that appeared in April 2002.)

Exhibit 1   Excerpt from AI's Justice for Torture Victims Publication, April 2001

Justice for torture victims

What you can do

● *You can help the people featured in this briefing:*
Please write appealing for:
- their cases to be impartially investigated;
- for them to be given prompt reparations from the state including financial compensation, medical care and rehabilitation; and
- for those responsible to be prosecuted and given a fair trial in proceedings which exclude the death penalty.

● *You can challenge your government to ensure that torture is not committed with impunity in your country:*
- torture should be expressly defined as a crime in national criminal law;
- all reports of torture should be promptly, independently, impartially and thoroughly investigated;
- decisions on whether to prosecute should be made by an independent prosecutor or investigating judge, not a political official;

- people suspected of torture should be brought to justice in fair trials;
- the rights of victims to an effective remedy against torture should be recognized in national law;
- victims of torture, witnesses and relatives should be protected before, during and after trials;
- victims of torture and their dependants should be entitled to reparation from the state including compensation and medical care.

● *You can challenge your government to ensure that your country is not a safe haven for torturers from other countries:*
- your country should ratify and implement the 1984 UN Convention against Torture, if it has not done so;
- your country should ratify and implement the 1998 Rome Statute of the International Criminal Court, if it has not done so;
- your country's legal system should allow the courts in your country to exercise universal jurisdiction over

alleged torturers (they should have the right to try cases no matter where the torture took place, and the nationality of the people involved);
- your country's legal system should allow people suspected of torture to be brought to justice in fair trials, or extradited to another country able and willing to prosecute them.

● *You can take a step to stamp out torture:*
- join Amnesty International's campaign against torture and impunity;
- join Amnesty International and other local and international human rights organizations which fight torture and impunity;
- make a donation to support Amnesty International's work;
- tell friends and family about the campaign and ask them to join too;
- register to take action against torture at *www.stoptorture.org* and campaign online. Visitors to the website will be able to appeal on behalf of individuals at risk of torture.

© Amnesty International Publications 2001
Original language: English.
All rights reserved.
Printed by Lynx Offset Ltd.

Amnesty International,
International Secretariat,
Peter Benenson House,
1 Easton Street,
London WC1X 0DW,
United Kingdom

www.amnesty.org

AI Index: ACT 40/022/2001

ISBN: 0-86210-309-6

ISBN 0-86210-309-6

9 780862 103095

Around the world, AI members and other human rights activists campaign against torture and impunity. Among their activities, they press the authorities in their countries to declare Torture Free Zones. One of the many ways of attracting attention is to wrap public buildings, former detention centres and other places of symbolic significance with Torture Free Zone tape
Photos: © AI

STAMP OUT TORTURE

Source: Amnesty International.

In 2002, AI worked on behalf of 2,813 named victims of human rights violations. AI's Urgent Action Network, made up of 80,000 volunteers in eighty-five countries, initiated 408 actions on behalf of people in eighty-one countries who were either at risk or had suffered human rights violations, including torture, disappearance, the death penalty, death in custody, or forcible return to countries where they would be in danger of human rights abuses. Of these urgent actions, 117 resulted in good news about the case. (See **Exhibit 2** for a direct-mail piece from Amnesty International USA describing the Urgent Action Network.)

AI's Web site contained more than 20,000 files and was visited by 10,000 people a day from all over the world. It featured a library of reports, press releases, and information on the latest campaigns, appeals for action, and online petitions. In 2002, more than 120,000 e-mail messages were sent to various governments as part of AI's Campaign Against Torture. AI also worked through a number of specialist networks to further its objectives. (See **Exhibit 3** for a description of AI's specialist networks.)

Expanding the scope of activities. Throughout the 1990s, AI had slowly expanded the scope of its activities from prisoners of conscience to include human rights abuses against refugees, women, children, ethnic minorities, and LGBT people. In addition, the organization broadened its target audience from governments to include intergovernmental organizations, armed political groups, companies, and other nonstate players. In 2001, AI also voted to expand its focus from human rights, narrowly defined, to include a whole spectrum of economic, social, cultural, and educational rights.

Organizational Structure.

In addition to the International Secretariat, the AI movement consisted of fifty-six national sections, pre-section coordination units in an additional twenty-four countries, and 7,800 local, youth, specialist, and professional groups in more than 100 countries.

AI was a democratic movement, self-governed by a nine-member Internal Executive Committee (IEC), whose members were elected every two years by an International Council (IC) representing the country sections. The IC's role was to set the organization's vision, mission, and core values and to discuss and approve AI's integrated strategic plan. The IEC's role was to provide leadership and stewardship for the organization as a whole. The day-to-day management of the organization was the responsibility of the International Secretariat.

The IC comprised 500 delegates from the different sections, with larger sections having a proportionally greater number of representatives. It met every two years, for twelve days, to debate and vote on resolutions. All major decisions concerning AI's human rights activities and the organization's internal operations were made by the IC. In 2001, forty-nine resolutions were put forward by various sections and voted on. They ranged from decisions about standardized financial reports to organizational development projects, the decision to take on the rights of internally displaced people, and the resolution to develop a corporate brand identity. In 2003, however, the roles of the IC, the IEC, and the International Secretariat were changing. Khan expanded on these changes:

> AI's mandate has grown over the years as sections or the IEC proposed resolutions, which were then debated and adopted by the IC. Over forty years, this has led to an incremental expansion of the mandate, which lacked a clear overall vision. Furthermore, it was very rigid because changes to the mandate could

Exhibit 2   Direct-Mail Piece from AI USA Describing the Urgent Action Network

Dear Friend,

I regret to inform you that we are faced with a severe crisis here at Amnesty International.

In plain English:

Our lifesaving Urgent Action Network to help prisoners of conscience and others threatened with torture or death is literally staggering under the weight of new emergencies.

However, you are not being asked to picket a prison in a foreign country, or attend a freedom demonstration, or in any way put yourself in jeopardy. Instead ...

... you can help us, quietly but effectively, right there in your own home.

And you can begin with the simple act of signing your name to the "Message of Hope" card that I'm enclosing with this letter.

Then mail it back to me, and I'll see that it is forwarded to a prisoner who is facing torture, or is being held in isolation for a political reason, or perhaps even faces the very real possibility of being executed.

For example, please listen to just one voice of the more than 45,000 individual prisoners whose cases were resolved with Amnesty International's help.

His name is Constantino, and for years he was held in a tiny cell; his only human contact was with his torturers. He said:

> "I did not experience a human face or see a green leaf, and my only company was cockroaches and mice.

> "The only daylight that entered my cell was through a small opening at the top of one wall. For eight months I had my hands and feet tied.

> "On Christmas Eve the door to my cell opened and the guard tossed in a crumpled piece of paper. I moved as best I could to pick it up.

> "It said simply, 'Constantino, do not be discouraged; we know you are alive.' It was signed 'Monica' and had the Amnesty International candle on it.

> "These words saved my life and my sanity. Eight months later, I was set free."

What happened here was the result of Amnesty's extraordinary programs, such as the Urgent Action Network.

AMNESTY INTERNATIONAL USA • 322 EIGHTH AVENUE • NEW YORK, NY 10001
(212) 807-8400 • www.amnestyusa.org

Source: Amnesty International USA.

Exhibit 2   continued

- 2 -

In the case of Constantino, we received reliable information, verified by our skilled researchers. The facts were fed into our massive worldwide network. And then, volunteers responded by sending urgent appeals, telegrams and telex letters to those responsible for detaining Constantino.

You see, our Urgent Action Network strips away the mask of secrecy that many governments hide behind.

We force them to ask the burning question: "Is this particular prisoner worth all of this negative publicity?"

Or: "Can we afford to further damage our domestic and international image?"

Sometimes prisoners do not know we are working on their behalf. Yet it can make a difference. Christine Anyanwu, a journalist long-imprisoned in Nigeria for reporting views in opposition to the ruling party, wrote to us upon her release:

> **"It has indeed been most reassuring to know that someone cares enough to hold one in his thoughts even for a second. I thank those friends who, undeterred by my silence, have continued to send messages of encouragement: 'We know you are there,' 'Hold on!' 'Stay strong.' Kindly convey my profound appreciation to the Amnesty International U.S. branch for its hard work and great effectiveness."**

A short message can give prisoners the needed courage to survive during the remaining days of their torture, because they know that they are not alone and that their captors are under pressure to release them.

Regrettably, other prisoners are not as fortunate.

Some die from torture, mistreatment or execution. But when that happens, we do everything possible to get the facts of that story told to the world.

The guilty must not have anywhere to hide!

We've exposed the shocking truth about the gouging out of a child's eyes in front of his or her parents, or mock execution by firing squad, or being buried alive, or spending weeks blindfolded and isolated and then the blindfold being removed and the prisoner forced to watch a family member being raped.

And we expose acts of torture, such as the case of one woman prisoner, who was taunted by the guards, saying, "We are God in here," ... while they applied electrical shocks to her body as she lay handcuffed to the springs of a metal bed.

Thank goodness many of us do not have to fear the kinds of atrocities described above, although serious violations do happen right here in the U.S.

But if you lived in certain other parts of the world ... your life might be far different, especially if you were a person who exercised the voice of your conscience and opposed an immoral and repressive government.

Exhibit 2   continued

- 3 -

Frankly, I'm sure that you yourself have a strong sense of right and wrong. And even though an injustice thousands of miles away from your home does not affect you physically – it does make you feel angry and frustrated. <u>And this is where Amnesty International comes in</u>. <u>We can help you express your moral indignation</u> – <u>and do something about it</u>.

But please understand. We seek the release of activists, civilians and others held because of their beliefs or identity. We do not take a stand on issues of political ideology. And frankly, that's what makes us so unique and effective ...

... <u>We demand that all prisoners of conscience be set free immediately and unconditionally</u> ...

... <u>We demand that political prisoners receive a fair trial within a reasonable time</u> ...

... <u>We demand that all forms of torture and ill-treatment stop at once and that the death penalty be abolished in all cases</u> ...

... <u>We demand that death squads which carry out extrajudicial executions be disbanded</u> ...

... <u>We demand that "disappearances," a form of state kidnapping, cease</u>

Naturally, we have our critics. <u>Some say we are too stern and unbending in our demands</u>.

But we look back to the year 1961 when Amnesty International was launched by a British lawyer named Peter Benenson, who published a newspaper appeal entitled: "The Forgotten Prisoners."

His appeal resulted in individuals in many countries offering to support the idea for an international campaign to protect human rights.

<u>And today</u>? <u>We are spreading the word faster and farther than ever</u>. <u>We have fax machines</u>. <u>We have satellite communications</u>. <u>We have e-mail and the World Wide Web</u>.

We have 1.1 million members in 162 countries and territories, including more than 80,000 Urgent Action Network volunteers in over 80 countries who are ready to go into action hundreds of times a year with letters, faxes, telegrams and phone calls appealing for justice and mercy.

And as a result, thousands of prisoners have been freed. Torture chambers have been closed, and executions have been stopped.

We deeply believe that: "The free must remember the forgotten."

<u>However</u>, in spite of our growth and our effectiveness, torture and political imprisonment and "disappearances" go on – seemingly at an accelerated rate.

<u>And our Urgent Action Network and other programs cannot keep up with demands</u>. <u>This is our dilemma</u>.

This is why I am writing you today, in the hope that you will sign your name to the enclosed card so it can be forwarded to a prisoner of conscience who needs your help. If you prefer not to sign the card, I will understand.

Exhibit 2   continued

- 4 -

But I trust you will still support our lifesaving mission ...

... and send a gift of $10, $15, $25 or even $50 so that Amnesty can respond to the growing number of urgent requests. Of course, if you wish to join with those who send $100, please do so. Any amount you are able to contribute will be deeply appreciated.

And, as a member of Amnesty, you will receive our informative quarterly newsmagazine, *Amnesty Now*.

Some of the stories you will read in this publication may shock you. Some stories will make you feel outrage. Some will break your heart. And some will give you a feeling of intense satisfaction.

You will realize that you are doing your share to help us stand up and fight back against those ruthless powers that throw people in jail, torture them and execute them for "crimes" such as simply criticizing the government.

Basic human rights are being violated right now – this very day. It is up to you to remember that important changes in the world often hinge on the actions of ordinary people. And Amnesty International is made up of ordinary people from across the political spectrum working with extraordinary levels of courage and commitment. Many display the decal I've enclosed for you.

You can share in this movement. I hope that you will.

Sincerely,

William F. Schulz
Executive Director

P.S. Please let me repeat just two things.

First, if you'll sign your name to the enclosed "Message of Hope" card, I'll do my best to see that it gets to a prisoner of conscience who is being tortured, or detained or possibly facing death.

(And even if the card never actually reaches the prisoner, when the jailers or those responsible are deluged with a flood of these cards, they are going to realize that they are no longer operating in secrecy. The word is out. Their prisoner is in the public eye. This could result in freedom or better conditions for the prisoner.)

And second, if you can send a gift of $10, $15, $25 or perhaps even $50, please do so right now.

As I said, our Urgent Action Network is sagging under the pressure of an extraordinary volume of requests. Never before in our history have we even considered the possibility that we could not honor these requests and could not go to the aid of a prisoner.

Help us keep this much-needed tradition alive.

Source: Amnesty International USA.

Exhibit 3	AI Specialist Networks in 2003

- The Lawyers Network worked as a member of the Coalition for an International Criminal Court, campaigning for states to sign and ratify the Rome Statute of the International Criminal Court (ICC). By 2002, more than 60 countries had ratified the Rome Statute, triggering the establishment of the International Criminal Court on February 5, 2002.

- The Military Security and Police (MSP) Network campaigned for effective controls on the transfer of arms and security assistance in order to prevent these being used for human rights abuses. In 2001, for example, the network campaigned for the suspension of electro-shock weapons.

- The Company Approaches Network worked with other NGOs to campaign for controls on the international diamond trade. Profits from the diamond trade were used to purchase weapons, which contributed to human rights abuses in Angola, the Democratic Republic of Congo, and Sierra Leone. In 2002, governments had made progress towards an international diamond certification system. In addition, the network worked with companies to help them develop policies which incorporated human rights standards.

- The Children's Network lobbied states to ratify the Optional Protocol to the UN Children's Convention on the involvement of children in armed conflict. This protocol entered into force in February 2002.

- The Women's Network and LGBT Network campaigned around two major reports: "Broken bodies, shattered minds: Torture and ill-treatment of women," and "Crimes of hate, conspiracy of silence: Torture and ill-treatment based on sexual identity."

- The Medical Network, which consisted of doctors, nurses, psychologists and other health professionals in over 30 countries, acted on behalf of sick prisoners denied access to medical care or health professionals who had been harassed by the authorities for providing treatment to opponents of the government. In 2001, the network acted on over 50 actions.

Source: AI Web site.

only be made through the democratic decision-making process involving all fifty-six sections. At the 2001 IC meeting, AI decided to move away from detailed development of its mandate through such a cumbersome decision-making process. The IC replaced AI's mandate with a "mission," defined in general terms and covering civil and political rights as well as economic, social, and cultural rights. The IC also agreed to adopt an integrated strategic plan which would focus on a broad set of themes and goals for a period of six years. Sections and the International Secretariat are expected to develop two- to three-year operational plans within the broad framework of the strategic plan. This gives us much greater flexibility and allows us to select issues strategically and to respond more quickly and effectively to the changes in the external world.

An AI section could be established in any country with the consent of the IEC. To be recognized, a section needed to demonstrate its ability to organize and maintain basic AI activities, consist of no fewer than two groups and twenty members, submit its statute to the IEC for approval, pay an annual fee, and be registered with the International Secretariat. Sections had to act in accordance with AI's core values and methods, strategic plans, working rules, and guidelines. Sections varied in size and culture. In some sections, members played a very strong role, such as in the United Kingdom and the United States. In other countries, sections were essentially staff-run. "Sections play a critical role," Khan said. "They campaign, raise funds, educate, and represent our members." Kerry Hutchinson, AI's U.K. director of marketing, added, "Sections raise all the money and are responsible for delivering the majority of our communications."

Evolving role of the International Secretariat. In 2002, the International Secretariat's budget was just under £21 million and was spent as follows: 24 percent for research and action (campaigning action), 17 percent for administrative costs, 15 percent for membership support, 14 percent for research and action support, 13 percent for publications and translations, 10 percent for campaigning activities, and 7 percent for deconcentrated offices.[6]

Traditionally, the International Secretariat was responsible for all human rights abuse research, government relations, and coordination with the United Nations and international media. In addition to taking a more active role in developing strategies and campaigns, the International Secretariat was becoming active in fund-raising and section development. "Fund-raising is traditionally a role managed by the sections," Khan explained. "However, traditional national boundaries are crumbling. For example, media is truly international, and online fund-raising is increasing in importance."

Mark Hengstler, director of international fund-raising, also said the International Secretariat's role is evolving. "The International Secretariat used to be a service organization that supported the decisions taken by the sections," he said. "Today that role is changing, and the secretariat is starting to play a greater role in the management of resources among and between sections." Poland, a new section established in 2001, derived most of its funding from the section development fund, managed by the International Secretariat. In 2002, the Danish AI section began training the Polish AI section in fund-raising techniques. AI UK was partnered with AI Benin to provide similar training. "The International Secretariat is moving from a service role to an advisory role and, increasingly, towards a guiding role for the whole organization," Hengstler concluded.

Balancing democracy and effectiveness. Although the democratic process by which AI developed strategies and made decisions was one of the organization's core values, some executives questioned its effectiveness, particularly as the organization continued to grow and expand its mission. Khan explained, "AI has always operated according to democratic principles, but the world at large functions on market principles, and this creates an inherent tension." In addition, many sections were managed and staffed by volunteers. The lack of professional staff, particularly in areas such as fund-raising, some believed, resulted in less than effective section organizations.

Differences among sections. Within AI were two main groups of members: older members who had joined the organization in the 1970s and 1980s, and newer and younger members in their twenties and thirties. These two groups were often reflected at the section level. Khan talked about some of the differences between them:

> *Canada, for example, has a high proportion of youth members. Australia has a number of board members who are in their twenties. This contrasts with the French section, for example, where the average age of board members is above*

sixty-five. The age difference is reflected in the positions each section takes. Older members tend to focus on AI's traditional roles such as prisoners of conscience and the elimination of torture, and they would like to see AI continue to focus on these issues. Younger members see human rights as covering a broader spectrum of human rights, including economic, social, and cultural rights. This creates a huge debate within the Amnesty movement not only on how much the organization should change, but also how fast it should change. In 2001, AI decided to expand its focus and address economic, social, and cultural rights, so one could say that the younger members are winning out. Another difference across sections is their interest in fund-raising. Some sections with a greater number of older members tend to reject modern methods of fund-raising as being overly aggressive.

A number of sections, such as those in Belgium and Switzerland, aware of the issue, were consciously trying to bring in new, younger members to their organizations.

BRAND MANAGEMENT.

Brand Trust.

In a study conducted by Edelman PR in January 2003, Amnesty International ranked number one in terms of public trust among brands in Europe, above all other NGOs and major corporations such as Microsoft, Coca-Cola, Nike, and McDonald's. In the United States, the Amnesty brand ranked tenth in brand trust, behind major U.S. corporations like Nike, and a few other major NGOs such as the World Wildlife Fund.

"The issue for the AI brand," said Sean Barrett, senior director of communications and campaigning at the International Secretariat, "is that while the International Secretariat is at the hub of the organization's wheel, it does not control how the AI brand is expressed in different countries." Different sections had distinct personalities and even used different logos. In 2002, for example, Amnesty International Israel used a logo depicting interlocking hands, and Amnesty International France used the symbol of a dove. "While the AI brand has great recall and is very powerful," Barrett added, "it has been modified around the world, and the challenge now is whether and how to standardize both the brand and the logo."

Despite the recently adopted vision and mission statements, no organization-wide brand identity existed. "We don't actively manage our brand," Hengstler commented, "but perhaps as a result, we do have a very strong brand reputation and recognition."

Funding.

No funds were sought or accepted from governments. All funds were contributed by AI's members, the public, and organizations such as trusts and foundations. Funds were accepted only from companies deemed ethical, and AI accepted no more than 10 percent of total funds from any one donor, with the exception of legacies. "It makes sense that the bulk of our funding should come from individuals," Khan explained, "because of our commitment to the individual." Increasingly, however, corporate funding and fee-for-service schemes were being developed. "In some sections," Khan said, "for example, Norway, AI provides companies with advice and training and charges consulting fees. Other sections, such as Germany, won't even talk to companies."

Corporate fund-raising. In 2003, AI UK put forward a resolution, to be discussed at the International Council, calling for a review of AI's corporate fund-raising strategy. AI UK members in particular believed it was important to understand the current and future levels of corporate fund-raising and its effect on AI's brand and reputation for impartiality. The desired outcome would be a transparent organization-wide corporate fund-raising policy. Corporate fund-raising included payments and funds from corporate entities, including donations, licensing arrangements, sponsorships, discounted services, gifts in kind, and consultancy fees. In 2002, guidelines for corporate fund-raising existed but required time-consuming and expensive screening of companies, and these guidelines were interpreted and implemented inconsistently throughout the AI movement.

AI had long maintained the principled position of not accepting funds or financial support from governments in order to preserve impartiality and credibility. Many believed this was still one of AI's most distinctive features. Some members believed it would be unrealistic to refuse all involvement with corporations, whereas others believed that the principle of refusing all government funding should be applied to corporate funding as well. The latter argued that AI needed to remain financially independent of the targets of its campaigning, including corporations, and be able to face any questions about conflicts of interest as a result of a relationship with a corporation.

Amnesty International UK. AI sections provided the International Secretariat with between 22 and 44 percent of the funds they raised in 2002. AI UK, for example, transferred 40 percent of its income to the International Secretariat, and the ten largest sections contributed more than 90 percent of AI's total revenues. AI UK's marketing income had risen over time, from £7.9 million in 1996 to £14.4 million in 2002, and was projected to reach £19 million in 2006. Expenditures over the same period had risen from £2 million to £4.5 million and were projected to reach £5.6 million by 2006. (See **Exhibit 4** for details of AI UK's forecasted marketing income and expenditures.)

AI UK's marketing strategy was based primarily on the recruitment and development of individual supporters. Using a variety of recruitment techniques, the section aimed to grow its supporter base as the key driver to increasing income. Supporters were recruited to committed-giving programs (paying by direct debit), and in 2002 more than 80 percent of AI UK's entire supporter base participated in these programs, providing a valuable and reliable platform on which to plan and build. These committed-giving programs and other membership payments accounted for 60 percent of AI UK's annual income.

Most fund-raising activities were holding steady or improving, with the exception of telefund-raising. Telefund-raising involved telephoning around 30,000 supporters to ask them to participate in a door-to-door collection program. This form of fund-raising had, in the past, generated annual net income for AI UK of around £200,000. In 2002, however, this had dropped to £40,000 against expenditures of £235,000. Hutchinson believed that this reflected a trend throughout the United Kingdom and was caused in part by the higher costs of telefund-raising and in part by the declining audience receptiveness to this type of activity. In 2002, AI UK was exploring new methods of fund-raising, including major donor development and community fund-raising and events. In addition, AI UK was planning to switch 50 percent of future recruitment activity to its trust fund. The trust enabled AI UK to

Exhibit 4	AI UK's Marketing Budget—Five-Year Forecast				
£'000	2002	2003	2004	2005	2006
INCOME					
Section[a]					
Fund-raising	1,734	1,410	1,500	1,600	1,700
Scotland	137	123	175	190	190
Appeals and PIF [c]	910	818	830	850	870
New Member Acquisition	1,012	676	678	678	678
Existing Individual Members	5,446	6,448	6,837	6,957	7,023
Shops	275	298	350	441	536
Trading	73	85	84	88	92
Corporate and Affinity	214	189	150	160	165
Welcome Members [d]	0	44	50	50	50
Total Section	9,801	10,090	10,653	11,013	11,304
Trust[b]					
Legacies	0	1,000	1,000	1,100	1,200
Committed Giving	0	1,483	2,651	3,516	4,293
Major Donor	0	376	450	490	670
Other Trust	0	1,021	1,175	1,389	1,576
Total Trust	4,645	3,880	5,276	6,495	7,740
Total Income	14,446	13,970	15,929	17,508	19,043
EXPENDITURES					
Fund-raising	795	784	814	883	1,032
Scotland	55	57	87	92	91
Trust	496	1,372	1,372	1,372	1,372
Trust Upgrade		35	35	35	35
Appeals and PIF	215	259	260	275	285
New Member Acquisition	2,209	1,548	1,610	1,674	1,741
Membership	179	263	271	279	287
Shops	167	199	252	298	320
Trading	52	14	25	27	28
Major Donor	8	17	94	115	171
Director	326	150	158	165	174
Welcome Members[d]	54	65	68	71	75
Total Expenditures	4,555	4,763	5,044	5,285	5,611
Net Income	9,891	9,207	10,885	12,224	13,433

Source: AI UK.

[a]Section referred to the main AI UK organization.

[b]Trust was a separate fund established by AI UK that benefited from earning gift aid on donations.

[c]PIF = Partners in Freedom, high-value supporter product. To be a PIF required an annual donation of £100. PIFs received specialized information about AI.

[d]Welcome members are new members who have not made a regular gift (direct debit) at the point of recruitment. They are sent a welcome pack introducing them to AI and two months later receive a telephone call asking them to convert to direct debit.

claim back inland revenue taxes of 28 percent through a scheme known as gift aid on behalf of willing supporters for their donations to the trust. AI UK also needed to use the trust for legal and administrative reasons to implement two new recruitment programs, house-to-house recruitment and direct-response TV. (**Exhibit 5** projects the size of the supporter base and associated income for both AI UK and the trust over time.)

Exhibit 5	AI UK Projected Supporters and Related Income				
	2002	**2003**	**2004**	**2005**	**2006**
Membership					
Supporter base	164,000	167,000	173,000	174,000	174,000
Income[a]	£5.4m	£6.6m	£6.8m	£6.9m	£7m
Trust Givers					
Supporter base	18,000	38,000	53,000	67,000	78,000
Income[a]	£1.5m	£1.4m	£2.6m	£3.5m	£4.3m
Gift Aid[b]	£0.4m	£0.4m	£0.5m	£0.7m	£0.8m
Total Income	£1.9m	£1.8m	£3.1m	£4.2m	£5.1m
Total					
Supporter base	182,000	205,000	226,000	241,000	252,000
Income	£7.3m	£8.4m	£9.9m	£11.1m	£12.1m

Source: AI UK.

[a]Corresponds to income from "Existing Individual Members" line and "Committed Giving" line in **Exhibit 4.**

[b]Gift Aid donations qualified for U.K. tax deductions.

Building section fund-raising capability. As noted in the membership development section of the 2001 key challenges, an increasing number of smaller, newer national sections depended on funding from the International Secretariat. Competitive research carried out in 2002, and outlined in detail below, suggested that in certain countries AI had not managed to raise funds even though other NGOs had been successful in doing so. In 2002, the International Secretariat established a Fund-raising Investment Fund with the aim of boosting certain dependent sections' own fund-raising capabilities over time, with the result of creating financially independent sections that would also contribute to the International Secretariat's expenses. (The expected resulting cash flow is outlined in **Exhibit 6.**)

Exhibit 6	Fund-raising Investment Fund—Cash Flow Over Time									
£'000	2001	2002	2003	2004	2005	2006	2007	2008	2009	2010
Loans to sections	(1,000)	(1,000)	(1,000)	(1,000)	(1,000)	(1,000)	(1,000)	(1,000)	(1,000)	(1,000)
Repayments from sections	0	300	550	800	1,000	1,000	1,000	1,000	1,000	1,000
Increased assessment from sections	0	0	0	700	1,309	1,849	2,328	2,752	3,128	3,461
Net inflow (outflow) for the year	(1,000)	(700)	(450)	500	1,309	1,849	2,328	2,752	3,128	3,461
Cumulative net inflow (outflow)	(1,000)	(1,700)	(2,150)	(1,650)	(341)	1,508	3,836	6,588	9,716	13,177

Source: AI International Secretariat.

Membership.

AI's integrated strategic plan called for an increase of 1 million members over a ten-year period and a doubling in global gross income. One complication, however, was that different sections measured membership differently. Although AI had more than 1.6 million members in 2002, an estimated 50 percent paid monthly dues and the rest were active letter writers. The International Secretariat's future fund-raising efforts would focus on committed or sustainable giving. "We don't want to have one-off donors," Hengstler explained. "We want to bring in long-term members who pay monthly dues over a number of years." AI's International Secretariat was urging sections to increase the proportion of sustainable or committed-giving programs through automatic credit card and electronic transfers. Studies showed that donors who gave through credit cards remained active for an average of three years, those who gave through electronic funds transfer remained active seven years, and those who gave onetime gifts remained active for only twelve months. Across the entire AI membership, an estimated 45 percent of donors gave through sustainable giving programs.

Supporter recruitment was also central to AI UK's income strategy. AI UK projected to grow the number of supporters from 182,000 in 2002 to 252,000 in 2007. The number of members was projected to grow from 164,000 to 174,000, and the number of trust and committed givers was expected to increase from 18,000 to 78,000. (See **Exhibit 5** for a forecast of AI UK supporter numbers over time.) Costs of recruiting new supporters were on the rise: in 2001 the average cost per recruit for AI UK was £48; in 2002, it was £60. "The majority of our members live in large urban areas such as London and Manchester," Hutchinson said, "and they are roughly 50 percent male, which is different from the competition, whose supporter base is predominantly female."

Hutchinson believed that, in the United Kingdom, several trends were affecting supporter recruitment. First, the overall costs of recruitment were increasing. Second, direct-dialogue recruits (those supporters recruited through a face-to-face interaction, principally on the street) formed the largest segment of AI UK's membership base (25 percent) but were not responsive to AI's traditional fund-raising approaches such as direct mail, telefund-raising, or raffles. Direct-dialogue recruits were very good value because they were recruited directly into a committed-giving program and generated, on average, £70 over four years. "While the new supporters we recruit are highly valuable," Hutchinson summarized, "they are not receptive to our current range of offers, and we need to develop a tailored plan for them." AI UK was also planning to test a new recruitment program in January 2003 called Caring Together, a house-to-house, committed-giving recruitment program that Hutchinson hoped had the potential to recruit supporters in the same volumes as direct dialogue used to recruit.

Competition.

In 2002, AI commissioned research to understand the organization's global positioning, particularly in the world's thirty-nine most important economies,[7] in relation to Greenpeace, the World Wide Fund for Nature (WWF), CARE, and Save the Children Fund. Although AI had the greatest number of offices, with thirty-eight sections out of thirty-nine countries, it lagged behind both WWF and Greenpeace in terms of number of supporters. (See **Exhibit 7** for a competitive comparison.) In terms of number of supporters per country office, AI averaged just below 50,000, far

| Exhibit 7 | Competitive Comparison of Numbers of Supporters and Offices, 2002 |

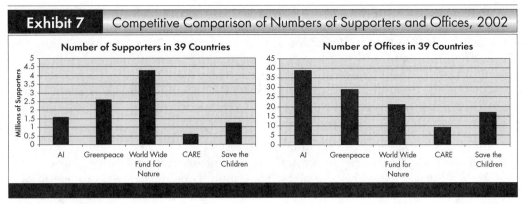

Source: Amnesty International.

behind WWF at 200,000, Greenpeace at nearly 100,000, and CARE and Save the Children at 60,000 and 70,000, respectively. In terms of income per supporter, CARE excelled, with the average supporter contributing £100 a year. Save the Children followed close behind, with the average supporter contributing £90, and AI, WWF, and Greenpeace followed at £55, £50, and £35, respectively.

AI believed that competition from many local NGOs had increased in the previous decade but that its only main global competitors in 2002 were Human Rights Watch and Greenpeace.

Human Rights Watch (HRW). HRW was an independent NGO founded in 1988 that investigated and exposed human rights violations and held abusers accountable. With operating revenues in fiscal year 2002 of $19.5 million and close to 200 professional staff, HRW tracked developments in more than seventy countries, published findings in dozens of books and reports every year, and sought to generate extensive coverage in local and international media. HRW met with government officials to urge changes in policy and practice and, in moments of crisis, provided up-to-the-minute information about conflicts to help shape the response of the international community.

HRW had a very small membership base; its main advocacy strategy was to shame offenders by generating press attention and enlisting influential governments and institutions to exert political and economic pressure. Initially focused on civil and political rights, HRW had increasingly addressed economic, social, and cultural rights as well. Similarly to AI, HRW prided itself on its impartiality and the accuracy of its reporting and accepted no government funding. Past campaigns had included prohibiting the use of child soldiers, banning the use of land mines, and documenting abuses in Kosovo and Rwanda. "Human Rights Watch is taking away our media exposure," Hengstler explained. "They are a young, dynamic organization and are much quicker at getting out a press release or condemning specific human rights abuses. AI might take two months to put out a report by the time it goes through our policy, legal, and media departments, but Human Rights Watch can get a similar report out in two weeks. In addition, they don't function along a democratic process so they can react more swiftly than we can." Although AI had lost a number of senior staff to HRW, HRW was perceived as U.S. focused and not as global in its reach as AI.

Greenpeace. Greenpeace was an independent, nonprofit organization that relied on contributions from individuals and foundation grants. It focused on threats to the planet's biodiversity and environment, and campaigned to stop climate change, protect forests, save the oceans, stop whaling, limit genetic engineering, stop nuclear threats, and eliminate toxic chemicals. Started in 1971 when a small boat of volunteers sailed into Amchitka, an area north of Alaska where the U.S. government was conducting underground nuclear tests, Greenpeace advocated bearing witness as a core component of the organization.

In 2002, Greenpeace had 2.8 million supporters and a total income of around $140 million. Headquartered in Amsterdam, the organization had forty-one national offices worldwide. "As a campaigning organization, Greenpeace tends to be top of mind for many people because they are in the news a lot," Hutchinson said. In some respects, Greenpeace and AI were similar; both were membership organizations based on bearing witness and campaigning, and they had collaborated on a number of occasions in campaigning and advertising.

Market Research.

In February 2000, AI USA conducted brand audit research, based on internal and external interviews and focus groups, in order to create a brand vision for the AI USA organization. During 2002, AI UK undertook a series of market research studies with the objective of understanding consumer awareness and perceptions to develop a marketing and communication strategy for the organization.

Brand awareness and recognition. In February 2000, external interviews and focus groups conducted in the United States revealed that people viewed the issue of human rights as closely linked to the U.S. Constitution, particularly freedom of speech, but did not include human rights in their "charity preference list." There was little recognition of the Amnesty International brand name or logo, although more people recognized the AI USA acronym. Even those focus group participants who recognized AI knew what the organization stood for but not what it did and could not recall any successes that AI USA had had. Most respondents were motivated by AI's mandate but unsure what membership involved. Those respondents who knew AI fairly well complained that "AI USA seems to have lost focus and is entering into areas that are related but fall outside their mandate." Or that "Amnesty is spreading themselves too thin." Others still worried that AI USA failed to take credit for success or take advantage of its worldwide membership base.

In April 2002, Haslam Callow and Partners was retained to conduct six two-hour focus groups in the United Kingdom designed to explore current perceptions of AI and reactions toward a range of advertising approaches. It found that the majority lacked awareness and were uncertain about AI and the work it did, with some people describing the organization as remote and impersonal. "The focus groups show that AI is not very accessible," Hutchinson commented, "and that we have an overly intellectual image."

Those consumers who did know AI recognized the organization's focus on human rights and described it as independent and centered on individuals and specific groups. The researchers also found that older consumers were more knowledgeable and interested in human rights issues and AI than the younger focus group participants. "In the United Kingdom," Hutchinson said, "we have some young members in school or at university, but there's a gap between them and another group of members in their forties. In the U.K., most people in their twenties and thirties are not really engaged in politics." The researchers recommended that AI communicate on human rights issues that involved innocent victims; were outside the arena of war; did not conflict with the values, laws, or religion of another society; and involved obvious abuse. Issues surrounding refugees and asylum seekers as well as the death penalty were seen by many as borderline and emotive.

In October 2002, nfp Synergy was retained to conduct a telephone poll of more than 1,000 adults. It found that AI's spontaneous awareness stood at 5 percent, behind the Red Cross at 11 percent and Oxfam at 26 percent. Semiprompted awareness, as defined by the question, "Which charities or NGOs have you heard of who work on human rights, international issues and overseas development?" stood at 27 percent for AI versus 55 percent for the Red Cross and 64 percent for Oxfam, and total aided-awareness figures were 78 percent for AI, 99 percent for the Red Cross, and 99 percent for Oxfam. "The AI brand has great potential and credibility," Hutchinson said. "People don't necessarily know what we do, but they think we're good."

Sixty-six percent of respondents could recall an advertisement for a charitable organization that they had seen in the last three months. Television ads and appeals, as well as letters, were the dominant form of communication. (See **Exhibit 8** for details of what people recalled.) "There is a sense," Hutchinson said, "that our media presence was greater in the past, but according to our records, AI's media exposure has actually increased." Seventy-four percent of respondents said they had given money to charity in the last three months, and 19 percent said they had volunteered their time. When asked, "Do you ever think you'd like to volunteer but don't know who to approach or where to go?" 81 percent responded no. When asked if there were any charity activities they found annoying, 50 percent responded no, and the remainder were spread fairly evenly over many fund-raising activities (outlined in **Exhibit 9**).

Communicating the brand. "We have learned," Hutchinson explained, "that communicating about a specific campaign is easy, but talking about AI as an organization is difficult. Because of the democratic nature of our organization, many people at AI UK expressed their own views about how best to communicate what AI stands for. We needed help channeling and condensing these opinions." In December 2002, Shaw Research Planning was retained to conduct focus groups with both AI members and staff and nonmembers to determine a communication platform that would attract new members to AI UK. First, the researchers found that throughout the focus groups, members had been drawn to AI by their belief in the importance of fairness and justice. Second, the researchers tested the appeal of five positioning boards designed to present AI in various ways: as a global force, as the world's eyes and ears, as relentless campaigners, as a people's movement, and as defiant for justice. (See **Exhibit 10** for a description of the concept areas.)

The global force concept was found to describe a manner of working but lacked emotional appeal and did not differentiate AI. The world's eyes and ears concept seemed to be a comfortable restatement of where the organization stood, and made members feel like "insiders." It inspired respect and admiration but implied distance. The relentless campaigners concept provoked an image of martyrdom, depressed members, and contained no benefit for nonmembers. The people's

Exhibit 8	Recalled Sources of Information About Charitable Organizations, AI UK 2002

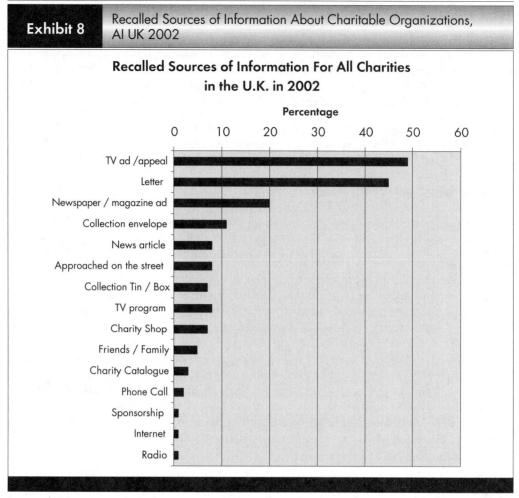

Source: nfp Synergy.

movement concept had a potent "feel" to it, but members thought they did not seek to "belong," and nonmembers thought it was vague, albeit interesting. The defiant for justice concept was by far the most appreciated and was seen by members as the spirit that had sustained AI for forty years. For a few, however, it was too strident, and for others it suggested an intense level of commitment that was off-putting. Hutchinson summarized as follows:

> *Although AI has an intellectual image, we elicit an emotional response, and so our communications have to reach people at the emotional level. We are also asking people to make a leap of faith. We don't build wells or vaccinate children, we are more values based. In a way, it's a state of mind. If you believe in justice and fairness, AI is attractive. Historically, AI has not been good at claiming success. We want the governments to claim success so that they enter a virtuous cycle of improving human rights in their countries. At the same time, it makes it difficult to promote the organization if we can't portray our effectiveness.*

| Exhibit 9 | Charitable Fund-raising Activities People Found Annoying— AI UK 2002 |

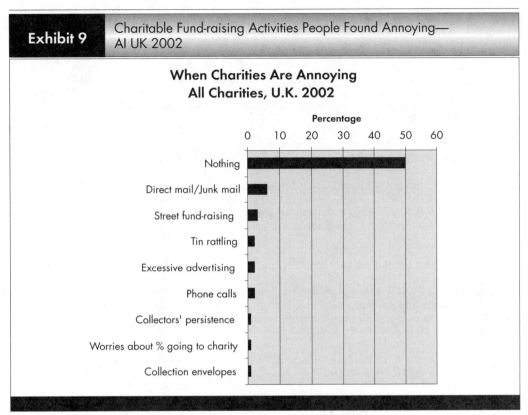

When Charities Are Annoying
All Charities, U.K. 2002

Source: nfp Synergy.

During internal interviews conducted in 2000 at AI USA, AI's main strengths were considered to be the ability to mobilize large groups of individuals to action, the deep network across the globe, and the integrity in research and calls to action. Weaknesses included the bureaucratic nature of the organization, too many meetings and different opinions, and a resulting slow decision-making process. In addition, AI was thought to be divorced from the world of "regular folks." Recommendations from external interviews and focus groups in the United States included communicating exactly what AI USA does and stands for and how to become a member. Positive communications focusing on achievements at the individual level were considered important, as were the use of the logo and the full Amnesty International brand name everywhere possible.

Khan concluded, "You need lofty goals to energize people but concrete examples of success."

Future Brand Management.

"People in NGOs are often uncomfortable and suspicious when you start talking about branding," Barrett said. "Brand management at AI must start with an education and discussion process. People need to build an appreciation that our brand is a considerable asset and that we have common ownership of the brand as well as a common duty to protect the brand and its value." Barrett also believed that the AI brand was strongly associated with the organization's history: "AI is on the cusp of

Exhibit 10	Descriptions of Concepts Used by Shaw Research Planning, 2002

GLOBAL FORCE

In today's global village, Amnesty International is the world's largest network of human rights campaigners. Amnesty believes that to make the world a safer place for all of us and achieve change on a global scale, international cooperation, international action, and international solutions are the only way.

THE WORLD'S EYES AND EARS

In a world of spin, bias, and superficial reporting, Amnesty International is a research-based organization that provides thorough and trusted reporting of human rights abuses. As it does not take money from governments or unethical companies, it is uniquely placed to provide impartial reporting and unbiased solutions.

THE RELENTLESS CAMPAIGNERS

In a complex world where problems can't be resolved overnight, Amnesty International refuses to accept that the way things are, is the way they will always be. So even though fighting for change and protecting human rights can be a struggle, Amnesty and its members will never give up hope.

A PEOPLE MOVEMENT NOT A CHARITY

In a world where individuals feel more and more powerless, Amnesty International demonstrates the power of many. Ordinary people—ready to stand shoulder to shoulder for their own rights and the rights of other ordinary people. Each individual part of a bigger community able to change the world together in a way they can't alone.

DEFIANT FOR JUSTICE

In a world where some people still do not have basic human rights, Amnesty International believes in justice for all without exception. This can mean standing firm or even confrontation. But Amnesty believes in doing what's right rather than what's easy, and if that means taking on the establishment, governments or the powerful, so be it.

Source: Shaw Research Planning.

entering new areas such as economic and social rights, and there is a very real danger that this will confuse the public, undermine the AI brand, and erode existing value." Barrett also believed that moving into new areas could give AI the opportunity to gain new supporters and members but that the key would be to communicate consistently and not allow a vacuum to develop into which the AI brand could fall.

In addition, the AI brand did not have a common global perception and awareness. Although in the developed countries, or "North," it was an established, well-known brand in its midlife, in the developing world, or "South," it was a very young, fairly unknown brand. "We are still perceived as a Western or Northern NGO," Khan said, "which is ironic because we have been the most active in the South and East."

AI also had aspirations to grow its membership base in the South, and Barrett wondered how best to position the brand to achieve this as well.

CONCLUSION.

Khan reflected on how to develop and manage a new global AI brand and how a new brand positioning would enable AI to achieve its membership and revenue growth goals.

First, she wondered how to maintain the brand's value in developing countries while communicating the organization's new mandate, particularly to new and prospective members throughout the world.

Second, she was concerned that the AI brand be strongly positioned relative to competition and that market research findings be incorporated in both the development and the communication of the new brand.

Third, Khan realized that, given the democratic nature of AI and the diversity within the movement's network, she would have to be creative and persuasive in her implementation of a global AI brand positioning.

Notes to Case

1   $1US = £0.65 on average in 2002.

2   Prisoners of conscience are defined by AI as people imprisoned solely because of their political or religious beliefs, sex, or racial or ethnic origin who have neither used nor advocated violence.

3   Much of this section is based on the 25th International Council Meeting Circular 36, July 2001.

4   This section is based on the book by Jonathan Power, *Like Water on Stone* (New York: Penguin Press, 2001).

5   Anecdote based on the book by Power, *Like Water on Stone* (New York: Penguin Press, 2001).

6   Deconcentrated offices played a coordination role similar to that of the International Secretariat but for specific geographic regions. There was a deconcentrated office, for example, in Kampala.

7   Countries were Argentina, Australia, Austria, Belgium, Brazil, Canada, Chile, the Czech Republic, Denmark, Finland, France, Germany, Greece, Hong Kong, Hungary, Iceland, Ireland, Israel, Italy, Japan, Korea, Luxembourg, Mexico, the Netherlands, New Zealand, Norway, Peru, Poland, Portugal, Russia, Slovakia, Slovenia, Spain, Sweden, Switzerland, Taiwan, Turkey, the United Kingdom, and the United States.

CASE 3
Oxfam America in 2002

On April 11, 2002, Raymond Offenheiser, president of Oxfam America (OA), held a press release in his hand that marked the launch of Oxfam's worldwide campaign *Make Trade Fair*. E-mail messages with the *Make Trade Fair* subject line had filled his inbox consistently over the past several months. This was the first time the entire family of Oxfam affiliates were launching a global campaign together—working to coordinate advocacy efforts, media communications, and even program activities to send a single global message. The campaign would be multiyear in nature and contain several targeted campaigns under the fair trade umbrella, such as a Fair Trade coffee campaign.

Although fair trade was the major campaign focus being coordinated across Oxfam's worldwide affiliates, Oxfam America was increasingly involved in a broad range of advocacy activities, both in its Washington, D.C., office and regional program offices. Managing advocacy efforts and coordinating them with the organization's core regional programs was one of Offenheiser's major concerns. He knew that a great deal of enthusiasm existed in the organization about the *Make Trade Fair* campaign. However, he also recognized that there was an equal amount of apprehension about Oxfam America's increasing efforts to link global advocacy to its regional programs around the world.

While the campaign launch was occupying a large share of Raymond Offenheiser's time, so was the development of the organization's next strategic plan. Oxfam America's vision and direction had become increasingly clarified in recent years with the development of a comprehensive strategic plan, *Partnerships for Impact,* in 1997. At the same time, the organization had experienced enormous growth, with contributions doubling in only five years. However, the organization's shift to a clear focus on "rights-based development" and increased collaboration with other Oxfam affiliates through Oxfam International was still a work in progress. Although important organizational changes had occurred, Offenheiser knew that significant internal and external challenges lay ahead for him and his staff.

Daniella Ballou (MBA '02) prepared this case under the supervision of Professor Reynold Levy. HBS cases are developed solely as the basis for class discussion. Cases are not intended to serve as endorsements, sources of primary data, or illustrations of effective or ineffective management.

INTERNATIONAL RELIEF AND DEVELOPMENT NGOS.[1]

The global relief and development NGO sector had experienced substantial growth since 1980, attributed in large part to the end of the cold war, the opening of previously closed societies, and the growth of intrastate conflict that followed in the 1990s. On the economic side, these political changes were paired with the growth of global markets and power of global economic institutions, such as the World Bank and the International Monetary Fund. These political and economic changes were believed to have increased the feasibility and necessity for growth in the international NGO sector.

See **Exhibit 1** for data on the growth of the relief and development NGO sector.

Players.

Relief and development NGOs take several forms. The first distinction is Northern versus Southern NGOs.[2] Oxfam America is one of the global Northern NGOs, indicating an organization based in the Northern Hemisphere, but serving primarily Southern or developing country communities. The Southern NGO sector consists of many thousands of small organizations in developing countries (estimated 20,000 to 250,000). In contrast to Southern NGOs, the Northern NGOs are fewer in number, estimated at 2,500 by the Organization for Economic and Development , and much larger in size. (See **Exhibit 2** for a list of the top Northern relief and development NGOs.) Fewer than ten very large organizations, or affiliate groups, generate the majority of revenues in the sector.

Like Oxfam America, many of the largest Northern NGOs operate as part of networks of affiliates, with relatively autonomous units based in various Northern countries. The major affiliated networks are Oxfam, CARE, Save the Children, MSF/Doctors Without Borders, World Vision, and Plan International. Several other operations have a single headquarters responsible for all programming and the majority of fund-raising—such as the International Rescue Committee and Mercy

| Exhibit 1 | Relief and Development NGO Sector |

| Exhibit 1a | Changes in U.S. International NGO Sector 1970–94 |

Year	Number of NGOs	NGO Revenues	US Total Giving	US GDP
1970	52	$.614bn	$23.4bn	$1010bn
1994	419	$6.839	$129.8	$6379

| Exhibit 1b | Growth in Revenue of Northern NGOs Involved in International Relief and Development |

Year	Private	Public	Total	US Share
1970	$800bn	$200bn	$1,000bn	50%
1997	$4,600	$2,600	$7,200	38%

Source for 1a: Marc Lindenberg and Coralie Bryant, *Going Global: Transforming Relief and Development NGOs* (Bloomfie CT: Kumarian Press, 2001), Table 1.1, p. 4.

Source for 1b: Marc Lindenberg and Coralie Bryant, *Going Global*, Table 1.2, p. 4.

Exhibit 2	Total Expenses and Expense Ratios for Major U.S. NGOs in Relief and Development (2000)	
Organization	Expenses ($m)	Efficiency (%)
CARE	$325	88
Catholic Relief Services	224	86
Christian Children's Fund	124	79
Doctors Without Borders	40	87
International Rescue Committee	143	93
Mercy Corp International	61	81
Oxfam America	22	78
Save the Children	123	81
World Vision	314	65–66

Source: Annual Reports; Charity Rating Guide; Watchdog Report by American Institute of Philanthropy.

Corp. All of these organizations have regional offices in the South that coordinate funding of programs/partner organizations focused on relief and development.

Evolving Context: Globalization.

Globalization, although not easily defined, was undoubtedly viewed as a driving factor in the evolving mission of Oxfam and other relief and development NGOs as they entered the twenty-first century. NGO leaders agreed that their organizations were facing a new set of challenges as a result of globalization. In September 1998, the Bellagio Conference on Globalization and Northern NGOs was held to explore the new challenges faced by global humanitarian aid NGOs. The NGO leaders at this conference, termed the Bellagio Group,[3] summarized these challenges as follows:[4] (1) new waves of complex emergencies; (2) new forms of global poverty; (3) declining capacity of national governments and changing private sector and NGO roles; (4) weak and outmoded global institutions; (5) new pressures for accountability and efficiency; (6) new pressures to respond globally; (7) recreating purpose and "mystique" of NGOs.

As a result of these new challenges many international NGOs, including OA, were evolving and seeking new approaches to providing relief and development aid. Throughout the second half of the 1990s, OA had been particularly concerned with creating an effective and relevant organizational mission and structure in the context of ongoing globalization.

OXFAM AMERICA.

Oxfam America is dedicated to creating lasting solutions to hunger, poverty, and social injustice through long-term partnerships with poor communities around the world. As a privately funded organization, we can speak with conviction and integrity as we challenge the structural barriers that foster conflict and human suffering and limit people from gaining the skills, resources, and power to become self-sufficient.

—Oxfam America Mission Statement

In 2001, Oxfam America (OA) was one of the major relief and development nongovernmental organizations in the United States. Although smaller than other wellknown organizations in the sector, in recent years OA had experienced substantial growth and in 2001, its revenues reached $29.2 million, doubling since 1995. This growth coincided with several major organizational changes: the appointment of Raymond Offenheiser as president in late 1995, a major strategic review in 1997, growing collaboration with Oxfam International, and changes in the board to expand the capabilities it offered the organization. At the same time the external context was marked by major international crises—including the wars in Kosovo and Sierra Leone, the destruction caused by Hurricane Mitch in Central America, ongoing turmoil in Colombia, the global shock of September 11th, and the ensuing war and humanitarian emergency in Afghanistan.

The 1997 strategic review had involved intense internal organizational reflection and led to several important strategic and organizational choices. The organization's strategic direction that emerged, titled *Partnerships for Impact: 1998–2002 Strategic Plan,* had clarified the organization's mission, vision, and approach to promoting sustainable development.[5] (See **Exhibit 3** for Oxfam America's statement of mission,

---

Exhibit 3 | Oxfam America Mission, Vision, and Values

The Oxfam Mission:

Oxfam America is dedicated to creating lasting solutions to hunger, poverty, and social injustice through long-term partnerships with poor communities around the world. As a privately funded organization, we can speak with conviction and integrity as we challenge the structural barriers that foster conflict and human suffering and limit people from gaining the skills, resources, and power to become self-sufficient.

Our Vision:

Oxfam America envisions a world in which all people shall one day know freedom—freedom to achieve their fullest potential and to live secure from the dangers of hunger, deprivation, and oppression—through the creation of a global movement for economic and social justice.

Our Values:

To create lasting solutions to hunger, poverty, and injustice, Oxfam America believes:

- In the essential dignity of all peoples and their right to pursue and shape the course of their own lives, and that respect for diversity of race, gender, religion, and ethnicity is essential to building just societies and vibrant communities.

- That poverty is a consequence of the systemic exclusion of distinct social groups from the rights, resources, and opportunities to achieve their fullest potential.

- That it is our responsibility to foster understanding of the root causes of poverty and injustice and promote the role each individual can play in a global movement for social change.

- That the distinctiveness of our partnerships is defined by mutual respect and a willingness to be innovative, share risks, and assume long-term relationships.

- That it is our obligation to be a responsive, efficient, and effective steward of our donor's resources and apply these resources in a way that will achieve maximum impact.

- That lasting solutions to global problems require sensible management of natural resources to ensure a stable quality of life for generations to come.

- That democratic participation and practice are primary and indispensable elements in enabling people and communities to secure freedom and access to the resources and opportunities they require.

- That it is our responsibility as global citizens to respond to human suffering in all its manifestations and to build an integrated global humanitarian response capability.

Source: Oxfam America.

vision, and values.) Overall, OA's four-tiered strategy for promoting development had evolved over its thirty-year history, but remained closely linked to its approach at its initial founding.[6] The key components were the following:

1. Provide financial, technical, and networking support to grassroots organizations to assist their community development initiatives.

2. Advocate among national and international policy makers for humane public policies that address the structural impediments to ending poverty and hunger.

3. Educate Americans about world hunger and poverty and the potential that poor communities have for designing and implementing sustainable development.

4. As a member of Oxfam International, increase organizational effectiveness by leveraging resources and drawing on the skills and efforts of like-minded agencies around the world.

OA had changed considerably in the previous five years, and by all accounts still was in the process of developing the type of organization required to fulfill its mission.

History.[7]

In 1942, a group led by Gilbert Murray, a professor of Greek literature at Oxford University in the UK, formed the Oxford Committee for Famine and Relief to consider the plight of hungry children in Greece during the Second World War. After the war, the committee, later abbreviated to Oxfam, continued to support refugees from wars and natural disasters around the world. From the beginning, Oxfam "sought donations from like-minded individuals trying to promote self-help efforts and relieve the suffering of people in the developing world."[8]

Over time the ideas of the original Oxfam were spread through international expansion and affiliates were launched in Australia (1953), the Netherlands (Novib founded in 1956, Oxfam affiliate since 1994), Belgium (1963), Canada (1963), USA (1970), Quebec (1973), Hong Kong (1984), New Zealand (1991), Spain (Intermon founded in 1956, Oxfam affiliate since 1997), Ireland (1998), and Germany (1995). Each international affiliate was managed as an autonomous organization with its own donor base and regional programs. Collectively these affiliates worked in eighty countries and raised more than $500 million annually.[9]

In 1996, the Oxfam International consortium was formed as a union of eleven Oxfams engaging in strategic collaboration in advocacy, grant making, marketing, communications, research, and emergency response. Although individual Oxfam affiliates remained independent, they sought to work together to gain the benefits of scale in programming and advocacy on a global basis.

OA was founded in 1970 by volunteers to respond to the refugee crisis in Bangladesh. During the thirty years of its existence the organization had grown from a small volunteer group working out of a borrowed room in a Boston suburban church to an important player in the international development field. Although its emphasis had always been on long-term sustainable development, revenue growth had historically been linked to periodic major disasters: Cambodia's "Killing Fields" in 1979, the 1984–85 Ethiopian famine, the 1991 Bangladesh floods, and the 1994 Rwandan tragedy. In the late 1990s, OA revenues nearly doubled, linked in part to the humanitarian emergencies caused by Hurricane Mitch in Central America and the war in Kosovo.

Within the nonprofit community, OA was known as an innovative international development organization. It was one of the first organizations to stress the importance of "sustainable development" when most other organizations were focused solely on crisis relief. Working with local, community-based organizations ("partners") and not imposing the views of expatriates were OA innovations that had become standard practice. Many community-based organizations that had received initial support from OA later developed into important Southern institutions. The 1992 Nobel Prize winner, Rigoberta Menchu of Guatemala, and the Peace and Justice Commission in Haiti were notable examples of organizations that had received early support from Oxfam. OA also engaged in advocacy before it had become the norm for U.S. humanitarian aid organizations.

By 2001, OA revenues had reached $29.2 million, up from $14.4 million in 1995. This was still one-tenth of the largest Oxfam affiliate, Oxfam Great Britain, whose FY 2001 revenues reached £187.3 million ($290US million). OA received almost all of its funds from individual donors, combined with periodic foundation grant support. OA did not accept government funding, in the interest of maintaining independence in both its programming choices and advocacy agenda. In 2001, 75 percent of funds came from individual donors, 5.5 percent from foundations, and 10 percent from other Oxfam Affiliates. OA distributed 78 percent of its funds to its programs and 22 percent to support administrative and fund-raising functions. (See **Exhibit 4** for Oxfam America's historical financial statements.)

Regional Programs.

As a result of the *Partnerships for Impact* strategic plan, OA regional programs focused on three thematic areas: community-based resource management, participation for equity, and development finance. Additionally, issues of gender, human rights, and culture were considered critical crosscutting areas of concern for all OA programs. In 2002, OA had regional program offices in Central and South America, Southeast Asia, southern Africa, west Africa, and the United States. The headquarters in Boston also served as the regional office for the organization's U.S. poverty-reduction programs. In the period from 1997 to 2002, the staff and budgets of each of the program offices had more than doubled as a result of the organization's overall growth.

Program offices primarily provided grants to partner organizations, typically local NGOs that provided direct service, and a limited number of other grants to the programs of other Oxfam affiliates (such as Oxfam Great Britain). OA had consciously chosen not to develop operational capacity on the ground, but to support regional partners as a means to promote sustainable development. In this way OA differed from many other major relief and development organizations that directly administered programs to local populations. Offenheiser described Oxfam's historical model as that of a "nonendowed foundation." Through *Partnerships for Impact*, the organization sought to enhance the effectiveness of its relationships with local NGOs based "on trust in order to optimize partners' capacity to achieve real impact on their own terms." (See **Exhibit 5** for a sample of OA's grants to partner organizations.) To complement its programs, OA also had several public education programs targeted toward American audiences, particularly young people.

| Exhibit 4 | Oxfam America Financial and Operating Performance |

($k)	1980	1990	1995	1998	1999	2000	2001
Revenues							
Contributed Revenues	5,487	11,407	$13,591	$15,178	$22,955	$25,919	27,202
Investments	63	255	432	449	691	1,065	1,108
Other	63	287	401	799	196	377	927
Total Revenue	**$5,613**	**$11,949**	**$14,452**	**$16,426**	**$23,886**	**$27,323**	**$29,238**
Expenses							
Programs							
—Regional & Emergency Programs	3,773	6,870	8,491	8,507	12,604	14,484	16,423
—Education	143	1,290	1,564	886	982	1,451	1,776
—Policy Change	-	-	-	776	1,020	1,147	1,397
Total Program	3916	8160	10,055	10,169	14,606	17,082	19,596
Support Services							
Management	104	621	573	672	755	967	959
Fund-raising/Member Recruitment	592	1,972	2,945	2,687	3,517	3,878	4,561
Total Support Svcs	696	2,593	3,518	3,360	4,273	4,845	5,520
Other	-	-	-	147	119	134	167
Total Expenses	**$4,612**	**$10,753**	**$13,724**	13,675	**$18,999**	**$22,061**	**$25,282**
Change in Net Assets	1,000	1,196	351	2,751	4,887	5,262	3,956
Net Assets, Beginning of Year	176	3,470	6,636	10,863	13,614	18,500	23,762
Net Assets, End of Year	**$1,176**	**$4,666**	**$6,986**	**$13,614**	**$18,500**	**$23,762**	**$27,718**

Sources of Contributions							
Individuals (includes Bequests)			84%	70%	77.4%	66.7%	75.2%
Foundations			10%[1]	18%	15.6%	22.0%[2]	5.5%
Corporations							1.4%	1.1%
Special Events			6%[3]	4%[4]	3.1%[5]	4.8%	1.5%
Oxfam Affiliates							9.7%
Other				8%	3.9%	5.1%	7.0%

Source: Oxfam America Company Documents and Annual Reports.

[1] Combined total for foundations and corporations.

[2] Includes total value of donation to be used over multiple years.

[3] Includes both groups and special events.

[4] Includes both groups and special events.

[5] Includes both groups and special events.

Advocacy.

In the late 1990s OA's efforts to influence public policy through advocacy grew substantially, from one person in 1996 to nine full-time staff members, plus several interns and consultants in 2001. The *Make Trade Fair* campaign and its coordinated launch with Oxfam International and Oxfam's global affiliates marked the culmination of efforts to create a single advocacy voice across Oxfam affiliates for major campaigns. (See **Exhibit 6** for the trade campaign press release.) Advocacy efforts went far beyond this single campaign and covered multiple issues of concern to regional partners and developing countries more broadly, such as the conduct of extractive industries and trade in conflict diamonds. OA, in its Washington, D.C., offices, engaged in policy research and lobbying of U.S. government decision makers. It also coordinated lobbying efforts with OI and joined with a wide range of other NGOs in support of specific issue campaigns that were in line with the organization's

| Exhibit 5 | Sample of Oxfam America Grants to Partner Organizations |

Agrarian Social and Economic Development Association: Agrarian Action (South America)

Strengthens the planning, monitoring, evaluation and learning capacities of partners to enable them to more successfully meet their own goals: $53,800

National Coordinator of Communities Affected by Mining (CONCAMI)—Peru

Trains and supports regional organizations of indigenous communities affected by the mining industry in Peru: $45,800

Fundacion Vamos—Mexico

Strengthens Women's Social Enterprises on the coast of Oaxaca through enterprise management and administration, training, networking, and expansion of local markets for their products: $50,000

Independent Federation of Shuar People of Ecuador (FIPSE)—Ecuador

For the Shuar people to legalize their territory and develop a plan for sustainable use of their land and natural resources: $32,550

Association of Women's Clubs (AWC)—Zimbabwe

Implemented gender-related social change programs, contributing to the ongoing empowerment of women in rural areas to participate in decision-making processes that affect their lives: $86,000

Cambodia Family Development Service (CFDS)—Cambodia

Funding to improve conditions for the people of the Kampong Plouk Commune by building resource management skills and knowledge among village leaders: $24,948

Farm Labor Research Project (FLRP)—North Carolina, U.S.

To organize and train migrant farm workers to expose oppressive working conditions in North Carolina: $50,000

Source: Oxfam America Annual Report 2001.

mission. Communication and education staff also grew considerably from 1997 to 2002, seeking to leverage advocacy work to reach the broader public and to build political and financial support.

Increasingly, OA's local partners were engaging in advocacy in their own countries, and OA sought to support their efforts. Offenheiser described the OA approach to advocacy in the South as one that "presumes that partners should be the leading actors and voices for development in their respective national contexts."[10]

See **Exhibit 7** for a list of OA advocacy campaigns.

Resource Development.

Donations from individuals, the nearly exclusive source of revenues for OA, supported the organization's growth. OA sought donations through several channels, including direct mail, the Internet, major gifts through direct solicitations, bequests, and special events. The strong growth in contributions in the late 1990s stemmed from a growth in the base of individual donors combined with several large grants from foundations. Humanitarian crises in the late 1990s, particularly Hurricane Mitch in Central America and the war in Kosovo, had helped to increase the donor base of OA.

See **Exhibit 4** for historical information on share of giving by donor category.

Organizational Structure and Management.

OA's staff were at its Boston headquarters, Washington, D.C., advocacy offices, and its five regional offices. Global Programs, Resource Development, Finance and Administration, Communications and Education, and Human Resources all operated out of the Boston headquarters. Advocacy and Policy and External Affairs were in the Washington, D.C., office. In each of the regional offices there was a director, program officers, administrators, and in some cases policy or advocacy officers. OA has regional offices in El Salvador, Peru, Zimbabwe, Senegal, and Cambodia.

Exhibit 6	Oxfam International Press Release at Launch of *Make Trade Fair* Campaign (April 11, 2002)

THE GREAT TRADE ROBBERY
Rich world swindles millions from the benefits of trade as global wealth divide widens to all time high

OXFAM today accused the rich world of robbing the poor world of $100 billion a year by abusing the rules governing world trade and denying millions of poor people their best escape route from poverty.

"For every dollar we give in aid two are stolen through unfair trade, costing the poor world $100 billion a year. Globalisation is leaving millions in despair, creating a world more unequal than ever before, when it could do the exact opposite. The wealth divide is at an all time high and the anger and social tensions that accompanies such morally unacceptable inequalities threaten us all," warned Jeremy Hobbs, Executive Director of Oxfam International during the launch of Make Trade Fair, a global campaign in 18 countries to change the rules of trade.

The campaign is launched as the 144 countries of the World Trade Organization start to work on a new agenda of trade negotiations that will determine how world trade will be regulated in the future. WTO negotiations risk widening the global divide unless the rich world changes its approach to the concerns of developing countries.

In a new report "Rigged Rules and Double Standards" Oxfam shows that 128 million people could be lifted out of poverty if Africa, Latin America, East Asia and South Asia each increased their share of world exports by just one percent.

However, rich world hypocrisy and double standards stop this from happening because the rich world is rigging global trade rules by:

- Subsidizing rich farmers $1bn a day. Over-production of agricultural surpluses is dumped onto world markets, suppressing world prices and destroying local markets in poor countries

- Influencing the International Monetary Fund and the World Bank polices to prise open poor countries' markets with little regard to the social consequences. These are policies the rich world has itself rejected.

- Stopping or penalizing poor countries from exporting their goods into rich world markets. Goods from poor countries are taxed at four times the rate of goods from rich countries.

- Being indifferent to erratic, falling commodity prices that condemn many poor economies to failure, while generating huge profits for big corporations.

- Allowing big corporations to ride rough shod over internationally recognized workers rights.

The report also highlights that while some countries appear to be successfully boosting their economies through increased exports this has had little impact on levels of poverty. Oxfam is calling on poor country governments to adopt policies so that the economic benefits of trade help to alleviate poverty and do not increase inequality.

People can join the campaign at a dedicated website: www.maketradefair.com

Exhibit 6   continued

Where the campaign will be launched

The campaign will be launched in New Zealand, Australia, Hong Kong, Bangladesh, India, South Africa Senegal, Switzerland, Germany, The Netherlands, Belgium, Spain, Great Britain, Ireland, Canada, United States, Mexico and Brazil.

Wealth divide widens

The wealth divide is at an all time high. In the last decade the world's poorest five percent lost almost a quarter of their real income while the top five percent gained 12 percent. Trade, though not exclusively, has been an important factor in this widening gap. For every $100 generated by world exports $97 goes to the high and middle income countries and only $3 go to low income countries.

Double standards

Nowhere in international relations is the rich world's double standards and hypocrisy so blatant as in its attitude to trade. It demands the poor world slash support for its farmers yet subsidizes its own farmers to the tune of $1bn a day. This leads to over production that is then dumped onto the world market, suppressing prices which poor farmers cannot compete against.

Topping the rogues' league of double standards is the European Union. It's dumping of surplus powdered milk on to the Jamaican economy has all but ruined the local dairy industry. The U.S. has done the same with dumping its subsidized rice on Haiti forcing thousands of poor rice farmers off the land. In Haiti's rice growing area child malnutrition is now among the most severe in the country.

IMF and World Bank

Through its influence at the International Monetary Fund and the World Bank the rich world demands the poor world open up its markets with no regard to the social consequences yet keeps its own markets tightly shut. It has created a race where the weakest have to jump the highest hurdles. The rich world taxes imports from poor countries four times the rates it charges imports from industrialized countries.

Aid debt and trade

For every dollar of aid to the poor world two dollars are swindled out of the poor world through unfair trade. Africa is of particular concern. A one percent increase in world exports for Africa is worth a staggering fives times the amount it receives in aid and debt relief combined. Yet Africa is increasingly sidelined from any benefits from trade.

Import tax hikes and the commodity crisis

Many poor countries are locked into only producing the raw food and materials we consume. The moment they begin to process these goods, therefore getting a higher price, they face high import taxes hikes, called tariff peaks, at rich world ports. Fully processed manufactured food products are subject in the EU and Japan to import taxes twice as high as products in the first stage of processing. In Canada, taxes on processed food lare as much as 13 times higher than those on unprocessed products. Thirty percent of all tariff peaks applied by the EU protect the food industry. These range from 12 to 100 percent and affect sugar-based products, cereals, and canned fruit. In the U.S., the food industry account for one-sixth of all tariff peaks, including orange juice (30 percent) and peanut butter (132 percent). Forty percent of all Japanese peak tariffs protect the food industry, affecting a wide range of products from cocoa powder and chocolate to canned meat and fruit juices.

Many poor economies are heavily dependent upon the export of a single commodity. Falling and erratic commodities prices are at crisis point. In 2000/01 poor countries sold nearly 20 percent more coffee than in 1997/98, yet they were paid 45 percent less. Had they sold it at the 1997/98 price, they would have been around $8 billion better off. This means less money for farmers but also cut backs in social spending on health and education. And this crisis is not restricted to coffee. Between 1996 and 2000 Ghana increased cocoa production by almost a third but was paid a third less.

Exhibit 6	continued

Corporations and workers' rights

When poor countries attempt to industrialize they also face many obstacles. Large trans-national corporations (TNCs) are powerful players in the globalized economy. Two-thirds of all trade takes place within TNCs. They are a major influence on labor standards in poor countries, either directly through the people they employ or more significantly through their sub-contractors.

The IMF and the World Bank trumpet successful export led economic growth of star pupils such as Mexico, Bangladesh and Honduras. However their export success does not trickle down to the rest of the economy. Their economic growth has been dominated by special export processing zones (EPZs). These are low wage ghettos for simple assembly of imported parts. The wealth it generates is spirited out of the country or left in the hands of a tiny minority.

Changing rules of the World Trade Organization

Many of the rules of the World Trade Organization (WTO), for example those on intellectual property, protect the interests of rich countries and powerful TNCs, while imposing huge costs on developing countries. This bias raises fundamental questions about the legitimacy of the WTO. By including new issues like investment, government procurement or competition rules, the new Doha trade round risks widening the global divide.

Women on the front line

Women workers are becoming increasingly crucial in these EPZs as cheap labor. They are the super-exploited in the new globalized economies. Women now make up about one-third of manufacturing workers in developing countries but they earn about three-quarters of their male colleagues. They may earn more money than before but they have fewer rights, less time to care for the family and more burden. In China they are forced to work 12-hour days in appalling conditions. In the sweatshops of Bangladesh they are denied the right to join a union. In the flower exporting market gardens of Colombia compulsory pregnancy testing is common before women are granted employment contracts. Summary dismissal has become standard practice for avoiding employer based maternity pay.

Oxfam is calling for a radical reform of the international trading system so that trade can become the engine for poverty reduction.

- Ending the use of conditions attached to IMF-World Bank programs which force poor countries to open their markets regardless of the impact on poor people.
- Improving market access for poor countries and ending the cycle of subsidized agricultural over-production and export dumping by rich countries, without demanding further concessions of developing countries.
- Creating a new international commodities institution to raise prices to levels consistent with a reasonable standard of living for producers, and changing corporate practices so that companies pay fair prices.
- Establishing new intellectual-property rules to ensure that poor countries are able to afford new technologies and basic medicines, and that farmers are able to save, exchange, and sell seeds.
- Prohibiting rules that force governments to liberalize or privatize basic services that are vital for poverty reduction.
- Enhancing the quality of private-sector investment and employment standards.
- Democratizing the WTO to give poor countries a stronger voice.
- Changing national policies on health, education, and governance so that people can develop their capabilities, realize their potential, and participate in markets on more equitable terms.

Exhibit 7	Oxfam America Campaigns (as of April 2002)

Make Trade Fair
Education Now
Oil, Gas & Mining
Conflict Diamonds
Fair Trade Coffee
US Food & Farm

Source: Oxfam America.

The OA board had twenty members who served up to two terms of three years each. Soon after his appointment as president of the organization, Offenheiser had sought to diversify the board, seeking new members with a range of personal and professional backgrounds. The board now had members from academia, the private sector, and other NGOs. See **Exhibit 8** for a list of Oxfam's board members.

OXFAM INTERNATIONAL.

> *Oxfam International is a global group of independent non-governmental organizations dedicated to fighting poverty and related injustice around the world. The Oxfams work together internationally to achieve greater impact by their collective efforts.*

—Oxfam International Mission Statement[11]

Exhibit 8	Oxfam America Board

Barbara D. Fiorito, Chair, New York, NY

The Honorable Chester Atkins, Director/Founder, ADS Ventures, Concord, MA

Dr. Seth Berkley, President and CEO, International AIDS Vaccine Initiative, New York, NY

Michael Carter, Professor, Dept. of Agricultural and Applied Economics, University of Wisconsin, Madison, WI

Susan Clare, Secretary/Treasurer, Wellesley, MA

Bradley J. Greenwald, VP of Business and Marketing Development, Wildblue Communications, Denver, CO

Paula Hayes, Director of Development, Environmental Defense, New York, NY

Wendy Johnson, Executive Director, the Southern Regional Council, Inc., Atlanta, GA

Dr. Jennifer Leaning, Senior Research Fellow, FXB Center for Health and Human Rights, Harvard School of Public Health, Boston, MA

Dr. Marc Lindenberg, Dean, Evans School of Public Affairs, University of Washington, Seattle, WA

Michael MacLeod, President, Public Interest Data, Inc., Alexandria, VA

Janet McKinley, Capital Research Company, New York, NY

Peter C. Munson, Senior Portfolio Counselor for Latin America, Citibank Global Asset Management, Citicorp/Citibank, New York, NY

Raymond C. Offenheiser, President, Oxfam America, Boston, MA

Mary Racelis, Director, Institute of Philippine culture, Ateneo de Manila University, Manila, Philippines

John Riggan, President and CEO, The Conservation Company, Philadelphia, PA

Kitt Sawitsky, Co-Managing Director, Goulston & Storrs, Boston, MA

Magdalena Villarreal, Senior Researcher, The Center for Research and Advanced Studies and Social Anthropology, Jalisco, Mexico

Beth Warren, President and CEO, WorkWorlds' Human Resource Corporation, Atlanta, GA

Jennifer Yablonski, West Africa Program Officer, Staff-Elected Board Member, Oxfam America, Boston, MA

Source: Oxfam America Annual Report 2001.

Founded in 1996, Oxfam International (OI) was a confederation of twelve Oxfam affiliates working together in more than eighty countries. OI was governed by the collective Oxfam affiliates and worked with them to align the programs, resources, and policies of its members. Each affiliate remained independently responsible for allocating resources and managing its own organization.

OI was governed by a board, comprising the chair of the board of each Oxfam member (or a specified board member) and the executive director of each Oxfam member. Committees comprising senior management of affiliates planned, coordinated, and managed OI's programs through three committees: the Program Directors' Committee, the Advocacy Coordinating Committee, and the Marketing Coordinating Committee.

OI's secretariat had a small body of staff to oversee strategy and activities and provide administrative support. OI also maintained a global advocacy team working in coordination with the advocacy staff of its affiliates. The team was based at the OI Advocacy Office in Washington, targeting the World Bank and the International Monetary Fund, with key advocacy staff in New York, Brussels, and Geneva, working on issues related to the United Nations, the European Union, and the World Trade Organization, respectively.

A RIGHTS-BASED APPROACH TO DEVELOPMENT.

The conscious choice to center all programming on a rights-based approach and to focus more particularly on economic, social and cultural rights has represented a major organizational shift for all Oxfam affiliates.[12]

A key development that was driving change at OA was OI's newly emphasized focus on a rights-based approach to development. OA identified two key reasons for this shift: disillusionment with the welfare model of international development and a belief that greater emphasis is required on economic, social, and cultural rights beyond the civil and political rights that have traditionally dominated the human rights agenda.[13] As a result, OA and OI as a whole put increased emphasis on promoting structural change through political advocacy and funding of on-the-ground programs oriented toward social justice. On the program side this has meant that funding of basic livelihood programs had declined, and funding of networks, human rights organizations, education programs, and local advocacy groups have all increased.

Campaigning in Extractive Industries: An Integrated Programming and Advocacy Effort.

OA's campaigning in extractive industries was viewed internally as a particularly effective implementation of the organization's right-based development agenda. OA's advocacy and regional programs supported the efforts of partner organizations to insert the voices of affected communities into national and international discussions about the various forms of economic development and their impacts. Both program and advocacy staff found that on this issue there had occurred a particularly successful alignment of political advocacy priorities with the realities of partner organizations working in the field. "The advocacy unit worked closely with the regional office and our local partners to understand their concerns and interests related to extractive industries. That process has heavily informed OA's approach to U.S. advocacy efforts and has helped make the campaign a success," expressed Thea Gelbspan, the South America Program Officer who worked out of the Boston office. Similarly, Keith Slack, Oxfam America's policy adviser in extractive industries explained, "Our regional staff and partners have been able to join us for meetings with the World Bank on this issue. Their perspective significantly strengthens our case to institutions like the bank."

As part of its work on extractive industries, OA commissioned a report in October 2001, *Extractive Industries and the Poor*.[14] OA argued that communities neighboring oil, gas, and mining projects were suffering from significant negative effects, while getting little or no economic benefit. The effects of such projects included widespread environmental damage, public health problems, devastating economic hardships, social disruption, and political repression.[15]

OA's work on this issue was integrated across multiple parts of the organization to help communities in three ways:

1. *Programs:* Oxfam's regional office in Lima, Peru, provided grants to partner organizations in Bolivia, Peru, and Ecuador. Grants supported capacity building so that partner organizations could advocate on their own behalf. Capacity-building activities included human rights training and networking. The main objective was strengthening partner organizations, and the leadership within them, to raise their own voices on issues that affect them.

2. *Advocacy:* The Washington D.C., staff had one individual dedicated exclusively to extractive industries and the office worked with local partners to persuade U.S.-based international companies and financial institutions, and the U.S. government to

   - Respect peoples' rights to consultation, participation, and compensation when affected by projects; and to free, prior, and informed consent;

   - Commit themselves to transparency and the goal of sustainable development; and

   - Promote projects that have positive impacts on poverty, equity, and human rights.

3. *Education:* OA's public education and outreach work supported campaigning by students and other activists to complement the initiatives of Oxfam's partners and advocacy programs.

NEW STRATEGIC AND ORGANIZATIONAL CHALLENGES.

Relationship with Oxfam International.

> *The degree of trust between affiliates and shared vision created by Oxfam International is allowing the affiliates to collaborate and leverage our collective global resources in a way that we would have not thought possible five years ago.*

> —Raymond Offenheiser, president, Oxfam America

Individuals throughout the organization agreed that one of the most significant changes that had occurred at OA in recent years was the extent of collaboration with Oxfam International. Historically, each Oxfam affiliate had worked more or less autonomously, with unique program strategies, advocacy priorities, and even organizational logos. With the formation of OI in 1996, that began to change, and by 2002 OA advocacy, programming, and marketing were increasingly linked to decisions made by OI's committees.

This had affected the organization in several ways. Programming and advocacy priorities increasingly stemmed from the vision of OI, and resources in both of these areas were now devoted to coordinating efforts with other Oxfam affiliates. From a marketing and fund-raising perspective, the first major change had been the unification of the Oxfam brand. As of 2001, all Oxfams shared a single logo to represent the Oxfam brand, which was used on all affiliate marketing and publications. See **Exhibit 9** for the new Oxfam logo.

In 2000, Oxfam International adopted a strategic plan titled *Toward Global Equity: Strategic Plan 2001–2004*. The strategic plan was based on the belief that globalization had been "selective and exclusive in its scope and benefits."[16] Thus, OI saw its role as an organization "campaigning for a model of economic and social development which is truly global and inclusive." Its strategic plan was based on three propositions about globalization: (1) the elimination of poverty through globalization requires *a focus on equity*, (2) *a new global movement* is required to change the course globalization for the better, and (3) *a break with business as usual* was required by Oxfam and other NGOs to make drastic improvements in the quality and coherence of their work. See **Exhibit 10** for more information on the OI strategic plan.

This broad sweeping and ambitious agenda posed significant opportunities and challenges to OA as it sought to create a coherent programming and advocacy agenda in line with OI's strategic vision.

Advocacy.

OA saw its growing emphasis on advocacy to influence public policy and corporate practice as a key part of promoting rights-based development and play its part in pursuing the collective goals of Oxfam International. This created two important issues for the advocacy unit: forging links with programming efforts and generating messages to donors, policy makers, and the general public. While OI presented the opportunity to leverage global advocacy, each affiliate was speaking to a unique national audience that influenced the types of messages that would be most appropriate. Gaining buy-in from all parts of the organization and the board was also seen as essential by staff if the organization were to engage in effective advocacy.

Another key component of effective advocacy was building a grassroots base of public support in the United States for OA's positions. This required mobilization of the donor base, the development of an online community of supporters, and the creation of links with related organizations and communities of support for campaigns.

Exhibit 9	Oxfam America Logo (logo shared by all Oxfam Affiliates)

Source: Oxfam America.

Jo Marie Griesgraber, director of policy and external affairs, who was based in the Washington, D.C., office, acknowledged that their office was "way understaffed" and needed additional research and media communication capacity to serve their growing advocacy agenda. However, she also thought the office "no longer operated in semi-isolation," as it spent more time coordinating with the Boston headquarters and the field operations than it had ever done in the past.

Exhibit 10	Excerpts from Oxfam International Toward Global Equity Strategic Plan

So why Oxfam?

In reaching out to the wider international community and trying to work more effectively towards global equity, what distinguishes the Oxfams? We are twelve autonomous organizations, each with its own history and supporters, but we nevertheless share a distinctive profile based on the combination of four approaches:

(1) The rights-based approach

The Oxfams focus on the realization of economic and social rights within the wider human rights continuum. Equity is key in the realization of these rights. Equity is about making the rules fair for poor people and ensuring that justice prevails. The five rights, which are enshrined in international agreements and covenants, are the foundation of this Strategic Plan.

(2) Humanitarian response *and* development action

A second feature of our shared identity is a "joined-up" approach to humanitarian response and longer-term development work. In many parts of the world the Oxfams are perhaps best known for speedy and effective response to man-made and "natural" disasters. Even where the name Oxfam is not associated with such responses, it is often the case that local organizations are supported by one or more of the Oxfams. Humanitarian action means saving lives: development action means building futures. Both share a common ethical basis and are rooted in a human rights framework.

(3) Action, advocacy and learning

While compassion and solidarity with those suffering poverty and injustice are the driving forces behind our work, we seek to achieve a threefold impact:

- Supporting the efforts of specific groups of people to make substantial and long-lasting improvements in their economic and social circumstances.

- Advocating changes in the policies and practices which cause poverty and injustice at all levels, and influencing the ideas and beliefs which sustain them.

- Contributing to developmental learning by identifying, demonstrating and documenting how these changes in policy and practice can be achieved.

(4) Working with autonomous, local partners

"The Oxfams at all times work through local and accountable organizations and/or towards strengthening or facilitating the establishment of such organizations or structures...and where and when local capacity is insufficient or inappropriate the Oxfams will help people directly ... while working simultaneously on strengthening local capacity (Oxfam International's Rules of Procedure, Article 52).

In 2000, the combined Oxfams were working with nearly three thousand local partner organizations in some 100 countries.

We believe that the empowerment of local organizations is vital to secure economic and social justice as well as for the achievement of civil and political rights. The Oxfams are distinctive for applying this principle on such a comparatively large scale.

Source: Oxfam International.

Exhibit 10   continued

A more user-friendly Oxfam

While Oxfam can be justly proud of the achievements of its partners, volunteers and staff, there are also areas that need to be developed. These include:

- Our relatively small membership base, which is mainly from the "North," and is not representative of the diversity which characterizes our work. We do not yet have members in influential countries such as Japan, France, India, Brazil, Mexico or South Africa.

- Membership conditions which present a high "threshold" for would-be new members (including brand licensing requirements, membership fees, time and cost of participation in a wide range of institutional activities).

- Although Oxfam has co-operated with other actors on specific campaigns, we need to become more open to co-operation as a core strategy.

- With our partners we have worked very effectively and gained enormous experience of working for change at local and sub-national levels. We need to build up our capacity to create powerful vertical links between the local and global levels.

Our three promises

All the Oxfams have signed up to three promises which underpin programmatic and institutional objectives set out in Towards Global Equity:

- First promise: *We will work to put economic and social justice at the top of the world's agenda.*

- Second promise: *We will co-operate in strengthening the emerging global citizens' movement for economic and social justice.*

- Third promise: *We will significantly improve the quality, efficiency and coherence of our work.*

We hold ourselves accountable to these commitments, and expect to be measured against them. The following chapters outline how we propose to honor them.

Source: Oxfam International.

Regional Programs.

As advocacy and education programs have grown in importance in the organization, the challenge is getting existing regional programs and these newer groups to work together to develop more effective, integrated initiatives.

—Raymond Offenheiser, president, Oxfam America

Aligning advocacy initiatives and programming goals posed an ongoing challenge to the organization. Programs were first concerned with the needs of their partners and viewed advocacy as a tool to further the interests of those they worked with on the ground. This meant that increasing capacity of local partners for advocacy in the regions where they operated was of particular interest. Although international advocacy efforts were viewed as important, the linkages between advocacy objectives in Washington, D.C., or Geneva and the realities in the regions were not always immediately apparent. Program staff remained concerned that their flexibility in supporting partners might be undermined by advocacy objectives that had little or no direct effect on their current programs in a region. Laura Roper, deputy director of global programs, expressed that for program staff it was important that advocacy priorities were not only "driven by the World Trade Organization (WTO)," but seriously engaged the regions in the prioritization process.

Greater communication with other affiliates through the OI Program Directors' Committee had significantly increased the collaboration between multiple affiliates working in a region. Transfers of funds between Oxfam affiliates to support programs in line with particular affiliates' programming objectives had also increased. Nonetheless, the degree of collaboration remained somewhat variable and dependent on the initiative of individual regional directors rather than being fully institutionalized.

Finally, although integration with OI called for increased coordination, OA had also been moving toward increasing the decision making and autonomy of field representatives through its commitment to becoming a learning organization. The relative influence of local decision makers versus global OI priorities remained unclear.

Resource Development.

OA had experienced unprecedented growth during the past five years, and the question now was whether that strong growth would continue. Although September 11th and the war in Afghanistan had heightened public awareness about global humanitarian issues, it remained to be seen how that would translate into donations during the next several years, especially with the marked slowdown in the U.S. economy. Furthermore, the market for private international aid dollars remained highly competitive.

Historically, messaging to OA donors had focused on ending hunger and poverty. In the late 1990s messaging had increasingly highlighted the organization's commitment to social justice and human rights. Stephanie Kurzina, director of resource development, explained, "[F]ive years ago we didn't talk about advocacy, we talked about hunger. Today we talk about social justice and reducing global poverty." However, developing a compelling case for rights-based development and campaigning for social justice to attract funds from multiple donor segments remained a major priority for the development staff. Kurzina also expressed that "much of the campaign messaging now comes out of OI. OA needs significant additional capacity to address the unique attributes of the U.S. audience. Another challenge for OA in comparison with other leading international NGOs is that its 100 percent private sector fund-raising program disallows the advantage of large government grants that come with lower costs and increase fund-raising efficiency."

Although media coverage of OA had increased in recent years, it remained targeted toward a particular segment—the *New York Times*, National Public Radio, and the *Washington Post* were the types of publications in which OA received coverage. Surveys showed that OA's brand recognition during the past five years had experienced little growth. Kurzina believed that a particularly exciting opportunity for the organization existed in the use of the Internet for relationship building, fund-raising, and campaigning.

Organizational Structure and Management.

As the organization prepared to engage in a new strategic review process, one of Offenheiser's main concerns was how OA would need to be organized to support the new emphasis on global campaigning. Changes in the number and type of staff across all organizational functions needed to be considered, as did board composition and whether new board members or experience should be added continued to be a possible issue to consider.

On a conceptual level, as part of the *Partnerships for Impact* strategic plan, OA had committed to becoming a learning organization. A key element of this model was increasing responsibility and authority of frontline staff and engaging broad participation across the organization in decision making. This meant that OA's strategic mission and values had to be clearly articulated to all staff and effective systems for accountability developed. Achieving this model was seen to be a continuous work in progress.

Staff members in all functions also viewed cross-functional collaboration as something that would be increasingly critical to the organization's success. However, collaboration across functions remained somewhat ad hoc.

INTEGRATING PROGRAMS AND CAMPAIGNING.

> *The campaign ... aims to change the rules that govern world trade to unleash the potential of trade to reduce poverty. It is motivated by a conviction that it is time to end double standards and to make trade fair.*
>
> —Make Trade Fair Campaign, Oxfam[17]

Raymond Offenheiser had only a short time to reflect on the enormous growth and changes that the organization had undergone in the past several years. He had much to consider as the organization moved forward. The new, shorter strategic planning process was under way, and leadership from regional programs, advocacy, development, and communications were all drafting their plans. Offenheiser and his staff were all considering what changes were needed to complete the transformation of OA required to do effective campaigning grounded on its field programs.

Equally demanding at the moment was managing the Fair Trade campaign, which required continuous external and internal communication. Although the initial launch and media attention was encouraging, it also was clear that campaigning would require new ways of working across the organization. Coordination and communication between Oxfam affiliates, program staff, advocacy and external affairs, development, communications, and the board were increasingly essential. Furthermore, the growing external relationships with the media, donors, Oxfam's growing online advocacy network, collaborating NGOs, and the general public required significant time and investment of resources.

Raymond Offenheiser put down the *Make Trade Fair* press release, looked at his watch, and realized that his short stop back in the Boston office was about to come to an end. He would soon be catching a flight to D.C., the start of a trip that included London and Brussels. While the full effect of becoming a campaigning organization and strengthening ties with Oxfam International was not yet fully clear, Offenheiser knew one thing with certainty: It definitely meant more transatlantic flights for the president of the organization.

Exhibit 11	Oxfam International Affiliates and Revenues (12 in Total)

Oxfam Great Britain: $281m (2000/01)
Novib Oxfam Netherlands: $184m (1999)
Intermón Oxfam (Spain): $34.9m (2000/01)
Oxfam America: $29m (2001)
Oxfam Quebec: $15.7m (FY 2000/01)
Oxfam Community Aid Abroad (Australia): $13.7m, (1999)
Oxfam Hong Kong: $11.2m (2000/01)
Oxfam Canada: $10.5m (2000)
Oxfam Ireland: $2.5m (2000/01)
Oxfam New Zealand: $1m (2000/01)
Oxfam Germany: $1m (1998)
Oxfam-in-Belgium

Source: Oxfam International.

Note: Exchange rate to U.S. dollars is based on average exchange rate for year of consideration.

Notes to Case

[1] This section is based in large part on Marc Lindenberg and Coralie Bryant, *Going Global: Transforming Relief and Development NGOs* (Bloomfield, CT: Kumarian Press, 2001), 1–31.

[2] This distinction is made in Lindenberg and Bryant, *Going Global.*

[3] The Bellagio Group consisted of the following NGO presidents: Peter Bell (CARE), David Bryer (Oxfam G.B.), Ray Offenheiser (Oxfam America), John Greensmith (Plan International), Philippe Biberson (Medecins Sans Frontieres), Jean Herve-Bradol (Medecins Sans Frontieres), Richard Stearns (World Vision U.S.), and Charles MacCormack (Save the Children U.S.).

[4] The Bellagio Group and the Bellagio Conference are described in Lindenberg and Bryant, *Going Global,* 18–22.

[5] Raymond Offenheiser, Susan Holcombe, and Nancy Hopkins, "Grappling with Globalization, Partnership and Learning: A Look Inside Oxfam America," *Nonprofit and Voluntary Sector Quarterly* 28, no. 4, Supplement 1999: 121–139.

[6] Offenheiser, Holcombe, and Hopkins.

[7] The history is taken in part from "Oxfam America," HBS Case 798-036 (Boston: Harvard Business School Publishing, 1997).

[8] Offenheiser, Holcombe, and Hopkins.

[9] Oxfam affiliate Annual Reports.

[10] Offenheiser, Holcombe, and Hopkins.

[11] Oxfam International Web site.

[12] Raymond Offenheiser and Susan Holcombe, "Challenges and Opportunities of Implementing a Rights-Based Approach to Development: An Oxfam America Perspective," Oxfam America, paper presented July 2–4, 2001.

[13] Offenheiser and Holcombe.

[14] Report authored by Michael Ross (Department of Political Science, University of California, Los Angeles).

[15] Oxfam America, "Oil, Gas and Mining: Communities Pay the Price," (2001).

[16] *Toward Global Equity*: Oxfam International Strategic Plan 2001–2004.

[17] More information on Make Trade Fair can be found at http://www.maketradefair.org.

PART 2

Progress and Performance

CASE 4
BRAC

BRAC has become a very large and diversified organization with an extensive network of field offices. We have experienced incredible growth over the past decade and are now on the brink of taking our activities international despite the many challenges we still need to overcome here in Bangladesh. The key issue, I think, is how to meet our objectives of poverty alleviation and empowerment of the poor, both here and abroad, while preserving the learning culture that defines BRAC, maintaining the quality and success of our initiatives, and building upon the strong BRAC brand.

—Dr. Salehuddin Ahmed, BRAC deputy executive director

Dr. Salehuddin Ahmed was an economist, educated at Dhaka University, who earned his Ph.D. in economics in the Ukraine. After working for the Bangladesh government, he was recruited to join BRAC in 1979. In 1983 he earned an executive master of business administration degree from the Asian Institute of Management and in 1999 was sponsored by the World Bank to attend an executive development program at Harvard Business School. "My horizon and mind-set has expanded over time as the organization has evolved," Ahmed explained. "Going forward, we must think out of the box but at the same time be experts in what we do every day, fully develop our capabilities, and continue to learn."

BANGLADESH.

Bangladesh gained its independence from Pakistan in 1971 after a long and bloody struggle. A war-torn country with 71 percent of the population living below the poverty line[1] and 10 million refuges to contend with, Bangladesh in the early 1970s was in desperate straits.

By 2003, Bangladesh was one of the most densely populated places in the world, with 130 million people living in an area the size of the U.S. state of Wisconsin, equivalent to more than 1,700 people per square mile. Around 83 percent of the population lived in rural areas, 87 percent were Muslims, and 12 percent were Hindus. The proportion of the population living in extreme poverty was estimated at 30 percent,

Professor John Quelch and Research Associate Nathalie Laidler prepared this case. HBS cases are developed solely as the basis for class discussion. Cases are not intended to serve as endorsements, sources of primary data, or illustrations of effective or ineffective management.

and an estimated 50 percent of children below the age of five were moderately or severely malnourished. In 2003, the official adult literacy rate was 60 percent, up from 24 percent in 1972. Because Hindus were a small minority, there was little evidence of a religious caste system. However, an estimated 40 percent of the women in Bangladesh were in purdah, meaning that they were heavily veiled, stayed close to their own compounds, and did not go out even to shop for food, although, thanks to the interventions of nongovernmental organizations (NGOs) and civil society, the status of women had improved substantially in the previous thirty years.

Over the thirty-two years of Bangladesh's existence, life expectancy and educational enrollment rates had increased, while infant mortality and fertility rates had dropped significantly. However, in 2003, Bangladesh remained a developing country in which nearly half the population struggled daily for survival and women were largely disadvantaged. (See **Exhibit 1** for gross domestic production [GDP] per capita and purchasing power parity over time.)

Located in a deltaic plain, Bangladesh is crisscrossed by several large river systems. Seasonal floods and rains, tropical cyclones and storms, and tidal bores often caused widespread damage and destruction. With agriculture accounting for 33 percent of the GDP and employing 65 percent of the labor force, Bangladesh in 2003 produced rice, wheat, jute, tea, sugarcane, oilseeds, and fruits and vegetables. Some light manufacturing, particularly in the garment industry, was also an important source of employment. Bangla was spoken by 98 percent of the population, and Bangladesh was a democracy with a multiparty parliamentary system.

BRAC HISTORY AND DEVELOPMENT THEORY.[2]

BRAC, formerly known as the Bangladesh Rehabilitation Assistance Committee, was established in 1972 by Fazle Hasan Abed as a small relief and rehabilitation organization to help resettle refugees in the Sylhet district after the country's war for liberation. Abed, a young Bangladeshi accounting executive working for Shell Oil, gathered a small team of concerned people who raised money and assembled a core staff to implement basic relief and reconstruction activities.

Abed and his colleagues thought that their efforts would be needed for two or three years and that the national government would then start carrying out necessary development functions. However, the development tasks proved to be huge and government agencies insufficiently equipped. Realizing that relief measures were

Exhibit 1	GDP per Capita and Purchasing Power Parity Over Time, Bangladesh		
Year Ending June	GDP (US$ billion)	GDP/Capita (US$)	PPP (US$)
1981	19.8	249	867
1991	31.0	274	1,165
2001	47.0	350	1,750

Source: BRAC.

not the answer to poor people's longer-term needs, Abed and his colleagues sought to develop programs that would build self-reliance among the poor. Early development efforts, focused at the village level, were unsuccessful, however, largely because village elites appropriated most of the resources. In 1977, BRAC assessed its existing programs and concluded that they had failed to benefit the poor. BRAC then changed its strategy to target the "poorest" people. Over time, an increasing proportion of those targeted were women. By 2003, BRAC's target group was defined as "households that own less than 0.5 decimals of land, own no implement of production, and in which the principal worker has to sell at least 100 days of manual labor a year in order to subsist." BRAC began providing support through village organizations (VOs), groups of about fifty individuals from target households.

In 1974, the organization's name was changed to the Bangladesh Rural Advancement Committee and, in 1992, reregistered simply as BRAC. On BRAC's early history, Abed commented, "Initially, in the 1970s, we made many mistakes, but these have helped us in the long run to understand that there is no fix-all strategy for development, and only through constant learning and adaptation can an organization develop the ability to serve the poor." BRAC had always attempted to pursue a holistic approach to poverty reduction and empowerment, and eight core principles had, over the years, emerged as the backbone of BRAC's development theory:[3]

1. BRAC believed that no matter how illiterate or poor a person was, he or she, if given the opportunity, could rise to the occasion and deal with problems. BRAC believed that a development organization should never become a patron, and when asked what he thought was the key to BRAC's success, Ahmed replied, "It's not so much BRAC that is behind the success we have had, but the millions of poor women in rural Bangladesh that have seized the opportunities we have offered, and who in turn have helped us shape our programs and products."

2. BRAC also believed that social awareness was necessary to empowerment and that self-reliance was essential. As conceptualized by Paolo Friere, the villagers BRAC worked with had to understand their own situations and the reasons why circumstances were as they were before they could reject fatalism and improve their position.

3. Participation and people-centeredness were evident not only in the BRAC development programs but also within the BRAC organization. Not only did BRAC encourage input from the village poor, but BRAC management encouraged discussion and creativity at all levels of the organization. "This is not a 'yes-sir' organization," explained Mohammad Abdur Rahman, senior trainer. "You'll find it hard to get top management to talk because they spend most of their time listening and observing."

4. Sustainability was another core principle, and BRAC believed that to achieve this, national systems and policies had to be changed and policies reoriented. BRAC field managers acted as catalysts of change in government agencies.

5. BRAC believed that there was no one "fix-all" approach to rural poverty. Although the creation of off-farm jobs above subsistence level was thought critical to moving beyond poverty, BRAC management realized that this depended on factors such as skills improvement, the availability of technical

services, infrastructure development, the availability of credit, and access to health care and education, as well as social development.

6. BRAC espoused the concept of going to scale, or expanding programs as rapidly as possible. Although all new initiatives were tested as pilot projects to assess their feasibility and viability, BRAC management believed that once a program had demonstrated clear benefits it should be expanded and made available to as many people as possible, as quickly as possible, in line with the mission of poverty alleviation.

7. Another key principle was that of keeping a market perspective and entrepreneurial spirit. Cost recovery of programs, through the financial participation of villagers, was implemented wherever possible and served the dual purpose of building self-reliance and business thinking for both the villagers and staff. Many of BRAC's support divisions also subcontracted and charged for their services outside the organization, and in the late 1990s, BRAC had diversified into a number of large and profitable commercial enterprises created to support development programs.

8. Last but not least, BRAC believed in the importance of women in the development process. Traditionally, women in Bangladesh had few rights and little choice about the course of their lives. Women worked nearly twice as many hours as men each day, were often pregnant or lactating, were frequently illiterate, ate last and least, and were often deserted when their husbands could not find income in the villages. However, research studies around the world, as well as BRAC's own experience, showed that women were the key to primary health care, nutrition, and family planning and that women were more reliable savers and borrowers. "We don't just listen to these women," Ahmed added. "We observe them over time and so are in a good position to understand the underlying tensions and forces that affect their lives."

BRAC IN 2003.

In the two decades before 2002, BRAC had experienced tremendous growth. In 1980, it employed 471 full-time staff. In 1990, this figure had climbed to 4,222, and by 2002, BRAC employed more than 26,000 full-time employees. Revenues and expenditures had followed a similar rate of growth, with annual expenditures in 1980 of $1.4 million growing to $21 million in 1990 and to $174 million by 2003. (See **Exhibit 2** for expenditures over time.)

By January 2003, BRAC was a multifaceted development organization with the twin objectives of "alleviation of poverty and empowerment of the poor." It employed 34,000 teachers in addition to its 26,000 full-time staff and was the nation's second-largest employer after the government and the largest NGO in the world.[4] BRAC worked in 60,000 out of 86,000 villages throughout Bangladesh, involving 3.8 million households, and its programs covered all aspects of the lives of the people with whom it worked. Within Bangladesh, BRAC was a household name and the BRAC brand implied a highly trustworthy, honest, and effective "poor-people-centered" organization.

In 2002, BRAC had initiated a new program to target the ultra-poor in Bangladesh. It had also ventured outside Bangladesh for the first time by registering as a foreign

Exhibit 2   BRAC Operating Expenditures, 1980–2002

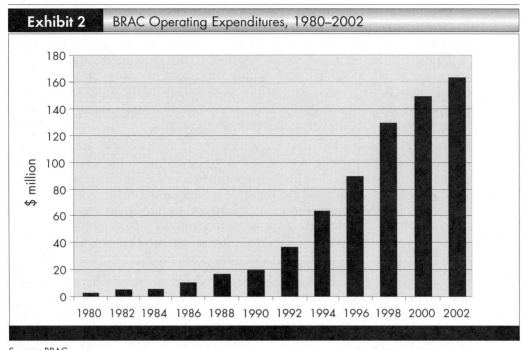

Source: BRAC.

NGO in Afghanistan, providing credit for the poor, primary education for girls, and several health clinics.

BRAC CORE DEVELOPMENT PROGRAMS.

BRAC's development activities were carried out through three different programs: the BRAC Development Program (BDP); the BRAC Education Program (BEP); and the Health, Nutrition, and Population Program (HNPP).

BRAC Development Program (BDP).

In 2003, the BDP focused on the socioeconomic development of underprivileged women through access to credit, capacity development, savings mobilization, institution building, and awareness creation. Formed in 1986 by integrating two BRAC programs, a rural credit and training program and a social awareness program, BDP had evolved over time, experimenting with new innovations and concepts to meet the needs of its target population. In 2003, BDP operated through a network of 1,500 field offices and fourteen training centers. (See **Exhibit 3** for a map of BRAC field office locations.)

Village organizations. VOs were at the heart of BDP and the channel through which BRAC introduced and delivered services to its members. Made up of thirty-five to fifty women from a single village, VOs met every week with a BRAC program organizer (PO) to discuss and carry out credit operations, learn about health issues, and discuss various socioeconomic and legal issues that affected their lives. In addition to facilitating weekly repayment of loans, the VO worked as a peer support group where members guaranteed one another's loans and supported one another through challenges and difficulties. In 2003, there were more than 113,000 VOs, up from 56,000 in 1998. (See **Exhibit 4** for a photograph of a VO meeting in March 2003.)

Exhibit 3   Map of BRAC Field Offices

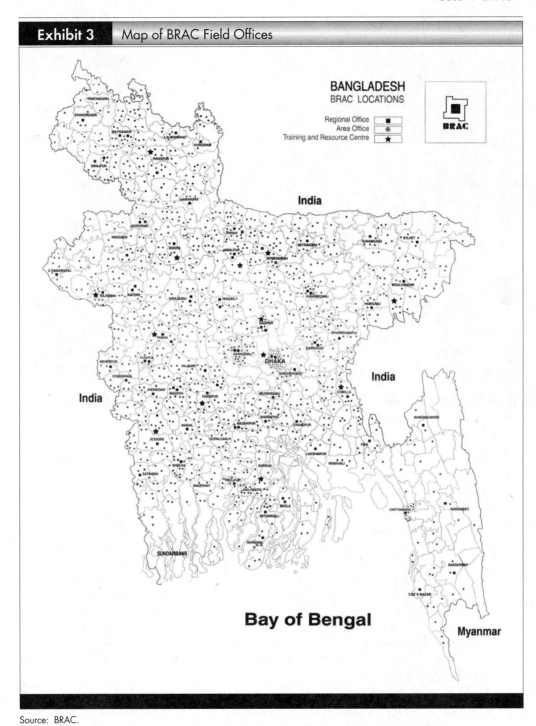

Source: BRAC.

Microfinance. Lack of access to reliable financial services was a major constraint
for the poor in their efforts to pull themselves out of poverty. By disbursing small
loans along with the technical assistance to enable households to generate their own

| **Exhibit 4** | Photograph of a VO Meeting in March 2003 |

Source: BRAC.

incomes, BRAC contributed to economic development by enabling millions of women to become income generators in their households. BRAC tailored credit programs to different target groups (see **Exhibit 5** for an overview of BRAC's financial services):

1. *The Rural Development Program/Rural Credit Program (RDP/RCP)* was the most common microfinance program operating through VOs and targeted the moderate poor. The difference between RDP and RCP was that the latter was self-sustaining. BRAC area offices, which managed the credit programs, typically became sustainable within four years, graduating from RDP to RCP. Three types of loans were offered under these programs: general loans, ranging from $20 to $200; program loans for areas such as poultry, livestock, agriculture, and sericulture, along with which BRAC provided technical assistance; and housing loans. BRAC also provided a savings program.

2. *BRAC Urban Program (BUP)*, started in 1997, was similar to the above but targeted the urban moderately poor. By 2003, 135,000 BUP members had a total of $6.5 million outstanding loans and $5.3 million in savings deposits. Senior BRAC executives thought they were still learning how to effectively serve this segment of the population.

3. *The Income Generation for Vulnerable Group Development Program (IGVGD)* provided credit and support services such as training and health

Exhibit 5   Overview of BRAC's Financial Services

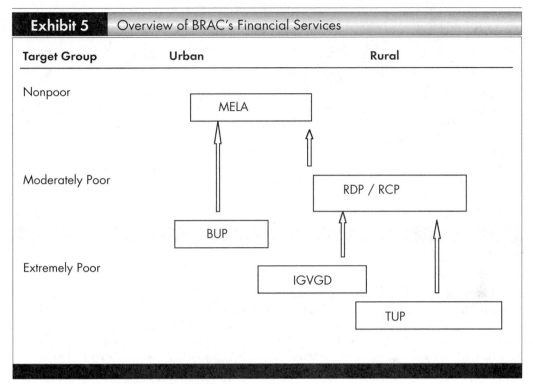

Source: BRAC Rural Development Program, Phase IV.

care to the extremely poor, who were also receiving food aid from the World Food Program through the government of Bangladesh. The objective, over time, was to advance these individuals from extremely poor to moderately poor and to promote them into the RDP/RCP or BUP programs.

4. ***Micro Enterprise Lending and Assistance Program (MELA)***, started in 1997, targeted the nonpoor and provided working capital credit to existing micro-entrepreneurs wishing to scale up. Clients included graduates of the RDP/RCP programs shifting from moderately poor to nonpoor status and people who were not members of the VOs. In 2003, there were more than 20,000 MELA borrowers with an average loan of 62,000 taka.

5. ***Targeting Ultra Poor Program (TUP)***, established in 2002, aimed to target, as the name suggested, the poorest segment of society. The expectation was that these individuals would also be able, over time, to climb into the moderately poor segment and feed into the RDP/RCP and BUP programs. The cost of this initiative was estimated at $300 per person.[5]

By 2003, BRAC's microfinance program was not only self-sustaining, requiring no donor funds, but was running a surplus. (See **Exhibit 6** for financial details of BRAC's microfinance program.) By January 2003, BRAC had made cumulative loans of $1.8 billion, had outstanding loans of $160 million, and had a repayment rate of more than 99 percent. Average loan size was around $100, and savings deposits by VO members totaled $86 million.

Exhibit 6	BRAC's Microfinance Program		
$ Million	**2001**	**2002**	**2003 (projected)**
Loan Disbursement	307	317	336
Loan Realization	269	281	302
Net Loan Increase	38	36	34
Fixed Asset Purchase	1	0	1
Project Income	48	49	50
Operational Activities	38	42	43
Net Surplus	10	7	8
Exchange rates	US$1 = Taka 52	US$1 = Taka 56.5	US$1 = Taka 58

Source: BRAC.

Employment and income generation (EIG). BRAC had learned that two major constraints preventing the poor from improving their lives were the absence of self-employment opportunities and a lack of skills to sustain those activities. "Microfinance alone cannot solve all the problems," Ahmed said. "We need to help people gain skills and become aware of their legal rights." Although BRAC members were free to initiate any income-generating activity they chose, training and support were provided for specific sector programs in which BRAC had demonstrated success and accumulated expertise. BRAC POs specific to each sector were responsible for interacting with VO members, motivating them, supplying basic inputs, organizing training sessions, and providing regular follow-up.

In 2003, eight categories of sector programs existed: poultry and livestock, fisheries, social forestry, agriculture extension, sericulture, rural enterprise, vegetable export, and program support enterprises. (Activities within each sector are summarized in **Exhibit 7**.) In 2002, these programs contributed to the employment of more than 2 million women and generated an estimated average annual household income of 17,250 taka. (**Exhibit 8** summarizes the employment opportunities and average income generated by sector.) By 2003, annual expenditures by BRAC of EIG programs were around 350 million taka, 70 percent of which were financed by service charges paid by VO members and 30 percent by BRAC. "These programs are run commercially," explained Gunendu K. Roy, program coordinator for BDP, "and enable members to play on a level playing field."

The poultry and livestock programs were the largest. Through a mix of BRAC, government, and private hatcheries, more than 1 million day-old chicks were supplied each month to village women, who raised them until they were two months old and sold them throughout the country. BRAC had trained 42,000 village women to provide vaccination services and also provided other VO members with poultry feed that they sold to other poultry rearers. Overall, more than 1.5 million village women were engaged in the poultry program. BRAC started the livestock program with the objectives of developing skilled, village-level paraveterinarians and improving local cattle breeds through credit and technical support. Recognizing the success and benefits of this program, the government of Bangladesh had, in 1990, adopted

Exhibit 7	Summary of EIG Sector Programs and Associated Actiities

Sector	Activities
Poultry and Livestock Program	Poultry and livestock extension work, chick rearing, key rearing, cage rearing, feed selling, minihatchery, pullet rearing, egg collecting, beef fattening, cow rearing, goat rearing, artificial insemination, fodder cultivation
Fisheries Program	Pond aquaculture development and extension, fish and prawn nursery, fish hatchery, pond reexcavation and reconstruction, experimental and development activities, marginal fish farmer, large-water body fisheries development program
Social Forestry Program	Timbers and fruit nursery, grafting nursery, roadside plantation, agroforestry, block plantation
Agriculture Extension Program	Vegetable cultivation, maize cultivation, cotton cultivation, crop diversification, hybrid seed production, processing and marketing, tissue culture
Sericulture Program	Mulberry tree cultivation, silkworm rearing, DFL production and rearing, cocoon dyeing and reeling
Rural Enterprise Project (REP)	Solar power, biogas, improved stoves, white salt production, rice seed production, netmaking, apiculture, Shuruchi (small hotel), Shupannya (grocery store), Shucharu (laundry), Shubesh (tailoring), Srijoni (carpentry shop), microenterprise development
Vegetable Export Program	French bean, green chili, potato, long-bean, broccoli, kantola, bitter gourd cultivation
Program Support Enterprises	Poultry farm and hatchery, feed mill, fish hatchery, seed production center, grainage

Source: BRAC. See "BRAC," HBS Case No. 395-107 (Boston: Harvard Business School Publishing, 1995).

BRAC's livestock development model for widespread implementation. "Many other private entrepreneurs have seen the success BRAC has had in poultry," said Roy, "and have entered this market as well."

Social development. The Social Development Program (SDP) aimed to promote greater awareness of social, political, and economic issues and knowledge of basic rights; provide legal assistance to members whose rights were being infringed upon; and build local-level social institutions. In 2003, there were six components to the SDP:

1. *Gram Shobha* was a forum of VO members, chaired by a PO, that met once a month to discuss social and economic issues that affected their lives. Not only did this forum provide an informal support and exchange platform for the women, but it helped BRAC staff understand the challenges these women faced.

2. *Human Rights and Legal Services (HRLS)* consisted of core BRAC trainers, trained by legal professionals, who trained Shebikas (community volunteers) selected from the VOs, who then conducted HRLS classes at the

Exhibit 8	Summary of Employment Opportunities and Income Generation by Sector		
Employment	**Number of People (000s), (2002)**	**Average Weekly Income (taka), (2000)**	
Poultry rearers	1,450,000	140	
Poultry vaccinators	40,675	N/A	
Paraveterinarians	3,645	N/A	
Cow rearers	85,166	N/A	
Goat rearers	81,035	N/A	
Fish farmers	48,277	400	
Vegetable growers	82,140	420	
Agroforestry farmers	19,284	600	
Silkworm rearers	6,584	N/A	
Restaurants	9,410	N/A	
Grocery stores	30,675	N/A	
Laundry	13,418	N/A	
Tailor shops	3,637	N/A	
Other micro-enterprise	3,637	N/A	

Source: BRAC.

village level. Legal-aid clinics had also been developed in partnership with Ain O Shalish Kendra, a Bangladesh lawyers organization, and were run once a week from BRAC area offices. By 2003, more than 87,000 courses had been held for more than 2 million participants.

3. *Local Community Leaders' Worskshops (LCLs)* were one-day workshops that took place at the BRAC area offices and aimed to influence and involve local community leaders in changing social practices that went against the law.

4. *Polli Shomaj* were organizations made up of representatives from three to seven VOs whose objectives were to build strong, democratic organizations, develop leaders among the poor, and give a political voice to poor women.

5. *Popular Theatre* was used to disseminate human and legal rights information. Through a series of plays given at the village level by a traveling troupe, social issues, laws, and basic rights were portrayed and explained. The troupes, consisting of ten village men and women who had followed a specialized training course, selected case studies based on actual events and gave a series of performances over a six-month period. Since its inception in 1998, more than 150 troupes had performed close to 500 stories nearly 9,000 times, reaching on average an audience of 600 people. (See **Exhibit 9** for a photograph of a Popular Theatre troupe rehearsing a new play.)

6. *Human Rights Violations* were addressed in cooperation with other legal and human rights organizations to assist women who had suffered from rapes or acid attacks (the latter being the practice of throwing acid into the face of a woman whom an attacker wished to punish).

Essential health care (EHC). In 1977, BRAC started training village health workers, known as Shastho Shebikas, to provide basic preventive and curative health services, as

Exhibit 9   Photograph of a Popular Theatre Troupe Rehearsing a New Play

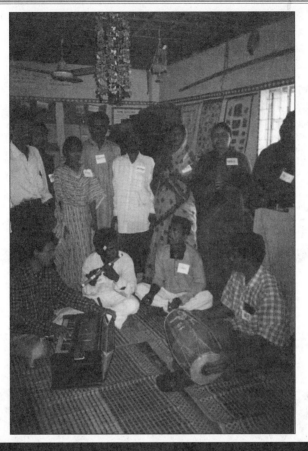

Source: BRAC.

well as training to fellow villagers. The Shastho Shebika, with the help of a BRAC PO, held regular health forums at the village level to discuss health, nutrition, and population issues. In addition, the Shastho Shebika visited, on average, fifteen households a day, providing basic health services, health and nutrition education, and referrals to other health service providers. (See **Exhibit 10** for an overview of the role of Shastho Shebikas.) She carried a small basic medical kit, developed by BRAC, containing family-planning supplies, medical supplies to treat common diseases, and basic health products such as iodized salt and sanitary napkins. The Shastho Shebika purchased these medical and paramedical products from BRAC and sold them to the community. The resulting profits provided these women with small incomes. By 2003, there were more than 22,000 Shastho Shebikas covering a population of 31 million. (See **Exhibit 11** for a photograph of Zulehka, a Shastho Shebika.)

During the 1980s and 1990s, BRAC had helped to implement the national Expanded Program on Immunization (EPI), which continued through the Shastho Shebikas. BRAC, in coordination with the government and other agencies, also constructed water and sanitation facilities, produced latrines, and provided revolving funds for tube-well sets. In 2003, major EHC goals included increasing the use of contraceptive methods to 55 percent of households served, increasing the number of slab latrine user families to 60 percent, ensuring safe water for all, and increasing vaccination rates of target children to 85 percent.

Exhibit 10	Overview of the Role of a Shastho Shebika

The Shastho Shebika (community health worker) is a VO member between 25 and 45 years of age and married. She is selected by her fellow group members to play this additional role in their community. The Shebika receives 18 days of training on health, nutrition, and population-control issues, as well as monthly refresher courses. Each Shebika is assigned to 300 households and provides basic preventative and curative health services to her area's VO members.

Shebikas are trained to treat the 10 most common diseases, advise on family-planning methods, identify danger signs in pregnancy, inform about immunization schedules and their importance, stimulate and encourage water sanitation programs, and participate in the health education of their communities. Shebikas also assist government health workers in their efforts to mobilize and organize satellite clinics and Expanded Program on Immunization (EPI) centers.

Source: BRAC RDP, Phase IV.

Exhibit 11	Photograph of Zulehka, a shastho Shebika, and Her Basic Medical Supplies

Source: BRAC.

IGVGD. BRAC estimated that half of those living below the poverty line in Bangladesh lived in extreme poverty. Despite the successes of BRAC and other NGOs in reaching the rural poor, those living in extreme poverty were less likely to benefit from their programs. For those individuals trapped in chronic food insecurity, with no asset base, traditional microfinance programs were not appropriate. In 1985, BRAC approached the World Food Program (WFP), which provided wheat to the government of Bangladesh, which in turn ran a Vulnerable Group Feeding (VGF) program. This program provided more than 330,000 vulnerable households in Bangladesh with a two-year supply of wheat. BRAC suggested implementing a new model for these VGF cardholders that would help them, over the two-year period, gain the skills and asset base necessary to escape extreme poverty. By 2003, a tailored development package had evolved, consisting of credit support, skills development training, technical assistance, basic health care, and social development, delivered through specific VGD VOs with the assistance of VGD POs.

The expectation was that the vulnerable women helped by this program would over time graduate to BRAC's core BDP activities or be eligible for other microfinance programs. (See **Exhibit 12** for Jorimon's story as an example.) By 2003, more than 1.5 million members were participating in the IGVGD program, and more than 80 percent of them graduated, after the two-year period, to become regular clients of BRAC BDP or other microfinance programs.

NGO cooperation. BRAC was the largest and most respected indigenous development NGO in the world. As such, it was considered a role model and was frequently solicited for advice and counsel, not only by local Bangladesh NGOs but by NGOs worldwide. To help build the capacities of other NGOs and promote information sharing, BRAC established in 1995 the NGO Cooperation Unit (NCU) to provide training, technical, logistical, and financial support to other, smaller NGOs.

Exhibit 12   Jorimon's Story

Jorimon's husband died of tuberculosis, leaving her with two small daughters, no assets, and a 5,000 taka debt. She worked for wealthier households in the village, sometimes earning very little, often begging for food. In 1994, she received a Vulnerable Group Feeding (VGF) card and 31.5 kg of grain each month.

Initially, Jorimon received a three-day training course from BRAC on poultry raising. She had kept chickens before, but she now learned about vaccinations, keeping the chickens clean, and the right types of feed to use. She also learned about the importance of savings and basic health issues. She then received a 1,000 taka loan from BRAC, spending part of the money to buy high-breed chickens from BRAC as well as some local variety chickens and investing part of the money with someone from the village who was a saree vendor. Jorimon did well with her investments and at the end of the first year sold her old chickens, bought new ones, and with an additional loan, bought two goats.

When her VGF cycle ended in 1996, BRAC workers asked her to join the regular BRAC BDP program. She did and received a loan for a cow. At first, Jorimon found it difficult without the free grain she was used to receiving, but the assets she had acquired during the two-year period, as well as the BRAC loans, helped her make the transition. In 1990, Jorimon still raised chickens and a number of goats, which she sold to slaughter each year, and kept a milking cow. The morning milk she sold to the community and the afternoon milk she kept to feed her daughters, who attended the local BRAC school every day. Jorimon then followed a tailoring course and used an additional BRAC loan to purchase a sewing machine. By 2002, Jorimon made clothing for children and women, which she sold to the village community; she had paid off her debts, was saving money regularly, and dreamed of owning a house one day. She was strict about her daughters' schooling and hoped for good marriages and prosperous lives for them.

Source: BRAC RDP, Phase IV.

BRAC Education Program (BEP).

BEP was designed to reduce mass illiteracy; contribute to the basic education of a significant portion of the country's children, particularly those of the poorest families; and ensure enhanced participation of girls. The program was initiated in 1985 after requests by VO members, who said to Abed, "BRAC does a lot to help us, but what about our children? Is there anything you can do to help them?" At that time, girls from poor families were typically not sent to school, and books and private tutors were unavailable and unaffordable for many families. "In addition," noted Erum Mariam, program head of BEP, "children were needed to help at home, and the typical school schedule of 9 a.m. to 5 p.m. was too much of a burden on families. With class sizes of fifty pupils and dropout rates of over 50 percent a year, there was a real need for a different kind of primary education system, one focused on girls, that would be low cost, child friendly, and close to home." By 2003, BRAC ran more than 34,000 village schools, constituting the largest private education system in the world and based on one of two models directed at two specific age groups. The first was the Non-Formal Primary Education (NFPE) program, a four-year program for children aged eight through ten who had never been enrolled in any school or had dropped out during their first year. The second was the Basic Education for Older Children (BEOC) program, a three-year program for children eleven through sixteen who had either dropped out or never attended school. By 2003, BRAC ran more than 10,000 BEOC schools, with nearly 300,000 members.[6]

NFPE class size was limited to thirty-three students, and the five-year primary curriculum was condensed into four years, with the same teacher teaching the same group of children for the duration of the program. (See **Exhibit 13** for a photograph of the inside of a BRAC NFPE classroom with the children performing a dance.) The teacher was recruited from the community and received a twelve-day training course, with monthly refreshers, and an annual five-day intensive training session before the start of the school year. School timing was flexible and agreed upon with the parents, who were encouraged to be actively involved in their children's education. "We constantly develop new educational material," Mariam explained, "and with the help of consultants, we strive to develop materials that will make it enjoyable for the children to learn. We emphasize social studies and critical thinking, which is a very different approach to the national system." On average, the annual cost per child was $18. By 2003, nearly 1.1 million children, 66 percent of them girls, attended BRAC schools, and of the 2.4 million children who had graduated from a BRAC school, 91 percent had moved on to attend formal schools at higher grade levels. By 2003, BRAC's yearly budget for its education program was just over $20 million. Donors contributed 95 percent of these costs, BRAC 2 percent, and student families 3 percent. Future plans included a request to the government of Bangladesh to bear the costs of teacher salaries and books and greater contributions by BRAC and parents.

In the true BRAC spirit of adapting and expanding programs to meet the needs of its members, a number of additional education initiatives had been established. These included more than 2,200 pre-primary schools; more than 700 rural libraries, 530 of which were self-financing; and 8,000 reading centers for adolescent girls. "We found that many of the girls who completed the BRAC school program but did not go on to high school were forgetting their literacy skills," Mariam explained. "They needed a forum to provide stimulation and access to materials. This program has

Exhibit 13   Photograph of the Inside of a BRAC NFPE Classroom

Source: BRAC.

evolved to become an opportunity for these young women to exchange, socialize, and build social awareness and confidence." The BRAC school model had been adopted by other eastern and southern African countries. Many organizations in South Asia, West Africa, and Central America had also modeled their primary education systems on the BRAC experience. "Many factors have contributed to our success," Mariam explained, "including the response from the communities, the availability of staff, the density of our population, the fact that we only have one language, and the increasingly good relationship and collaboration with the government."

Health, Nutrition, and Population Program (HNPP).

BRAC's health care programs had also evolved over time. In addition to the EHC program run under the BRAC development program, BRAC HNPP ran nearly 100 health centers throughout the country, which treated more than 550,000 patients in 2002. Typically staffed by a medical doctor and two nurses and equipped with laboratory facilities, essential drugs, and basic outpatient facilities (including those for infant deliveries), these health centers provided secondary-level clinical services and technical backup for the EHC programs. (See **Exhibit 14** for a photograph of a BRAC health center physician and his patient.) The health centers delivered services at a cost price, waiving user fees for extremely poor households, and average center cost recovery was around 60 percent. Reproductive health and disease control was the focus of BRAC's EHC program and rural health centers. With one of the world's highest maternal morbidity and mortality rates, pregnancy care and family-planning services dominated the health care services they provided. In 2002, more than

Exhibit 14   Photograph of a BRAC Health Center Physician and His Patient

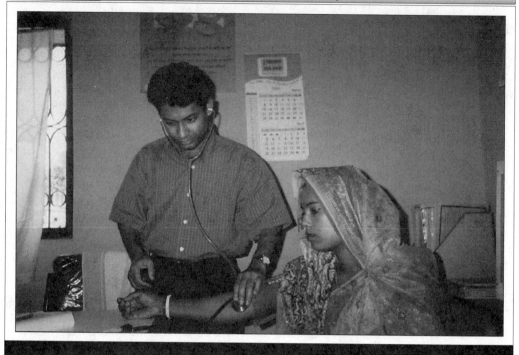

Source: BRAC.

725,000 pregnant women received prenatal care and more than 5 million couples received family-planning advice.

BRAC also collaborated with the Bangladesh government on different national health programs in the fields of nutrition, immunization, and tuberculosis control. Under these government-supported programs, BRAC ran more than 7,000 community nutrition programs targeting pregnant and lactating mothers and children under the age of two. Managed by a community nutrition promoter, a woman from the village who followed twenty-four days of intensive training, these community nutrition programs provided birth-weight and growth-monitoring sessions to close to 500,000 mothers of infants and young children and 300,000 pregnant and lactating women.

"Despite having implemented successful health programs that have demonstrated real results," said Dr. Shamsher Ali Khan, program coordinator for HNPP, "we still face many challenges." He continued:

> *Although fertility rates are down to 3.3 compared to six twenty years ago, 15 percent of all pregnancies involve complications, and 10 percent of these require surgery. In addition, 30 percent of adolescent girls suffer from malnutrition and anemia, which makes them more likely to suffer from complications during delivery. Over 50 percent of infant deaths occur in the first week of life, and we have a new program called Saving Newborn Life, which attempts to target this specifically. Arsenic levels in the water are also a big problem in*

Bangladesh, as are tuberculosis and hepatitis. BRAC attempts to get to tackle and solve the source of any health problem. Our strength as an organization lies in the fact that we have multidimensional programs. For rural women in Bangladesh, health status is linked to knowledge of basic sanitary precautions, access to income-generation opportunities, education, social development, and knowledge of legal rights. BRAC provides support in all these areas and is therefore in a better position to positively impact the lives of these women than, say, a more focused organization. You could say we are a one-stop shop.

BRAC SUPPORT SYSTEMS.

BRAC Training Division (BTD).

Training and dissemination of information had always been key components of BRAC's development activities and philosophy. In 2003, through fourteen training and resource centers and a broad network of specialized trainers, BRAC provided capacity building, professional development, and skills training to both BRAC staff and VO members. About 25 percent of the training facilities capacity was subcontracted each year to other organizations. Training courses fell into two broad categories: human development and management, and occupational skills development. The first focused on enhancing the quality and skills of BRAC staff and maintaining the BRAC culture. The second provided the development of new need-based training modules for members of BRAC's development programs. In 2002, more than 60,000 people were trained by BTD.

Collaborative training programs had also been initiated with both the government and other NGOs, such as the development of materials for early-childhood development, a joint program among the government, UNICEF, and BRAC. In addition, the Global Partnership for NGO Studies, Education and Training, a consortium of three organizations (BRAC, the Organization of Rural Associations in Zimbabwe, and the School for International Training in the United States), offered diploma and master's degrees in NGO leadership and management.

Research and Evaluation Division (RED).

Research was an inextricable part of BRAC, and RED had been working independently since 1975 to provide an unbiased analytical basis for BRAC's program evaluations and decisions. It was largely because of RED's input and BRAC's ability to integrate the division's findings and recommendations that David Korten, in 1979, characterized BRAC as "coming as near to a pure example of a learning organization as one is likely to find."[7] In 2003, RED conducted a wide range of multidisciplinary studies in areas such as socioeconomic development, agriculture, nutrition, population, education, environment, and gender. Although it maintained a focus on BRAC program areas, it also worked in collaboration with NGOs and government and academic bodies throughout the world (including Harvard University) and had earned a reputation as an excellent research organization. In 2003, RED generated nearly two-thirds of its income from external consultancy and commissioned research projects. Professor Muazzam Husain, director of RED, expanded:

I have not come across any NGOs that have such a strong research organization. We are now a respected research organization. Last year, the World Bank, before financing a major bridge construction project, requested that BRAC be entrusted with the assessment of its impact on 6,000 households. The challenge, however, given the number of external research requests we receive, is to balance internal and external projects. We also lose many of our top research staff to better-paying organizations.

RED undertook both impact and evaluation studies and broader thematic research. As of December 2001, RED had produced 855 research reports and papers, the findings of which were disseminated through conferences, seminars, symposia, workshops, book chapters, national and international journals (including prestigious journals such as the *New England Journal of Medicine*, *Lancet*, and *World Development*) and newspaper articles, and internal newsletters. (See **Exhibit 15** for an overview of RED's ongoing studies in December 2001.) By 2003, RED employed more than fifty professional staff and seventy-five support staff.

Support Programs.

Other key divisions included monitoring, human resources, construction, public affairs and communications, and audit and accounts. The latter was particularly capable, possibly because Abed was a chartered accountant. In addition, BRAC had, in the 1990s, expanded into a number of different commercial, profit-making ventures. In some cases, these commercial entities provided inputs to BDP sector programs; in other cases they provided access to the commercial markets for the goods produced by BDP sector programs. In 2003, these enterprises included a bull station, twelve fish and prawn hatcheries, thirteen grainage and sericulture operations, two seed-processing plants, three poultry-feed mills, five poultry farms, one poultry-processing plant (planned), a dairy-processing plant, cold storage, a printer, eight handicraft production centers, and eight handicraft retail stores. (See **Exhibit 16** for recent revenues and net income figures from these enterprises.)

The Aarong, meaning "village fair," production centers and retail stores were the oldest of BRAC's commercial ventures and were established in 1978 with the objective of bringing support and market access within the reach of rural artisans and expanding the market for their goods both domestically and internationally. In 2003, more than 30,000 artisans were involved in the production of pottery, woven baskets, and silk and luxury garments that were sold through eight department-store-like outlets in the major cities of Dhaka, Chittagong, Sylhet, and Khulna. Over the years the Aarong brand had become known as one of the finest producers of rural crafts and was synonymous with high quality.

Other commercial ventures were not necessarily directly linked to BRAC's development programs. For example, BRAC was a major shareholder in the BDH-Delta BRAC Housing Finance Corporation, a public limited company and nonbanking financial institution that promoted affordable home ownership by financing and contributing to the growth of the housing sector. BRAC was also involved in the field of information technology through BDMAIL Network Limited, an Internet service provider, and BRAC Information Technology Institute, which provided training and education to develop information technology professionals. In addition, BRAC Bank was formed in 2001 and functioned as a full-fledged commercial bank focusing on providing financial services to small and medium-sized enterprises, and BRAC University was inaugurated in 2001 with the mission of providing broad-based, high-quality education.

Exhibit 15	Overview of RED's Ongoing Studies in 2001

Field	Study
Education	1. An analysis of the workload of the Non Formal Primary Education (NFPE) teachers of grades IV and V
	2. Competency achievement of BRAC school graduates
	3. Education Watch 2001: revisit of Education Watch 1999 indicators
	4. Evaluation of curriculum toward a research-led curriculum development: two studies, on mathematics and social studies
	5. Impact of BRAC's NFPE program
	6. Socioeconomic background of the learners' households and the issue of financial sustainability: the case of BRAC primary school
	7. Socioeconomic differentials of the members of BRAC Gonokendra Pathagar
	8. Time distribution in different teaching-learning activities in BRAC schools
	9. Tracer study on assessment of basic competencies of BRAC school graduates
Environmental	1. Arsenic mitigation and epidemiological study in Matlab upazila
	2. Assessment of the activities of arsenic mitigation project of BRAC in Sonargaon and Jhikargachha
	3. Assessment of BRAC's forestry program with special reference to ecological distribution
	4. Assessment of the status of arsenicosis patients in Sonargaon and Jhikargachha
	5. Baseline survey of arsenic issues on four upazilas
	6. Dugwell—a potential alternative safe water option to combat the deadly menace of arsenic poisoning in rural Bangladesh
	7. Functionality of Ward arsenic mitigation and option maintenance committee of BRAC arsenic project
	8. Has arsenic concentration in tube-well water changed over time? A comparative analysis of water samples from two upazilas.
	9. Study on willingness to pay for arsenic-free safe drinking water in Bangladesh
	10. Assessment of environmental awareness of the students who completed the primary level
	11. Perception and knowledge about the arsenic in water at Matlab in rural Bangladesh
	12. Preparing maps of all tube-well locations of Sonargaon, Barura, and Monirampur
	13. Testing of tube-well water for arsenic and preparing mitigation plans for all CNCs of Bangladesh
	14 Use of GIS and remote sensing techniques to compensate river erosion-affected people due to the construction of the Hamuna bridge project in Bangladesh
Health, Population, and Nutrition	1. Assessing compliance with iron supplementation during pregnancy: a comparison between methods
	2. Bangladesh health equity watch
	3. CFPRP-health component
	4. Changing health-seeking behavior in the context of development interventions: experiences from Matlab, Bangladesh
	5. Early-childhood development

Source: BRAC Research 2001, BRAC RED.

| Exhibit 15 | continued |

Field	Study
	6. Effectiveness of daily and weekly doses of iron supplementation program for postpartum women
	7. Impact of development interventions on neonatal health
	8. Microcredit programs and health of the poor
	9. Micronutrient beverage supplementation for adolescent girls at nonformal schools in rural Bangladesh
	10. National survey on anemia and low birth weight
	11. Patterns and risk factors of childhood morbidity in rural Bangladesh
	12. Poverty mapping of BRAC-ICDDR, B study households
	13. Reaching the disadvantaged: identification of gaps and needed interventions to promote health equity in rural Bangladesh
	14. Secondary analysis of BRAC-ICDDR, B joint research paper
	15. Side effects have limited impact on compliance to iron supplementation
	16. Gender and TB: an assessment of gender-sensitive community-based DOTS program in Bangladesh
Socioeconomics	1. Assessing portfolio quality in BRAC's MELA program: a trend analysis
	2. BRAC federation and its role in village shalish: an exploratory study
	3. Dynamics of impact of BRAC BDP on the livelihoods of participant households
	4. Extension for the sustainable livelihoods study: a case of the BRAC poultry program
	5. Extremely poor households and BRAC interventions: is there any impact?
	6. GQAL: a study on VO members
	7. The impact of BRAC's poultry program at beneficiaries' level
	8. Impact of BDP on employment generation
	9. Impact of BDP on food security
	10. The Jamalpur flood rehabilitation program: experiences and lessons
	11. Patterns and trends in food consumption in poor rural and urban households in Bangladesh
	12. Relative profitability analysis of selected vegetables over other alternative crops and its impact
	13. The seed delivery system in Bangladesh
	14. Socioeconomic baseline survey of villages under open water fisheries of the Fourth Fisheries project of the government of Bangladesh
	15. Socioeconomic differentiation among male, female, and Karbari-headed households
	16. Strategic plan for BRAC advocacy on empathy
	17. Third impact assessment study of BDP
	18. To produce or not to produce? Tackling the tobacco dilemma
	19. Managing pneumonia by community health volunteers: the case of ARI control program of BRAC
	20. Risk factors of violent death in rural Bangladesh
	21. Integrating ARI prevention with microcredit programs: experience of BRAC
	22. Changes in the land ownership and use in rural Bangladesh
	23. Post-election violence on non-Muslims in Bangladesh
	24. Sustainability and institution building of BRAC village organizations

Source: BRAC Research 2001, BRAC RED.

Exhibit 16	Revenues and Net Income Generated by BRAC's Commercial Enterprises and Program Support Enterprises			
Millions of Taka	Revenues 2001	Net Income 2001	Revenues 2002	Net Income 2002
Aarong Shops	627	48	651	64
BRAC Printers	163	11	182	14
BRAC Dairy and Food	309	10	353	19
Poultry Enterprises	122	27	128	19
Seed Enterprises	373	34	447	23
Feed Enterprises	641	29	465	8
Fish and Prawn Hatchery	23	5	33	8
Nursery	39	11	37	3
TOTAL	2,297	175	2,296	158
Exchange rates	US$1 = Taka 52		US$1 = Taka 56.5	

Source: BRAC.

THE BRAC BRAND.

Although BRAC, and to a lesser extent the Aarong brands, were respected household names in Bangladesh, BRAC did not actively promote either the organization or the brand names. It was virtually unknown outside Bangladesh and the international development community. This was in sharp contrast to its main competitor, Grameen Bank, which was known worldwide and actively promoted itself, drawing some criticism from competitors, particularly in the international microfinance field.

BRAC's Competition—Grameen Bank.

Grameen Bank was a nonprofit NGO established in 1976 by Muhammad Yunus. It was the best-known microfinance organization in the world and followed a lending model known as the "village banking method" or "Grameen method," focusing on poor women in rural Bangladesh. In 2002, Grameen Bank employed 11,770 staff and worked in more than 41,000 villages in Bangladesh, providing US$287 million in loans. The average loan size was just under $110, 95 percent of the bank's customers were women, and loan recovery rates stood at 98 percent. Grameen Bank said to outperform all other banks in Bangladesh and most banks around the world. However, in November 2001, a negative *Wall Street Journal* article said that "Grameen's performance in recent years hasn't lived up to the bank's own hype."[8] Specifically, the article said that repayment rates were inflated by Grameen as a result of the rescheduling of bad loans.

Grameen operated in a similar way to BRAC, through village organizations managed by a Grameen employee, but it did not train members and ran no community health or education services. (See **Exhibit 17** for a comparison table of BRAC and Grameen.) "The major difference between BRAC and Grameen," Ahmed said, "is that Grameen believes that credit is a fundamental right of the people and that market forces will take care of the rest. BRAC believes that, in Bangladesh right now, poor people cannot compete in the market. Basic infrastructure and inputs don't

Exhibit 17	Comparative Table of BRAC and Grameen		
		BRAC	**Grameen**
Members served (microfinance)		3.8 million	2.4 million
Members served (health)		31 million	0
Members served (education)		1.1 million	0
Members trained		600,000	0
Number of villages covered		64,000	41,000
Number of employees		26,000 full-time, and 34,000 part-time	11,752
Annual loans disbursed ($ millions)		317	171
Average loan size		$100	$110
% activities funded by donors		20%	0%
Number of countries present in		2	24 (through network)
Income generated by commercial activities (taka million)		2,881	150 (est.)

Source: http://www.brac.net and http://www.grameen-info.org

exist. There is no way for poor people to even access the markets, and that's where we come in."

Grameen had expanded the scope of its activities and now operated a family of Grameen enterprises including a telecom company, a knitwear factory, an Internet service provider, a venture capital fund, and a trust whose mission was to replicate the Grameen model worldwide through a network of partner organizations. BRAC, on the other hand, had expanded organically, focusing inward on its members and meeting their needs. "We are a very shy organization," explained Shabbir A. Chowdhury, program head of microfinance. "We believe our work will speak for itself."

"We have never proactively marketed BRAC," Ahmed added. "Our ethos has been that we focus on the work and that recognition will come by itself."

Management, Culture, and Image.

Effective management had been identified as the key to BRAC's success. In interviews given in the early 1990s, Abed underlined the importance of participation, decentralization, entrepreneurial spirit, and a shared set of core values. As Catherine Lovell noted in her book profiling the organization, BRAC also maintained a flat organizational structure and a small head office staff and stressed the importance of staff training and regular meetings at all levels of the organization.[9] "We are a values-driven, people-centered organization," Ahmed concluded. (See **Exhibit 18** for a list of BRAC values in 2003.)

"We have also had a consistent and visionary leadership combined with a democratic organizational environment," Shabbir Chowdhury added, "and that has kept the organization moving forward."

BRAC was also used to solving problems. "We are used to dealing with the unknown and the unpredictable," explained Abdul-Muyeed Chowdhury, executive director. "That capability is genetically ingrained in the organization now. Because we listen to our members, we take initiatives that attempt to address issues that they raise."

Exhibit 18	BRAC Values 2003

- Concern for the people
- Human dignity
- People's capacity
- Gender equity
- Fairness
- Honesty and integrity
- Discipline
- Creativity and innovation
- Participation
- Accountability
- Cost consciousness
- Teamwork
- Openness
- Sharing information
- Transparency
- Professionalism
- High-quality products and services
- Concern for the environment

Source: BRAC.

"BRAC always sets high goals," added Faruq A. Choudhury, adviser to BRAC, "and that is why we have grown so fast."

"BRAC is known for excellence," Shabbir Chowdhury added. "In Bangladesh everyone knows and respects BRAC, and people who work for BRAC enjoy a special status." BRAC top executives shared these sentiments and believed that BRAC, over its thirty years, had, through its programs, created an image that afforded the organization access to and acceptance by people in rural Bangladesh.

Government Relations.

"Government relations are important," Choudhury explained, "because governments can interfere with our work by trying to bring discipline and regulation without fully understanding the situation on the ground. Although in the past government and NGO relations have been bumpy, to say the least, the current and future relationship between the government and BRAC looks excellent." In 2003, BRAC not only partnered with the government in the implementation of field programs, but advised the government in sectors such as education.

CHALLENGES AND CONSTRAINTS.

Growth and International Expansion.

Ahmed commented on BRAC's further development:

> Until the mid-1980s, BRAC was thinking at the local level. In 1982 we managed our first national program in oral hydration and we started thinking more nationally. Now we are involved in nation-building activities. The BRAC University and BRAC Bank, for example, are institutions necessary to create an environment from which the future leaders of our country will emerge, and through our education programs we are shaping the future generation of Bangladesh. Getting involved in business was just a logical extension of our

> *development work, and now we feel ready for an international role, with Afghanistan as the pilot. We don't think that we can replicate BRAC in other countries, but we can adapt lessons learnt and share our experience. One of the main challenges as we continue to grow is how to maintain our unique BRAC culture and hold on to our key people.*

By June 2003, BRAC-Afghanistan employed 158 staff members, 137 of whom were Afghans. The organization served 378 VOs, just under 10,000 members, and 5,500 microfinance borrowers. It operated twenty-four schools for 727 students and ten health clinics. In the area of education, BRAC's approach was to support government efforts to achieve "Education for All," and its program targeted adolescent girls eleven through fifteen years of age and was based on a three-year curriculum. In the area of health, BRAC was in the process of establishing community health volunteers, a network of health clinics, and mobile clinics. The components of health care included health and nutrition, pregnancy-related care, family planning, water and sanitation, and basic curative care. BRAC-Afghanistan had also developed livelihood and small-enterprise programs, which provided microfinance for poor women and small enterprise loans for men.

"A key question," added Choudhury, "is how fast should we continue to grow and in what areas." Another key question facing the growing organization was how much advocacy work to take on. Dr. Imran, head of BRAC's new Targeting Ultra Poor program (TUP), expanded, "We need to define how BRAC addresses the policies and institutions that create the mess that BRAC is trying to clean up. BRAC now truly has the clout and reputation to start effectively working on concrete advocacy issues." In 2002, BRAC established a human rights and advocacy unit to support, in particular, the needs of the ultra-poor in Bangladesh. The unit promoted socioeconomic equity at the local, national, and international level through workshops, social mobilization activities, and the development of communication materials.

Human Resources.

As BRAC's reputation and scope of operations expanded, it became increasingly difficult for BRAC to retain its senior top-performing staff, who were increasingly wooed away by organizations such as the World Bank. "One of our major constraints," Ahmed explained, "is the shortage of qualified human resources to sustain our growth and diversification, particularly at top management levels."

Added Abdul-Muyeed Chowdhury:

> *Our international expansion, for example, is limited by lack of people at all levels. We just don't currently have the staff to go into several countries at the same time. In addition, every year we need to recruit hundreds of people to work in the field in Bangladesh as POs. Life in the field is pretty tough, and we have very high attrition rates. We typically recruit college graduates and provide training for them, but roughly 50 percent of them don't make it through their first year.*

"Over the past few years," added Choudhury, "we have recruited high-caliber people from the private sector in order to manage our commercial ventures. We have had to pay them commercial rates that are far higher than the rates we pay staff in our development operations. This imbalance has obvious repercussions for the organization, and we need to find a way to get back on an even keel." Another human resource challenge was the hiring and retaining of female staff. Despite its stated focus on women, only 25 percent of BRAC's field staff positions were held by women, and there were very few female top executives.

Financial Independence.

Over the years, the proportion of BRAC's expenditures funded by donors had decreased from 72 percent in 1994 to an estimated 18 percent in 2003. (See **Exhibit 19** for details.) "We want to fill that funding gap and become as self-reliant as possible," explained Abdul-Muyeed Chowdhury, "but we also need to find the resources that can continue to fuel our growth." BRAC's stated financial strategy was to continue to decrease dependence on donor contributions for both its health and education programs. The plan called for 50 percent of all education program expenses to be borne by BRAC, the government, and parents by 2010. Beyond 2006, BRAC expected to self-fund all its health programs through service charges, profits from the sale of health commodities, and income generated by BRAC commercial projects.

Culture and Societal Norms.

Muslim fundamentalists had long been critical of BRAC's influence on women and children and had even set fire to or destroyed BRAC program assets in the past. However, as Mariam described it, BRAC made small, incremental, nonthreatening changes that, over time, gradually reshaped attitudes and perceptions. "We work at the grass-roots level," Mariam explained, "and when people in rural areas see women teachers, women BRAC POs, and women health volunteers, their attitudes towards women and their role in society start to shift." She continued:

BRAC is a strong positive brand in many people's minds. Whenever we do anything new in a community, we involve that community and hold meetings

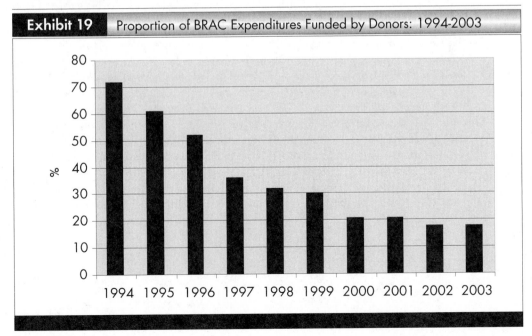

Exhibit 19   Proportion of BRAC Expenditures Funded by Donors: 1994-2003

Source: BRAC.

> *and forums. For example, we explain the necessity and rationale behind women POs riding bicycles, because they need to get from village to village efficiently. Because they are part of BRAC and doing good work for people in the villages, the fact that they ride bicycles and, increasingly, motorbikes has been largely accepted. This, in turn, paves the way for increased freedom for many women and girls.*

Ahmed expanded:

> *This society is conservative and our culture keeps women at home, raising children and taking care of domestic issues. It takes time to change. We have chosen to support activities that can be undertaken by women without clashing with our culture, such as poultry rearing, but we are also promoting activities such as restaurant and grocery store ownership, and our use of women health workers is a subtle way of releasing forces that can fundamentally shift our culture. Another example is the adolescent forums and programs that promote literacy and health among young women, two critical elements in their empowerment. These young women know their legal rights, have built up greater self-esteem, and have role models such as BRAC teachers and POs.*

Fulfilling the Mission—Reaching the Ultra-Poor.

"Despite our many successes," said Choudhury, "we have not managed to reach the bottom 25 percent of the population. They are difficult to find, they have no addresses, they don't even officially exist in many cases. To date, we have failed to find innovative ways to access them." Imran expanded on the challenges this target group presented:

> *We estimate that 25 percent of the population is not effectively being reached. To date, most BRAC and other programs have targeted people with some economic resources who are able to climb out of poverty more easily and quickly. The hard-core poor such as widows, single mothers, people living in more remote areas, and those that cannot get access to programs such as the WFP's Vulnerable Group Feeding program don't have any breathing room that would allow them to participate in our existing programs. BRAC has therefore developed the TUP program to provide them, free of charge, with a small asset base of poultry, vegetable seeds, or livestock on which they can build and grow. We also incorporate health and social development programs, and we have found that, in order to be successful, we need one PO per fifty TUP members, compared to the normal one PO per 300 members in our other microfinance programs. BRAC has historically been good at service delivery and scaling up, but I believe that TUP is a real challenge that requires a different mind-set, a different approach, and different measures of success. For example, the time frame required for this program will be much longer than for other programs, and it is not set up to be self-financing.*

CONCLUSION.

Given BRAC's impressive growth and success to date, as well as the challenges it currently faced, Ahmed reflected on the best future strategy for the organization. He pondered the following questions:

1. Was it possible to pursue a strategy of financial independence while at the same time refocusing programs on the ultra-poor segment of the population?

2. Could BRAC continue to maintain and nourish those elements of the organization that had made it so successful to date and yet pursue growth and diversification?

3. Should BRAC bother with international activities? If so, where and how, and with what focus?

4. What was the role of the BRAC brand in accomplishing the organization's mission, and what, if anything, could be done to manage it better?

Notes to Case

[1] The World Health Organization (WHO) defined the poverty line as having insufficient income and household production for a daily intake of 2,112 calories.

[2] This section based on "Globalization, NGOs and Multisectoral Relations," Hauser Center, Harvard University, 2000.

[3] This section based on Catherine Lovell, BRAC: Breaking the Cycle of Poverty (Bloomfield, CT: Kumarian Press, 1992).

[4] The New York Times, March 25, 2003.

[5] Ibid.

[6] The 10,000 BEOC schools were part of the 34,000 schools run by BRAC.

[7] David C. Korten, "Population and social development management: a challenge for management schools," 1979.

[8] Daniel Pearl and Michael M. Phillips, "Grameen Bank has hit a repayment snag," The Wall Street Journal, November 27, 2001.

[9] Lovell, BRAC: Breaking the Cycle of Poverty.

CASE 5
ACCION International

The challenge we face at ACCION is how to take an organization whose network of micro-finance institutions currently serves close to 1 million people, to one that reaches 10, or even 100 million borrowers. Our mission is to use microfinance to make a real difference in address-ing world poverty. In order to meet this mission, we now have to take ACCION to the next level and overcome any barriers to our ability to grow.

—Maria Otero, CEO ACCION International

ACCION International was an independent, not-for-profit organization based in Boston and one of the world's premier microfinance organizations. ACCION worked with twenty-seven financial institution partners in twenty-one countries in Latin America, the Caribbean, and Africa, many of which ACCION had helped create and to which ACCION provided technical assistance and training.[1] These institutions offered small individual loans and, for borrowers who lacked collateral, small group loans, in which each client cross-guaranteed the other's share. Between 1992 and 2002, ACCION's network of institutions had reached 2.7 million clients and disbursed $4.6 billion in loans, with a repayment rate of 97.5 percent. ACCION's own operating budget for 2002 was $10.7 million, with 52 percent of funding coming from private contributions, 19 percent from U.S. government grants, and the remaining 29 percent comprising international grants, interest, investment income, and contract and training fees.

History.

ACCION International was founded in 1961 by Joseph Blatchford, a law student and amateur tennis player, who completed a goodwill tennis tour of thirty Latin American cities in 1960, returning to the United States haunted by images of Latin America's urban poor. Determined to help, Blatchford and his law school friends raised $90,000 from private companies to start a community development organization designed to help the poor help themselves. In the summer of 1961, Blatchford and thirty volunteers flew to Venezuela and set to work. Initially greeted with skepticism, the fledgling "ACCIONistas" were soon working closely with local residents

Professor John Quelch and Research Associate Nathalie Laidler prepared this case. HBS cases are developed solely as the basis for class discussion. Cases are not intended to serve as endorsements, sources of primary data, or illustrations of effective or ineffective management.

to identify the most pressing community needs. Together, volunteers and residents installed electricity and sewer lines, started nutrition programs, and built schools and community centers.

Over the next ten years, ACCION started programs in three additional countries (Brazil, Peru, and Colombia), placed more than 1,000 volunteers, and contributed more than $9 million to development in some of the poorest communities of Latin America. By the early 1970s, ACCION's leaders had become increasingly aware that these projects did not address the major cause of urban poverty in Latin America: the lack of economic opportunity. "We began to sense that a school or water system didn't necessarily have long-term impact. We were simply reorganizing the resources that a community already had within it, rather than increasing their resources," said former ACCION director Terry Holcombe.

The employment situation in many of the Latin American urban areas in the 1970s was dire. Drawn by the mirage of industrial employment, thousands of rural migrants flocked to the cities each year. Once there, however, few found jobs. Those that were available often did not pay a living wage. Unable to find work and lacking a social safety net, many of these urban poor survived by starting their own small businesses or "microenterprises." They made shoes, banged out pots, or sold household goods or vegetables. Lacking the means to grow their tiny businesses and to buy supplies, they often borrowed from local loan sharks at rates as high as 10 percent a day. Consequently, most of their profits went to interest payments, leaving them locked in a daily struggle for survival.

In 1973, ACCION staff members in Recife, Brazil, contended that if the many small-scale entrepreneurs could borrow capital at commercial interest rates, they might be able to lift themselves out of poverty. ACCION coined the term "microenterprise" and began issuing small loans, effectively launching the field of microcredit. The experiment proved successful, and within four years the organization had provided 885 loans and helped stabilize 1,386 jobs.

Over the next decade, ACCION helped start microlending programs in fourteen countries in Latin America. ACCION and its affiliates, the ACCION Network, developed a lending method that met the distinct needs of microenterprises: small, short-term loans that built confidence and a credit record combined with site visits by loan officers. With a loan repayment rate of close to 99 percent in those early years, ACCION Network borrowers soon shattered the myth that the poor were bad credit risks. ACCION also found that microlending could pay for itself, with the interest each borrower paid helping to cover the cost of lending to another. In the mid-1980s, the demonstrated ability to cover the costs of lending, enhanced by ACCION's new loan guarantee fund, the Bridge Fund, enabled ACCION's affiliates to borrow from the local banking sector and dramatically increase the number of microentrepreneurs they reached. Between 1989 and 1995, the amount of money lent by ACCION's Latin American Network multiplied more than twenty times. Yet the ACCION Network was reaching fewer than 2 percent of the microentrepreneurs in need of its services. "In the 1980s," explained Michael Chu, president and CEO of ACCION International from 1994 to 1999 and current board member, "we created nonprofit organizations, gained support of key business leaders, and proved that microfinancing worked. Initially, most of our loans were group loans, based on what became known as the solidarity model, but increasingly they have declined relative to individual loans."

ACCION remained convinced that microlending had the potential to transform the economic landscape of Latin America. To do so, however, ACCION knew that microlenders would need access to a much larger pool of capital. In response, ACCION helped create BancoSol, the first commercial bank in the world dedicated solely to microenterprise. Founded in Bolivia in 1992, BancoSol was the bank of the poor: its clients were typically market vendors, sandal makers, and seamstresses. By 2002, however, BancoSol offered its 45,000 clients an impressive range of financial services, including savings accounts, credit cards, and housing loans (products that as late as the mid-1990s were accessible only to Bolivia's upper classes). BancoSol was no longer unique, and in 2002 the majority of ACCION partners in Latin America were regulated financial institutions, with the power to access the financial markets and the potential to reach not just thousands, but millions of the poor. Carlos Castello, senior vice president of international operations for Latin America and the Caribbean, explained, "About five years ago, ACCION decided to support and focus on what we call the commercial approach to microfinance. Since then, most of our partner organizations have radically changed, and today most of the major players are for-profit financial institutions."

In 1991, concerned about growing income inequality and unemployment in the United States, ACCION brought its microlending model home, starting a program in Brooklyn, New York. Over the next five years, ACCION worked to adapt its lending model to the very different social and economic context of the United States. In 2000, ACCION's U.S. initiative was renamed ACCION USA. In 2002, ACCION USA was the largest microlender in the country, with lending locations in California, Georgia, Illinois, Massachusetts, New Mexico, New York, Rhode Island, and Texas. By year-end 2002, the ACCION USA Network had lent more than $62 million to more than 8,000 low-income entrepreneurs.

A nonprofit subsidiary of ACCION International, ACCION USA's goal was to serve microentrepreneurs throughout the United States, regardless of location. In 2001, ACCION USA merged with Working Capital, a New England–based microlender, adding five new lending locations to the ACCION USA Network, and in 2002, ACCION USA was centralizing its loan processing, exploring Internet-based lending and call centers and opening new lending offices.

In October 2000, ACCION made the strategic decision to begin working in partnership with microlending organizations in sub-Saharan Africa, marking its first initiative outside the Americas. According to Otero, "ACCION recognized the vital need for microcredit throughout Africa and believed it could fulfill its mission of addressing poverty by reaching increasing numbers of the continent's poor." In 2002, ACCION was providing technical assistance to microlenders in Benin, Mozambique, South Africa, Uganda, and Zimbabwe. (See **Exhibit 1** for a timeline of the major milestones in ACCION's history.) "What has been critical to ACCION's success," Chu explained, "has been the organization's ability to question itself and its lending models, and to adapt to the very environment it has contributed to change."

Mission and Activities.

In 2002, ACCION International's mission was to give people the tools they needed to work their way out of poverty. By providing microloans and business training to poor women and men who started their own businesses, ACCION's partner lending organizations helped people work their own way up the economic ladder with

Exhibit 1	Timeline of ACCION's Major Milestones

Time period	Characteristics and Innovation
1960–1972	*ACCION Created as a "Private Peace Corps"* Programs in Venezuela, Brazil, Colombia, and Peru. ACCION deploys volunteers in the field with a major focus on community development.
1973–1980	*Microlending Experiment Begins* First microloans made in Recife, Brazil, 1973. Replication efforts in other countries: Ecuador, Colombia. Shift from volunteers to professionals with staff of 5 people.
1981–1985	*Developing a New Technology* ACCION begins to test "Solidarity Group" lending in the late 1970s. It is deployed widely by the mid-1980s. Expansion to Dominican Republic, Ecuador, Mexico, and Peru in the early 1980s. Focus on self-sustainability of microenterprise lending institutions via commercial interest rates and the belief that the poor can pay commercial rates of interest. Early successes in reaching much poorer clientele and women. Staff of 10.
1986–1990	*Building a Network* Pro-active expansion with new affiliates in Bolivia, Brazil, Chile, Costa Rica, and Guatemala and Honduras. Emphasis on increasing scale and outreach and establishment of a formal network. Establishment of reporting standards for network affiliates, including standard definitions for key ratios. ACCION collects data on a monthly basis. ACCION creates the Bridge Fund, a guarantee mechanism that will facilitate access to commercial (bank) funds by network members (active in 1986). Emphasis on institutional development, ACCION launches publication series designed to document its experience and disseminate it to others. Staff of 18.
1991–1994	*The "Gran Salto" Expanding an Industry* Network commits to lending $1 billion in 5 years and accomplishes this goal. 1992 inauguration of BancoSol, La Paz, Bolivia, as the first commercial bank specializing in microfinance, after transformation of PRODEM, the microlending NGO ACCION and local business leaders established in 1987. Creation of Centro ACCION Microempresarial, ACCION International's training and technical assistance arm, in Bogota, Colombia. Widespread use of Bridge Fund enables rapid program growth in terms of number of loans, new clients, and total portfolio. Number of clients grows from 40,000 to 259,000 and portfolio from $13.7 million to $137.3 million. Expansion to Argentina, Nicaragua, and Panama. Design and implementation of ACCION CAMEL. Network establishes standards of financial performance and develops rigor and transparency in this area. ACCION plays active role in members' efforts to transform into or create regulated microfinance institutions. Corposol/Finansol in Colombia comes close to bankruptcy because of poor management and flawed governance. ACCION takes the lead in re-capitalizing and managing the institution. Launch of U.S. microlending initiative in NYC. Total staff of 40 people.
1995–1999	*The Commercialization of Microfinance: New Players / New Models* Strong emphasis on accessing financial markets through the issuance by microfinance institutions of financial instruments such as bonds and CDs. New mechanisms for providing equity and loans, ACCION creates the Gateway Fund and is one of the founders of PROFUND, to invest in MFIs in Latin America. ACCION takes on a significant role in the governance of investee microfinance institutions by participating on the board of directors. Competition begins, especially in Bolivia.

Source: ACCION Board Members Manual 2002 and interviews.

Exhibit 1	continued

Time period	Characteristics and Innovation
	Expansion to Honduras and Venezuela.
	Near collapse of Finansol in Columbia absorbs staff time, causes loss of funds; teaches ACCION hard lessons about the importance of strong governance and financial transparency. ACCION rebuilds the institution, now Finamérica.
	Lending methodology evolves. New products designed to face increased competition.
	U.S. program expands to 6 sites and model undergoes reengineering.
	Staff increases to 65.
2000–2002	*Current Situation*
	Strong emphasis on performance and commonality of vision results in departure from the Network of several institutions. MFIs in Mexico, Haiti, Ecuador, and Brazil join the network. 27 ACCION partners in 14 countries in Latin America, the Caribbean, and 5 countries in Africa.
	Five associated lending programs serving more than 30 cities and towns in 5 U.S. states, and direct lending by ACCION USA in 5 states.
	Creation of ACCION Investments SPC, an investment company capitalized at $18 million by 9 investors and managed by ACCION's for-profit arm, GAIM.
	Total number of active clients = 798,031
	Active portfolio = $440 million

Source: ACCION Board Members Manual 2002 and interviews.

dignity and pride. ACCION strove to bring this opportunity to as many of the world's self-employed poor as possible by developing microfinance institutions that were financially self-sustaining and together, capable of reaching millions of people.

ACCION's Partners. Initially, many partners were NGOs (nongovernmental organizations); many later became commercial banks. Chu explained:

> At first, microfinance was so new, and so inconceivable to the established financial sector and regulatory bodies, that we had to start with nonprofit organizations. Our objective has always been to make microfinance economically viable, so we developed nonprofits with a business approach. For many years we then worked on transitioning these NGOs to financial institutions, and now ACCION is starting to work with established banks and get them involved in microfinance.

"We currently have four partner models," Castello explained. "NGOs that have transformed into banks or finance companies, boutique microfinance banks, large national or international banks that have created microfinance subsidiaries, and NGOs." See **Exhibit 2** for a list of ACCION partners in December 2002.

1. *NGOs that had transformed into banks.* This was the dominant model, with eight ACCION partners having gone this route, and two partners in transition.

"We have struggled with these transformations," admitted Castello.

> All of our affiliates would agree that these transformations have been time consuming and expensive, and institutions have had difficulties with cultural issues. For example, in most cases, we have found that people with banking backgrounds tend to instinctively implement controls for managing risk, thereby increasing hurdles for clients to obtain credit and pulling the institution up-market. While there are exceptions, we have found that what works best is

Exhibit 2	ACCION International Partners 2002

Partner Name	Country	Model	ACCION's Role T.A. Technical Assistance Inv = Investor Brd = Board Member R.A. = Resident Adviser
BancoSol—Banco Solidario S.A.	Bolivia	NGO to commercial bank	T.A. / Inv / Brd / R.A.
Finamérica—Financiera América S.A.	Colombia	NGO to finance company	T.A. / Inv / Brd / R.A.
Cooperativa Emprender	Colombia	Cooperative (regulated)	T.A. / Inv / Brd
Fundación Mario Santo Domingo	Colombia	NGO	
FED—Fundación Ecuatoriana de Desarrollo	Ecuador	NGO	
Banco Solidario S.A.	Ecuador	Boutique bank	T.A. / Inv / Brd / R.A.
Génesis— BancaSol	Guatemala	NGO to commercial bank (in-process)	T.A. / Inv / Brd / R.A.
FINSOL— Financiera Solidaria S.A.	Honduras	NGO to finance co.	T.A/ R.A.
ADMIC—ADMIC Nacional A.C.	Mexico	NGO	T.A /R.A.
Compartamos—Financiera Compartamos	Mexico	NGO to finance company	T.A. / Inv / Brd / R.A.
CREDIFE	Ecuador	Service co. of a major bank	T.A. / Inv / R.A.
FAMA—Fundacion para el Apoyo a la Microempresa	Nicaragua	NGO	T.A. / R.A.
Multicredit Bank	Panama	Commercial bank	
Fundación Paraguaya	Paraguay	NGO to finance company (in-process)	T.A. /R.A.
BanGente—El Banco de la Gente Emprendedora	Venezuela	Boutique bank	T.A. / Inv / Brd
Integral—Apoyo Intergral S.A.	El Salvador	NGO to finance co.	T.A. / Inv / Brd / R.A.
SogeSol— Societe Generale de Solidarite	Haiti	Service co. of major bank	T.A. / Inv / Brd / R.A.
El Comercio—El Comercio Financiero SAECA	Paraguay	Finance company	T.A. / R.A.
CML—Caribbean Microfinance Limited	Trinidad and Tobago	Commercial bank	T.A.
MicroKing—MicroKing Finance	Zimbabwe	Subsidiary of major bank	T.A. / Brd / R.A.
Nkwe—Nkwe Enterprise Finance*	South Africa	NGO	T.A.
Padme—Association pour la Promotion et l'Appui au Developpement de MicroEntreprises	Benin	NGO	T.A. / R.A.
Tchuma	Mozambique	Credit Union	T.A. / Brd / R.A.
UMU—Uganda Microfinance Union	Uganda	NGO to finance company	T.A. /R.A.
Mibanco	Peru	NGO to commercial bank	Inv / Brd
Réal Microcrédito	Brazil	Service co. of a major bank	T.A. / Inv / Brd / 2 R.A.

Source: ACCION International.
* ACCION withdraws in early 2003 because of very poor performance and Nkwe's lack of funds to grow the institution.

a president with an NGO background, loan officers who know microfinance, and bankers in the rest of the organization.

Despite the demands of transformation, most of ACCION's affiliates had, however, transferred successfully and were reaching their mission objectives while expanding the range of products they offered their clients. "Many other players are now following our lead in transforming NGOs," Castello said, "but I believe that this model has run its course in Latin America because nearly all the NGOs capable of transforming have taken this step, and because it is so expensive and cumbersome when compared to other new recently developed models."

2. *Boutique banks.* This model began in the mid-1990s and was represented by two partners in the ACCION network in 2002. Castello explained:

> *These organizations started off as for-profit entities, with the backing of social or multilateral investors, focused on microfinance. The problem with this model is that it takes time to build up a portfolio and register returns, and you need patient, long-term investors. In the case of Banco Solidario in Ecuador, it started with larger loans to facilitate funding while building up a microfinance portfolio, and these larger loans are now being phased out. The advantage of this model is that the organizations don't have to undergo internal reporting changes and are already regulated, so they don't have to wait to receive a banking license.*

In both cases, the bank president had a banking background but the credit area was still staffed with microfinance experts.

3. *Large banks with a microfinance subsidiary.* This was the most recent and promising ACCION model, represented by three partners in 2002. Under this model, ACCION helped to set up a service company as a separate subsidiary of a large bank. The service company originated and managed microloans that were then booked by the bank. The service subsidiary was not a regulated financial institution and was therefore lean and flexible, requiring only minimum operating funds. Typically, the bank would hold 80 percent of the service organization's shares and ACCION the remaining 20 percent. Castello explained the advantages of having a separate service company:

> *We have found that this does not work when the bank views microfinance loans simply as an additional product. There's too much of a culture clash because a bank, which is set up for low-risk and high-profit clients (by original standards), just cannot accommodate microfinance loans. By establishing a separate entity staffed with microfinance experts, one can build up a profitable portfolio that can be maintained separately or gradually integrated into the bank in five or six years.*

The main advantages of this model were that there was no pressure to go up-market since the service organization's major shareholder, the bank, was already competing in that segment. In addition, the infrastructure of the existing bank could be leveraged to allow relatively low-cost and very fast expansion of lending.

SogeSol in Haiti. Valerie Kindt, director of international operations, had been a resident adviser to Sogebank, the leading national Haitian bank, for more than two years. She helped establish SogeSol, which was a direct subsidiary of the bank and focused on microloans. She explained the challenges she had encountered:

> *Haiti has a population of around 8 million, an ineffective government with no legislation or restrictions on interest rates, and a thriving informal economy.*

The Haitian microfinance industry is well developed and competitive, with the majority of institutions being NGOs and rural cooperatives. To date, five major banks have entered into microfinance. The first, Banque Union Haitienne, incorporated microloans as an additional bank product and did not establish a subsidiary. Unibank, with the help of IPC, a German consulting firm, established a subsidiary called MCN (Micro-Crédit National), which offers slightly larger loans than SogeSol, who was the third player to enter the market. Since then, two additional players have entered what is an increasingly competitive marketplace.

Kindt believed that much of SogeSol's success stemmed from the fact that ACCION focused on technical assistance and training of local management, rather than running the project itself. Pierre Marie Boisson, president of SogeSol, Sogebank's chief economist and a Harvard graduate, was committed to the project from the outset and had secured the funding required to implement the methodology, technology, and systems required. Challenges had included the in-class training time required for loan officers (five weeks compared with an average of two weeks in other countries) and overcoming the perception that it was "dirty work." "Haiti has a strong hierarchical society," Kindt explained, "and one of the challenges has been overcoming Sogebank staff perceptions of SogeSol." She expanded on the resulting problems that this caused for SogeSol:

One of the main problems is that SogeSol customers must come into Sogebank branches to make their loan payments. These customers are often treated very rudely by the bank tellers, who believe that they are their social superiors. They might refuse to take small change as part of a loan payment, for example, resulting in the customer defaulting on his or her loan. Although we provide very fast, efficient service at SogeSol, it is difficult to control behavior at Sogebank. The result is that our customers often feel more comfortable with a really good NGO competitor such as ACME. We are working on ways to resolve this issue.

Boisson spoke of other challenges SogeSol faced. "This is still a young industry," he said, "with significant competition and virtually no regulation. SogeSol is also still a young organization and we need to continue to grow and manage our client base." Boisson was particularly concerned about keeping delinquency rates low and client retention rates high. He expanded on the two issues:

Our current thirty-day delinquency rates are 3.7 percent, which, compared to our competitors, is pretty good. The concern I have, however, is that the judicial system in Haiti is so slow that lawyers used by SogeSol can take up to a year to collect collaterals of delinquent clients. This means that SogeSol may be wrongly presenting an image of tolerance towards bad clients, encouraging other clients to become delinquent, therefore reducing overall portfolio quality. Our client retention is currently around 80 percent, which is a little lower than I would like. However, this is also influenced by the fact that we are unlikely to renew a client who misses payments and we tend to encourage clients to be more conservative.

4. **NGOs.** NGOs made up the fourth group of ACCION partners. In 2002, there were six such partners in the Latin American Network. Castello explained, "Many successful NGOs operate just as efficiently as commercial

organizations, and as long as they don't have financing constraints, they may not need to become commercial entities." This had been ACCION's initial partner model and, in some countries, particularly in Africa, remained a viable option.

In Latin America, ACCION provided all of its partners with technical assistance services and financing, and held minority shareholder positions (between 6 and 24 percent), giving ACCION board representation. ACCION professionals worked with local partner management, as resident advisers, often with profit and loss responsibility, to build lending operations capable of reaching hundreds of thousands of microentrepreneurs. In December 2002, nine of the of eighteen resident advisers in Latin America held temporary line positions within partner organizations. Additional services ranged from business planning to staff training and new product development. By strengthening partners, ACCION hoped to help them become a permanent part of the financial fabric of the countries where they operated. See **Exhibit 3** for an overview of ACCION requirements of its partners. "Because ACCION does not own its partners," Kindt said, "influence is based on bringing solutions. ACCION has to stay relevant and continue to ask the question, what is the best way forward to achieve our mission?"

ACCIONs Lending Model. ACCION's loan methodology was designed to both meet the needs of microentrepreneurs and ensure that their microfinance partners were financially sustainable. ACCION considered microentrepreneurs skilled businesspeople, not objects of charity. Like traditional banks, ACCION partners evaluated potential borrowers using measurements such as business assets, amount and cost of goods sold, cost of raw materials, and household expenses. Unlike traditional banks, loan officers met potential borrowers at their places of business, where they also weighed intangibles such as references from customers and neighbors, and the loan officer's own "gut feeling" about the microentrepreneur's drive to succeed. This character-based lending allowed ACCION to go "beyond the numbers" and develop a more complete picture of a potential borrower than could be obtained from a traditional credit score.

Exhibit 3	ACCION Requirements of Its Partners

1. Private and independent.

2. Specialize in the provision of financial services to the poor households.

3. Understand the markets they serve and commit to improving services to these markets.

4. Have strong board leadership drawn from the private sector.

5. Have the objective of achieving massive reach in their operations.

6. Strive toward financial sustainability or have achieved economic viability.

7. Access the financial markets as their main source of capital.

8. Do not depend on, or provide, subsidized credit.

Source: ACCION International.

Loan officers themselves varied from individuals with university degrees and a sense of social mission to individuals with less formal education. Most worked on an incentive system based on the number of active clients they managed and portfolio quality. "A loan officer's background is less important than his or her personality," Castello said. "They need to be people-people, with sales skills, an ability to work in the field, and adaptable in nature."

Boisson expanded, "Loan officers cannot be traditional bankers. They need to be close to the social groups they serve in order to be accepted by them, but also need to be highly competent. The best loan officers are young, outgoing commercial types for whom this is often their first job."

The focus on financial sustainability had enabled ACCION's partner programs to increase the number of active borrowers from 13,000 in 1988 to nearly 800,000 in 2002. ACCION's experience over thirty years had demonstrated that microlending could both help the poor and be profitable. In Mexico, for example, ACCION's partner, Financiera Compartamos, served 143,000 poor and low-income entrepreneurs by year-end 2002, and turned a substantial profit. Financial viability enabled microlenders to break free from the limitations of donor funds because they could attract private investment and had the potential to access billions of dollars in the international financial markets to help the very people that traditional banking systems had excluded.

ACCION Clients. In 2002, an estimated 3 billion people lived on less than $2 a day, and 40 to 60 percent of people working in the developing world were self-employed. ACCION's borrowers were self-employed women and men who relied on microenterprise as their main source of income. They included the very poor and those who had some assets but remained marginalized from the mainstream economy and society. ACCION's Latin American, Caribbean, and African borrowers were among the region's poorest people at the time of their first loan. They usually had no collateral, might not read or write, and sometimes did not even have enough capital to open for business every day. Sixty-five percent of them were women. (See **Exhibit 4** for details on ACCION's borrowers and loans.) According to the IDB (Inter-American Development Bank), in 2001 there were more than 50 million microenterprises, providing jobs to more than 150 million people, in Latin America alone. Microlending in Latin America had a thirty-year track record, and studies

Exhibit 4	ACCION Borrowers and Loans in 2002			
	ACCION Latin American Network	ACCION African Partners	ACCION USA	Totals
Active clients at year-end	740,321	57,710	3,807	801,838
Total amount disbursed	$785.3 million	$34 million	$18.1 million	$837.4 million
Active portfolio at year-end	$420 million	$18.4 million	$20.4 million	$458.8 million
Average loan	$581	$317	$5,976	

Source: ACCION Web site

from the 1980s clearly demonstrated microlending's positive effect on business income and family welfare.

Services and Products.

ACCION had helped to found, build, and strengthen some of the most successful microlending institutions in the world. More than half the partners in Latin America, including all the regulated institutions, with the exception of BanGente in troubled Venezuela, earned a profit in 2002. ACCION had pioneered many of the best practices and standards in the industry, including individual and solidarity group lending methodologies, the CAMEL diagnostic system to assess and compare microfinance institutions' performances, and guarantees and equity funds for microfinance institutions. About 30 percent of ACCION's operating costs were paid for directly by partners, either from their profits or from funds made available by multilateral or bilateral institutions specifically for technical assistance or product development.

ACCION CAMEL™. This was a diagnostic and management tool that measured the **c**apital adequacy, **a**sset quality, **m**anagement capability, **e**arnings, and **l**iquidity of microfinance institutions. (See **Exhibit 5** for details of the ACCION CAMEL tool.) Designed to help managers assess an organization's financial health and overall performance, and initially developed by the U.S. Federal Reserve to evaluate the solvency of U.S. banks, CAMEL was adapted to the field of microfinance by ACCION in 1993. Since then, ACCION had performed more than forty CAMEL evaluations, and CAMEL had been adopted by government regulators, such as the Bolivian bank superintendency as the evaluation tool for all microfinance institutions in the country. It was also being implemented as a due diligence tool for Banco Centro Americano de Integracion Economica based in Honduras, by the SIDBI Foundation for Microcredit in India, and for training staff members from supervisory entities from eight African countries.

Deborah Drake, vice president of the policy and analysis division, expanded on the importance of the CAMEL tool. "The analysis is similar to that carried out of traditional financial institutions," she said. "The CAMEL reviews the same areas and indicators, but the relative weightings and ranges that we use for microfinance institutions are different. For example, it is much more expensive to manage a microfinance institution, and operating expenses are more likely to amount to 20 percent instead of the less than 5 percent of average loan portfolio recorded by traditional banks." Although the ACCION CAMEL issues a rating, its primary purpose has been to provide a diagnostic tool for ACCION network members. Drake explained further, "It is really a working tool. A CAMEL team, composed of ACCION staff, will go to a partner institution and carry out an in-depth, on-site assessment that can take up to two weeks. The ACCION Camel team provides a presentation of initial findings to the institution's senior management and board of directors, followed by a comprehensive written report. Not only is the process quite time consuming, but it is also fairly expensive, with a full evaluation costing around $25,000 to complete."

Given widespread demand for this type of analysis, other organizations had begun to offer their own evaluations and ratings. "Until last year, we did not offer CAMEL outside our own network," Drake said, "but, as a result, we missed an opportunity to shape the industry by implementing more widely what many consider to be the best tool in the industry, and we let a number of competitor products, some less expensive,

Exhibit 5	Details of ACCION CAMEL, 2002

The CAMEL methodology was originally adopted by North American bank regulators to evaluate the financial and managerial soundness of U.S. commercial lending institutions. The CAMEL reviews and rates five areas of financial and managerial performance: <u>C</u>apital Adequacy, <u>A</u>sset Quality, <u>M</u>anagement, <u>E</u>arnings, and <u>L</u>iquidity Management. As microfinance institutions (MFIs) increasingly reach out to formal financial markets to access capital, there is a need for a similar tool to gather and evaluate data on MFI performance.

Based on the conceptual framework of the original CAMEL, ACCION developed its own instrument. Although the ACCION CAMEL reviews the same five areas, the indicators and ratings used by ACCION reflect the unique challenges and conditions facing the microfinance industry. The ACCION CAMEL analyzes and rates twenty-one key indicators, with each indicator given an individual weighting. Eight quantitative indicators account for 47 percent of the rating, and thirteen qualitative indicators make up the remaining 53 percent. The final CAMEL composite rating is a number on a scale of zero to five, with five as the measure of excellence. This numerical rating, in turn, corresponds to an alphabetical rating (AAA, AA, A; BBB, BB, B; C; D; and not rated).

CAMEL Information and Adjustments

The MFI is required to gather the following information for a CAMEL examination: 1) Financial statements; 2) Budgets and cash flow projections; 3) Portfolio aging schedules; 4) Funding sources; 5) Information about the board of directors, operations/staffing, and macroeconomic information. Financial statements form the basis of the CAMELS' quantitative analysis, and MFIs are required to present audited financial statements from the last three years and interim statements for the most recent twelve-month period. The other required materials provide programmatic information and show the evolution of the institution. These documents demonstrate to CAMEL analysts the level and structure of loan operations and the quality of the MFIs' infrastructure and staffing.

Once the financial statements have been compiled, adjustments need to be made. These serve two purposes: They place the MFIs' current financial performances in the context of a financial intermediary, and they enable comparisons among the different institutions in the industry. The CAMEL performs six adjustments: for the scope of the microfinance activity, loan loss provision, loan write-offs, explicit and implicit subsidies, effects of inflation, and accrued interest income.

CAMEL Scoring

Based on the results of the adjusted financial statements and interviews with the MFIs' management and staffs, a rating of one to five is assigned to each of the CAMEL's twenty-one indicators and weighted accordingly.

<u>Capital Adequacy</u>. The objective of the capital adequacy analysis is to measure the financial solvency of an MFI by determining whether the risks it has incurred are adequately offset with capital and reserves to absorb potential losses. One indicator is *leverage,* which illustrates the relationship between the risk-weighted assets of the MFI and its equity. Another indicator, *ability to raise equity,* is a qualitative assessment of an MFI's ability to respond to a need to replenish or increase equity at any given time. A third indicator, *adequacy of reserves,* is a quantitative measure of the MFI's loan loss reserve and the degree to which the institution can absorb potential loan losses.

<u>Asset Quality</u>. The analysis of asset quality is divided into three components: portfolio quality, portfolio classification system, and fixed assets. Portfolio quality includes two quantitative indicators: *portfolio at risk,* which measures the portfolio past due over thirty days; and *write-offs/write-off policy,* which measures the MFI's adjusted write-offs based on CAMEL criteria. Portfolio classification system entails reviewing the portfolio's aging schedules and assessing the institution's policies associated with assessing portfolio risk. Under fixed assets, one indicator is the *productivity of long-term assets,* which evaluates the MFIs' policies for investing in fixed assets. The other indicator concerns the institution's *infrastructure,* which is evaluated to determine whether it meets the needs of both staff and clients.

<u>Management</u>. Five qualitative indicators make up this area of analysis: governance; human resources; processes, controls, and audit; information technology system; and strategic planning and budgeting. *Governance* focuses on how well the institution's board of directors functions, including the diversity of its technical expertise, its independence from management, and its ability to make decisions flexibly and effectively. The second indicator, *human resources,* evaluates whether the department of human resources provides clear guidance and support to operations staff, including recruitment and training of new personnel, incentive systems for personnel, and performance evaluation systems.

Source: Adapted from Sonia Saltzman and Darcy Salinger "The ACCION CAMEL Technical Note," September 1998.

Exhibit 5	continued

The third indicator, *processes, controls, and audit*, focuses on the degree to which the MFI has formalized key processes and the effectiveness with which it control srisk throughout the organization, as measured by its control environment and the quality of its internal and external audit. The fourth indicator, *information technology system*, assesses whether computerized information systems are operating effectively and efficiently, and are generating reports for management purposes in a timely and accurate manner. This analysis reviews the information technology environment and the extent and quality of the specific information technology controls. The fifth indicator, *strategic planning and budgeting*, looks at whether the institution undertakes a comprehensive and participatory process for generating short- and long-term financial projections and whether the plan is updated as needed and used in the decision-making process.

Earnings. The ACCION CAMEL chooses three quantitative and one qualitative indicator to measure the profitability of MFIs: adjusted return on equity, operational efficiency, adjusted return on assets, and interest rate policy. *Adjusted return on equity (ROE)* measures the ability of the institution to maintain and increase its net worth through earnings from operations. *Operational efficiency* measures the efficiency of the institution and monitors its progress toward achieving a cost structure that is closer to the level achieved by formal financial institutions. *Adjusted return on assets (ROA)* measures how well the MFI's assets are utilized, or the institution's ability to generate earnings with a given asset base. CAMEL analysts also study the MFI's *interest rate policy* to assess the degree to which management analyzes and adjusts the institution's interest rates on microenterprise loans, based on the costs of funds, profitability targets, and macroeconomic environment.

Liquidity Management. This area evaluates the MFI's ability to accommodate decreases in funding sources and increases in assets and to pay expenses at a reasonable cost. Indicators in this area are *liability structure, availability of funds to meet credit demand, cash flow projections,* and *productivity of other assets.* Under liability structure, CAMEL analysts review the composition of the institution's liabilities, including their tenor, interest rate, payment terms, and sensitivity to changes in the macroeconomic environment. The types of guarantees required on credit facilities, sources of credit available to the MFI, and the extent of resource diversification are analyzed as well. This indicator also focuses on the MFI's relationship with banks in terms of leverage achieved based on guarantees, the level of credibility the institution has with regard to the banking sector, and the ease with which the institution can obtain funds when required. *Availability of funds to meet credit demand* measured the degree to which the institution had delivered credit in a timely and agile manner. *Cash flow projections* evaluate the degree to which the institution is successful in projecting its cash flow requirements. The analysis looks at current and past cash flow projections prepared by the MFI to determine whether they have been prepared with sufficient detail and analytical rigor, and whether past projections have accurately predicted cash inflows and outflows. *Productivity of other assets* focuses on the management of current assets other than the loan portfolio, primarily cash and short-term investments. The MFI is rated on the extent to which it maximizes the use of its cash, bank accounts, and short-term investments by investing in a timely fashion and at the highest returns, commensurate with its liquidity needs.

Source: Adapted from Sonia Saltzman and Darcy Salinger "The ACCION CAMEL Technical Note," September 1998.

gain a foothold." Drake was looking at developing versions of the ACCION CAMEL that would focus on specific audiences such as investors. She explained,

> *Our strong point is assessing the strengths and weaknesses of an institution and their impact on financial performance. We don't want to become a rating agency. We are designing a shorter, less expensive CAMEL that will be piloted in 2003, with modules that can be added onto the CAMEL evaluation as needed. For example, there is a specific module when the CAMEL is being used for investor due diligence. We have also developed a CAMEL update product that can be used by institutions that have already been through the full analysis, and there may be other possibilities that we have not yet fully explored.*

Other products included training programs for partner staff and microentrepreneurs, credit scoring, market research and product development tools, and automation technology. See **Exhibit 6** for details of selected products.

Financing for Partners. ACCION's Capital Markets Department helped partners obtain equity financing, debt financing, and other commercial funding. By enabling

| Exhibit 6 | Details of Selected ACCION Products |

ACCION's Dialágo de Gestiones (Client Training Program)   This was a training program designed to help microentrepreneurs to better manage their small businesses. Created by Centro ACCION in Bogota, Colombia, with support from the Mulit-lateral Investment Fund of the IDB, and launched in 1999, Diálogo is based on feedback from microentrepreneurs that revealed that traditional, lecture-based courses were not as effective for learning as participatory workshops. Encompassing interactive role-plays, games, and discussions, Diálogo's forty modules taught business basics: pricing, quality control, marketing, customer service, dealing with competition, in an accessible and practical way. Since its launch, more than 230,000 microentrepreneurs, 62 percent of them women, had participated in the training program, which charged a fee for service established by each Diálogo licensee. The program was licensed to twenty-eight partners in fourteen countries, some of them microfinance affiliates of ACCION, and others entities specially dedicated to training. Licensees all received ACCION training of their own trainers, assistance in marketing the program, promotional materials, and monitoring visits. ACCION had trained 650 trainers for its licensees and additionally had brought them together as a network to conduct impact evaluations of the business training. Based on such feedback, ACCION had developed new training modules and materials. Through 2002, sales of workbooks to licensees yielded more than $100,000 in royalty fees for ACCION.

Credit Scoring for Microenterprise   This credit-scoring model provided partners with an easy-to use tool to rate prospective borrowers and calculate the risk of extending credit to them. The model was developed in partnership with LISIM, a professional credit scoring firm based in Bogota, Colombia. In 2002, the model was in use at BancoSol in Bolivia, Banco Solidario in Ecuador, FINAMERICA in Colombia, and Mibanco in Peru.

Market Research and New Product Development   ACCION had developed a range of tools to help partners attract and retain clients. These tools included qualitative market research, such as focus groups and interviews, and quantitative surveys on specific issues, such as brand image in the marketplace. The results helped partners understand their clients' needs in order to provide them with appropriate products and services. Building on the market research, ACCION helped a partner improve existing products and develop new ones. In 2002, ACCION was developing and testing a number of new products, including home improvement loans, rural lending, remittances from relatives in developed countries, and savings plans.

PortaCredit   PortaCredit was microloan processing software for personal digital assistants (PDAs), developed by ACCION to reduce the time required to make a microloan and to reduce operating costs. Using handheld computers equipped with the software, loan officers could record the necessary data and upload to the microfinance institutions' centralized database, thereby standardizing and streamlining the credit process. Initially implemented in Mexico City in 1999, PortaCredit was now being used in ACCION partner programs in Bolivia, Colombia, Ecuador, and Venezuela.

Source: ACCION International.

partners to link directly with investors and commercial banks, ACCION helped them become independent of donor funds and develop as commercial financial institutions. Equity financing options included the following:

- ACCION's Latin America Bridge Fund was established in 1984 and was the first loan guarantee fund for microfinance institutions. By providing standby letters of credit, the Bridge Fund enabled ACCION's partners to borrow from local banks. Capitalized at more than $7 million in 2002, with loans from socially responsible investors, the fund had provided guarantees averaging $5 million per year and enabled twenty-seven institutions in twelve countries to access local commercial funding.

- The Gateway Fund LLC, ACCION's wholly owned equity fund, made equity, quasi-equity, and debt investments in its affiliate microfinance institutions with a proven track record in Latin America and the Caribbean. The fund was capitalized at $7 million in 2002 and was managed by Gateway ACCION International Manager Inc. (GAIM), a wholly owned, for-profit subsidiary of ACCION international.

- The IDB/MIF Fund, a $2.5 million investment fund, was administered by GAIM for the Multilateral Investment Fund of the Inter-American Development Bank (IDB/MIF). The fund invested in equity, quasi-equity, and debt of microfinance institutions in Latin America and the Caribbean. Investment objectives were to leverage private investment in microfinance institutions while generating long-term gains.

- ProFund, a $21 million equity fund for small and microenterprise lenders in Latin America and the Caribbean, was created in 1994. ACCION was one of four founding members. Over the next eight years, ProFund invested in, or made quasi-equity available to, eleven microfinance institutions in the region. ACCION held a board seat and was a member of its investment committee.

- The AfriCap Microfinance Fund was an investment fund created by ACCION and Calmeadow, a Canadian foundation. The fund was dedicated to financing commercial microfinance institutions in Africa, in which ACCION was a founding investor and held the board chair. AfriCap aimed to underwrite Africa's emerging microfinance sector by investing in selected microlending institutions and financing technical assistance to those institutions. With capital of $13.8 million, the fund made its first investments in 2003.

- ACCION created ACCION Investments in Microfinance SPC in March 2003. A worldwide investment company for microfinance capitalized at $18 million, it was initially funded by nine investors, including both multi- and bilateral governmental entities, private investors from the United States and Europe, and ACCION. The company was managed by ACCION's for-profit arm, GAIM, and had a board made up of its investors. ACCION Investments would allow ACCION to take on the new responsibility of managing funds on behalf of other investors, such as the IFC (International Finance Corporation, a part of the World Bank) and the IDB (Inter-American Development Bank). Otero noted that GAIM's management of ACCION Investments would affect ACCION's investment approach to new microfinance institutions and would have an influence on ACCION's operations. She also believed that ACCION could leverage ACCION Investments to attract new investors and commercial partners. See **Exhibit 7** for *The New York Times* announcement.

Castello summarized ACCION's partnership role as follows:

> *Today we provide our partners with three things: investment and financing; technical assistance, including training, new product development, and technology; and management advice. As the markets in Latin America evolve, ACCION will take on more of an investor (through GAIM) and governance role, with technical assistance providing our point of entry to other areas of the world. I also see ACCION adding value by connecting investors and technology providers, and by matchmaking strategic alliances. Because ACCION aims to establish long-term and intense partnerships, this precludes us from having more than one or two partners in any county, given the issues of competition. So in order to achieve our mission, we have to play a role in leading the industry, establishing and sharing best practices.*

Exhibit 7	*New York Times* Announcement on ACCION Investments, March 2003.

This announcement appears as a matter of record only.

ACCION Investments in Microfinance, SPC

A company investing in microfinance institutions
in Latin America, the Caribbean and Africa
has been formed with a capital of

$18,023,000

was the sponsor

Investors are:
Inter-American Development Bank (IDB)
Kreditanstalt für Wiederaufbau (KfW)
International Finance Corporation (IFC)
ACCION International
Netherlands Development Finance Company (FMO)
Belgian Investment Company for Developing Countries (BIO)
The Finnish Fund for Industrial Cooperation Ltd. (FINNFUND)
Andromeda Fund
Arthur Rock 2000 Trust

Source: ACCION International.

Boisson described how ACCION had helped him establish SogeSol as follows:

> *Microfinance is a very specialized business, and you need the right business model to succeed. When I first presented the idea of getting into microfinance to my board in 1998, the fact that ACCION would provide technical assistance was critical. In practice, ACCION helped in four key areas: client selection, speed of implementation, establishing procedures and systems, and human resource selection and training. In terms of client targeting, for example, we had originally thought about going after existing bank clients who were*

microentrepreneurs and had savings accounts. ACCION suggested doing a market survey of potential clients branch by branch to segment the market and divide each area per credit officer. This enabled us to access a large number of clients quickly and gain the economies of scale that are so critical in this business. ACCION's experience helped us define the roles and responsibilities of the credit officers and implement time management processes that were key to productivity. The only area we are still having trouble with is the information systems, which we have had to adapt, but these were not supplied by ACCION.

Organizational Structure and Funding.

In December 2002, ACCION implemented a new organizational structure in which ACCION International, ACCION USA, and GAIM were managed separately. ACCION International's staff included a team of microfinance and investment specialists in the United States (in Boston and Washington, D.C.); Centro ACCION, a nonprofit Colombian NGO that served as ACCION's technical assistance arm for Latin America; and nineteen resident advisers working with local partners. ACCION's key competitive strength lay in the extensive microfinance experience of its staff.

- twenty technical specialists
- nineteen resident advisers
- four technology/management information system (MIS) specialists
- four CAMEL specialists
- three business-training specialists
- four investment experts.

The new International Operations division had two pillars: Latin America/Caribbean, and Africa, with functional specialists in research and development reporting to the two regional senior vice presidents to improve ACCION's ability to respond to the field. The CAMEL team reported to the Policy and Analysis department, and the Financial Services department oversaw ACCION's direct investments and governance work. (See **Exhibit 8** for ACCION's most recent organizational chart.).

More than 50 percent of ACCION International's revenues in 2001 came from private contributions, including individuals, corporations, and foundations. (See **Exhibit 9** for ACCION International's consolidated statement of revenues and expenses over time.) Roy Jacobowitz, vice president for resource development, expected this trend to continue in the future. "ACCION's income has doubled in size in the last eight years," Jacobowitz explained. "This is largely due to an increased recognition of the power of microfinancing. Over the same period we have reduced the percent of our funding from public sources from 60 percent to 25 percent, and our funding from private sources has risen from 20 percent to 55 percent."

Otero expanded on this increasing role of private sector funding. "Accessing resources to sustain our future growth is a challenge," she said. "Although public funds come in large dollar amounts, an organization can become dependent on a public donor and beholden to it. Private funds are more labor-intensive and expensive to bring in, but ultimately give an organization more freedom to act. Also, if we really want to grow, we need to tap into the private sector more efficiently." **Exhibit 10** shows ACCION's communication and fund-raising budgets over time. Otero believed, however, that ACCION's main funding achievement was that by 2002, ACCION

Exhibit 8	ACCION International Organizational Chart, December 2002

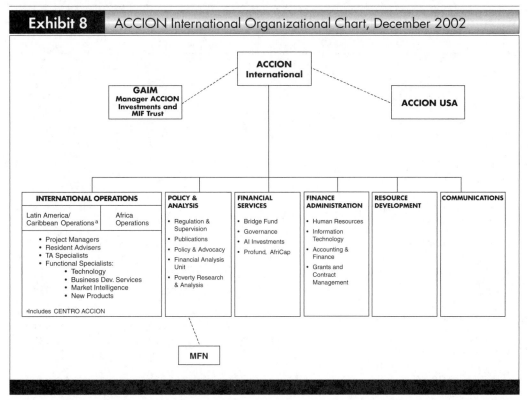

Source: ACCION International.

Note: GAIM (for profit), ACCION USA, and CENTRO ACCION are separate, wholly owned institutions. GAIM is the company
        manager of ACCION Investments, which is not a subsidiary of ACCION International. GAIM also manages the MIF Trust.
        ACCION International is the host organization for MFN (MicroFinance Network), a global network of microfinance
        institutions.

partners had managed to grow their combined lending portfolio to $440 million, nearly all funded from capital markets sources. "Although ACCION's operating budget is only $10 million," she explained, "ACCION's real impact comes from helping our partners access commercial sources of funding and operate independently of subsidies. This is the kind of leverage we want to continue to achieve."

Branding.

Although the ACCION brand was very well known in the worlds of microfinance and international development, it lacked broader public awareness. Robin Ratcliffe, vice president for communications, said, "To date, high recognition and awareness for our brand has been limited to players in microfinance, multilateral, and governmental development agencies. This has been sufficient in the past, but is not so going forward." A focus group of a dozen direct mail donors who contribute to international relief organizations, conducted in the United States in October 1998, revealed the following: No one had heard of ACCION International and no one knew about the concept of microfinancing. However, once the group was shown a short videotape and given a number of handouts, response to ACCION and its mission was overwhelmingly positive. Specifically, the emotional appeal of case studies combined with ACCION's pragmatic approach to alleviating poverty was considered

Exhibit 9	ACCION International Consolidated Statements of Activities		
$000	**1990**	**1995**	**2002**
REVENUES			
Private contributions	1,033	2,463	6,306
United States government grants	1,866	1,828	1,908
International grants	0	1,645	808
Investment and fee income	224	914	949
Contracts and training fees	0	437	2,246
TOTAL	3,123	7,287	12,217
FUNCTIONAL EXPENSES			
Program Services			
Latin America and	1,936	1,448	
Caribbean microenterprise			3,619
Africa microenterprise	N/A	N/A	681
Unites States microenterprise*	61	836	2,281
Capital markets	227	741	1,062
Research, development and	180	266	
policy			1,020
Communications	84	134	597
TOTAL	2,488	3,426	9,260
Supporting Services			
General and administrative	302	767	1,641
Fund-raising	109	443	901
TOTAL	411	1,210	2,542
Total functional expense	2,899	4,636	11,804
Net increase in assets from	223	2,651	413
operations			
Equity in BancoSol net income	N/A	N/A	60
Change in accounting principles	N/A	1,416	N/A
Currency translation loss	0	0	(116)
Loss on Investments in Affiliates			(33)
Total increase in net assets	223	4,067	324
Board-designated for liquidity reserve			250
Net assets, beginning of year	258	1,400	19,456
Net assets at 31 December	481	5,467	19,781

Source: ACCION International Annual Reports.
* ACCION USA line item of $2.5 million includes the lending staff, not just technical assistance, as is the case in LA and Africa.

very powerful. (See **Exhibit 11** for an example of an ACCION print ad.) Some confusion, however, was evident around whether ACCION was more a bank or a charity. Otero commented:

> *We need to be known by our target market, but we probably don't need to become a household name. The interesting thing about ACCION is that although we work in the field, through our partners, with over 800,000 clients, all of whom have wonderful stories to tell, our partners don't carry the ACCION brand name. Consequently, when a media story is run on one of our Latin American or African partners and their clients, the ACCION name hardly ever appears. In the U.S., however, all ACCION programs are branded as ACCION, and we are gaining some brand awareness for our activities in the United States. One question we ask ourselves is whether it is feasible or even desirable to attempt to ask all our partners to carry the ACCION brand name.*

Exhibit 10	ACCION Communication and Fund-raising Budgets			
$'000	2000	2001	2002	2003 (budget)
COMMUNICATIONS				
Salaries	136	203	262	225
Professional services	44	76	104	116
Travel and conferences	15	24	90	25
Office and occupancy	100	108	126	130
Depreciation and amortization	6	7	7	4
Total Functional Expenses	301	418	592	500
FUND-RAISING				
Salaries	314	440	515	454
Professional services	49	185	65	103
Travel and conferences	46	58	23	141
Office and occupancy	176	264	233	235
Awards and grants	2	14	2	N/A
Interest and fees	3	4	3	5
Depreciation and amortization	8	14	12	5
Miscellaneous	1	9	3	0
Total Functional Expenses	599	988	856	973

Source: ACCION International.

ACCION's tagline was "ACCION—More than hope, success" and the brand promise was "Facilitating permanent access to financial services for poor households by building locally run, sustainable microfinance institutions together capable of reaching millions of people." Key brand attributes were derived as part of an internal strategic examination of the ACCION brand that began in 2000. They are summarized in the brand map on **Exhibit 12.** Ratcliffe expanded:

> *Members of ACCION's communications department, along with the pro-bono counsel of a marketing executive from American Express, created a list of key attributes we felt were essential to ACCION. This list was a compilation of thoughts from the management, fund-raising, and communications teams. The list was then honed and combined to form an initial "Brand Map," which aimed to express ACCION's unique value proposition, backed up by these key attributes. In 2002, in conjunction with an analysis of ACCION's competitors in the marketing and PR areas, the Brand Map was fine-tuned to crystallize those attributes that most set ACCION apart from the competition. This resulted in a new, more comprehensive map, with more definitive language.*

Chu believed that branding was particularly important as a means of differentiating ACCION from its competitors. He explained, "We need to build the ACCION brand and position it properly. In order to be true to our mission, we need donors

| Exhibit 11 | Example of ACCION Print Ad, 2002 |

The loan, she'll pay back.
Her dignity, she'll keep.

SHE MAY BE POOR, but she doesn't want charity. She just wants to grow her tiny business and make enough to feed her family. Thanks to ACCION, there's hope. For over 25 years we've provided business loans as small as $100 to hardworking people like her. But we can't do it without your help. Please call (617) 625-7080 or visit www.accion.org today.

More than hope, success.

ACCION International, 56 Roland Street, Suite 300, Boston, MA 02129 USA
617-625-7080 • www.accion.org

Source: ACCION International.

Exhibit 12	ACCION International Brand Map, 2003

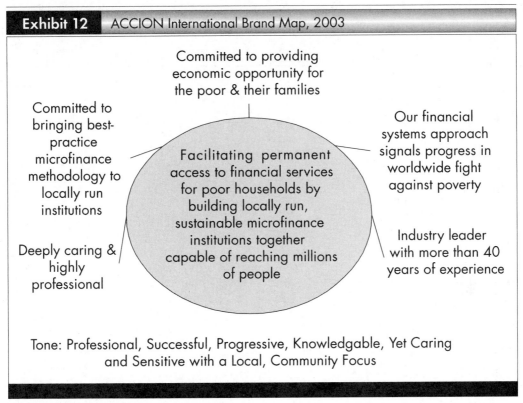

Committed to providing economic opportunity for the poor & their families

Committed to bringing best-practice microfinance methodology to locally run institutions

Our financial systems approach signals progress in worldwide fight against poverty

Facilitating permanent access to financial services for poor households by building locally run, sustainable microfinance institutions together capable of reaching millions of people

Deeply caring & highly professional

Industry leader with more than 40 years of experience

Tone: Professional, Successful, Progressive, Knowledgable, Yet Caring and Sensitive with a Local, Community Focus

Source: ACCION International.

to accept that we do things a bit ahead of when it's rational to do them. That's what makes advances in this field happen."

Otero added:

> We need to communicate clearly and simply our model and achievements. In the private sector, a company's success is determined by its bottom line; measures for success are clear and quantifiable. In the not-for-profit world, there is often a disconnect between flow of funds and results in the field, and as long as you can present what you do in an appealing way, you can raise funds even if you are not particularly effective. That is why branding ACCION and clearly differentiating ACCION from its competitors are so important for us.

Competition.[2]

In 2002, ACCION shared the spotlight with five major competitors in the field of microfinance: Grameen Bank/Grameen Foundation, Opportunity International, FINCA, Freedom from Hunger, and IPC. (See **Exhibit 13** for an overview of ACCION's major competitors.)

Grameen Bank. A nonprofit NGO established in 1976 by Muhammad Yunus, Grameen Bank was the best-known microfinance organization in the world. Their lending model was known as the "village banking method" or "Grameen method" and they focused on the poor women in rural Bangladesh. In 2002, Grameen bank

Exhibit 13	Overview of ACCION and Competitors 2002				
	ACCION International	**Grameen Bank**	**Opportunity International**	**FINCA**	**Freedom from Hunger**
Tagline	More than hope, success	Banking for the poor	Giving the poor a working chance	Small loans, big changes	Health, self-reliance. Dignity
Target	Microentrepreneurs/ poor households	Rural poor	Family	Family (credit as a human right)	Women, building healthy lives
Number of countries	21	1	27	20	16
Geographical focus	Latin America, Caribbean, and Africa	Bangladesh	Africa, Asia, Eastern Europe, and Latin America	Latin America, Africa, former Soviet Union	Latin America and Africa
Number of active clients at year end 2002	798,031	2.4 million	397,489	189,587	240,000
Total number of clients served over last 10 years	2.7 million	N/A	800,000	N/A	N/A
% Women clients	60%	95%	86%	N/A	100%
Loans outstanding year-end 2002	$440 million	$263 million	$64 million	$40 million	$18 million (estimated)
Total lent in 2002	$820 million	$292 million	$127 million	$98 million	N/A
Average loan	$575	$110	$237	$518	$75
Payback rate	97.5%	98%	98%	97%	N/A

Source: ACCION International, Web sites and interviews.

employed 11,770 staff and worked in more than 41,000 villages, providing US$292 million in loans. The average loan size was just under $110, 95 percent of the bank's customers were women, and loan recovery rates stood at 98 percent. Grameen Bank claimed to outperform all other banks in Bangladesh and most banks around the world. In November 2001, a negative Wall Street Journal article said that "Grameen's performance in recent years hasn't lived up to the bank's own hype." Specifically, the article said that repayment rates were misrepresented by Grameen and were in fact considerably lower than the organization said because of the rescheduling of bad loans.

In the early 1990s, Grameen partnered with Results Educational Fund, a U.S.-based lobbying organization with close to 40,000 volunteers who sought to create the political will to end hunger and used Grameen as a model, thereby putting Grameen on the map. Building on its strong brand name, in 1999 Grameen created the Grameen Foundation USA, based in Washington, D.C. It served as Grameen's fund-raising arm in the United States with the objective of replicating the Grameen model in other countries.

Otero believed that Grameen's model was dated and had not evolved over time. She explained:

> Grameen demonstrated that it's possible to reach the poor with credit in massive numbers. This was very important. But Grameen did not build sustainability into its model, depending on decades for subsidies, and yet it does a very good job of marketing itself. In the U.S., Grameen Foundation is serious competition when it comes to fund-raising. They have offices in Washington, D.C., Dallas, and Seattle, and whomever we call on they have already been there. They have a different business model from ours and their fund-raising strength is based in large part on the charisma of Dr. Yunus. I just met with people from the UNDP, and the first organization they think of when you say microfinance is Grameen.

Opportunity International. A nonprofit humanitarian organization, founded in 1971 by Al Whittaker, president of Bristol-Myers International Corporation, Opportunity International aimed to help poor families transform their lives, emotionally, spiritually, and materially, with loans and basic business training. Opportunity International's commitment was religious in nature and "motivated by Jesus Christ's call to serve the poor." Forty-two autonomous but affiliated partners delivered the loan program in twenty-seven countries in Africa, Asia, Eastern Europe, and Latin America. In 2002, Opportunity International served 397,489 clients (86 percent of them women) and lent $127 million, with a 98 percent repayment rate.

FINCA. FINCA (Foundation for International Community Assistance) was a nonprofit NGO established in 1984 by American economist John Hatch, and saw its role as creating employment, raising family incomes, and reducing poverty worldwide. The emphasis was on building hope for the future and promoting financial independence. FINCA used models and terminology similar to those used by Grameen and also emphasized access to credit as a "human right." FINCA's vision was to tap into community spirit, enabling one family to help another family escape poverty. In 2002, FINCA served 189,587 clients and had outstanding loans of $40 million, administered through twenty partner programs in Latin America, Africa, and the former Soviet Union, and arrears estimated at 3 percent.

Both FINCA and Opportunity International said in 2002 that they were focused on commercialization, transforming NGOs (nongovernmental organizations) and village banks into regulated institutions, and that they were following the "financial systems" approach of ACCION. Both presented models like ACCION's but claimed to reach even poorer segments of the population. "Both organizations are following the transformation model, which we started over ten years ago," Otero commented. "They are beginning to experience the demands of converting. In a way, by following the path we have opened, they are validating what we have done at ACCION and underscoring our model. As colleagues, we interact in a variety of settings. But from a business model perspective, we have very little to learn from these competitors, and this may make us seem a little arrogant."

Freedom from Hunger. Freedom from Hunger was a nonprofit NGO established in 1946 as Meals for Millions, which provided Multi-Purpose Food, a high-protein powdered food supplement. The organization shifted its focus in 1970 to the implementation of applied nutrition programs, focusing almost exclusively on the health and nutrition of mothers and children. In 1988, Freedom from Hunger developed an integrated microcredit/health and nutrition education program. By 2002, Freedom from Hunger was an international development organization, focused on supporting women with innovative and self-sustaining solutions to poverty and chronic hunger. FFH stressed the importance of empowering the poor through nutrition information. In 2002, according to its Web site, the organization worked in sixteen countries through twenty local partners serving 240,000 families. The average loan size was $75, and outstanding loans were estimated at more than $18 million.

IPC. (Internationale Projekt Consult GmbH) was a for-profit German consulting company founded in 1981 to improve the opportunities for micro- and small enterprises to access formal financial services, and bank loans in particular. IPC's objective was to reduce the degree to which micro- and small enterprises were dependent on informal providers of credit. IPC's services covered three areas:

1. *Consulting services*: IPC helped central banks, banking supervision bodies, private commercial banks, and development banks in areas such as organizational development; product development; the regulation of financial institutions (especially microfinance institutions); and the definition of coherent policies in the field of micro-, small- and medium-enterprise development.

2. *Project management*: IPC had a track record of long-term collaborations with commercial banks in microlending projects, including those in Russia, Ukraine, Kazakhstan, Armenia, and Paraguay.

3. *Bank management services*: By 2002, IPC had management services agreements with fifteen target microfinance-oriented institutions in Eastern and southeastern Europe, South America, Africa, and Asia. Under these agreements, IPC staff occupied key positions at the financial institutions (general manager, credit manager, and finance manager). IPC often took an investment stake in those institutions with which it had management services agreements. IPC was respected for its technical excellence and had received substantial funds from multilateral and bilateral donors. "They are our main competitor in the field," said Elisabeth Rhyne, a leading microfinance expert and Harvard PhD. "They take a similar approach to ACCION, in terms of technical assistance and governance, and in many countries our partners are in direct competition with theirs." Otero added, "IPC is more hands-on and directive; they own and manage most of their partner institutions. We do, however, share a commitment to commercial microfinance and its integration into the financial system, and we can learn from IPC's innovative and coherent strategy."

FUTURE CHALLENGES AND OPPORTUNITIES.

Changing Client Base and Industry Dynamics.

Several microfinance markets in Latin America were becoming increasingly competitive. In a few countries, particularly Bolivia and Nicaragua, market penetration was approaching saturation. With increased competition, attracting and retaining clients was becoming more important. However, in some countries, client over-borrowing and increased delinquency were causing concern. Growth expectations were lowered as markets reached saturation, and the prospect of mergers and consolidation in the microfinance industry was on the horizon. This resulted in pressure, particularly in Bolivia, to move up-market, providing larger loans to established or new clients, or to impose restrictions on access to the remaining poorest clients. The latter approach could risk compromising ACCION's mission. "It's difficult to measure market saturation," Castello explained, "but there are two main indicators in microfinance that saturation is starting to occur. First, you see a deterioration of portfolio quality over time and among multiple institutions. For example, in Bolivia, arrears have risen to a range of 7 percent to 9 percent, as opposed to just 2 percent a few years ago. Second, as competition increases, interest rates drop. In this way, market saturation actually empowers the small entrepreneur." Recent analysis of BancoSol clients, however, showed that the majority of first-time loans continued to be less than $500.

In Haiti, Boisson was interested in expanding SogeSol's customer base to include what he called small loans rather than microloans, the former being loans between $300 and $3,000 and the latter being loans from $500 to $5,000. He explained his rationale, "We have found that small loans perform even better than microloans, and we would like to go beyond ACCION's traditional focus on microloans to include these types of clients."

Within the microfinance industry there was also a growing division between those institutions that used a commercial approach, including ACCION's partners, and those that did not, the latter characterizing themselves as more poverty focused. The trend toward microfinance services being delivered via licensed, regulated financial institutions continued in Latin America and was beginning in Africa. Commercially oriented microfinance institutions increasingly needed equity capital to grow, consolidate, and launch new operations. In 2002, equity capital was available primarily from specialized equity funds as well as from multilateral and bilateral agencies and socially responsible financial institutions. Equity in microfinance was receiving a lot more attention, and additional sources of equity could include regional investors, foundations, universities, pension funds, individual socially responsible investors, and potentially, international and local commercial investors. In 2003, ACCION sponsored the creation of the Council of Microfinance Equity Funds, which brought together twelve private equity funds to examine equity investment issues and provide guidance in this area.

Regulators.

As the number of licensed microfinance institutions grew, government agencies such as banking superintendencies became more involved in assessing and regulating the industry, although they lacked knowledge and experience of the sector. In 2002, regulations for microfinance were being revised and devised in countries throughout Latin America and Africa, sometimes to the industry's benefit, sometimes not. "ACCION can help by educating regulators on the differences between traditional banking and microfinance lending," Otero said. "The interest and knowledge level of central bankers varies widely from country to country."

Otero noted that regulatory bodies for financial institutions protected the public and kept the financial systems of their countries solvent. She continued, "The existing global banking standards are not applicable to microfinance, and regulators must develop norms and regulations that ensure proper supervision of microfinance institutions. This is difficult to achieve because in many countries microfinance is not a priority since it represents such a small proportion of the financial system. However, if the necessary frameworks are not in place, it will hinder the development of the microfinance industry." ACCION had established an internal policy department to work with regulatory bodies. Otero wondered whether ACCION should be devoting more resources to this area.

Drake believed that the ACCION CAMEL tool could be adapted to help regulators. "We can either impact regulatory bodies at the legislative level, but that's really more a role for the World Bank," she explained, "or we can work with central banks and train key individuals using an instrument that has been tried and tested for over ten years."

Geographic or Product Expansion?

Otero had championed the recent expansion into Africa. She viewed the move as essential for ACCION to maintain its leadership. "Microfinance is an industry," she asserted, "whose leaders must be global in their perspective. If you are not global, you cannot be a leader, and we want ACCION to continue to be a leader."

Africa. During the 1990s, microfinance was growing not only in Latin America but in Africa, Eastern Europe, and Asia. Funding was increasingly available for microfinance in these regions, and ACCION's main competitors, with the exception of Grameen, were international in scope. "Our mission is to reach as many people as possible," explained Otero, "and we felt that, at ACCION, we had learned a lot that we could contribute to other areas of the world. In addition, it could be a competitive weakness to focus on just one geographical area."

In May 2000, Otero drafted a proposal to the board for initiating work outside the Americas and suggesting an initiative in Africa. She believed that ACCION should focus on a single region beyond Latin America and that a focus on Africa might be preferable to Asia or Eastern Europe: First, ACCION's learning curve would be faster in Africa because subregions would vary less in context and culture; second, ACCION's technical assistance capabilities would add greater value to institutions addressing issues of institution building; and third, donor funding, especially from international aid organizations, was readily available for initiatives in Africa and would not take away from ACCION's donor support for Latin America. "Africa was the natural next step," Otero explained. "In Asia there were already several well-established microfinance organizations. In Africa there was great need, the opportunity for high potential impact, and a funding base different from that for our work in Latin America."

Otero proposed building on the work of a Canadian foundation called Calmeadow (whose founder had been on ACCION's board) that had initiated microfinancing in several African countries in 1996. Working with a South African for-profit consulting firm called Vulindlela, in a joint-venture agreement, Calmeadow had secured four projects to provide technical assistance to microfinance institutions in Benin, Zimbabwe, and South Africa. In 2000, the majority of Calmeadow funding came the Canadian International Development Agency and the organization had been looking to spin off its Africa program to concentrate its efforts on developing an equity fund for microfinance for Africa.

Otero proposed a phased approach to ACCION assuming responsibility for Calmeadow's Africa program, and recruited Elisabeth Rhyne to both head up the Africa initiative and direct ACCION's Research and Development department. Although the Calmeadow strategy enabled ACCION to expand its geographical reach quickly and with relatively low risk and cost, Otero recognized the challenges and suggested a two-year learning period for ACCION. Some of the challenges when comparing Latin America and Africa included much lower per capita incomes, higher proportion of rural populations, less developed financial sectors, high HIV infection rates, and political instability. In addition to these market differences, many of ACCION's microfinance experts spoke only Spanish and ACCION's manuals and documentation were mainly in Spanish as well.

ACCION found that Africa differed from Latin America in a number of ways. For example, microentrepreneurs in Africa had lower incomes than their counterparts in Latin America, resulting in the need for smaller loans. In addition, since the financial systems in many African countries were less developed, ACCION believed that it had a key role to play in influencing government policies and regulations. (See **Exhibit 14** for targets for ACCION partners in Africa.)

A key challenge for ACCION moving forward was the choice of partners in Africa. "ACCION does not yet have the history or depth of knowledge in Africa that it does in Latin America," Rhyne explained. "We have a choice between partnering with existing organizations or starting new organizations. Most competitors in Africa have used the village-banking model so ACCION's greater focus on individual loans can be a competitive advantage, especially in urban areas."

The Uganda Experience. Victoria White, senior director of international operations, had been living and working in Uganda since early 2002. In December 2002, she was deeply involved in providing technical assistance to an ACCION partner, Uganda Microfinance Union (UMU), an NGO, which was transforming into a regulated financial institution and hoped to become licensed under the new legislation covering microfinance institutions in May 2003. She expanded on the environment in Uganda and the challenges facing UMU:

> Uganda, with a population of 25 million, is still largely rural. The lengthy civil war destroyed many aspects of civil society, including the financial sector, which has a history of bank failures. Currently, about fifteen major banks, including a number of international banks such as Citibank and Barclays, are present in Uganda, but they target the upper income segments of the population and corporate clients. Microfinance has been very vibrant in Uganda, appearing in the early 1990s and currently reaching 500,000 borrowers. The most popular model has been a modified village-banking model, based on lending groups providing guarantees for individual loans. In December 2002, legislation was passed establishing a legal structure for microfinance institutions. Currently, there are a dozen strong players providing financial services (including both UMU and FINCA), but, under the new legislation only three to five organizations will become licensed, regulated microfinance institutions.

Exhibit 14	Targets for ACCION Partners in Africa 2002 to 2005				
	2001	2002 projection	2003 projection	2004 projection	2005 projection
Active Clients	35,000	57,000	85,000	112,000	137,000
Active Portfolio	$11 million	$19 million	$29 million	$40 million	$52 million

Source: ACCION Strategic Plan.

In December 2002, UMU served more than 32,000 clients, of which 16,000 were borrowers, and was in the process of becoming a for-profit financial institution with an initial capital base of between $3 million and $4 million. "We are looking for five or six initial investors," White explained, "and enough capital to support our aggressive growth plans. For this we will be relying on help from ACCION's financial services group." Much of the transformation work involved the implementation of MIS and management systems, as well as training of staff in financial and treasury management skills. "To date, we have fully automated two branches," White said. "It has gone very smoothly and productivity levels have increased significantly.

"Now that there is legislation, ACCION can play a key role in training bank supervisors, using a modified CAMEL tool. In Africa we are still working with NGOs who need more basic financial management skills. In addition, most of the organizations we are dealing with in Africa have been up and running for a while and our approach needs to be more collaborative."

New Products. In several countries—Bolivia, Chile, Paraguay, Ecuador, El Salvador, Nicaragua, and Guatemala—urban microfinance markets were becoming increasingly competitive. To stimulate growth, ACCION was considering helping partners expand their range of products to include home improvement finance, rural lending, savings, and remittances.

However, ACCION's area of competence was on business credit. ACCION had little expertise in areas such as remittances. In addition, some ACCION executives wondered if this shift to other products would compromise ACCION's mission of providing access to credit for the poor. Several of ACCION's partners were moving toward becoming full-service banks, developing additional products and services without ACCION assistance or approval. Chu expanded on the dilemma:

> It's good business to hold on to one's existing customers and provide them with products and services they want. We cannot forget that new credit customers represent a feeder into the system, and that our mission is to reach the greatest number of poor people and provide them with access to whatever financial tools help them out of poverty. I believe that we need to constantly redefine the best way to serve the poor, and extend our notion beyond microloans to other services that can be profitable, for example by providing health insurance. But not all ACCION professionals necessarily agree.

Boisson expanded on ACCION's future role: "ACCION can continue to help SogeSol and other partners by providing new products and access to new clients, helping us grow and improve our technical management, and improving management information systems dedicated to microfinance. ACCION has tremendous strength in its network, and can leverage this to help partners."

ACCION's three-year strategic plan addressed some of the challenges and opportunities outlined above, and reiterated the organization's commitment to achieving its social mission through the commercialization of microfinance via the three current models and the strengthening of its investment activities. (See **Exhibit 15** for a summary of the main points of the strategic plan and **Exhibit 16** for the associated financial forecast.) As part of this strategic plan, ACCION defined four new products in which it would concentrate its efforts: rural lending, home improvement financing, remittances, and savings products.

Exhibit 15	Summary of ACCION Strategic Plan 2002–2005

ACCION's medium-term strategic plan said the organization would continue to serve as clients the poor and people previously excluded from the financial system, with a focus on the microentrepreneur and his or her family, and with an emphasis on extending the boundaries of the financial system to include those excluded from it.

Although ACCION has established the goal of reaching 1 million borrowers by 2005, it would in fact, exceed this goal by the end of 2003. ACCION was dedicated to the integration of microfinance into the mainstream financial system and the commercialization of microfinance services. Support for microfinance institutions would continue via long-term partnerships and would include technical assistance, investment, and governance.

With the exception of CAMEL, products would not be made available on a one-off basis. ACCION would remain a mission-driven NGO, operating in a businesslike manner on commercial principles, and the organization would continue to grow in a way that combined the agility of a small organization with the productivity and resources of a larger one.

Channels   ACCION would continue for the period of the strategic plan to balance its efforts across the three main approaches to microfinance commercialization: transformation of NGOs into financial institutions, establishment of specialized financial institutions, and launching of microfinancial services by existing commercial banks.

Products   The plan called for ACCION to continue providing microfinance institutions with both technical assistance, on the one hand, and debt and equity instruments on the other. In line with this was the additional goal of contributing to the development of the microfinance industry through policy advocacy and research and the use of the CAMEL assessment tool.

Source: ACCION Strategic Plan.

Barriers to Growth.

Chu believed that the main barrier to ACCION's growth and expansion involved the ability of its affiliates to demonstrate sustained, reliable profitability over the long term. He explained further:

> BancoSol's profitability, for example, has been erratic. Its success spawned an industry, drawing in competitors, and resulting in client over-indebtedness and lower repayment rates. In addition, the economic turmoil in Latin America requires nimble management that can navigate the ups and downs to achieve consistent returns. I believe that ACCION's strengths today lie in technical assistance, but we need to ensure that the knowledge we transfer is up-to-date as the reality we operate in changes. We need to become better at helping our partners develop business strategies and we also need staff members who can manage the capital markets side of our business. In addition, we need to leverage our minority positions in the governance of our partner institutions.

CONCLUSION.

Keeping in mind ACCION's overall objective to dramatically increase the number of borrowers and reduce world poverty, Otero prepared for a strategic retreat with her key managers and identified three issues that she especially wanted her team to address:

1. Was ACCION poised for a shift in both its activities and priorities? If so, what were the key changes Otero and her staff would have implement to take the organization into the next phase of its development?

2. Should ACCION remain focused on business credit and continue to expand geographically, or should it broaden its technical assistance to

Exhibit 16	ACCION International Financial Plan Summary 2002–2005		
$'000	2003 projected	2004 projected	2005 projected
REVENUE			
Private grants and donations	6,294	9,122	9,902
Public grants	3,087	3,050	2,600
Interest and fees	1,038	1,047	1,107
Contracts, fees, public, and other	2,721	3,228	3,993
Total	13,140	16,447	17,602
EXPENSES			
Program services			
USA (includes network support)	3,325	4,156	4,511
Latin America operations	2,225	2,493	2,771
Africa operations	1,230	1,591	1,822
Technical teams	1,205	1,419	1,490
Financial services	823	1,671	1,813
Policy and financial Assessment	747	618	648
GAIM	501	N/A	N/A
Communications	500	514	566
TOTAL	10,555	12,462	13,621
Supporting Services			
USA supporting services		622	639
Resource development	972	1,026	1,077
General and administrative	1,150	1,425	1,496
TOTAL	2,122	3,073	3,212
Total	12,880	15,535	16,833
Revenue less operating expenses	463	912	769
Additions to liquidity reserve	250	336	365
Investments	154	550	400
NET REVENUE	10	26	4

Source: ACCION Strategic Plan.

Note: Does not include ACCION USA.

cover a wider variety of banking services, responding to the needs of its existing partners in Latin America? Could the organization do both and were these parallel ways of evolving compatible?

3. How should ACCION promote its brand, particularly in light of the growing proportion of funds coming from private donors? In the current challenging fund-raising environment, which strategy would maximize private donations?

Notes to Case

[1] As of May 2003 Benin, Bolivia, Brazil, Colombia, Ecuador, El Salvador, Guatemala, Haiti, Honduras, Mexico, Mozambique, Nicaragua, Panama, Paraguay, Peru, Tanzania, Trinidad and Tobago, Uganda, the United States, Venezuela, and Zimbabwe.

[2] This section based largely on Web site information for each organization in December 2002.

CASE 6
International Federation of Red Cross and Red Crescent Societies

My primary role is to fully implement Strategy 2010.[1] I need to take the International Federation from being an actor in the disaster-response arena, where we are somewhat in competition with our National Societies, to being a facilitator, playing a coordination role, supporting and building capacity at the National Society level. As we build up our National Societies' capabilities, we will increase our visibility and image and strengthen our brand, enabling us to carry out our mission of improving the lives of vulnerable people and achieving our longer-term goal of becoming the world's most respected and reliable civil society partner.

—Didier Cherpitel, Secretary General and CEO, International Federation of Red Cross and Red Crescent Societies

Cherpitel joined the International Federation in 2000, having previously spent thirty years with JP Morgan. "My appointment to this post was a big surprise for many people, both inside and outside of the organization," he said. For many, Cherpitel symbolized the increasingly strategic and businesslike focus of the International Federation Secretariat. Central to the implementation of Strategy 2010, the International Federation had started to deploy a best-practices tool known as the National Society Self-Assessment. Although it was only in its initial phase in 2002, Cherpitel wondered how best to make the self-assessment process achieve what it was intended to: self-analysis to help make National Societies become more effective, accountable, and better managed. He also reflected on the additional steps that the organization might take to resolve outstanding challenges and strengthen its brand.

THE INTERNATIONAL FEDERATION.

In 2002, the International Federation of Red Cross and Red Crescent Societies (the International Federation) was the world's largest humanitarian organization. It operated through a network of National Societies, with the help of nearly 100 million volunteers and members worldwide, assisting close to 233 million people a year, with

Professor John Quelch and Research Associate Nathalie Laidler prepared this case. HBS cases are developed solely as the basis for class discussion. Cases are not intended to serve as endorsements, sources of primary data, or illustrations of effective or ineffective management.

an annual domestic and international expenditure of more than 24 billion Swiss francs (CHF).[2]

Founded in 1919, the International Federation comprised 178 member Red Cross and Red Crescent Societies, a secretariat in Geneva, fourteen regional offices, sixty-three country delegations, six sub-delegations, and two regional logistics centers. The International Federation was a volunteer-driven organization that aimed to assist the world's most vulnerable people. Core activities included the promotion of humanitarian values, providing health care in communities, building and strengthening systems to prepare for disasters, and responding when disasters occurred.

History.

The Red Cross was originally the idea of a young Swiss man, Henry Dunant, who in 1859 came upon the bloody scene of a battle in Solferino, Italy, between the armies of imperial Austria and the Franco-Sardinian alliance. Some 40,000 men lay dead or dying, and Dunant organized the local people to attend to the soldiers' wounds and feed and comfort them. He later called for the creation of national relief societies to assist those wounded in war and paved the way for the future Geneva Conventions.

In 1863, five men from Geneva, including Dunant, set up the International Committee for Relief to the Wounded, later to become the International Committee of the Red Cross. The organization's emblem was a red cross on a white background, the inverse of the Swiss flag. The following year, twelve governments adopted the first Geneva Convention, offering care for the wounded and defining medical services as "neutral" on the battlefield.

World War I, however, demonstrated that cooperation between the already existing Red Cross Societies was necessary. In 1919, Henry Davison, president of the American Red Cross War Committee, proposed the formation of an International Federation, initially named the League of Red Cross Societies, that joined the five founding member societies of Britain, France, Italy, Japan, and the United States. The organization was first renamed in 1983 as the League of Red Cross and Red Crescent Societies, and in 1991 became the International Federation of Red Cross and Red Crescent Societies. "The International Federation was created around the same time as the United Nations," Cherpitel explained, "and we were structured in a similar way." The first objective of the International Federation was to improve the health of people in countries that had been most affected by World War I, and the initial stated goal was to "strengthen and unite already existing Red Cross Societies and promote the creation of new Societies." "Our role has expanded," Cherpitel added, "to improving the lives of vulnerable people everywhere by mobilizing the power of humanity in the four core areas of disaster response, disaster preparedness, health and care in the community, and humanitarian principles and values."

Emblem.

In 2002, the International Federation used as its logo two globally recognized emblems: the red cross and the red crescent, set on a white background within a red rectangle. (See **Exhibit 1** for the International Federation's logo.) The International Federation's member National Societies used one or the other of these emblems, either the cross or the crescent. The red cross was formally adopted by the first Geneva Convention of 1864, and the red crescent, initially used by the Ottoman Empire in 1876, was adopted by the 1929 Geneva Convention.

Exhibit 1	International Federation Logo in 2002

 International Federation of Red Cross and Red Crescent Societies

Source: IFRC.

For National Societies, the emblem served two purposes: It acted as their logo of identification; and it protected their organizations, their personnel, and their country's medical services in times of conflict. Rules on the use of the emblems were defined by international law. Under the Geneva Convention of 1949, states and their National Societies could use only one of the two emblems for the protection of the medical services of their armed forces. The red cross or red crescent logos belonged to the nation-states themselves, not to the National Societies.

Organizational Structure.

The International Federation, together with the National Societies and the International Committee of the Red Cross (ICRC), made up the International Red Cross and Red Crescent Movement. The three components of the movement were independent; each had its own status and exercised no authority over the other two.

The International Committee of the Red Cross (ICRC). The ICRC was an impartial, neutral, and independent organization whose exclusively humanitarian mission was to protect the lives and dignity of victims of war and internal violence and to assist them. It directed and coordinated the international relief activities conducted by the movement in situations of conflict and promoted humanitarian law and universal humanitarian principles. Established in 1863, the ICRC was at the origin of the International Red Cross and Red Crescent Movement.

The network of 178 National Societies. The National Societies covered nearly every country in the world. National Societies acted as auxiliaries to the public authorities of their own countries in the humanitarian field. During wartime, National Societies assisted the affected civilian populations and supported military medical personnel where appropriate. Cooperation among National Societies enabled the International Federation to develop its capabilities, assist those most in need, and reach out to individual communities. National Society programs met both immediate and long-term needs and covered a range of services such as disaster relief and health and social activities. The promotion of humanitarian values was an intrinsic part of all Red Cross and Red Crescent activities. National Societies conducted campaigns on behalf of vulnerable people in their own countries and promoted awareness of international humanitarian laws.

National Societies were auxiliaries to their governments. The decrees or partnerships with the governments could be loose or strict, depending on the country, but the Red Cross Red Crescent emblem, the logo, image, and brand, belonged to each nation-state. Cherpitel explained, "National Societies and the International Federation have a role to play that is supplementary and complementary to that of public authorities and NGOs [nongovernmental organizations] and cannot strictly be compared to that of relief or development NGOs."

The International Federation. The secretariat, in Geneva, coordinated and mobilized relief assistance for international emergencies, promoted cooperation among the National Societies, and represented them in the international arena. Within the secretariat, six divisions supported the International Federation's objectives: cooperation and development, disaster management and coordination, external relations, support services, monitoring and evaluation, and governance and planning. In addition, the International Federation had fourteen regional offices, sixty-three country delegations, six sub-delegations, and two regional logistics centers that supported the National Societies worldwide.

Role and Mission.

The International Federation's stated mission was to "improve the lives of vulnerable people by mobilizing the power of humanity." Vulnerable people were defined as those who are at the greatest risk from situations that threaten their survival or their capacity to live with an acceptable level of social and economic security and human dignity. Often, they were victims of natural disasters or poverty brought about by socioeconomic crises, refugees, or victims of health emergencies. The International Federation's employees and volunteers shared seven fundamental principles, developed in 1965, that outlined the impartial, neutral approach of the organization and its voluntary and humanitarian principles. (See **Exhibit 2** for the seven fundamental principles.)

Cherpitel expanded on the nature of the organization and its ability to fulfill its role and mission:

> We are a volunteer organization, operating at the grass-roots level with more than 100 million volunteers, local people, working to help their fellow citizens. That is our key strength and advantage. Volunteers have a particular dedication and commitment, and the sheer number of our volunteers enables us to truly mobilize the "power of humanity" at the local-communities level worldwide. This makes the International Federation truly unique and exceptional. No one will ever be able to replicate or match this.

Exhibit 2	The Seven Fundamental Principles of the International Federation of the Red Cross and Red Crescent Societies, Established in 1965

1. Humanity: Protect life and health and ensure respect for human beings.

2. Impartiality: No discrimination as to nationality, race, religious beliefs, class or political opinion.

3. Neutrality: Does not take sides in hostilities or engage in controversies of a political, racial, religious or ideological nature.

4. Independence: National Societies are auxiliaries in the humanitarian services of their governments but must maintain autonomy to be able to act in accordance with the principles of the Movement.

5. Voluntary service: Is a voluntary relief movement.

6. Unity: There can only be one Red Cross or Red Crescent Society in any one country.

7. Universality: The International Red Cross and Red Crescent Movement is worldwide.

Source: IFRC.

Core Activities.

In 2002, the secretariat of the International Federation and each individual National Society focused on four core areas: promoting humanitarian values, disaster response, disaster preparedness, and health and community care. Disaster response accounted for nearly 50 percent of the International Federation secretariat's operations and special programs and continued to be the organization's main activity. (See **Exhibit 3** for a breakdown of contributions to operations and special programs over time.) Guiding and supporting the development of member National Societies was increasingly becoming the International Federation secretariat's core role. Capacity-building programs included management and volunteer training; strengthening branch structures; helping with planning, fund-raising, and gender equality; and creating the opportunity for National Societies to network with each other.

Promoting humanitarian values. The aim of the International Federation was to influence the behavior of people within member Red Cross and Red Crescent Societies, in public and private positions of authority, and among members of the communities where the organization worked through a better understanding of seven fundamental principles: humanity, impartiality, neutrality, independence, voluntary service, unity, and universality.

In May 1999, "The Power of Humanity" was chosen as the Red Cross Red Crescent slogan for activities worldwide. (See **Exhibit 4** for a visual example.) From May 1999

Exhibit 3	Voluntary Cash Contributions to Operations and Special Programs, 1998–2002				
CHF Millions Category	1998	1999	2000	2001	2002 (estimated as of 9/02)
Disaster response	135	229	185	130	86
Disaster preparedness	8	8	17	21	14
Health and care	25	32	45	45	38
Humanitarian values	0.6	0.9	1	2	2
Organizational development	17	19	24	32	18
Coordination & management	22	33	26	19	15
Regional cooperation	0.9	4	1	1	1
Other Programs	0.1	0.5	0	0	0
TOTAL	208.6	326.4	299	250	174

Source: Internal audits.

US$1 = CHF 1.45.

Exhibit 4 | Reproduction of the "Power of Humanity" Logo, 2001

Source: IFRC.

---

to May 2000, hundreds of events, seminars, competitions, publications, and programs were carried out and promoted by National Societies under this banner. The slogan aimed to capture the organization's capacity to bring out the best in people and their willingness to work together. It also sought to position the organization as a channel for people who wished to make a commitment to human rights and as a partner, cooperating with people and organizations to achieve common solutions.

Disaster response. The International Federation's response system was based on the right of the National Societies to request support in a crisis. The secretariat's role was that of coordinator. It launched international appeals to raise funds and mobilized personnel and relief goods. Through its regional and country field offices, the International Federation provided managerial, technical, and administrative support.

Between 1990 and 1999, almost 2 billion people were affected by disasters, and more than 90 percent of total disaster-related deaths occurred in developing countries. In 2001, the International Federation disaster-response programs reached 34.6 million beneficiaries throughout the world. The organization had developed a number of approaches and teams to respond rapidly to disasters:

- Field assessment and coordination teams (FACTs) consisted of a core group of 200 experienced disaster managers within the International Federation secretariat and different National Societies who stood ready to participate, at twelve to twenty-four hours' notice, in a FACT team for two to four weeks. In the event of an emergency, the disaster management and coordination division at the secretariat composed a team that was immediately deployed to the disaster area. The FACT team assessed the situation, developed a plan of action, and facilitated the start of relief activities. The secretariat launched an appeal (fund-raising for a specific project) based on the FACT report.

- Emergency response units (ERUs) were pretrained teams of volunteers who already knew one another and were familiar with prepacked sets of standardized equipment. The International Federation secretariat was responsible for the coordination, monitoring, and evaluation of ERU deployment. Standard operating procedures and technical specifications for the different ERUs had been developed, and regular ERU working groups met to further refine standards and rapid-response mechanisms.

- The Disaster Relief Emergency Fund (DREF) was a pool of nonearmarked money used to guarantee immediate funding in response to emergencies. Managed by the secretariat, DREF funds were sought through an annual appeal and used to either start up operations in major disaster areas or support smaller or less visible emergencies.

Disaster preparedness. The sharp increase in natural disasters in recent years had prompted the International Federation secretariat to devote more attention to disaster-preparedness activities that aimed to make National Societies more aware of the risks they faced and how to reduce their vulnerability and cope when disaster struck. In 1999, an estimated 212 million people were affected by disasters. Estimated financial losses attributable to natural disasters stood at more than $100 billion in 1999, compared with $50 billion in 1990 and $1 billion in 1960. The International Federation believed that disaster preparedness was the most effective way of reducing the effect of disasters and that it required effective links between emergency response, rehabilitation, and development programs. The organization saw its role in disaster preparedness as complementary to national government activities but believed there was a need for more advocacy and raising awareness of the hazards, levels of risk, and coping mechanisms for at-risk populations.

The International Federation carried out research, developed tools, and drafted policies in the areas of post-conflict environments, climate change and disasters, refugees, and migration. Through the annual publication of its *World Disaster Report*, the International Federation aimed to play an advocacy role by analyzing, examining, and making available to the public the key issues in humanitarian preparedness and response.

Health and community care. By 2002, infectious diseases were killing 13 million people every year. Poverty was the primary cause of the spread of diseases, and the lack of information and services for the 3 billion people living on less than $2 per day meant that they suffered the most.

Health and social welfare services, delivered domestically, accounted for the largest portion of National Societies' CHF 24 billion annual expenditures. Internationally, health was a major component of most emergency appeals, and health programs represented 30 percent of the International Federation's appeal for 2002–2003. In 1998, the International Federation initiated the African Red Cross/Red Crescent Health Initiative 2010 (ARCHI 2010), a ten-year effort of the fifty-three African Red Cross/Red Crescent National Societies that aimed to build capacities to address high-priority public health problems across the continent. Working with many partners (ministries of health, the African academic world, WHO, UNICEF, UNFPA, UNAIDS[3]), data on major health problems were collected, analyzed, and prioritized. Consensus was reached on the major public health interventions that African National Societies should address as priorities during the next decade. These priorities were community-level promotion and prevention activities focused on HIV/AIDS, childhood preventable diseases, women's and pregnancy-related issues, and initial responses to accidents and injuries.

Other major activities in the area of health and community care were the following:

1. Blood services. (More than 75 million units of blood were collected per annum.)

2. First-aid training, in which the International Federation was the world leader.

3. HIV/AIDS, which was predicted to kill more people from 2000–2009 than all the wars and disasters in the previous fifty years. (Since the epidemic had begun, 25 million people had died, 42 million were now living with HIV and AIDS, and 5 million people became infected worldwide in 2001 alone.)

4. The Roll Back Malaria initiative: With 300 to 500 million cases each year (90 percent of which were in Africa), an estimated 3,000 children died from malaria every day.

5. Measles vaccination programs. (Measles could be prevented by a simple vaccination, but in 2002 more than 1 million children died.)

6. Polio, which had seen a huge drop in numbers; the International Federation, along with other organizations, was striving for its global eradication.

7. Tuberculosis, which killed an estimated 2 million people a year.

8. Psychological support.

9. Relief health programs (resulting from earthquakes, cyclones, floods, refugees, post-conflict, famine).

10. Water and sanitation projects.

11. Programs focused on women and children.

Capacity building. Guiding and supporting the development of its member National Societies was becoming the International Federation's most important task. It worked through both its secretariat in Geneva and its country and regional delegations to provide this help. A set of indicators had been produced to help National Societies plan and measure their progress in capacity building. These "customized assessment and performance indicators" listed 120 checkpoints toward achieving the defined characteristics of a well-functioning National Society (CWFNS) and had been built into a National Society self-assessment tool piloted in 2001. (See **Exhibit 5** for the CWFNS.) From the CWFNS, policies had been developed to guide the International Federation and National Societies to ensure a basic quality and consistency of approach for Red Cross and Red Crescent action worldwide.

Building the capacities of volunteers, training leaders, and managers, was also a key element in strengthening National Societies. The International Federation supported its members by preparing manuals, for example, on disaster preparedness and quality standards for blood programs. To assist National Societies with their long-term fund-raising, the International Federation also provided technical assistance, training materials, and performance indicators.

Exhibit 5	Characteristics of a Well-Functioning National Society

Foundation

Mission

a) A well-functioning National Society has a clearly stated mission, in other words, a clear purpose, a clear idea of what it is trying to do. The mission is well understood and broadly supported by members at all levels of the society.

b) It is guided by the Fundamental Principles of the Movement and operates in conformity with these Fundamental Principles throughout the society.

c) It maintains a position of autonomy and independence, while working closely, as a responsible partner, with the government and with others.

d) Its mission reflects the Mission of the Red Cross and Red Crescent as well as the challenge as defined in the International Federation's Strategy 2010.

e) It demonstrates understanding and acceptance of its responsibilities as a member of the International Federation and part of the Movement.

f) It strikes the right balance between the preservation of established values on the one hand and the innovation needed to meet new challenges on the other.

g) It has a positive public image that properly reflects its mission and its values.

Legal base

a) A well-functioning Society has up-to-date and relevant statutes, modified only after concurrence of the ICRC and the International Federation.

b) It is constituted on the territory of an independent country, as the only Red Cross or Red Crescent society.

c) It uses the title and emblem of the Red Cross or Red Crescent in conformity with the Geneva Conventions and the relevant regulations.

d) The Red Cross or Red Crescent law or decree under which it is recognized by its government is still relevant.

e) The statutes are being respected; in particular, the general assembly (or equivalent governing body) is being convened regularly and elections are held in accordance with the statutes.

Constituency

a) A well-functioning Society extends its activities to the entire territory of the country, through either an adequate branch network based on a territorial structure, or through another form of territorial coverage.

b) It recruits its voluntary members and staff without consideration of race, color, ethnic origin, sex, class, religion or political beliefs, pursuing widespread and popular membership, and seeking to ensure that membership and leadership are a true reflection of the general population.

c) It has a clear definition of the various types of membership.

d) It makes special efforts to attract and involve the youth of the country.

Capacity

Leadership

a) A well-functioning Society has a clear and straightforward governing structure with well-defined roles for its general assembly, for the central or executive committee, for the chairman or president, and for the chief executive officer; accountability has been well-established at all levels of governance and management.

b) It avoids domination of the governing body by one person, one group or by the government; it also avoids exclusion of certain people or groups from membership.

c) Decision making is widely shared, with all volunteers having access to the decision-making process and with provision for consultation and a wide expression of views.

d) Leaders are committed to the Red Cross/Red Crescent and have the necessary background and skills, with special efforts made to ensure regular succession of leaders.

e) Leadership training as well as leadership opportunities are provided at all levels, especially for women and youth.

Human resources

a) A well-functioning Society engages a sufficient number of properly qualified persons (staff and volunteers) to carry out its services, and taps professional advice and expertise beyond its own membership.

b) It has explicit policies regarding the recruitment, training, appraisal and reward of staff and volunteers, and it actively implements these policies.

c) It actively recruits volunteers from all sections of the community, including vulnerable groups that it is trying to assist, and engages in programs that rely on volunteers as well as on financial inputs.

Financial and material resources

a) It finances its activities on a planned basis, covering the expenses of administration and other core activities from its own core resources.

Source: IFRC.

Exhibit 5   continued

b) It seeks to minimize dependence on foreign or government assistance through active local fund-raising combined with sound financial management.

c) It carries out local fund-raising on a systematic basis, seeking broad support within the population.

d) It diversifies its sources of funding in order to protect its independence and reduce risks while ensuring high ethical standards and avoiding support from sources or on conditions that are inconsistent with its mission.

e) It keeps administrative and other overhead costs under control to ensure that as many of its resources as possible are used to improve the situation of the most vulnerable.

f) It has available the basic material infrastructure (buildings, transport and other means) adequate for its purposes, consistent with its desired public image and sustainable in terms of operation and maintenance.

g) It has regular external audits, and regular publication of audited annual accounts.

Organization

a) A well-functioning Society has the structures, systems and procedures in place that allow it to fulfill its mission.

b) Its organization is flexible, prepared to respond immediately to disasters.

c) It has a headquarters, which gives leadership and support to local units.

d) It has an up-to-date, comprehensive development plan that brings together its mission, its specific objectives, its relief and development programs, and its financing.

e) It has a sound system of financial management, budgeting, accounting and external, independent auditing, with clear accountability for the use of funds.

f) It works closely with other organizations, national and international, public and private, taking into account what others are doing, coordinating its activities with them and sharing resources, information and expertise.

g) It actively supports the International Federation, participating in its affairs, implementing its policies, and assisting the International Federation, the ICRC and other societies to the limits of its abilities, including the sharing of experiences, knowledge and expertise.

Performance

Activities

a) A well-functioning Society carries out a set of activities that is well selected, planned and evaluated.

b) It ensures that activities are consistent with its mission and with its desired public image, thus enhancing public confidence.

c) It adheres to relevant International Federation policies, including the Principles and Rules for Disaster Relief and for Development Cooperation, and other policy decisions of the General Assembly, the Council of Delegates and the International Conference.

d) It actively disseminates the Fundamental Principles and humanitarian law. It cooperates with the government to ensure respect for international humanitarian law and to protect the Red Cross and Red Crescent emblem. While respecting the principle of neutrality, it is not indifferent in the face of situations that adversely affect the most vulnerable.

e) It is prepared to take prompt and effective action in response to disasters, in accordance with its specific role in disaster relief; it is prepared in peacetime for its statutory tasks in case of armed conflict; it actively assists in relief operations after natural disasters; and it selectively undertakes development programmes aimed at strengthening the capacities of vulnerable communities.

f) It implements a set of core programs in line with regional requirements as determined by respective regional conferences.

Relevance

a) A well-functioning Society concentrates its activities on the most vulnerable, enhancing their capacity to help themselves.

b) It pursues the active participation of program target groups in its membership, in the decision-making process, and in contributing to the costs of services.

Effectiveness

a) A well-functioning Society monitors continuously whether its activities have the desired effect and whether results are achieved efficiently, taking prompt corrective action where needed and feeding the results back into the planning process.

b) It enjoys a good reputation for the quality of its work, both amongst the country's leading opinion makers and the public at large. To help enhance its public image, it keeps the press well informed about its activities.

c) It prepares regular progress reports and keeps the International Federation, its members, its donors and the public at large regularly informed about its activities, finances and achievements.

d) It regularly evaluates and assesses the quality and impact of its activities and makes adjustments where needed.

Source: IFRC.

Enabling National Societies to cooperate and learn from one another was considered vital and was achieved through regional meetings (such as a Pan-African conference in September 2000), workshops (such as "youth power" in Sweden in July 1999), and networks (for example, an HIV/AIDS network in Asia).

Partners.

In 2002, the International Federation worked in partnership with a number of entities in three areas to enhance effectiveness:

1. Humanitarian assistance—The International Federation worked with many different NGOs, the European Union's ECHO, and many United Nations (UN) agencies. ECHO remained a key donor and partner, and the International Federation had developed an ECHO Framework Partnership Agreement to further strengthen the relationship. Bilateral relations between the International Federation and many UN agencies continued to grow in 2001, particularly with UNHCR, UNICEF, WHO, UNAIDS, and the UNDP.[4] Mathew Varghese, head of the evaluation department, explained, "We want to work in partnership with other organizations. We have UN observer status and work with the UN agencies as one of their implementing partners in the field."

2. Development—To ensure sustainable and consistent assistance, the International Federation had initiated a tripartite process with twelve donor governments and their National Societies. For example, a three-year partnership with the U.K. Department for International Development, the British Red Cross, and the International Federation contributed CHF 31 million.

3. Research—The International Federation worked with research institutions, universities, and the private sector to monitor trends in humanitarian assistance.

At the international level, the International Federation was considered a major humanitarian player. The International Federation had UN observer status and worked with the UN in developing policies and reports and implementing field programs. At the local and regional levels, National Societies also partnered with community groups, businesses, and government ministries.

CURRENT CHALLENGES.

Funding.

In 2001, the International Federation secretariat recorded total income of CHF 289 million, versus total income for 2000 of CHF 335 million. In fact, income had been on the decline since 1999, and the trend was expected to continue in 2002. "Part of the reason for this decline," Varghese explained, "is that our income is linked to the number of disasters that strike within a given year. In addition, as the International Secretariat moves into its new role of coordinator, many of the funds will be channeled through bilateral agreements between member societies rather than through the secretariat."

Income was divided into statutory and voluntary, with the latter representing more than 90 percent of total income. (See **Exhibit 6** for a statement of income and expenditures.) Close to 54 percent of the 2001 income came from voluntary contributions from governments and government agencies, and a further 28 percent came

Exhibit 6	Statement of Income and Expenditures, 2001		
	Statutory 2001 000' CHF	Voluntary 2001 000' CHF	Total 2001 000' CHF
INCOME			
Statutory contributions	26,659	0	26,659
Voluntary contributions:			
National Societies	12	81,717	81,729
Government and governmental agencies	0	155,031	155,031
Others	527	13,212	13,739
Other Income	3,889	7,799	11,688
Total Income	31,087	257,759	288,846
EXPENDITURES			
Contributions to National Societies	0	10,544	10,544
Contributions to other organizations	0	210	210
Expenditures incurred by Federation:			
Relief supplies	0	75,852	75,852
Transportation and storage	0	22,705	22,705
Capital equipment	0	14,084	14,084
Personnel	18,584	87,095	105,679
Travel and communication	1,731	10,854	12,585
Information	921	6,011	6,932
Administration, office and general	4,786	29,376	34,162
Depreciation	457	3,529	3,986
Total Expenditures	26,479	260,260	286,739

Source: International Federation of Red Cross and Red Crescent Societies Annual Report 2001.

from voluntary donations from National Societies. National Societies also provided the secretariat with income through statutory contributions. Christopher Sorek, head of communications at the International Federation, explained, "These are membership fees, not of a fixed amount but based on an agreement between the secretariat and each society." Varghese added, "These fees are guided by five factors, which include a percentage of each National Society's annual income with a fixed minimum and maximum. It is very similar to the UN system."

The International Federation raised funds every year through a series of "appeals" that identified specific needs by geography and program. In addition to those appeals established at the start of the financial year, new appeals were launched throughout the year in response to specific disasters and crises. (**Exhibit 7** summarizes the appeals for 2002–2003.)

As early as 1993, the International Federation established a forum for global revenue generation to develop innovative fund-raising strategies and create opportunities for cooperation that would increase revenues for the International Federation as a whole. A framework was established that underlined the primary role of National Societies in revenue generation and the role of the secretariat as a coordinator and supporter, and that covered the areas of data sharing, multinational corporations, and merchandising and commercial endeavors. Initiatives during the 1990s included use of the Internet, lotteries, and partnerships with corporations.

In 1999, the executive council reviewed the issue of global revenue generation and concluded that efforts should be concentrated on sources of revenues unavailable to

Exhibit 7	Summary of Appeals, 2002–2003: Preliminary Budget by Region and Category (000' CHF)							
Region/ Category	Disaster Response	Disaster Preparedness	Health and Care	Humanitarian Values	Organization Development	Coordination Management	Regional Cooperation	Total
MENA[a]	4,948	2,094	6,051	846	2,766	2,008		18,713
Americas	1,108	4,796	2,921	657	3,530	2,077	574	15,662
Asia/Pacific	2,230	12,177	22,893	1,431	9,078	6,277	496	54,582
Africa	15,365	8,247	27,482	2,885	8,653	9,366	1,219	73,217
Europe	20,230	7,353	21,744	1,872	8,728	6,424	473	66,825
Funds[b]	7,500				4,000			11,500
Global[c]	2,684	4,562	4,443	1,024	6,608	1,326	8,845	29,491
Total	54,065	39,229	85,533	8,715	43,363	27,478	11,607	269,899
% total	20%	15%	32%	3%	16%	10%	4%	100%

Source: International Federation "Appeal 2002–2003" document.

[a]Middle East and North Africa.

[b]Includes disaster-relief emergency fund and capacity-building fund.

[c]Global programs.

a National Society working independently and that new sources of revenues should not detract from National Societies' existing revenue sources. In addition, the council ruled that new initiatives should open opportunities for National Societies to enhance their own fund-raising opportunities and that the use of the emblem of the red cross or red crescent should be tightly regulated.

Criteria for corporate partnerships were established in 1999 and can be seen in **Exhibit 8.** In 2002, private-sector partnerships included global alliances with Unilever, Nestle, BP, and Royal and SunAlliance. Betsy Thurston, head of private-sector marketing at the International Federation, believed that corporate partnerships had not yet been developed to their full potential. "Private-sector funding only represents 2 percent of our income," Thurston explained. "Although there exists great potential for revenue generation, we have not yet committed the resources necessary for its development. For corporate partnerships, it all boils down to the strength of our brand. We are not extracting the full value from our existing partnerships, and we are selling our brand short. We treat each partner differently and don't extract all we can from a relationship." (See **Exhibit 9** for an overview of voluntary cash contributions by source.)

Online fund-raising was also being developed at the International Secretariat with e-commerce for the processing of donations, banner campaigns on portals of companies the International Federation wished to be associated with, and a more donor-friendly Web site that simplified the message to increase funds raised online. Some National Societies, however, worried that international fund-raising efforts, particularly through the Internet, would hurt their own fund-raising efforts. In 2002, an estimated 50 percent of National Societies had well-maintained Web sites; most National Societies in developing countries did not. About 20 percent of National Societies had a robust online fund-raising capability.

Brand Image.

In July 2001, the International Federation commissioned the Young and Rubicam (Y&R) Advertising Agency to review the strength of the Red Cross brand in fifteen countries. Y&R's brand asset valuator (BAV) viewed brand strength as a function of

Exhibit 8	Criteria for Corporate Relationships, Established 1999

The following criteria were to be used:

1. In assisting the Secretariat in selecting corporations for global fund-raising approaches.

2. In assisting the Secretariat in deciding whether unsolicited corporate donations can be accepted.

3. Serving as a means for determining suitable contractual partners for other forms of cause-related marketing activities.

CRITERIA

- The Secretariat will only enter into commercial relations with established corporations whose activities are compatible with the International Federation's humanitarian principles. Each company will be screened to ensure its main activities are not in contradiction with the International Federation's principles and strategy.

- All terms and conditions of a relationship with a company have to be confirmed in a written and signed agreement, specifying the parties to the agreement, the description of the program or activity, the National Societies involved, the use of the name and emblem, cost allocation, duration, exclusivity . . .

- In those events when a company benefits immediately from the relationship with the International Federation, an appropriate percentage of the target amount should be paid as an up-front donation or guaranteed by the company in some other way.

- The Secretariat will acknowledge the support of the companies appropriately but will not undertake active commercial promotion of any kind, nor endorse products.

- An issues management committee, chaired by the Secretary General, will respond to eventual controversial issues created by the relationship between the International Federation and the company.

Source: IFRC.

Exhibit 9	Voluntary Cash Contributions by Source, 1998–2002

CHF Millions Category	1998	1999	2000	2001	2002 (estimated as of 9/02)
(estimated as of 9/02)					
Government direct	18	46	34	50	41
Government via N.S.	68	64	78	67	36
ECHO direct	43	53	34	27	27
ECHO through N.S.	0.5	0.8	1	13	
National Societies	65	119	128	82	51
International org / NGOs	10	35	14	9	11
Private donors	2	7	10	10	8
Other	0.1	0.3	0	4	-3
TOTAL	206.6	325.1	299	250	174

Source: Internal audits, IFRC.

brand vitality and brand stature. Based on consumer research, brand vitality was a function of a brand's differentiation (how distinctive the brand was perceived to be). Similarly, brand stature was a function of a brand's esteem (how highly regarded the brand was) and brand knowledge (how well known the brand was). The main conclusions of the study were as follows:

- The Red Cross brand stature was high in all countries and across all consumer groups.

- The Red Cross brand strength was more variable, with signs of weak differentiation (rather than low relevance) in Asian markets, especially in Japan and Malaysia. (See **Exhibit 10** for the Red Cross BAV model.)

- The image of the Red Cross evoked feminine and nurturing associations. The Red Cross was seen as a group of focused and helpful people, of good value and high quality, but traditional, lacking an "edge," and not missionary in its goals.

Sorek drew the distinction between the Red Cross and NGOs:

> *Although our brand was compared to major NGO brands, we are not an NGO, and at the International Secretariat level don't really compete with them. Most of our funds come from governments, and we are really competing for funds with many of the UN agencies. At the National Society level, however,*

Exhibit 10 Brand Asset Valuator Model for the Red Cross, 2001

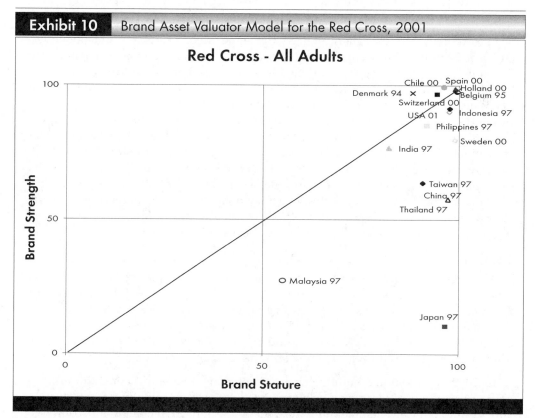

Source: IFRC/Young and Rubicam.

competition with national and international NGOs is obviously stronger, although our mandate and function make us distinct from NGOs and the major competitors vary by country.

Young and Rubicam suggested that the Red Cross brand could be strengthened if it were more differentiated in the minds of consumers. They believed that an opportunity existed to "bridge the female, passive supporter" characteristics of the existing brand with the "male, change agent and difference maker" of more "missionary" brand images of organizations such as Médecins Sans Frontières (Doctors Without Borders). "We were seen as a great, trustworthy organization that everyone knows and respects," Sorek said. "We are very well known, but what we are known for is rather fuzzy. The key question is, what do we want to be known for?" Sorek believed that given the strategic redirection of the International Secretariat's role, the organization had a perfect rebranding opportunity.

In 2000, Smith Beers Yunker and Company conducted a series of interviews with corporations specifically on the Red Cross Red Crescent brand. They found that the organization enjoyed a solid reputation and was viewed by the corporate community as a global organization "worthy of partnership." The International Federation was perceived as among the least adversarial humanitarian organizations and accepted by the establishment, which many corporations viewed as a positive trait. However, the International Federation and its members were considered old-fashioned and "shackled by inflexible structures," and there was no understanding, in the minds of those interviewed, of the different roles of the International Federation, the ICRC, and the National Societies.

In November 2001, the American Red Cross came under a barrage of well-publicized criticism for its handling of the Liberty Fund, which grouped funds collected after the September 11, 2001, tragedy, causing then-president Bernadine Healy to resign. Specifically, the organization was criticized by the local and national press for planning to use nearly 50 percent of the $550 million it had collected on a variety of other projects and administrative costs. Following closely on its heels, another scandal hit San Diego's Red Cross chapter in January 2002. The chapter had raised $400,000 for disaster relief after a series of wildfires in the San Diego area, but fewer than half the funds reached the victims. At the time, the local press reported that the San Diego Red Cross president was earning more than $300,000 a year.[5] These scandals hurt the organization's brand in the United States, which saw a significant drop in revenues in 2002. How other National Societies and the Red Cross Red Crescent Movement as a whole suffered from the negative publicity had not been quantified.

Emblem.

Although the red cross and red crescent emblems had worked well for a long time, a number of problems had arisen by 2002. First, in some conflicts, the cross or the crescent had been interpreted as having religious significance. Second, some National Societies, such as those in Israel and Eritrea, felt uncomfortable using either the red cross or red crescent, and the former used a red shield of David, whereas the latter used both the cross and the crescent together.

In 2002, an additional emblem, with no religious or political connotations, was being proposed to resolve these problems. It would be used in conflicts for protection and as the indicative emblem of a National Society. Implementation, however, involved changing both international law and the statutes of the Red Cross and Red

Crescent Movement. Specifically, a third additional protocol to the Geneva Convention would need to be adopted, requiring a diplomatic conference, convened by the Swiss government, of all 188 parties to the Geneva Conventions. In addition, a full International Conference of the Red Cross and Red Crescent, comprising 188 governments and 179 National Societies,[6] would be required to change the statutes.

Network Coordination.

Since each Red Cross or Red Crescent National Society was an independent organization, uncoordinated bilateralism, often consisting of agreements between two National Societies, one with funds and the other needing funds, were frequent. "All these activities are undertaken with the best of intentions," Varghese explained, "but when they are not coordinated, they often don't result in the maximum favorable impact." In many cases, these activities did not focus on the right priorities or long-term objectives of sustainability.

In response to the January 2001 earthquake in India, for example, a number of Red Cross Societies started to send in their own technical personnel. Varghese said:

> India had all the educated technical personnel it needed, and so bringing excess international capacity bilaterally when local skills existed affected the quality of the disaster response. The challenge we face is to help build the National Society's capacity to respond locally and empower the International Secretariat to coordinate activities so that we maximize resource utilization and benefits across the entire network.

STRATEGY 2010 AND SELF-ASSESSMENT.

Strategy 2010 was the International Federation's ten-year strategic plan. It was the result of a two-year process of consultation with National Societies, the analysis of trends in the external environment, and an internal capabilities assessment summarized in the report "Learning from the Nineties." Adopted by the International Federation's general assembly in October 1999, it outlined three strategic directions and ten expected results. (See **Exhibit 11** for details on Strategy 2010.) In essence, Strategy 2010 defined the four previously mentioned core activity areas as the common denominators on which the International Federation would build its reputation. Well-functioning National Societies would be strengthened through capacity building, using the self-assessment tool and networkwide programs of cooperation.

Strategy 2010 required that a new capacity-building culture be developed alongside the strong emergency-response culture that dominated the organization. Many people saw the International Federation, in its emergency-response role, as very different from the development organization that built National Societies' capabilities and promoted cooperation among them. In October 2002, Cherpitel expanded on the drivers and nature of the strategic changes:

> We are in the middle of a change process. We were previously short-term oriented, focused on emergencies, a doer/actor type of organization. Both external and internal forces have caused us to rethink our role and strategy. Externally, we have witnessed an explosion in the number of NGOs internationally and domestically. In many countries there is increasing confusion about the role of the state, and we have experienced a substantial decrease in funding. Internally,

many National Societies have built up important international capacity [ability to provide international assistance], and the International Federation and various National Societies were often in competition operationally, resulting not only in inefficiencies but also in a negative impact on our image. In the Balkans in 1995, for example, within two weeks there were sixteen National Societies in the field tripping over each other. Now the International Federation must take a supportive leadership role, serving all National Societies, becoming a facilitator and a coordinator. Building the capabilities and reputation of each member of the network will enable us to build our overall visibility and image and attract more funding. Longer term, this strategy will enable us to become the most respected and reliable civil society partner.

Exhibit 11   Strategy 2010

Three Strategic Directions:

1. National Society programs, responsive to local vulnerabilities and focused on the areas where they could add the greatest value within four core areas: promoting humanitarian values; disaster response; disaster preparedness; and health and community care. The core areas were seen as the common denominators that constituted the backbone on which the International Federation would build its collective experience and reputation.

2. Well-functioning National Societies, which could mobilize support and carry out their humanitarian mission, contributing to the building of civil society. Strengthening of National Societies through capacity building.

3. Working together through networkwide program cooperation, long-term partnerships and funding, as well as more active advocacy.

Ten Expected Results:

1. National Society programs that were established, continued, and discontinued on the basis of local vulnerability, potential impact, capacity of other institutions, and Red Cross/Red Crescent comparative advantages.

2. Quality criteria for service delivery and advocacy in each of the core areas, adopted through policy decisions at national and international levels.

3. A Federationwide evaluation system that showed measurable progress in all core areas and a process for achieving the characteristics of a well-functioning National Society.

4. National Societies that worked with different models of volunteer engagement. Decision-making bodies that reflected the population with balanced gender, ethnic, and youth representation.

5. National Societies with a more diversified and sustainable financial resource base.

6. An organization that mobilized people and influenced decisions in each core area.

7. Cooperation strategies agreed upon by all, framing humanitarian and capacity-building cooperation programs between National Societies.

8. Increased availability of information, demonstrated information sharing, and learning from experience, regionally and globally.

9. More National Societies contributing internationally on a long-term basis to development cooperation.

10. All components developed and implemented in parallel against a common strategy for the movement.

Source: IFRC.

National Society Self-Assessment 2002[7].

The need for an assessment system was clearly identified in Strategy 2010 "to ensure that Governance, supported by the Secretariat, will actively monitor and provide timely support to National Societies towards achieving the characteristics of a Well-Functioning National Society." A questionnaire, titled Self-Assessment Against Strategy 2010, was developed and piloted in fifteen National Societies in 2000. After the pilot phase and extensive input from the spectrum of National Societies to ensure relevance and utility, the board requested that the secretariat administer the self-assessment questionnaire to all member societies over three years. (**Exhibit 12** summarizes the basic assumptions and principles behind the self-assessment.) "The self-assessment tool was created as a monitoring and compliance mechanism," Varghese explained:

> *Self-assessment ensures that all members are playing by the rules of the game, the thinking being that the movement is only as strong as its weakest link. By making governance and self-monitoring priorities, we can help protect the brand. In addition, self-assessment enables the International Federation to get a picture of the global situation and understand trends in order to formulate policies, while at the same time ensuring quality and accountability at the individual society level.*

Exhibit 12   Basic Assumptions and Principles Behind the Self-Assessment

1. Global Indicators with Local Understanding—Given the diversity of National Societies, it is not possible to have a standard prescription and therefore there is a case-by-case approach to each National Society self-assessment, against the guidance of a well-functioning National Society.

2. Trust—If National Societies are not transparent and honest of their weaknesses, it is not possible to mobilize external support to address problems they face.

3. Ownership—The National Society owns the self-assessment process. Encouraging the societies to share the self-assessment report with other societies for transparency as well as to link assessments to capacity building is key.

4. Scale—Building support at all levels by a scale of about 60 societies worldwide undergoing the self-assessment process every year.

5. Credibility—Of the main findings through constantly improving on key indicators, rigor of analysis and timely availability of findings.

6. Participation—Encouraging participation at all levels of the organization through discussion and questionnaire completion.

7. Timeliness and Regularity—Making the self-assessment a regular business process.

8. Tracking Performance—Regularly checking on progress against key findings. The questionnaire will be administered in 2003 to those National Societies that underwent the self-assessment in 2001.

9. Learning—Continuous correction of methodological weakness and documenting practices.

10. Quality Assurance—Ensuring self-assessment points are relevant and useful.

11. Usefulness—Combining results orientation, governance, management and operational utility with long-term sustainable approach.

12. Simplicity of Language—and telling the truth.

Source: IFRC.

In 2002, sixty National Societies were requested to participate in the first phase of a self-assessment program, compared with forty National Societies in 2001. The revised questionnaire contained indicators to measure societies' performance against the CWFNS within the framework of Strategy 2010 and contained eight sections, outlined below. The results of the data analyses of the responses in both 2001 and 2002 are summarized below.

Legal base. To be recognized by the International Red Cross and Red Crescent Movement, a National Society had to fulfill certain legal conditions. It had to be recognized by its government as the only Red Cross/Red Crescent Society in the country, adhere formally to the fundamental principles, and use the title and emblem of the red cross or red crescent.

According to the CWFNS, a National Society had to ensure that the law or decree under which it was recognized by its government was up-to-date and relevant. (**Exhibit 13** summarizes responses in this area.) Up-to-date and relevant statutes were also considered necessary for a well-functioning National Society, and 67 percent of responding societies had revised their existing statutes within the previous ten years (22 percent had not done so). In addition, 67 percent of National Societies perceived a need in 2002 for revision of their statutes.

National Societies were asked to provide information about the existence and enforcement of the legal provisions governing the use of emblems. (**Exhibit 14** summarizes responses in the emblem protection area, which was closely associated with protection of the society's brand and image.)

Governance. Good governance required that a general assembly be held regularly. It was recommended that general assemblies be convened once a year; however, it was also recognized that that might not be feasible for all National Societies. Nevertheless, the characteristics prescribed that a general assembly had to be held at least once in four years. (**Exhibit 15** shows the frequency of general assemblies.) The CWFNS also required that decision making be widely shared, and placed particular emphasis on the participation of members from branches at the general assemblies. For 35 percent of National Societies, the proportion of branch representatives lay between 75 percent and 100 percent. For an additional 5 percent of

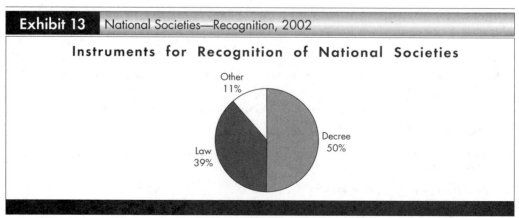

Exhibit 13 National Societies—Recognition, 2002

Instruments for Recognition of National Societies

Other
11%

Decree
50%

Law
39%

Source: IFRC.

Exhibit 14   National Societies—Emblem Protection, 2002

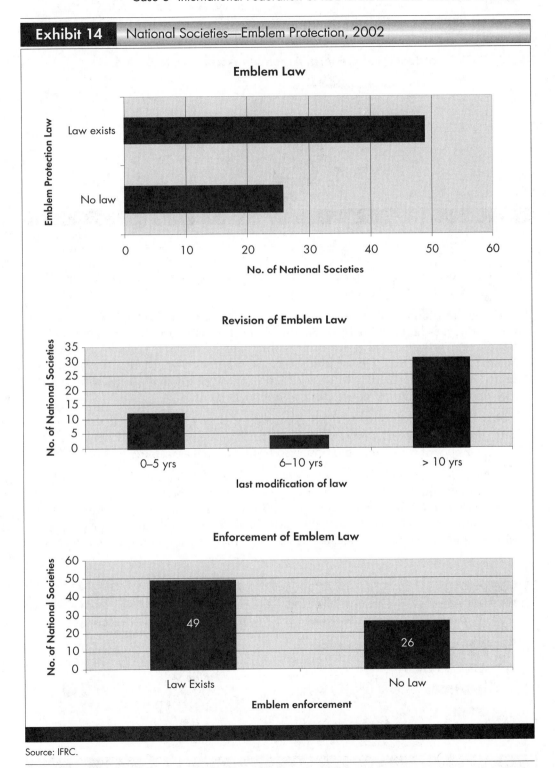

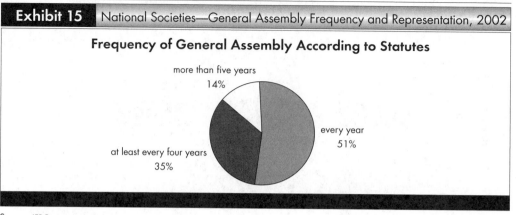

Exhibit 15 National Societies—General Assembly Frequency and Representation, 2002

Source: IFRC.

National Societies, this representation was below 25 percent. The remaining National Societies did not answer this question.

The composition and election of the governing boards of the National Societies were also reviewed. (**Exhibit 16** shows the proportion of board members elected to the function.) Given the need for transparency and accountability, it was also important that the respective roles of the governing board and the secretary general be clearly defined. (See **Exhibit 16** for a review of those National Societies with guidelines on the separation of governance and management.)

Human resources. The CWFNS contained explicit policies about the recruitment, training, appraisal, and reward of staff and volunteers. (**Exhibit 17** gives details on the number of volunteers and observed trends, as well as training for volunteers.)

In 1999, for example, the Zimbabwe Red Cross noted that only 20 percent of its trainees in community-based health care were male. The society expressed the wish to encourage more participation by male trainees and developed a program within the community to this end. In 2000, the Chad Red Cross created a division for "women and development" because it believed that issues relating to gender and

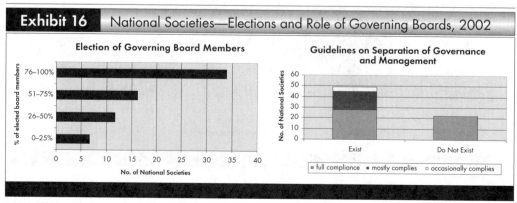

Exhibit 16 National Societies—Elections and Role of Governing Boards, 2002

Source: IFRC.

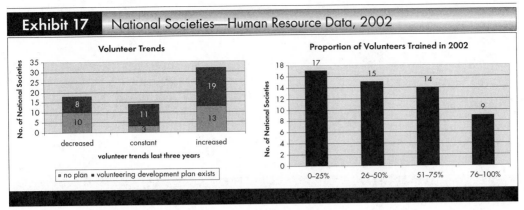

Exhibit 17   National Societies—Human Resource Data, 2002

Source: IFRC.

representation of women in society required special attention. According to a demographic survey, 77 percent of the women in Chad had never been to school, and a large part of the female population had no access to maternity services even though the average number of births per woman was 6.6.

Financial management. An expected result of Strategy 2010 was that National Societies would develop a diversified and sustainable financial resource base. The CWFNS said National Societies should seek to minimize dependence on foreign or government assistance through active local fund-raising and sound financial management. (**Exhibit 18** reviews sources of income and auditing for National Societies.)

Self-monitoring. Mechanisms for the monitoring of integrity and image were considered essential. As emphasized in Strategy 2010, integrity problems in one National Society could affect the entire Red Cross/Red Crescent Movement. This had recently been demonstrated by the wide-ranging effect of the scandals surrounding the American Red Cross in 2001 and 2002, as described earlier.

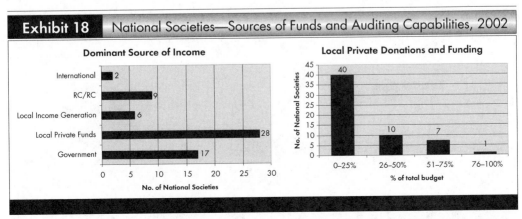

Exhibit 18   National Societies—Sources of Funds and Auditing Capabilities, 2002

Source: IFRC.

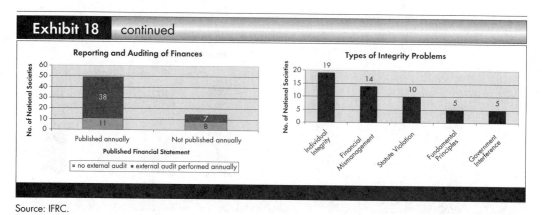

Exhibit 18 continued

Reporting and Auditing of Finances

Types of Integrity Problems

Source: IFRC.

"Within the organization," Sorek explained, "when one National Society has a serious image problem, it can affect everyone." Varghese added, "Problems relating to integrity are thought to stem from one of the following: government interference, violation of fundamental principles, nonrespect for statutes, issues of leadership, problems of financial management, and problems of individual integrity." (**Exhibit 19** reviews the image problems facing National Societies and the existence of mechanisms for monitoring integrity.)

According to the CWFNS, a National Society should enjoy a good reputation for the quality of its work. To help ensure its public image, a society had to keep the press well informed, systematically promote and monitor its reputation through a communication plan, and move quickly in response to any image problem. For example, throughout 2000, the Azerbaijan Red Crescent Society worked to build its public image and was regularly mentioned in the mass media. More than 220 articles were published, and thirty-five accounts of the organization's activities aired on different TV channels. Two documentary films were produced and broadcast on national television, and close cooperation with radio channels in Baku ensured that reports of the society's activities were regularly aired.

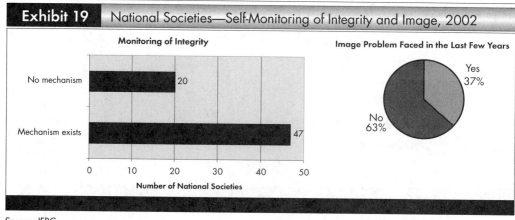

Exhibit 19 National Societies—Self-Monitoring of Integrity and Image, 2002

Monitoring of Integrity

Image Problem Faced in the Last Few Years

Source: IFRC.

Branch monitoring. Effective branch monitoring was a challenge facing National Societies since branch activities affect the overall effectiveness of a society's operations and programs, as well as the integrity and image of a National Society. Mechanisms for branch monitoring varied with socioeconomic and geographical conditions. (**Exhibit 20** reports on the types and adequacy of existing mechanisms.)

Strategy 2010. According to the CWFNS, a society should have an up-to-date development plan that specified its mission, objectives, relief and development programs, and financing. In addition, these plans should address the four core areas of Strategy 2010. In 2002, more than 80 percent of National Societies had a development plan that had been updated within the last five years.

After an extensive decentralization process in 1998, the Sudanese Red Crescent Society conducted a strategic assessment of its role, program orientation, objectives, and overall performance. Members of the board, management, and branch representatives were consulted, and in 1999 a workshop on the design and formulation of a five-year strategic plan was organized. The resulting plan contained revised mission and vision statements and six strategic goals.

Cooperation and partnerships. Strategy 2010 required National Societies to increase collaboration within the movement and to seek long-term partnerships and funding in both the public and private sectors. Specifically, better information sharing and cooperation were expected to result in improved program effectiveness and efficiency. (**Exhibit 21** reviews National Societies' key agreements and partnerships.)

The International Federation believed that the capabilities and capacities of national and local Red Cross members were an important determinant of the quality of service provided to the most vulnerable. Therefore, the value of the information provided by the assessment system was dependent on the ability of the International Federation to provide practical support to help the National Societies improve. To this end, individual assessment reports were prepared for each of the National Societies. Having participated in the assessment and after further discussions, each participating society was expected to produce and agree upon a plan of action. Varghese expanded on the importance of this phase:

> *The purpose of the feedback is to help individual societies identify their strengths and weaknesses and, with the help of technical and regional departments of the*

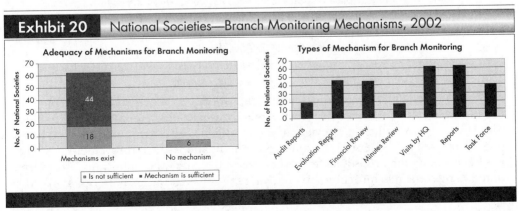

Exhibit 20   National Societies—Branch Monitoring Mechanisms, 2002

Adequacy of Mechanisms for Branch Monitoring

Types of Mechanism for Branch Monitoring

Source: IFRC.

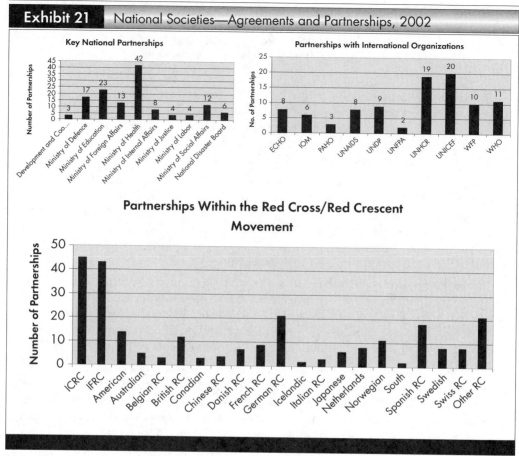

Exhibit 21   National Societies—Agreements and Partnerships, 2002

Source: IFRC.

ECHO = European Commission Humanitarian Aid Office; IOM = International Organization for Migration; PAHO = Pan American Health Organization; UNAIDS = United Nations Aids Organization; UNDP = United Nations Development Programme; UNFPA = United Nations Population Fund; UNHCR = United Nations Refugee Agency; UNICEF = United Nations Children's Fund; WFP = World Food Programme; WHO = World Health Organization.

secretariat, build a plan to address them. The process not only requires direct feedback by the National Societies but full participation and ownership of the self-assessment by National Societies. There is no set standard or median we are striving to achieve for each criteria. Rather, the idea is to address all the issues identified in an individual society's report and work with the governance, management, and staff of that society to address them.

By the end of 2003, it was expected that all National Societies would participate in the self-assessment and that a peer-review mechanism would be implemented to help with compliance. Under peer review, member societies would mutually validate findings of the self-assessment and frame recommendations for improvement. "There has been some initial resistance to participate and change the status quo," Varghese noted, "and some real difficulties in rectifying the issues the assessment raised in individual countries. However, everyone has so much to gain from the process that it is quickly becoming adopted by most National Societies." The peer-review process was expected to be particularly important in increasing collaboration within the movement and respecting the diversity of National Societies through a common accountability framework.

Challenges Facing Different National Societies.

In 2002, many of the National Societies in developed countries were faced with the challenge of an aging organization: aging volunteers and an aging group of beneficiaries. In 2000, in the Netherlands for example, the average volunteer age was 52, and the average beneficiary was 58. An estimated 45 percent of funding came from government sources, and some 78 percent of funds were spent on programs addressing the elderly. The Dutch Red Cross was struggling to find new sources of funds and, in 2001, decided to refocus on the 17-to-40 age group with programs such as HIV/AIDS awareness, day care for young children, and first-aid courses. "With this reorientation," Sorek explained, "the organization has begun to recruit younger volunteers and so broaden its image and brand appeal."

In a country in southern Africa, however, the sources of funding were radically different: only 1 percent came from local donors, with the rest from six developed-country National Societies, the UN, and other international organizations. Many field programs were run directly by the other National Societies, and the local Red Cross Society had relatively few volunteers working in collaboration with other organizations for most of its programs. On the other hand, in other developing countries such as the Philippines, the Red Cross had attracted a large number of local volunteers with strong roots in their communities.

Sorek expanded on the different types of National Societies: "Not every National Society is the same. Different local needs, structures, relationships with the government, funding characteristics, and engagement with the community help create the National Society's space in civil society. This, in turn, drives the development of its image and perception."

India Red Cross Society (IRCS). Founded in 1920, by 2002 the IRCS comprised 32 state branches and 650 district branches. The president of India was also the president of the society, and the managing body was composed of nineteen members, six of them nominated by the president and the remaining elected by the state branches through an electoral college. In 2002 Dr. Vimala Ramalingam was the society's secretary general and CEO.

The society's main activities focused on providing relief to the victims of natural disasters such as floods, earthquakes, and cyclones in India. "The vast majority of our work," Ramalingam said, "has been to respond to emergencies within our own country." In June and July of 2002, for example, monsoon floods in the northern and eastern states of India affected 20 million people and were responsible for more than 500 deaths. The IRCS states affected responded by supplying shelter, clothing, and food. In addition, the American Red Cross dispatched an assessment team that later provided food rations, and the International Federation launched an appeal for CHF 2.9 million to support the IRCS in providing food, shelter, and basic health care for 200,000 people over a six-month period. (**Exhibit 22** gives details of the January 2001 earthquake in India and the Red Cross's successful response.) Ramalingam explained:

We first participated in the self-assessment study three years ago. At that time, we did not really know what our strengths and weaknesses were, or who

Exhibit 22	Details of January 2001 Earthquake in India and Red Cross Response

On January 26, 2001, an earthquake of magnitude 7.9 struck Gujarat in India. Some 20,000 people lost their lives and hundreds of thousands of homes were destroyed.

Within two days of the disaster, the India Red Cross Society (IRCS) invited the International Federation to mount a disaster-response operation in partnership with the IRCS. In total, some 50 National Societies made donations and sent delegates to assist with the operation. On January 20, 2001, the International Federation Secretariat launched an appeal for CHF 25.6 million and received over CHF 40 million in goods, services, and cash donations.

The emergency operation exceeded its target of 300,000 beneficiaries. Personnel reached the epicenter in Bhuj within 48 hours, and emergency response units (ERUs) were mobilized by eight National Societies to provide medical, water and sanitation, and logistics relief. A 310-bed Red Cross ERU hospital was operational in Bhuj in less than a week, and the hospital became the flagship of the International Federation operation and an important component of the public relations success for both the IRCS and the International Federation.

The International Federation was the first agency to reach Bhuj and was able to provide critical information to other agencies and the international press. The emergency period lasted 120 days, and during this time 228,000 blankets, 117,000 tarpaulins, 35,000 tents, 53,000 kitchen sets, and 61,000 water containers were distributed. This successful emergency operation was made possible in large part because of the personal commitment of staff and delegates and the high levels of coordination between National Societies, both in the field and at the Secretariat level.

Source: IFRC.

was in the best position to address certain issues: the Indian government, the International Federation, or the IRCS. For example, as a result of consecutive self-assessments, we are aiming to add the manpower and physical infrastructure required for a nationwide disaster-preparedness/disaster-response program. With the International Federation's support, we have initiated training programs and workshops and are in the process of establishing state branch disaster coordinators and a national disaster-response team.

The International Federation had provided the IRCS with a delegation of ten technical assistance experts. Ramalingam expanded on their role: "The delegation is very helpful. They act as consultants to the IRCS and have been supportive."

Although planning and coordination were done at the IRCS headquarters, all society activities were conducted at the state level. The state organizations raised funds, managed volunteers and resources, and ran relief operations. "The key challenge now," Ramalingam said, "is to take aspects of the self-assessment to the states themselves."

Danish Red Cross (DRC). Founded in 1876, the DRC had 250 local branches in 2002 serving 130,000 members and supporters, of whom 15,000 members were active volunteers, making the DRC Denmark's largest voluntary humanitarian organization. Some two-thirds of funds were spent on national programs. The DRC's main focus was running the country's asylum centers. These centers provided refugees with a secure home while they waited for decisions on their applications for political asylum. Many asylum seekers waited years for a decision, and the DRC provided them with Danish-language lessons and the opportunity to earn or maintain their skills and qualifications.

The DRC allocated one-third of its resources, or 120 million Danish krona (DKK) annually,[8] to the world's conflict and natural disaster areas. The DRC worked with International Federation and Red Cross and Red Crescent societies, primarily in

Asia, in assisting refugees and offering relief to victims of natural disasters and with the ICRC in war and conflict zones.

Dr. Pedersen, DRC secretary general, discussed the self-assessment tool and the changes at the International Federation level:

> The self-assessment has highlighted a couple of areas which we were already aware of as challenges for the DRC. The main recommendation was to diversify the source of our donations, since two-thirds of our funds come from the Danish government. However, this is difficult to do, and we have not yet followed through. I agree with the changes at the International Federation level, but as yet, nothing has really changed in the relationship between the DRC and the International Federation. In terms of our international work, sometimes we work in coordination with them, sometimes we work bilaterally, directly with other National Societies. The stated goal of the International Federation has been to develop the National Societies' capabilities, and I don't think that they have achieved this yet. Across the globe, some National Societies face important integrity problems that I'm not sure that the self-assessment study alone can resolve.

South African Red Cross Society (SARCS). Founded in 1921 with the amalgamation of various Red Cross entities present in the country, in 2002 the SARCS comprised more than 3,000 volunteers and 160 staff and had annual expenditures of more than CHF 10 million. Made up of five regions, thirty-one branches, and eighty affiliated local committees, the organization also had a voluntary aid corps and air-mercy service that operated under a separate trust.

With an estimated 20 percent of South Africa's sexually active population infected with HIV or living with AIDS, the SARCS health programs focused on preventive health training and home-based care for HIV/AIDS victims. The organization also provided first-aid training, youth skills-training programs, and disaster relief.

In 1994, the SARCS started to undergo a number of organizational changes. The transition was not smooth and resulted in internal management struggles, major integrity issues, and the gross mismanagement of funds. Personality clashes and bitter legal battles came to a head in 1997, and the local newspapers were full of criticism for the organization and its management. The SARCS became considerably indebted and, in 2003, was still in default of contributions to the International Federation. In 2000, a new secretary general was appointed, and a recovery plan was initiated. Recovery, was slow, however, and in 2001 the SARCS appealed to the International Federation for full-time assistance for the transitional period and embarked upon a full self-assessment process.

Seija Tyrninoksa, an International Federation representative with substantial self-assessment experience, was appointed in August 2002 to assist with the implementation of the self-assessment as part of the SARCS overall change process, led by new leadership. She explained:

> Given the tumultuous last ten years or so, the SARCS really needed an in-depth analysis of its key challenges and a concrete, detailed report of recommendations. The self-assessment was implemented throughout the organization, but, with hindsight, it was perhaps implemented a little too aggressively, with many of the guidelines not having been fully understood. The key is to make the self-assessment process participatory, so that everyone in the organization sees the

value of the process and has the capacity and desire to participate in it. We are now organizing regional workshops and implementing a second series of questionnaires. In essence, the self-assessment tool is one component of an annual monitoring and accountability/evaluation system that has helped the SARCS overcome major organizational and image issues.

CONCLUSION.

Cherpitel believed that the International Federation was moving in the right direction and that the self-assessment tool was one of the best ways to implement Strategy 2010 and achieve the organization's mission and longer-term goals. He confided:

> *The question is not only what we do, it's how do we do it. This new focus for the secretariat represents a major cultural change, and we need to gain the buy-in of all our network members. It's going to take at least five years for all National Societies to trust the secretariat delegates. At the same time, we will need to help each National Society develop its own capabilities around the four core areas of disaster response, disaster preparedness, health and community care, and humanitarian principles and values. This will require a whole new set of skills and talents to the ones we currently have within the secretariat.*

In addition to successfully implementing the self-assessment, Cherpitel wondered what other specific actions he should be taking to strengthen the organization's brand and image.

Notes to Case

[1] Strategy 2010 was the central guide for the International Federation of Red Cross and Red Crescent Societies in the first decade of the twenty-first century.

[2] US$1 = CHF1.35.

[3] WHO: World Health Organization; UNICEF: United Nations Children's Fund; UNFPA: United Nations Population Fund; UNAIDS: The Joint U.N. Program on HIV/AIDS.

[4] ECHO = European Commission Humanitarian Aid Office; UNHCR = UN High Commission for Refugees; UNDP = UN Development Programme.

[5] This section is based on an article by J. Stryker Meyer, "Bad News for the Red Cross," *North County Times*, April 28, 2002.

[6] The number of National Societies was 179, 178 of which were members of the International Federation and one of which was awaiting admission at the next general assembly.

[7] This section is based on the "National Society Self-Assessment, 2002" report.

[8] US$1 = DKK 7.

PART 3

Brand Meaning

CASE 7
UNICEF

In September 2002, Marjorie Newman-Williams, director of communications, was about to present the results of a United Nations Children's Fund (UNICEF) rebranding exercise to the 47th Annual Meeting of National Committees for UNICEF in New York. The rebranding effort flowed from the desire to ensure that the UNICEF identity reflected its evolving mission. As Newman-Williams said, "UNICEF's public image and awareness is very different from who we are, and who we want to be." The rebranding process had taken more than two years, and Newman-Williams described it as "a challenge in an organization that had little understanding of the importance of branding and not much stomach for it." She expanded:

> Four forces drove the branding effort. First, UNICEF's internal shift towards a rights-based organization, increasingly appreciating the importance of advocacy as a strategy to achieve its goals. Second, an increasingly challenging external donor environment, combining a decline in multilateralism and an increase in restricted funds. Third, market research conducted at national levels, which showed that the UNICEF image did not match with whom we thought we were. Fourth, a need to provide greater clarity and consistency in our communication strategy. The objective was to refresh and revitalize UNICEF's image and reputation, uncover what UNICEF stands for, and find a way to express this individuality in a clear and focused way and reflect it in everything we do as an organization. We started the rebranding process in 1999, and I think we are very close to implementation now.

UNITED NATIONS CHILDREN'S FUND.

UNICEF was mandated by the United Nations General Assembly to advocate for the protection of children's rights and was guided by the Convention on the Rights of the Child. UNICEF's stated mission was to "reduce childhood death and illness, protect children in the midst of war and natural disaster, promote education for girls and boys alike, and strive to build a world in which all children live with dignity and security."

Professor John Quelch and Research Associate Nathalie Laidler prepared this case. HBS cases are developed solely as the basis for class discussion. Cases are not intended to serve as endorsements, sources of primary data, or illustrations of effective or ineffective management.

In 2002, UNICEF worked in 162 countries and territories and had 6,000 staff people, 14 percent of whom worked at headquarter locations. In 2001, total income was more than $1.2 billion, with governments and intergovernmental organizations accounting for 64 percent of contributions. An additional 33 percent was derived from the private sector (individuals, foundations, businesses, and nongovernmental organizations), mostly through National Committees, with the remaining 3 percent coming from other sources.

History.

Founded in December 1946, UNICEF (the United Nations International Children's Emergency Fund) was established to help children after World War II in Europe. In 1950, its task was expanded to help children living in poverty in developing countries, and in October 1953, UNICEF became a permanent part of the United Nations system. Its name was changed to the United Nations Children's Fund, although it maintained the acronym UNICEF.

In 1953 actor Danny Kaye became UNICEF's "ambassador," and he made a film for the organization called, *Assignment Children*, that was seen by more than 100 million people. In 1959, the U.N. General Assembly adopted the Declaration of the Rights of the Child, focusing on children's rights to education, health care, and nutrition. As of 1962, UNICEF had begun to support teacher training and provide classroom supplies in the newly independent African countries. By 1965, education made up 43 percent of the organization's assistance to Africa. UNICEF was awarded the Nobel Peace Prize in 1965, and in 1983, the organization launched a drive to save the lives of millions of children through programs focusing on oral rehydration, immunization, breast-feeding, and good nutrition.

In 1987, a UNICEF study called "Adjustment with a Human Face" prompted global debate on how to protect women and children from the negative effects of economic reform, and in 1989, the U.N. General Assembly adopted the Convention on the Rights of the Child. In 1990, the World Summit for Children set ten-year goals for children's health, nutrition, and education, and in 1996, UNICEF supported a study called "The Impact of Armed Conflict on Children," raising awareness of war's effect on children. In 2001, the Global Movement for Children and the Say Yes for Children campaigns mobilized millions of children and adults around the world, and on May 10, 2002, the Special Session of the General Assembly on Children released its official outcome document, "A World Fit for Children."

Over the previous five decades, UNICEF had evolved from an organization focused on providing supplies and services to a rights-based organization that combined field support and services with broader advocacy work. Newman-Williams explained:

> *In the 1950s and 1960s, UNICEF was a supply and logistics organization that could provide a steady supply of goods in turbulent times, and to troubled and hard-to-access regions. In the 1970s, a tug-of-war developed between advocacy programs and supply operations, and in the 1980s and 1990s, the concept of children having rights really started taking hold. In the 1990s, UNICEF began to realize that the organization could do more to bring about the sustainable change it hoped to achieve, and we therefore gave greater emphasis to advocacy work. Today, the supply and service programs in the field*

buy us a seat at the national policymaking table, to address broader issues of children's rights. There is some debate internally as to whether we are going too far, and it is true that, unless we can show tangible results for children, our credibility is at stake.

Mission and Objectives.

Mandated by the U.N. General Assembly to advocate for the protection of children's rights, help meet children's basic needs, and establish opportunities for children to reach their full potential, UNICEF was guided by the Convention on the Rights of the Child, an international human rights treaty ratified in 2002 by 191 countries, with the notable exception of the United States. The United States refused to sign any multilateral agreement that conceded power to any authority other than itself. (See **Exhibit 1** for UNICEF's mission statement.)

UNICEF cooperated with 162 countries and territories, in partnership with governments, to focus on nine key areas: child protection, education, health, HIV/AIDS, nutrition, water and environmental sanitation, early childhood development, gender concerns, and emergency aid. Providing essential supplies for children was a core component of UNICEF programs. In 2001, UNICEF provided nearly $600 million worth of supplies, including vaccines, essential drugs, food, medical equipment, education supplies, transport, and information technology (IT) equipment.

Exhibit 1	UNICEF's Mission Statement, 2002

UNICEF is mandated by the United Nations General Assembly to advocate for the protection of children's rights, to help meet their basic needs and to expand their opportunities to reach their full potential.

UNICEF is guided by the Convention on the Rights of the Child and strives to establish children's rights as enduring ethical principles and international standards of behavior towards children.

UNICEF insists that the survival, protection and development of children are universal development imperatives that are integral to human progress.

UNICEF mobilizes political will and material resources to help countries, particularly developing countries, ensure a "first call for children" and to build their capacity to form appropriate policies and deliver services for children and their families.

UNICEF is committed to ensuring special protection for the most disadvantaged children—victims of war, disasters, extreme poverty, all forms of violence and exploitation and those with disabilities.

UNICEF responds in emergencies to protect the rights of children. In coordination with United Nations partners and humanitarian agencies, UNICEF makes its unique facilities for rapid response available to its partners to relieve the suffering of children and those who provide their care.

UNICEF is non-partisan and its cooperation is free of discrimination. In everything it does, the most disadvantaged children and the countries in greatest need have priority.

UNICEF aims, through its country programs, to promote the equal rights of women and girls and to support their full participation in the political, social and economic development of their communities.

UNICEF works with all its partners towards the attainment of the sustainable human development goals adopted by the world community and the realization of the vision of peace and social progress enshrined in the Charter of the United Nations.

Source: UNICEF Annual Report, 2002.

UNICEF's medium-term strategic plan (MTSP) for the period 2002–2005 combined a results-based management approach and a human rights-based approach and was developed to serve three functions: (1) outline the role and contribution of UNICEF to the document called "A World Fit for Children" (see **Exhibit 2** for key elements of the document), (2) describe UNICEF's organizational priorities and objectives, and (3) serve as a framework of accountability for UNICEF and its stakeholders. (See **Exhibit 3** for UNICEF's financial forecast in the MTSP.)

The MTSP also established the following five organizational priorities, for each of which both service and advocacy activities were identified: girls education, integrated early childhood development, immunization "plus," HIV/AIDS, and child protection. In 2001, UNICEF spent just over $1 billion on direct program assistance, broken down

Exhibit 2	Key Elements of "A World Fit for Children"

"A World Fit for Children" was a document, adopted by the U.N. General Assembly at the 27th special session in May 2002, that comprised a declaration and a plan of action.

DECLARATION

We reaffirm our obligation to take action to promote and protect the rights of each child—every human being below the age of 18 years including adolescents. We are determined to respect the dignity and to secure the well-being of all children.

We hereby call on all members of society to join us in a global movement that will help build a world fit for children through upholding our commitments to the following principles and objectives:

1. Put children first.
2. Eradicate poverty: invest in children.
3. Leave no child behind.
4. Care for every child.
5. Educate every child.
6. Protect children from harm and exploitation.
7. Protect children from war.
8. Combat HIV/AIDS.
9. Listen to children and ensure their participation.
10. Protect the earth for children.

PLAN OF ACTION

1. Promote healthy lives . . . through access to primary health care systems, adequate water and sanitation systems.

2. Provide quality education . . . ensure that all children have access to and complete primary education that is free, compulsory and of good quality.

3. Protect against abuse, exploitation and violence.

   • General protection
   • Protection from armed conflict
   • Combating child labor
   • Elimination of trafficking and sexual exploitation of children

4. Combat HIV/AIDS.

5. Mobilize resources.

Exhibit 3	Financial Forecasts for UNICEF's MTSP				
Millions US$	**2001**	**2002**	**2003**	**2004**	**2005**
INCOME					
Regular Resources	$ 545	$ 588	$ 629	$673	$ 720
Governments	340	343	355	362	370
Private Sector	170	210	195	205	215
Other	35	35	35	35	35
Other Resources	423	420	420	420	420
Governments	283	280	280	280	280
Private Sector	140	140	140	140	140
Other	0	0	0	0	0
Emergencies	192	190	190	190	190
TOTAL INCOME	1,160	1,198	1,195	1,212	1,230
EXPENDITURES					
Program Assistance	900	925	925	932	942
Program Support	230	243	252	260	268
TOTAL EXPENDITURES	1,130	1,168	1,177	1,192	1,210
Income less Expenditures	30	30	18	20	20
Movements noncash assets/liabilities	30	8	-9	-9	-9
Year-end cash balance					
Convertible currencies	479	517	526	537	548
Nonconvertible currencies	8	8	8	8	8
TOTAL CASH BALANCE	$ 487	$ 525	$ 534	$ 545	$ 556

Source: UNICEF MTSP, November 7, 2002.

into the above-mentioned priorities as follows: 15 percent for girls education, 36 percent for integrated early childhood development, 24 percent for immunization "plus," 7 percent for HIV/AIDS, 14 percent for child protection, and 4 percent for other programs. Key to its effort to promote these organizational priorities, UNICEF planned to use information, communication, and advocacy to influence the actions of others. UNICEF's MTSP made its goals clear:

> *We will put children at the heart of every agenda and ensure that the voice of children is heard. We will expose disparities, confront discrimination and end violations of children's rights. We will continually develop our knowledge and expertise to create, deliver and inspire solutions. We will maximize the resources devoted to children, both by acting directly and by building powerful alliances to force action and change.*

The majority of UNICEF's top management believed that two factors made UNICEF unique:

1. UNICEF was mandated by the United Nations and had global agreement with governments about its strategy and frameworks. "We are a multilateral agency that works at all levels," said Anupama Rao Singh, one of the deputy directors of headquarters' (HQ's) program division. "Our success is that we have privileged access and relationships with local governments."

2. UNICEF was firmly anchored in the developing countries in which it operated, and the organization's rigorous approach and integrity allowed it to be a player in all countries. "This is our core competence," commented Cecilia Lotse, director of HQ's program funding office. "Even if our

environment changes, UNICEF must maintain its competitive advantage in the field." Omar Abdi, deputy director of HQ's program division, expanded on this idea: "The strength of UNICEF is in the field. Programs are decentralized and developed at the local level. The difference between UNICEF and NGOs [nongovernmental organizations] is that we have lengthy track records in many countries and unique access to a range of partners."

Increasing focus on advocacy. UNICEF's advocacy work was both national and global in scope. National advocacy work was considered an inherent part of the field programs. "These two missions are different sides of the same coin," said Philip O'Brien, regional director for the CEE/CIS[1] region. "For example, in Albania our field programs and analysis resulted in policy changes at the national level." Global advocacy work was based on extensive data and research gathered by the field offices and compiled by UNICEF's research arm in Florence, resulting in major studies with a global effect. For example, "Adjustment with a Human Face," which was fairly controversial when published, and "Children on the Frontline" were both part of UNICEF's global advocacy work.

Being an international organization financed in large part by voluntary contributions from individual governments did, however, create a certain conflict for UNICEF's advocacy work. "We have a responsibility to be the world advocate for children," O'Brien explained, "but there is a tension inherent with any government that is a major partner. We can never become an organization like Human Rights Watch because we are an intergovernmental body. We can have the same message, but we will say it in a different way."

"We might be criticized for not speaking out against certain governments," Abdi added, "but we have the kind of access that most other organizations do not have, and we use that special privilege to challenge governments behind the scenes when we feel it is necessary."

Organizational Structure.

In 2002, UNICEF was a subsidiary body of the General Assembly, reporting through the U.N. Economic and Social Council, and an integral part of the United Nations. It maintained its own staff and facilities and was financed by its own sources, received as voluntary contributions from governments, intergovernmental agencies, NGOs, and individuals. UNICEF was governed by a thirty-six-member executive board, members of which were elected by the Economic and Social Council and served a three-year term.

UNICEF comprised an HQ in New York, eight regional offices, 126 country offices worldwide, offices in Tokyo and Brussels that supported fund-raising, a research center based in Florence, and a supply operation based in Copenhagen. Thirty-seven National Committees, based mostly in industrialized countries, raised funds and spread awareness about the organization's mission and work. (See **Exhibit 4** for UNICEF's organizational chart.)

The role of HQ was to provide overall strategic direction and guidance and lead the development of the global UNICEF perspective by integrating the experiences and contributions of all parts of the UNICEF system.

Seven regional offices provided guidance, support, oversight, and coordination to the country field offices, and one regional office (Europe) served as the focal

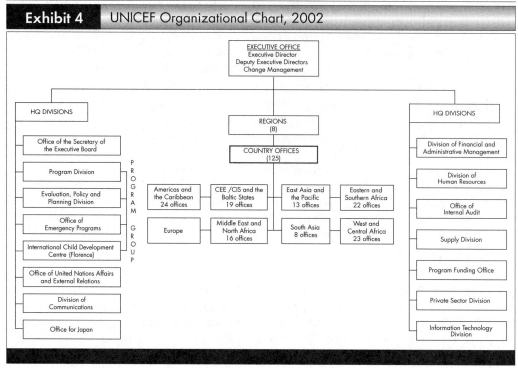

Exhibit 4   UNICEF Organizational Chart, 2002

Source: UNICEF Communications Division.

point for relations with the National Committees for UNICEF. Regional offices also provided technical support to the field, and each region had a management team that met twice a year to develop regional strategies and share best practices.

The field offices supported the planning, implementation, and monitoring of country programs in collaboration with national governments. In recent years, UNICEF had pushed for increased financial decentralization, giving field offices more accountability and responsibility for their budgets. From the broad strategies developed in the MTSP, countries developed their operational plans and, every year, annual work plans were submitted, along with country reports, to both the regional offices and HQ. The program division was responsible for defining the criteria for unrestricted country allocations and establishing the planning ceilings for programs in field offices. Country ceilings were determined by three criteria: child mortality, per capita income, and absolute number of children under the age of five. These unrestricted funds were used to support a five-year program in each country.

National Committees. The National Committees' main task was to raise funds from private donations, but they also played a role in advocacy, communication, and education. National Committees were separate legal entities and NGOs that had a standard agreement with UNICEF, similar to that of a franchise, enabling them to use the UNICEF logo. In exchange, they were required to provide, on average, 75 percent of their gross revenues to UNICEF, although some variations existed, with countries such as Japan and Germany providing 85 percent and 90 percent, respectively, and smaller Eastern European countries around 25 percent. (See **Exhibit 5** for details of contributions from National Committees.)

| Exhibit 5 | National Committee Contributions, 1998 |

National Committee	Proceeds to UNICEF ($000s)	Performance Index[a]	Fund-raising as % of Total Proceeds
San Marino	$ 82	9.11	NA
Netherlands	41,060	7.05	87%
Luxembourg	1,849	6.82	51
Slovenia	1,296	4.60	22
Hong Kong	6,573	4.22	93
Switzerland	15,856	3.51	67
Spain	22,581	2.73	53
Greece	4,258	2.40	49
Portugal	3,316	2.12	39
Belgium	7,630	1.96	69
Estonia	106	1.54	0
Germany	47,362	1.42	68
France	30,597	1.38	58
Italy	22,092	1.33	52
Finland	2,218	1.21	50
Austria	6,589	1.20	54
Bulgaria	164	1.17	0
Japan	76,490	1.10	82
Slovakia	310	1.09	23
Ireland	855	0.91	76
United Kingdom	15,025	0.85	89
Austria	2,629	0.80	61
Denmark	2,019	0.76	24
Lithuania	90	0.75	0
Canada	5,569	0.64	0
Sweden	2,051	0.61	51
Norway	1,196	0.52	7
Hungary	304	0.46	5
Rep. Korea	2,738	0.39	74
New Zealand	308	0.36	100
Czech Republic	270	0.35	17
Turkey	971	0.33	4
Latvia	26	0.31	0
Poland	529	0.26	3
United States	21,600	0.19	70
Israel	NA	9.11	0
Andorra	NA	NA	NA

Source: UNICEF internal documents.

[a]National Committees with a performance index over 1.0 generate above-average proceeds for their countries, controlling for both population size and GNP per capita.

Each National Committee had a board of directors drawn from civil society, with line management reporting to these boards. "The caliber of the board is vital," commented Steve Woodhouse, director of the Geneva regional office. "There is a direct correlation between the success of a National Committee and the strength of its board." UNICEF HQ maintained the power to close down a National Committee by withdrawing recognition and use of the logo. This had occurred several times in the past.

Funding.

UNICEF derived its income entirely from voluntary contributions from two main sources: governments and intergovernmental organizations, and nongovernmental private sector groups and individuals. In 2001, the former accounted for 64 percent of UNICEF's total income of $1.2 billion and the latter for 33 percent. Regular resources (core funds) were unrestricted funds used to support country programs and finance the management and administration of UNICEF; other funds were resources restricted for special projects. (See **Exhibit 6** for a breakdown of UNICEF income by major donor country.) In 2001, regular resources made up 45 percent of contributions and had been shrinking as a percentage of total contributions (down from 55 percent in 1999), causing some concern within the organization. Ellen Yaffe, UNICEF's chief financial officer, summarized as follows:

> *UNICEF's key challenge is the decline in core income. Further declines seem likely, and this will restrict our ability to manage long-term projects and maintain operational field offices. If our field capabilities are eroded because the unrestricted funds, which are used to maintain these offices and our field staff, decline, then our ability to manage the growing restricted funds will also be jeopardized, and our business model will have to change. If we essentially become a contractor for donors of restricted funds, which by the way are much more cumbersome to manage, our relationship with local governments will also change, and we may not have the same ability to conduct our advocacy work.*

Private sector funds. In 2001, National Committees contributed 33 percent of UNICEF's total income, with fund-raising as the prime income driver as compared with the more established greeting card sector. The larger committees had more than a million regular supporters. Although net revenues from greeting cards in 1991 still represented 80 percent of private sector funds, they represented less than 20 percent in 2001. A fairly wide variation existed among countries, with the poorer countries still deriving a higher proportion of revenues from greeting card sales. In 2002, the private sector division at HQ had 200 dedicated staff members focused on product development and selecting lines of greeting cards, marketing, and fund-raising support.

Many National Committees oversaw highly professional fund-raising organizations, often relying heavily on direct mailings. National Committees assured 80 percent of

Exhibit 6	Sources of UNICEF 2002 Income by Major Donor Country					
Country	Government Regular (US$000s)	Per Capita Contribution ($)	Government Other (US$000s)	National Committee Regular (US$000s)	Per Capita Contribution ($)	National Committee Other (US$000s)	TOTAL (US$000s)
Australia	$ 2,625	$0.14	$ 6,853	$ 64	$0.003	$ 2,463	$ 12,006
Belgium	3,131	0.31	6,652	2,841	0.28	2,056	14,681
Canada	8,599	0.28	29,626	461	0.02	5,273	43,951
Denmark	22,456	4.22	8,250	1,625	0.31	408	32,739
Finland	10,480	2.03	3,276	2,101	0.41	1,834	17,691
France	6,631	0.11	1,732	18,156	0.31	7,370	33,889
Germany	3,870	0.05	610	28,620	0.35	30,411	63,616
Italy	11,621	0.20	24,758	21,352	0.37	6,749	64,480
Japan	25,596	0.20	72,007	66,332	0.52	21,648	185,592
Netherlands	31,744	2.00	37,062	24,928	1.57	8,241	101,975
Norway	34,510	7.72	29,805	835	0.19	90	65,240
Spain	1,606	0.04	140	12,923	0.32	9,740	24,409
Sweden	29,748	3.36	30,358	1,306	0.15	1,078	62,490
Switzerland	9,551	1.33	1,759	7,103	0.99	3,256	21,715
United Kingdom	24,638	0.41	49,244	8,093	0.14	14,465	96,440
United States	109,758	0.39	106,619	9,463	0.03	36,560	262,456

Source: UNICEF Annual Report, 2002.

fund-raising costs, and activities were by and large decentralized. HQ provided know-how, guidelines, and support as well as investment funds to promising fund-raising or marketing projects. "Being able to provide seed capital for certain projects gives us some leverage with the National Committees," explained Rudolf Deutekom, director of the private sector division.

UNICEF's typical donor was a woman forty-five to sixty-five years old. In 2002, UNICEF fund-raising efforts in addition to direct mail focused on committed giving and legacy development. "Part of our big challenge," Deutekom added, "is that most of our volunteers are now over fifty years old. Even though we have great brand awareness, if we continue to reach out through our traditional constituencies, we will have a hard time changing our image or attracting new donors."

In 2002, UNICEF and its National Committees were facing increased competition, particularly from child-sponsorship organizations such as Save the Children and World Vision. In Canada, for example, World Vision had raised $200 million in 2001, whereas UNICEF had raised only $25 million. "We are often viewed as being part of the United Nations," Deutekom commented, "rich and not cost conscious."

An important part of the private sector division's work was the management of corporate partnerships and alliances. Through the National Committees, UNICEF had, over the previous twenty years, built ties with corporations and businesses throughout the world (see **Exhibit 7** for an overview of UNICEF's key corporate partnerships in 2002). "The key is to tap into the logistical resources of a partner and use an indirect approach to cobranding, more of an association of brands, in fact," Deutekom said. "The best partnerships are with insurance or financial services companies because they represent a low risk for UNICEF. Other good partnerships involve promotional projects, where point-of-sale materials make a reference to UNICEF and we get a percentage of proceeds." A coordinating committee, made up of top executives at HQ, reviewed all major international proposals, and by August 2002, UNICEF had screened more than 850 companies in three years and approved close to 200 while typically managing 120 alliances at any point. (See **Exhibit 8** for results of the corporate partnerships and alliances program.)

UNICEF had developed selection guidelines for the National Committees based on two guiding principles: find the best ally, and find the best alliance. Two steps were taken to determine whether a corporation was the best ally for UNICEF. First, UNICEF had to undertake research and conduct due diligence on the potential ally. Second, UNICEF evaluated the potential partner against UNICEF's mission, mandate, and brand values. The best alliance involved a strong corporate fit with UNICEF's values, program, advocacy, and fund-raising goals. Certain sectors were considered unacceptable: armaments and weapons makers, toy manufacturers selling imitation weapons, alcohol and tobacco companies, companies employing child labor, and companies involved in pornography. Any companies that violated U.N. sanctions, or those found in violation of environmental laws, were also excluded. In addition, UNICEF never endorsed products, goods, or services and would not grant sector exclusivity to any company.

In 2002, UNICEF entered into a partnership with McDonald's in North America that, apart from a significant cash donation, consisted of the distribution, through McDonald's franchises, of trick-or-treat "Change for UNICEF" collection boxes. The partnership was driven by the U.S. National Committee, which had a strong ongoing

Exhibit 7	UNICEF's Key Corporate Partnerships in 2001	

Program	Description	Impact
Change for Good on International Airlines	For more than a decade passengers have donated change.	In 2001, the program raised $37.4 million.
Procter & Gamble	"Clean up for kids"/trick-or-treat for UNICEF	$550,000
Pier 1	Largest seller of UNICEF cards	$1.5 million in 2001 in the U.S.
MobiNil (Egypt)	Three-day promotional sale of mobile phones	Percentage of proceeds to UNICEF
MasterCard	Use of credit card at defined times	Percentage of proceeds to UNICEF
Ta-Ta (Uruguay supermarket chain)	Fund-raising campaign at checkout	One peso per customer at checkout
Amway	Purchase of UNICEF Christmas cards	0.5 million cards in 2001 ($200,000)
Aeon (Japan)	Promotions, customer and employee campaigns	$845,000 (2001)
Diners Club International	Affinity card in Ecuador	$100,000 (2001)
Esselunga (supermarket chain in Italy)	Matched donations of customers	$220,000 (2001)
Fater (JV between Angelini and P&G)	Promotion linked to the sale of Pampers	$120,000 (2001)
FTSE International	FTSE4Good Index/license fees	$500,000 (by end 2001)
IKEA	Code of conduct and financial support	
Manchester United (football club)	"United for UNICEF"	$1.5 million (2001)

Source: UNICEF Annual Report, 2002, and published sources.

relationship with McDonald's but had the potential for fund-raising in other countries. Once approved, global partnerships were open to all countries, but given resistance from some National Committees, particularly in Europe, HQ allowed an opt-out to the McDonald's partnership, which most National Committees chose to take. To publicize the partnership, McDonald's published a photograph of the secretary-general of the United Nations and the executive director of UNICEF with the CEO of McDonald's. The media and the NGO community reacted negatively. Deutekom summarized the effect and next steps for UNICEF as follows:

> Corporate partnerships will continue to grow, but the McDonald's experience will slow us down and make us more stringent in our requirements. Going forward, we will be even more careful about any partnership that suggests UNICEF is endorsing a product or a service. Note, however, that in spite of its growth potential and visible role, corporate alliances still only represent about 10 percent of all funding. Our main source of revenue, therefore, is still heavily secured through and by individual donors, i.e., the general public.

Exhibit 8	Review of UNICEF's Corporate Partnership and Alliance Program

7/98 through 8/02 Worldwide	Number	US$ Million (estimated total benefits to UNICEF)
Number of proposals reviewed	222	$64
Number of proposals approved	193	57
Number of proposals declined	15	4
Number of proposals in process	14	3

Number of proposals submitted for review 7/98 through 8/02	By National Committees	By Field Offices
1998	5	18
1999	9	31
2000	15	40
2001	20	42
2002	24	19

Approved Alliances by Type, 2001	US$000s	Approved Alliances by Industry Sector	US$000s
Customer fund-raising	$5,600	Banking and finance	$1,630
Events and sponsorship	4,050	Soaps, cosmetics	720
Promotional licensing	3,100	Telecommunications	510
On-product promotional licensing	400	Diversified financials	500
Employee fund-raising	150	Food and drug chains	430
Cash donation	90	Other retail	310
Licensed-product royalties	20	Media	220
		Beverage	220
		Pharmaceuticals	200
		Food	150
		Health care	120
		Automotive	100
		Other	100

Source: Internal documents.

Key Challenges Facing UNICEF.

Positioning the organization. Some top UNICEF executives worried that the increasing rights-based focus of the organization would stretch its capabilities too thin and possibly dilute the organization's effect. Specifically, previous programs focused on children in the first five years of life, but in 2002, programs covered children from birth through adolescence. In addition, two human rights principles promised to extend UNICEF's potential scope. Rights were considered universal, so the focus of programs could no longer be solely on developing nations. In addition, rights were considered indivisible, which brought into play a whole spectrum of rights (the right to access to health, education, safety, and so on). "In the past," Abdi said, "our reputation was built on immunization and education programs, and our impact was clearly measurable. In the advocacy arena, how do we measure and communicate our results?"

Other executives highlighted UNICEF's unique position and role. UNICEF was in essence part NGO and also part of the U.N. system. The organization differed from NGOs in that its mandate came from the United Nations, giving UNICEF a unique legitimacy with member governments and access to discuss sensitive issues such as the reform of national legal systems for protecting children's rights. The disadvantages, however, were that states and governments were very protective of sovereignty and resistant to change. "Consensus building takes time and is challenging," Singh said. "Right now, there is a sense of cynicism towards the U.N. system, although UNICEF has an advantage in that we focus on children, which is less contentious than other issues."

Global funds. In 2002, there was a continued shift toward an increasing number of bilateral development agreements, with developing countries increasingly wanting to drive their own development agendas. This drove the creation of "global funds" for specific sectors and areas, and donors were asked to participate directly with these funds. The global funds were, by definition, restricted, and the question for many UNICEF executives was how UNICEF would adapt to these changes. Lotse explained, "UNICEF ends up acting like a conduit or channel for these earmarked funds. We are asked to help at the local level to play a management role, but we want to be more than a consultant." Yaffe expanded on this idea: "For example, in one country, the World Bank might like the program UNICEF was doing in the area of education, and they would give money to the government's global education fund. The government would then turn around and give the money to UNICEF to manage, effectively becoming UNICEF's boss."

The rise in global funds was therefore directly linked to the decrease in general, or unrestricted, funds. Yaffe worried that the decrease in unrestricted funds would reduce income predictability and affect existing field operations. Singh was also concerned: "Because of our work we have a presence on the ground at the community level which represents experiential learning that has been built over time. The concern is that we may not have the same comparative advantage if we don't have funds to maintain this presence."

REBRANDING UNICEF.

UNICEF Brand Image and Research.

Research interviews conducted between 1999 and 2002, both externally and internally, revealed the following trends. Externally, although the UNICEF image was positive, the organization appeared distant, institutional, cold, and rigid. Like other bureaucracies, UNICEF was seen as a necessary but cumbersome institution that had a role but no longer projected leadership and hope. UNICEF was regarded as worthy but inefficient, important but not current. The communications team thought the UNICEF brand was living off the past and not providing a vision for the future.

UNICEF had changed its logo and emblem twice in the past: once in 1960, after the United Nations adopted the Declaration of the Rights of the Child, and once in 1985/1986 to celebrate UNICEF's fortieth anniversary. (See **Exhibit 9** for a pictorial history of the UNICEF logo.) In 2002, UNICEF and its National Committees were using a wide variety of different logos, emblems, and taglines in different countries. (See **Exhibit 10** for an overview of some of the different logos and taglines being used in 2002.) "It is very important for UNICEF to have just one look," explained Kjersti Gjestvang, secretary general of the Norwegian National Committee. "At this point, each National Committee has done its own branding exercise and developed a slightly different approach, but that dilutes our brand, and we need to get behind a single image."

Exhibit 9 Pictorial History of UNICEF Logo

1946

1960

1985

Source: UNICEF Communications Division.

Exhibit 10 Overview of Different Logos and Straplines Used in 2002

Source: UNICEF Communications Division.

In 1999, Censydiam Worldwide conducted market research on UNICEF's logo and positioning in four countries: Japan, Germany, France, and Italy. The common public perception was that UNICEF was a well-structured, competent organization that took care of children in poor countries in the areas of health, food, housing, and clothing and focused on the long term. UNICEF's vocation was clear, but many people were confused about how and where UNICEF realized its objectives. UNICEF appeared too abstract, vague, and uncontrollable. The link with the United Nations gave an impression of solidity, trust, and credibility but also caused UNICEF to seem distant and bureaucratic. Hardly anyone knew that UNICEF stood for United Nations Children's Fund, but most had the impression that UNICEF was centrally organized with a strong link to the United Nations. There was no awareness that each country had its own National Committee. The term "committee" was also perceived as creating distance and associated with more administration. The term "fund," however, was found to imply raising money and came across as more friendly and flexible.

Spontaneous recognition of the logo was generally vague. Aspects that were remembered included the blue color, the mother and child symbol, and sometimes the globe. The logo was thought by some to project a message of warmth and care. To others, it depicted UNICEF as stable and reliable but also strict. The logo came across as authoritative without being dominant but was also considered old-fashioned. There was a general preference for lowercase letters rather than capital letters.

In 1999, UNICEF conducted a survey in Norway and found that, although UNICEF's brand recognition (prompted awareness) was high, only 13 percent of the Norwegian adult population knew that UNICEF worked with children, whereas 24 percent were able to spontaneously mention UNICEF as one of the organizations selling greeting cards. In the same survey, respondents were also asked to rate issues people were facing in developing countries (such as hunger, health, education, etc.) in terms of importance. In 1999, only 46 percent of respondents rated the lack of education as a very important issue, compared with 84 percent for hunger, 81 percent for children in need, 77 percent for war, and 63 percent for HIV/AIDS. UNICEF was seen as a leader in education and, consequently, Gjestvang focused communication efforts on education. A new survey conducted in 2001 revealed that UNICEF's spontaneous brand awareness had increased significantly to 36 percent versus 15 percent in 1999, and that 21 percent of the Norwegian population now recognized that UNICEF worked for children. Funds raised over this period went from 10 million krone ($1.3 million) in 1999 to 27 million krone ($3.5 million) in 2002.

In 2001, UNICEF Canada also conducted a brand audit, which revealed that all child-focused organizations were struggling for consumer donations and most consumers did not easily differentiate between them. UNICEF Canada's communication materials were found to be informative but too ponderous, with no unified UNICEF look or tagline and no communication piece that spoke directly to donors. Internally, employees and volunteers thought that UNICEF should be known as the advocate for children and that the image needed to become more modern, aggressive, and proactive. UNICEF's name was well known, but its work was not. In donor focus groups, participants were unclear about the purpose of UNICEF and what differentiated it from the major child-focused NGOs. The concept of children's rights was not well understood. Some perceived UNICEF as a "fat cat" and funded by the United Nations. The current brand footprint was found to be traditional, unassuming, and principled, but the ideal brand footprint needed to be confident, effective, and compassionate.

Internal Branding Workshops and Focus Groups.

Phase one. In July 2000, the advertising agency TBWA conducted more than 100 questionnaires and face-to-face interviews across the entire UNICEF organization. The interviews generated insights into staff perceptions of UNICEF's strengths and weaknesses. (UNICEF's perceived strengths and weaknesses resulting from these interviews are summarized in **Exhibit 11**.)

In August 2000, TBWA helped UNICEF design a branding workshop with fifteen key UNICEF individuals from the field, HQ, and the National Committees, split into two groups, to explore the brand essence. Internal discussions about the difference between a children's-rights organization and a children's charity were initially very important. "Some people believed that people who are starving don't worry about dignity," Newman-Williams said. "Others responded that the thing people in refugee camps worry about the most is their dignity." The first day of the workshop, two groups worked in parallel to develop a series of working definitions of UNICEF's vision, mission, and positioning, outlined below:

- *Vision:* To be the passionate driving force that builds, with children, a better world in which every child's right to dignity, security, and self-fulfillment is achieved.

- *Mission:* We will put children at the heart of every agenda and ensure that the voice of children is heard worldwide. We will expose disparities, confront discrimination, and work to end violations of children's rights. We will continually develop our knowledge and expertise to create, deliver, and

Exhibit 11	UNICEF Perceived Strengths and Weaknesses

Perceived Strengths	Perceived Weaknesses
• Reputation and track record	• Task too big to deal with
• Being global	• Bureaucracy
• Focused on children	• Rift between HQ and field/National Committees
• Unique mandate from governments	• Elephant (slow and inflexible)
• Powerful international force via U.N. agency status	• Old-fashioned (aging in style, image, supporter base)
• No political or religious affiliations	• Too diplomatic
• Dedicated staff	• Lack of public faith in the U.N. system
• Intellectual leadership	• Internally poor communicator (no shared direction)
• Field program (action, not just words)	• Externally poor communicator (messages too complex and academic)
• Decentralization	• Competition with clearer, sharper messages
• Logo	

Source: Summarized from UNICEF internal interviews and workshops.

inspire solutions. We will maximize the resources devoted to children both by acting directly and by building powerful alliances to force action and change.

- *Positioning:* For people who want to make a lasting difference, UNICEF is the champion of rights for all the world's children, with the authority, knowledge, and resources to get things done.

The second day, the two groups worked toward a brand profile for UNICEF made up of rational and emotional values. TBWA defined rational values as those appealing to the consumer's head ("gives consumers something to buy") and emotional values as those appealing to the heart ("gives consumers something to buy into"). The agreed-upon profile of the combined groups was as follows:

- Rational values: principled, leading, credible, influential, innovative, "gets things done"

- Emotional values: passionate, courageous, inspirational, visionary, loving, and wired

The two groups were also asked to develop a brand essence that "encapsulates how consumers connect with the brand, represents the core—heart, sole, spirit, DNA—of the brand, and illustrates how UNICEF would want consumers to think and feel about the brand." TBWA cautioned that the brand essence was not "a reflection of current consumer attitudes, short term in its approach, just brand personality and character or an advertising proposition." Four components were used to build the brand essence: form, personality, differentiation, and authority. (The resulting brand essence is presented in **Exhibit 12**.)

Follow-up work with TBWA combined this brand essence with the above definitions of vision, mission, positioning, and rational and emotional values and resulted in the UNICEF brand model depicted in **Exhibit 13**. The brand model was seen as central to the MTSP, communication strategy, and all future communication plans, including those for fund-raising.

In June 2001, UNICEF's division of communications summarized the results of the branding exercise in an internal presentation as follows:

> *What do we mean by the UNICEF brand? We mean the organization, its reputation, and everything it does and stands for. Everything we do contributes to building the UNICEF brand and builds trust in the organization. Whatever the nature of the interaction with UNICEF, a common personality should be evident, a sort of DNA that runs through everything we do: in our policies, programs, and operations, in our relationship with donors, partners, and suppliers, and in the way we recruit, manage, and develop our staff.*

Phase two. In November 2001, the brand agency Wolff Olins was retained to develop UNICEF's information architecture and the organization's key message. It proposed a communication framework consisting of three elements—issue, action, and impact—and a UNICEF identity that included guidelines on imagery, voice, layout grids, color palate, typeface, a new tagline, and a modified logo. (See **Exhibit 14** for proposed the new logo emblem, tagline, and color scheme compared with those of the existing identity.)

Exhibit 12 UNICEF Brand Essence, 2001

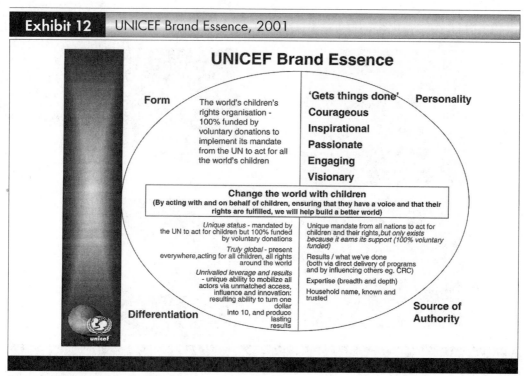

Source: UNICEF Communications Division.

Exhibit 13   UNICEF Brand Model, 2001

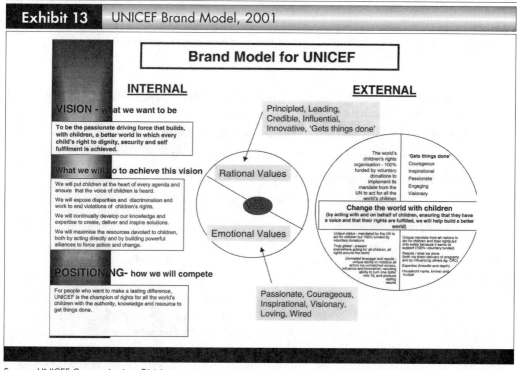

Source: UNICEF Communications Division.

Exhibit 14 Proposed New Logo Emblem and Color Scheme

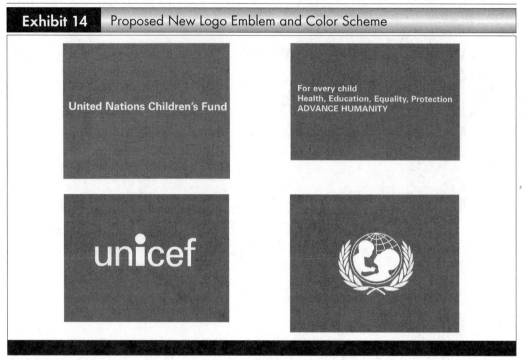

Source: UNICEF Communications Division.

As part of the new brand toolkit, which combined all the elements of the proposed new identity, a number of changes were proposed:

- Initially, it was suggested that the mother and child emblem be removed, but this was later changed to suggesting that the emblem and logo be separated.
- The proposed tagline was "For every child, health, education, equality, protection. Advance Humanity."
- The central "I" in the UNICEF logo should be made more dominant.
- UNICEF should adopt a more vibrant cyan blue color.

Reactions to the Rebranding Process and Toolkit.

Overall, the first phase of the rebranding exercise was well received internally. Most executives recognized the need for revitalizing the brand and believed the development of the brand essence and brand model had been worthwhile. Abdi commented, "Brand is important in the field because of increasing clutter. Being able to differentiate the brand can really help you get attention from customers, governments, and populations."

"As we move towards a rights-based approach, the organization needs a sense of common values and ethics," Singh said. "The values dimension of the brand model could be a great unifying force for UNICEF, but the challenge seems to be internal communication. We need everyone down the line to understand the brand essence." Gjestvang added, "The brand essence was excellent, and I recently saw a version of it in a recruitment slide, so I think it has been well adopted by the entire UNICEF organization."

Many executives thought that the second phase of the branding exercise had not been fully understood within UNICEF and that too much focus was being placed on the logo and the emblem. The suggested changes presented in the brand toolkit stimulated widespread comment, the last part of the "Advance Humanity" tagline and the issue of separating the logo from the mother and child emblem prompting the strongest reactions. "The second consultant that was used," explained Jacques Hintzy, president of the French National Committee, "did not take into account the excellent work that was done before on the brand model. The tagline was perceived as pretentious, and abandoning the mother and child symbol met with a lot of resistance. The process to date has been successful; it is now just the design phase that is a problem. It is an execution issue rather than a philosophical concern."

"The National Committees felt that their views had not been taken into account in the second phase," Woodhouse explained. "Separating the signature from the emblem particularly caused grave concern, and the tagline was considered too long." Abdi said, "When I was a child growing up in Mogadishu, there was an area in the city known as UNICEF. It was associated with services that were delivered there, and the symbol was the sign that everyone recognized, particularly if they couldn't read. The explicit link to the U.N. through the mother and child symbol is critical." Some thought the tagline had too much of a U.S. focus and would not work in other cultures. Others thought that there was nothing unique about "Advance Humanity" and that the general public would not link it especially to UNICEF. Still others thought "equality" was not easily measurable and was more of an aspirational goal. Gjestvang expanded on the second phase of the brand exercise: "In the development of the toolkit, the feedback from the field and National Committees was not taken into account. I felt more like a hostage than a participant. I am concerned about the tagline because if we say that we advance humanity, it sounds like bragging, and we will put off potential partners."

Newman-Williams acknowledged the above arguments but urged that in certain moments in UNICEF's history the organization had gone against the tide and advanced its mission:

> "Advance Humanity" is another example. Our donor base is bolder on these issues than we think they are. UNICEF executives have a low tolerance for external consultants and tend to become nervous when confronted by unfamiliar marketing speak. The risk is that the central purpose gets lost. The process has been challenging. There have been a lot of different opinions and influences. And the logo redesign is a real stretch for everyone, especially the National Committees.

In early 2002, the National Committees had raised concerns about the logo to the executive board, and it had become a highly political issue. "This organization operates on consensus," Newman-Williams added, "and ultimately you're changing the way the organization behaves. Implementation will be the critical part of the whole rebranding process."

Three UNICEFs. Some executives thought there were three distinct groups within UNICEF: the HQ staff, the National Committees, and the field offices. UNICEF had three corresponding roles as a children's-rights organization, a fund-raiser in developed countries, and an implementer of field programs in developing countries. Considered the bolder and more long-term-focused part of UNICEF, HQ staff was sometimes thought to be wrapped up in ideology, with concepts that were too cerebral to be understood by the general public. The National Committees and field offices were thought to be slower to embrace change and more short term in perspective. The older National Committees were considered part of the old guard and were thought to be particularly resistant to change. "These three UNICEFs each see the brand in different ways," Deutekom commented. "Their roles are all slightly different and so are their messages and target audiences."

Testing the new brand identity. In August 2002, the Sofres market research company was retained to evaluate the new brand identity. Consumer focus groups were carried out in France and the United States, and exploration of the current logo revealed that the emblem was critical. Some thought the laurel leaves were old-fashioned or represented wheat. The logo was well liked for its lowercase font. Without the emblem, the logo was found to be cold, rigid, and bureaucratic. The descriptor (United Nations Children's Fund) evoked limited recall but did bring into focus the link to the United Nations and the organization's target: children.

Initial reactions to the new brand identity as a whole were that the changes were not noticed much. The new brand identity seemed to function but did not bring any real changes or evolution. The cyan blue color and larger "I" were noticed the most, but most people did not decode the meaning of the larger "I." It appeared that the descriptor became slightly more prominent alongside the new logo. Different degrees of modernity were associated with the three elements, with the logo perceived as young and dynamic but the emblem perceived as outdated. An analysis of the tagline: "For every child, health, education, equality and protection. Advance Humanity" revealed that "Advance Humanity" was considered pretentious and overpromising. In addition, the word "equality" seemed to some to be unachievable.

Recommendations from the study were the following: keep the logo with the large "I"; always accompany the logo with the emblem but renew the emblem, perhaps by removing the laurel leaves; keep the descriptor unchanged; and consider returning to original dark blue rather than cyan. As for the tagline, the details of the first sentence could be preserved (without reference to equality), but the second sentence needed to be modified.

CONCLUSION.

Newman-Williams was at a crossroads. Should she move ahead with the implementation of the brand toolkit as it stood, with the new color scheme, the larger "I," the unmodified emblem, and the proposed tagline? Or should she attempt to adapt and modify some of the elements of the toolkit, and if so, which ones? Newman-Williams wondered how long further modifications would take and doubted that she would be able to satisfy everyone. She believed the second sentence of the tagline, "Advance Humanity," truly symbolized the new UNICEF and felt strongly that it should remain unchanged. As she prepared for her presentation to the heads of the National Committees and key HQ directors (see **Exhibit 15** for a list of attendees), she wondered what questions would be asked and how she would answer them.

Exhibit 15	List of Attendees of 47th Annual Meeting of National Committees, September 2–4, 2002

National Committees	Participant	Title
Andorra	Mr. Marc Vila Amigo	President
Australia	Ms. Gaye Phillips	Executive Director
Austria	Dr. Martha Kyrle	President
	Dr. Gudrun Berger	Executive Director
Belgium	Mr. Marc Van Boven	Chairman
Bulgaria	Mr. Zdravko Popov	President
	Ms. Jetchka Karaslavova	Executive Director
Canada	Ms. Laura Ludwin	Chairperson
	Mr. David Agnew	President and CEO
Czech Republic	Ms. Pavla Gomba	Executive Director
Denmark	Mr. Ole Kyed	Chairperson
	Mr. Steen Andersen	Executive Director
Estonia	Ms. Elle Kull	President
	Mr. Toomas Palu	Executive Director
Finland	Ms. Astrid Thors	President of the Board
	Mr. Kalle Justander	Senior Adviser, Member of the Board
France	Mr. Jacques Hintzy	President
	Mr. Gilles Paillard	Executive Director
Germany	Mr. Reinhard Schlagintweit	Chairman
	Dr. Deitrich Garlichs	Executive Director
Greece	Ms. Joanna Manganara	Executive Board Member
	Mr. Ilias Liberis	Information, EDev. & Fund-raising Officer
Hong Kong	Mr. Robert Fung	Chairman
	Mr. Matthew Mo	Executive Director
	Ms. Teresa Wong	General Manager, Fund-raising
Hungary	Ms. Edit Kecskeméti	Executive Director
Ireland	Mr. William Early	Chairman
	Dr. Chris Horn	Incoming Chairman
	Ms. Maura Quinn	Executive Director
Israel	Ms. Evi Adams	Board Member & BFHI Coordinator
Italy	Dr. Giovanni Micali	President
	Mr. Giacomo Guerrera	Vice President
	Mr. Roberto Salvan	Executive Director
Japan	Mr. Yoshihisa Togo	Executive Director
South Korea	Ms. Dong-Eun Park	Executive Director
Latvia	Ms. Ilze Doskina	Executive Director
Lithuania	Mr. Jaunius Pusvaskis	Executive Director
New Zealand	Mr. Dennis McKinlay	Executive Director
Norway	Ms. Kjersti Gjestvang	Executive Director
Poland	Mr. Marek Pietkiewicz	Executive Director
Portugal	Mr. Manuel Pina	President
	Ms. Madalena Marçal Grilo	Executive Director
Slovakia	Ms. Veronika Lehotska	President
	Mr. Miroslav Kana	Executive Director
Slovenia	Ms. Andreja Crnak-Meglic	President
	Ms. Maja Vojnovic	Executive Director
	Ms. Zora Tomic	Member of the Executive Board
	Ms. Barbara Volcic-Lombergar	Member of the Executive Board
Spain	Mr. Francisco Gonzalez-Bueno	President
	Ms. Consuelo Crespo	First Vice President
	Mr. Jaime Gonez-Pineda	General Treasurer
	Mr. Victor Soler-Sala	Adviser for International Affairs
Sweden	Mr. Kent Harstedt	Chairperson
	Mr. Ingvar Hjärtsjö	Secretary-General
Switzerland	Mr. Wolfgang Wörnhard	President
	Ms. Elsbeth Müller	Executive Director

Source: UNICEF Communications Division.

Exhibit 15   continued

National Committees	Participant	Title
Turkey	Ms. Ayse Sevinc Soysal	Executive Director
United Kingdom	Sir John Waite	Chairman
	Mr. David Bull	Executive Director
	Ms. Anita Tiessen	Deputy Executive Director, Program
	Mr. William Cottle	Deputy Executive Director, Finance & Services
United States	Mr. Anthony Lake	Vice Chair, Board of Directors
	Mr. Charles Lyons	President

UNICEF Office		
New York Headquarters	Ms. Carol Bellamy	Executive Director
	Ms. Marjorie Newman-Williams	Director, Division of Communications
	Ms. Cecilia Lotse	Director, Program Funding Office
Geneva Regional Office	Mr. Stephen Woodhouse	Regional Director
	Ms. Janet Nelson	Deputy Regional Director
	Mr. Hans Olsen	Chief, Communications Section
	Mr. Ken Maskall	Senior Program Officer
	Ms. Katharina Borchardt	Planning Officer
	Mr. Jean Metenier	Planning Officer
	Mr. Eduardo Rodriguez	Planning Officer
	Ms. Valérie Pascal-Billebaud	Assistant Project Officer
Private Sector Division, Geneva	Mr. Rudolf Deutekom	Director
	Mr. Prom Chopra	Deputy Director, Operation & Finance
	Mr. Per Stenbeck	Deputy Director, Fund-raising
	Mr. Sergio Furman	Marketing Officer
	Mr. Roger Keczkes	Marketing Officer
	Ms. Helene Reymann	Marketing Officer
	Mr. John Winston	Brand Manager
Private Sector Div., New York	Mr. Alejandro Palacios	Chief, International Accounts
India Office	Ms. Maria Calivis	Representative
Support Staff	Mr. Oktavijan Aran	Fund-raising & Sales Assistant
	Ms. Ana Beauclair	Senior Secretary

Source: UNICEF Communications Division.

Notes to Case

[1] CEE = European Economic Community. CIS = Commonwealth of Independent States (former USSR).

CASE 8
CARE USA

In January 2003, Marilyn Grist, senior vice president of external relations for CARE USA, sat at her desk in downtown Atlanta evaluating the success of the organization's new brand, released just one year previously. She reflected on the long process of creating and implementing the new brand and considered what might have been done differently. She knew that CARE faced a number of challenges, including a changing international organizational structure, a shrinking donor pool, and the need to reestablish CARE as part of the American culture. She wondered how best to leverage the new brand to address these issues.

History.

CARE USA was founded in 1945, when twenty-two American organizations came together to distribute lifesaving food packages to survivors of World War II in Europe. In May 1946, the first 20,000 CARE Packages®[1] reached the port of Le Havre, France, and over the following two decades some 100 million additional "CARE Packages" reached people in need, first in Europe and later in Asia and other parts of the developing world. The first CARE Packages were U.S. Army surplus "10-in-1" food parcels, intended to supply ten soldiers with one meal. When these ran out, CARE USA began assembling its own food packages. Initially, individuals in the United States bought packages and sent them to friends and family in Europe. Ten dollars bought a CARE Package and guaranteed that its addressee would receive it within four months. Soon, though, CARE USA was inundated with requests to send CARE Packages to "a hungry occupant of a thatched cottage" or "a schoolteacher in Germany" and expanded its activities accordingly. Later CARE Packages included food for different cultural diets and nonfood items such as tools, blankets, school supplies, and medicines. Although the CARE Packages program had been phased out by the 1980s, it remained a powerful symbol for the organization. (See **Exhibit 1** for an early CARE USA advertisement featuring the CARE Package.)

The acronym "CARE" had not changed, but the meaning behind the words for which the letters stood had evolved with the organization. Originally, CARE had

Professor John Quelch and Research Associate Nathalie Laidler prepared this case. HBS cases are developed solely as the basis for class discussion. Cases are not intended to serve as endorsements, sources of primary data, or illustrations of effective or ineffective management.

Exhibit 1 | Early CARE Advertisement Featuring the CARE Package

CHRISTMAS is not far away for us. But for many families in other lands, Christmas, when it comes, may be just like any other day—full of fatigue and hopelessness and hunger.

You can brighten Christmas for a family abroad by sending a CARE FOOD CRUSADE package. One dollar will send 22 pounds of America's food surplus to a needy family for Christmas. Do it now! Send your dollars to CARE — New York, CARE—San Francisco or your local CARE office.

FOOD CRUSADE PACKAGES MAY NOT BE SENT TO A SPECIFIC INDIVIDUAL OF YOUR CHOICE

Source: CARE USA.

stood for Cooperative for American Remittances to Europe. Subsequently, this was changed to Cooperative for American Relief Everywhere, and in 1993 it changed again, to Cooperative for Assistance and Relief Everywhere, Inc. Over the years, CARE expanded its work to address the world's most threatening problems. In the 1950s, the organization extended its activities into developing countries and used

U.S. surplus food to feed the hungry. In the 1960s, CARE pioneered a number of primary health care programs, and in the 1970s, CARE responded to the massive famines in Africa with both emergency relief and long-term agroforestry projects, integrating environmentally sound tree- and land-management practices with farming programs. In the 1980s, CARE developed microcredit and HIV/AIDS programs, and in the 1990s expanded into basic education. CARE had evolved to work with communities in developing countries on a wide range of programs spanning education, health care, safe water, basic sanitation, and farming and agriculture.

By 2002, CARE was one of the world's largest international humanitarian organizations, committed to helping families in poor communities improve their lives and achieve lasting victories over poverty. CARE worked in sixty-eight countries across Africa, Asia, Europe, Latin America, and the Middle East and had a staff of 12,000, the great majority of whom were citizens of the countries in which CARE ran programs. In fiscal year 2002, ending June 30, CARE USA's total income was just over $427 million, 67 percent of which came from government grants. More than 250,000 individuals, corporations, and foundations supported the organization, and it was estimated that CARE USA had directly improved the lives of 31 million people during 2002. (See **Exhibit 2** for CARE USA's statement of activities.)

Mission and Activities.

CARE believed that every person in the world was entitled to a minimum standard to live in dignity and security, which meant having enough food to eat and clean water to drink; having access to basic health care, basic education, and economic opportunity; and having the ability to participate in decisions affecting one's family and community. CARE sought "a world of hope, tolerance and social justice, where poverty has been overcome and people live in dignity and security." CARE's new mission statement, developed as part of the rebranding process in 2000, was to

> [s]erve individuals and families in the poorest communities in the world. Drawing strength from our global diversity, resources and experiences, we promote innovative solutions and are advocates for global responsibility. We facilitate lasting changes by strengthening capacity for self-help; providing economic opportunity; delivering relief in emergencies; influencing policy decisions at all levels; and addressing discrimination in all its forms.

CARE was guided by the aspirations of local communities and said, "We pursue our mission with both excellence and compassion because the people whom we serve deserve nothing less." CARE worked at the community level but took a "big picture" approach to poverty, going beyond the symptoms to the underlying causes, seeking to tap human potential in a broad range of programs based on empowerment, equality, and sustainability. In 2002, CARE USA allocated 90 percent of its expenses to program activities and 10 percent to support services and fund-raising. Of its programs, 80 percent were community development programs and 20 percent were emergency or rehabilitation programs.

Of CARE USA's $392 million program expenditures for 2002, 40 percent was allocated to Asia, 28 percent to Africa, 22 percent to Latin America and the Caribbean, 6 percent to Europe and the Middle East, and 4 percent to multiregional programs. In addition, program expenses were broken down by different sectors as follows: 26 percent for nutritional support, 32 percent for multisector programs, 15 percent

| Exhibit 2 | CARE USA Consolidated Statement of Activities | | |

$ millions	FY 2000	FY 2001	FY 2002
Public Support			
General purpose	42	43	44
Temporarily restricted	17	22	15
Addition to endowment	0.5	0	0
CARE International	68	60	70
Interest and dividends	4	4	5
Net assets released from restrictions	18	17	19
Satisfaction of program restrictions	(18)	(17)	(19)
TOTAL	131	128	134
Government and Other Support			
U.S. government	251	239	245
Host governments	28	23	22
Others	31	25	20
TOTAL	310	287	287
Other Revenue	5	4	7
TOTAL REVENUES	446	415	421
Expenses			
Programs	409	380	392
Fund-raising	17	18	19
Management and general	16	19	18
Public information	3	3	4
Grants to CARE International	3	2	2
TOTAL EXPENSES	448	422	435
Support (under) / over expenses	(2)	(3)	(7)
Other Changes in Net Assets	(3)	(6)	(11)
TOTAL CHANGE IN NET ASSETS	(5)	(9)	(18)
Net Assets Beginning of Year	215	210	201
Net Assets End of Year	210	201	183

Source: CARE USA annual reports.

Note: Fiscal year runs through June 30.

for agriculture and natural resources, 12 percent for health, 4 percent for water and sanitation, 4 percent for infrastructure, 3 percent for small economic activity development, and 4 percent for basic and girls education. (See **Exhibit 3** for details of CARE USA's program expenses.) Specific accomplishments during fiscal year 2002 included the following:

- More than 1.5 million farmers in forty-three countries were trained in activities relating to agriculture and natural resources, providing long-term solutions to hunger.

- More than 182,000 survivors of war, famine, and natural disasters were provided with emergency assistance, including food, shelter, water, and health care.

- More than 128,000 acres of land in three countries were cleared of land mines, creating safe areas in which families could live and work.

- Nearly 470,000 people in thirty-three countries received basic education, providing the foundation necessary to improve their lives.

| Exhibit 3 | CARE USA Program Expenses FY 2002 |

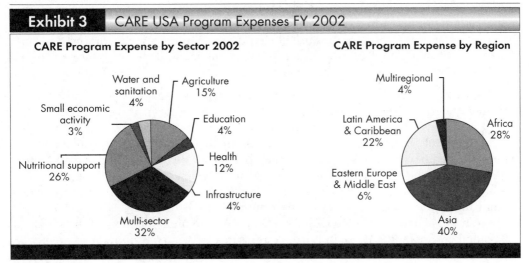

CARE Program Expense by Sector 2002

- Water and sanitation 4%
- Agriculture 15%
- Small economic activity 3%
- Education 4%
- Health 12%
- Nutritional support 26%
- Infrastructure 4%
- Multi-sector 32%

CARE Program Expense by Region

- Multiregional 4%
- Latin America & Caribbean 22%
- Africa 28%
- Eastern Europe & Middle East 6%
- Asia 40%

Source: CARE USA.

- Almost 10 million children in twenty-six countries benefited from child health projects, reducing their vulnerability to disease.

- More than 3 million people in thirty-four countries gained access to clean water and sanitation services, improving health and reducing time spent gathering water.

- More than 785,000 people in thirty-nine countries received training and assistance through projects in credit, savings, and marketing, expanding income-generating skills.

CARE's programmatic strategy for the five years beginning fiscal year 2002 was to focus especially on three key factors affecting poor communities: education, HIV/AIDS, and emergency relief and preparedness. Education was seen as a cornerstone to reducing poverty. By helping children gain the knowledge and skills to succeed, CARE believed that the foundation was laid for healthier, more productive families, communities, and societies. Poverty was both a cause and consequence of HIV/AIDS. CARE armed people with the information and tools to protect themselves and promoted grassroots efforts to mitigate the effects of HIV/AIDS in poor communities. CARE worked with communities to assess the risk of, and prepare for, natural disasters and other emergencies, protecting hard-won victories over poverty.

Organizational Structure and Funding.

CARE International (CI) was a federation of twelve CARE organizations in Australia, Austria, Canada, Denmark, Germany, France, Japan, the Netherlands, Norway, Thailand, the United Kingdom, and the United States. In addition to an International Secretariat in Brussels, there were five regional management units for East and Central Africa, Latin America, South and West Africa, the Middle East and Europe, and Asia—and country offices in each of the sixty-eight countries in which CARE operated field programs. Regional management units coordinated CARE USA activities within particular regions of the world and reported back to CARE USA.

The CI secretariat's role was one of coordination and, increasingly, of arbitration and tracking of individual CI members. In 2001, the secretariat adopted a five-year strategic plan that drove organizational changes such as the use of working groups, made up of members from the different CI members, and the appointment of a smaller, more active international board.

CARE operated on a "lead-member" model, where one of three CI members (the United States, Canada, or Australia) took a leadership role in the management of field programs within a certain country.[2] Lead members were responsible for all program development, program management, financing, and the reporting of activities. CI members that were not lead members acted as fund-raising centers, and their funds were channeled through one of the three lead members, depending on the programs they were financing. For example, in 2002, CARE UK received bilateral funds earmarked for Malawi. These funds flowed through CARE USA to the programs in Malawi, for which CARE USA was the lead member. Most of the smaller CI members, including those in Europe, were uncomfortable with the lead-member model and wanted to be more directly involved in program development and management. In addition, some CI members brought specific program expertise to the federation. For example, CARE UK had expertise in urban programming and CARE Denmark in agriculture and forestry.

In 2002, CARE USA income and expenditures represented more than 65 percent of CI. "CARE USA was historically the 800-pound gorilla within CI," Grist explained. "CARE USA was the original organization, followed by CARE Canada, which was also involved in the distribution of CARE Packages. However, bringing the other CARE countries on board has been a long and laborious process and has required CARE USA to invest substantially in establishing these other CI members." Although each CARE member had the same representation and, in theory, an equal voice within the international federation, many executives conceded that CARE USA strongly influenced the decision-making process at the international level. In addition, some of the European CI members such as CARE France and CARE Germany were perceived as outposts of an American organization by bilateral and European Union donors and struggled to create separate identities as legitimate national organizations.

In early 2003, CI evaluated a number of proposed changes in the way the international organization was structured and operated. The organization wanted to ensure a single CARE presence in each country to avoid confusion and duplication of effort. At the same time, senior management explored organizational options other than the lead-member model. The goal was to establish a shared management structure whereby all members could have a say and a vote in international project operations. It was, however, unclear how best to achieve this. As an experiment, in 2003 it was proposed that the management of the country offices in the Middle East and Europe region report to a single regional manager. This manager in turn reported to an oversight committee composed of representatives of interested CI members. Initially, it was proposed that the regional management units report directly to the International Secretariat, but this was strongly resisted by the lead members. Another experiment, also undertaken in 2003, established regional emergency response units consisting of individuals from each of the CARE member organizations reporting to an emergency response director at the International Secretariat level.

In 2002, the U.S. government provided CARE with more than $159 million in cash, $84 million in agricultural commodities, and nearly $400,000 in nonfood in-kind

contributions, for a total support of nearly $245 million. Host governments pro-
vided more than $19 million in cash and $3 million in nonfood in-kind support. The
United Nations provided an additional $7 million in cash and $1.2 million in agricultural commodities. In addition, other CI members provided more than $68
million in cash and $1.5 million in agricultural commodities (mainly through their
governments). Public support accounted for a further $63 million in cash and
$1 million in nonfood in-kind contributions; combined, this represented only 15
percent of total income, but it was critical for driving other income. (See **Exhibit 4** for
details of CARE sources of support.)

Fiscal year 2002 was one of the most challenging fund-raising years in CARE
USA's history. The sluggish U.S. economy, the weakening of the stock market, and
the events of September 11th, 2001, resulted in the lowest single-quarter amount of
unrestricted revenue in more than seven years in the first quarter of fiscal year 2002.
Almost immediately after September 11th, 2001, the number of gifts received
dropped by 71 percent. In contrast to the typical 1,500 to 3,000 gifts received each
day, on September 28, CARE USA received only five gifts. Grist had developed a set
of aggressive revenue goals for fiscal year 2003. She planned to raise unrestricted
private revenue by 11.7 percent ($53.7 million) and restricted private revenue by
7.8 percent ($18 million) versus revenue raised in fiscal year 2002.[3] In addition, she

Exhibit 4	CARE USA Sources of Support ($ millions)				
Donor	Cash	Agricultural Commodities	Non food In-kind	2002 Total	2001 Total
U.S. government	160	85	0.4	245	239
U.S. direct public support	63	0	1	64	68
CARE Australia	0.6	0	0	0.6	2
CARE Canada	10	0	0	10	12
CARE Denmark	6	0	0	6	7
CARE Germany	2	0	0	2	2
CARE France	1	0	0	1	1
CARE Japan	0.1	0	0	0.1	0.1
CARE Netherlands	7	0	0	7	N/A
CARE Norway	5	0	0	5	5
CARE Austria	2	0	0	2	2
CARE U.K.	35	1	0	36	30
Host governments	19	0	3	22	23
UNHCR	1	0	0	1	2
UNICEF	0.5	0	0	0.5	0.5
WFP	2	1	1	4	3
Other U.N. agencies	3	0	0	3	2
Dutch government	0	0	0	0	5
Luxembourg government	0.1	0	0	0.1	0.3
Swiss government	3	0	0	3	2
World Bank	1	0	0	1	0.5
Other (grants and contracts)	7	0	0	7	8
Other revenue (interest)	7	0	0	7	4
Total FY 2002	336	87	5	428	
Total FY 2001	328	86	5		419

Source: CARE USA Annual Report FY 2002.

Note: UNHCR = United Nations High Commission for Refugees; UNICEF = United Nations Children's Fund;
WFP = World Food Program

proposed to spend $25.1 million to achieve these goals, producing net revenues of $46.6 million. (See **Exhibit 5** for details of CARE USA's external relations division revenue and expenses.)

THE CARE BRAND.

The Need for a New Brand.

Tony Williams, director of brand management and creative production message creation at CARE, described the evolution of CARE USA's activities and brand positioning:

> *Initially CARE was all about CARE Packages. As time went on and the term "care package" became generic, the organization began to expand into self-help programs in developing countries and CARE began to talk about development activities. The messages were simple, reflecting CARE's basic activities in the*

Exhibit 5	CARE External Relations Revenue and Expenses ($ thousands)		
$'000	**FY 2001**	**FY 2002**	**FY 2003 (plan)**
REVENUE			
Unrestricted Revenue			
Direct marketing	22,554	24,213	24,865
Planned giving	7,900	8,229	8,406
Major gifts	10,765	10,254	12,908
Other	5,099	5,843	7,497
Total	46,318	48,539	53,676
Restricted Revenue			
Direct marketing	1,695	1,998	1,768
Planned giving	141	46	0
Major gifts	18,614	11,674	15,277
Other	1,704	1,706	996
Total	22,154	15,424	18,041
Total Revenue			
Direct marketing	24,249	26,211	26,633
Planned giving	8,041	8,275	8,406
Major gifts	29,379	21,928	28,185
Other	6,803	7,549	8,493
Total	68,472	63,963	71,717
EXPENSE			
Fund-raising			
Direct marketing	9,054	9,686	10,501
Planned giving	1,135	1,078	1,292
Major gifts	5,112	4,368	5,129
Other	0	0	1,250
Total	15,301	15,132	18,172
Management and Operations	3,021	3,754	3,863
Public Information	3,002	3,562	3,066
Total	21,324	22,448	25,101
NET REVENUE	47,148	41,515	46,616
Expense to Revenue Ratio	31.1%	35.1%	35%
Net Unrestricted Revenues	25,168	26,520	28,590

Source: CARE External Relations Department.

field. As we entered the 1970s, our field activities became increasingly complex and varied, and our messages and communications began to reflect this increasing diversity. By the early 1990s, the organization was a hodgepodge of activities, and we projected a somewhat confused image.

In 1994, CARE undertook its first logo change and developed a visual identity to help unify the organization at the CI level. The stenciled green logo was developed for CARE's fiftieth anniversary. (See **Exhibit 6** for a reproduction of the old CARE logo and communications style from the fiscal year 1999 annual report.) This effort, however, was not supported by a mission statement or vision and did not take into account any market research.

In January 1998, Grist initiated an international fund-raising and communications working group within CI to address a number of issues facing the organization. "Although CI members were using the green logo, many still included their country name, and there were many inconsistencies in styles and messages throughout the CARE world," she recalled. (See **Exhibit 7** for visual representation.) Although CARE's programming had changed over the years, the picture the public and even many CARE supporters had of what CARE did was vague. There was a gap between perceptions about CARE and the reality of what CARE did. In 1999, CARE therefore conducted focus groups in the United States to understand the donor attrition it had experienced. "We found that there was substantial confusion in the minds of the focus group participants about what CARE did and a lack of connection between the brand image and our fieldwork," Grist explained.

Creating the New Brand.

In 1999, CARE USA retained the pro bono services of McCann-Erickson Worldwide to help develop a brand identity and strategy for CARE. Grist recalled the task:

> *This was a huge pro bono project that took three years and was worth millions of dollars. The people we worked with from McCann-Erickson really became part of the team and took great pride in the work and its results. The first issue we needed to decide on was whether the brand would be developed for use by CARE USA or CI. Joe Plummer, from McCann, and I had to use all our powers of persuasion to bring representatives throughout the whole CARE organization on board. "Brand" was a dirty word back then, and we had to start by explaining what a brand was and why it was important.*

Grist expanded: "This is a very consensus-driven organization. I realized that if there was no joint ownership of the process in developing the brand, it would never work." CARE therefore established a global branding task force comprising eleven members, six from different CI members and five from the field and program divisions.

McCann-Erickson defined the global branding challenge as follows: "To develop a brand strategy that will establish CI as a distinctive, consistent, and relevant global brand—among donors, partners, recipients, and other stakeholders." Initially, as CI first worked to develop a new vision and mission statement, McCann-Erickson acted as a supportive observer. Then McCann-Erickson led the organization through extensive analysis of current communication strategies and market research, developed the brand position, objectives, and footprint, and, with the help of one of its partner agencies, FutureBrand, developed the creative visuals, brand logo, and tagline. "What we discovered," explained Jonathan Louw, one of the international task-force members, "was that managing change within an international organization

Exhibit 6 CARE Stenciled Green Logo and Communication Style, Annual Report 1999

For further information, please contact:

CARE
151 Ellis Street, NE
Atlanta, Georgia 30303-2440
1-800-422-7385
www.care.org

CARE'S REASON FOR BEING IS TO AFFIRM
THE DIGNITY AND WORTH OF INDIVIDUALS
AND FAMILIES IN SOME OF THE POOREST
COMMUNITIES OF THE WORLD.

WE SEEK TO RELIEVE HUMAN SUFFERING,
TO PROVIDE ECONOMIC OPPORTUNITY,
TO BUILD SUSTAINED CAPACITY FOR SELF-HELP,
AND TO AFFIRM THE TIES OF HUMAN
BEINGS EVERYWHERE.

WE ARE COMMITTED TO PURSUING OUR MISSION
WITH EXCELLENCE BECAUSE THE PEOPLE WHOM
WE SERVE, BENEFICIARIES AND DONORS,
DESERVE NOTHING LESS.

Source: CARE USA.

Exhibit 7   CARE Logos and Taglines Throughout the World in 1994

CARE Canada   B.P./P.O. Box 9000   6 Antares   Ottawa K1G 4X6

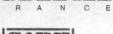

CARE Danmark
Borgergade 14
1300 København K

Telefon 33 15 00 07
Telefax 33 15 39 07

Telex 15928 msdk
Giro   9 51 51 51

CARE DEUTSCHLAND e.V.
Mitglied in CARE INTERNATIONAL
Herbert-Rabius-Straße 24-26 · Postfach 30 03 51
5300 Bonn 3 (Beuel)
Telefax 02 28/9 75 63-51 · Telex 886445 care d
Telefon 02 28/9 75 63-0

F R A N C E   40, Rue de Paradis - 75010 PARIS - Tél. (1) 45 23 22 55 - Fax (1) 45 23 22 56

 ITALIA

Via Lazio, 14 - 00187 ROMA
Tel. (06) 4882427 - 4819571
Fax (06) 4819571
C/C N. 42970 BNL Roma Bissolati
C/C Postale N. 443002 - C.F. 96059630580

ケア　ジャパン
 〒171 東京都豊島区雑司ヶ谷2-3-2
国際援助機関   TEL. 03 (5950) 1335 FAX. 03 (5950) 1375

U-hjelp som nytter!

Verein für Entwicklungszusammenarbeit
Mitglied von CARE International
Spendenkonto: PSK 1236.000
Bankverbindung: Schoeller & Co.
Kto. Nr. 308.802

ÖSTERREICH

Invalidenstraße 11
A - 1030 Wien
Telefon: (0222) 715 0 715 0
Telefax: (0222) 715 9 715
DVR. Nr.: 0504386

660 First Avenue · New York, NY 10016 · (212) 686-3110 · Fax: (212) 686-2467

Source: CARE USA.

was a complex challenge. The politically unbalanced structure of CARE, given the dominance of CARE USA, made multiple buy-in from individual CARE organizations even more difficult."

Vision and mission. In 1999, members of CI convened in Thailand to work with outside facilitators to develop a common vision and mission. "Prior to this," explained Adam Hicks, vice president of marketing and communications for CARE USA, who had previously spent twelve years with Coca-Cola, "CARE was perceived as a generic humanitarian organization. The vision exercise helped us to think big but be specific. We are now clearly positioned as an organization focused on ending poverty." (See **Exhibit 8** for CARE International's vision and mission statements.) Grist believed that establishing the vision and mission up front had been critical for developing a cohesive brand strategy with integrity.

Market research. Between November 1999 and April 2000, McCann-Erickson explored CARE's previous brand-perception research and conducted twenty-nine focus groups in six countries. CARE had low awareness, lacked clear imagery beyond current donors, and was viewed as an empathetic but not particularly effective organization. Focus groups' perceptions were of "a big organization that has been around for a while." Although CARE was perceived as a "good" organization, it was not seen as compelling or distinctive. Perceptions of its warmth and humanity were mostly

Exhibit 8	CARE International's Vision and Mission Statements

VISION

We seek a world of hope, tolerance and social justice, where poverty has been overcome and people live in dignity and security.

CARE International will be a global force and partner of choice within a worldwide movement dedicated to ending poverty. We will be known everywhere for our unshakable commitment to the dignity of people.

MISSION

CARE International's mission is to serve the individuals and families in the poorest communities in the world. Drawing strength from our global diversity, resources and experience, we promote innovative solutions and are advocates for global responsibility. We facilitate lasting change by:

- Strengthening capacity for self-help

- Providing economic opportunity

- Delivering relief in emergencies

- Influencing policy decisions at all levels

- Addressing discrimination in all its forms

Guided by the aspirations of local communities, we pursue our mission with both excellence and compassion because the people whom we serve deserve nothing less.

Source: CARE International.

confined to the Anglophone markets, and even there, associations with the CARE program were fading. Some of the focus groups also compared CARE to the Red Cross and UNICEF. "Our brand inventory appeared shallow and incorrect," Hicks said. "We saw a real weakness compared to some competitor brands; our unaided awareness was 4 percent, and aided awareness stood at 56 percent."

CARE's target donors were identified as "skeptical progressives," typically individuals older than thirty-five, with incomes above $75,000, who were college educated and well traveled. It was estimated that skeptical progressives made up close to 15 percent of the U.S. population. In 2003, CARE's donor portfolio was diverse, and the organization had a broader spectrum of donors than competitors such as Oxfam or World Vision, which tended to attract a certain political or religious group of donors. Some executives believed that this donor diversity was an advantage; others argued that CARE needed to focus on recruiting "true believers" to the CARE vision and mission.

Brand strategy. In May and June of 2000, McCann-Erickson helped develop CI's brand strategy and brand footprint. (See **Exhibits 9** and **10**.) One element of the CARE brand strategy was to "confront the root causes of poverty head on in order to fuel change that matters and lasts, enabling the world's poorest communities to

Exhibit 9	CARE International's Brand Strategy

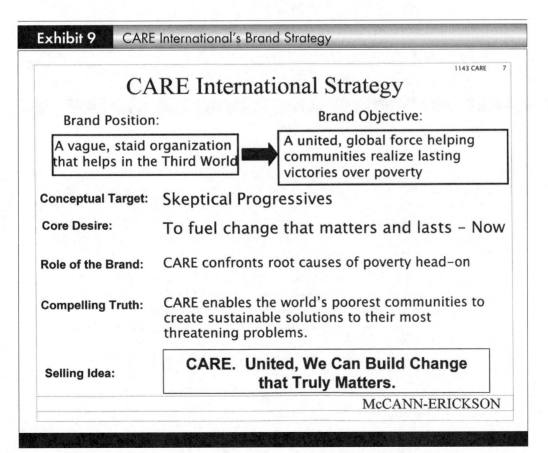

Source: CARE International.

| Exhibit 10 | CARE International's Brand Footprint |

1143 CARE   8

Desired CARE International Brand Footprint

CARE means

- A united global force for the eradication of poverty and its injustices
- Sustainable solutions to root causes of poverty
- Community self-reliance

CARE is

- A Bold Visionary
- Compassionate Strategist
- "In-the-thick of it"

McCANN-ERICKSON

Source: CARE International.

create sustainable solutions to their most threatening problems." McCann-Erickson argued that CARE needed to move from the position of a vague, staid organization that helped in the third world to a "united, global force in a worldwide movement, helping communities realize lasting victories over poverty." (**Exhibit 11** shows the elements needed to shift the portrait of CARE.) "The development of the brand footprint was managed in English," Louw recalled.

> We had difficulty in some countries with the word "movement," which carried connotations of the Nazi movement in Germany in the 1930s. Many people were uncomfortable and did not understand the concept the words were conveying. We learned that it is not enough to translate the words; you must translate the concept behind the words. In France, for example, we spent several hours grappling with the phrase "in the thick of it." Eventually, we came up with a phrase roughly translated as, "I am an agent of change." It was amazing; the room lit up and came alive as people started to capture the concept and buy in to it.

Hicks expanded:

> We wanted to be perceived as united both with our project participants and partners, many of whom are local nongovernmental organizations, and with our donors. We chose communities as our focus because this best reflects our

Exhibit 11   Elements to Shift the Portrait of CARE International

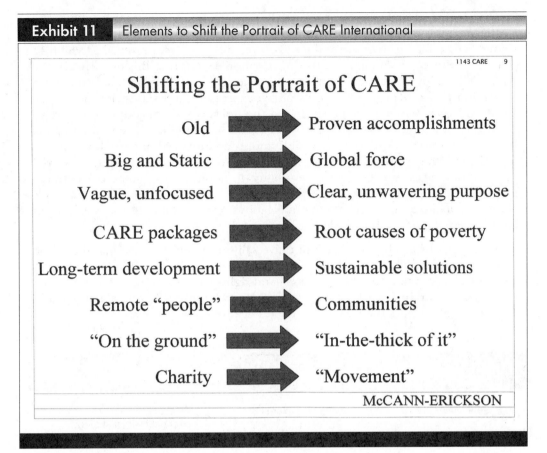

1143 CARE   9

Shifting the Portrait of CARE

Old	Proven accomplishments
Big and Static	Global force
Vague, unfocused	Clear, unwavering purpose
CARE packages	Root causes of poverty
Long-term development	Sustainable solutions
Remote "people"	Communities
"On the ground"	"In-the-thick of it"
Charity	"Movement"

McCANN-ERICKSON

Source: CARE International.

activities in the field, and people can conceive and conceptualize change at the community level. "Lasting victories" is a term that is aspirational but still believable. The real shift for us was to position CARE as treating the sources of poverty, not just the symptoms, and this is very true to the way our programming around the world works. The term "root causes," for example, came from our program strategy and really resonates with people.

During the same period, opinions on the brand strategy were solicited from the entire organization, using an intranet Web site. "I wasn't sure that this was a wise move," Hicks commented. "Consensus is a good and bad thing at the same time. When you ask people what they think, they expect to see changes that reflect their input, and when they don't, they're not very happy."

The logo. In November 2000, FutureBrand, McCann-Erickson's partner, presented initial artwork to the CI board. "This was a critical meeting," Grist remembered. "We were now starting to look at logos and taglines. It was not just an intellectual exercise anymore but a reality, and people started thinking about all the documents that would have to be reprinted and all the signs that would have to be changed, on trucks, for example. People started asking: How much is all this going to cost?"

The creative directives given to FutureBrand were to capture the essence of the CARE brand, as defined by the CARE brand strategy. The logo had to engage the viewer, and had to be evocative and provocative, distinctive yet universal. (**Exhibit 12** gives a graphic representation of the logos considered during this process.) In the end, CARE adopted a logo featuring a "community of hands" that symbolized humanism and evoked the concepts of self-expression and industriousness. (See **Exhibit 13**.) The circular shape suggested the holistic and collaborative nature of CARE's work and its global scope, as well as unity and diversity. The new lowercase logotype portrayed CARE as an accessible and straightforward organization and distanced the organization from its past acronym. The earth-toned palette conveyed warmth, optimism, and grounded sensibility. In addition, the many color photographs showing positive imagery of people caught in their daily activities and lives added a human component to communications. (See **Exhibit 14** for examples of CARE's new communication style.)

Initially, however, the logo was not universally accepted. In Australia, the colors used were very similar to traditional aboriginal colors, which CARE Australia worried would communicate that it was a land-rights organization, thereby causing donor confusion. In Japan, the logo looked somewhat like a Buddhist symbol, and the direction in which the hands faced had negative connotations.

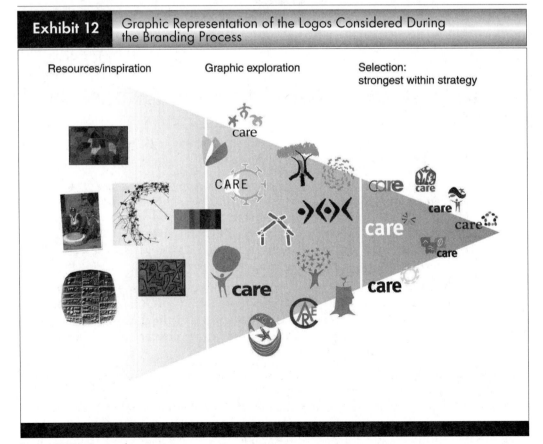

Exhibit 12	Graphic Representation of the Logos Considered During the Branding Process

Source: CARE International.

Exhibit 13 CARE International New Logo and Tagline, Adopted January 2002

where the end of poverty begins

Source: CARE International.

Note: The SM (service mark) was then changed to a ® registered mark.

The tagline. McCann-Erickson described a tagline as "a high-profile opportunity to say one thing about the organization." A tagline could be considered a call to action, a descriptor of the brand itself, or an attitude. In each case, however, it was important that the new tagline be true to CARE's brand essence and prove compelling. Given the low brand awareness and perception of CARE as a vague or lumbering organization, it was thought that the tagline should both provide context and communicate a clear and powerful vision. In addition, in order to have an effect on the target audience of skeptical progressives, the tagline needed to respond to their desire for progress and achievable goals.

The new tagline that met the above requirements was "Where the end of poverty begins." It communicated CARE's core purpose of creating a world in which poverty has been overcome and people live in dignity, acknowledged the magnitude of the mission, and was thought to inspire others to believe in and support it. The play on words was meant to convey CARE's commitment to progress, and the word "where" referred to the people who were building this new world: the project participants, partners, supporters, and staff. "The tagline was the most contentious aspect of the new brand," Grist recalled. "It was hotly debated right up until the very end. Many of the CARE European members and our field staff felt that it was arrogant and that it would put off our partners in the field. In the end, we decided to allow the country offices to use a modified tagline that added the word 'together': 'Together,

Exhibit 14   Example of CARE's New Brand and Communication Style

imagine

Imagine a farmer's satisfaction when he grows enough food to feed his family. Imagine a mother's pride when her daughter becomes the first girl in the family to go to school. Imagine the joyful smile of a healthy child who is protected against preventable illnesses such as polio.

In the battle to overcome poverty, these are small victories we see each day. Whether teaching new farming techniques, training teachers or improving access to health care, CARE works to create lasting solutions.

In more than 60 countries around the world, CARE is partnered with communities, local groups and international organizations in an effort to identify and confront root causes of poverty. And in one community after another, we see the proof that a better tomorrow is possible.

CARE is one of the world's leading international poverty-fighting organizations. Our integrated programs include emergency relief, community rehabilitation and long-term solutions to poverty.

care

victories over

poverty solutions to poverty
every day

Source: CARE USA.

where the end of poverty begins.'" CI executives also agreed that the tagline would be used in the broader context of CARE's many partners.

The new brand was scheduled for launch in the United States in September 2001, but, given the events of September 11th, the launch was postponed until January 2002.

Implementing the New Brand through Direct Mail.

In the fall of 2001, CARE USA conducted four focus groups to test potential new messages arising from the rebranding work that might be used in direct mailings and other communications. CARE learned from these focus groups that its messages should highlight solutions to help people understand how their donations make a difference. In addition, on the continuum of charitable crisis to the vision of ending global poverty, CARE should marry the two, reframing global poverty as a crisis. Hicks added, "It was critical, in order to encourage donations, to emphasize lifesaving work and the correction of circumstances that threatened life to begin with." On the basis of this research, new direct, donor-acquisition mail campaigns were developed and tested in the summer of 2002.

Six direct-mail pieces were tested first in a series of one-on-one interviews and second in a direct-mailing program. Two of the direct-mail pieces, "Children in Crisis" and "Mommy,"[4] were crisis pieces, high on the emotion continuum, whose main message centered on hungry children. (See **Exhibit 15** for sample letter of the "Children in Crisis" piece.) Two other direct-mail pieces, "Meals and More" and

---

Exhibit 15	Sample Direct-Mail Letter for "Children in Crisis" Program

EMERGENCY: FOOD FOR THE CHILDREN!

Dear Mr. Tony Williams, millions of the world's children are going hungry. Please join CARE's Atlanta Campaign by sending your gift today!

Please join CARE's Atlanta Campaign to help children in the world's poorest countries!

Here's an example of how your gift could help:
- ☐ $10 to feed 60 hungry children
- ☐ $20 to feed 120 hungry children
- ☐ $50 to feed 295 hungry children
- ☐ $_____ (my best gift to help children)

Mr. Tony Williams
151 Ellis St. NE
Atlanta, GA 30303-2420
I.I.II.II......II.II....II...I.I.I.I.I.I.II...I.I.I.I...I.I.I

0451635114   010304130SED7

☐ I'd like to make my gift by credit card (see back).

Thank you for your gift! You will receive a receipt. Please send this form, along with your gift, to: CARE, P.O. Box 1871, Merrifield, VA 22116-9753.
Questions? Call
1-800-422-7385.

Just 17¢ can provide a hot, nutritious meal for a hungry, hurting child.

Thank you for making a difference!

care℠

151 Ellis Street NE
Atlanta, GA 30303
1-800-422-7385
www.care.org

Dear Mr. Tony Williams,

I believe you're someone who cares about the poorest and most vulnerable people of the world — especially the children. That's why I'm writing today.

You see, tonight literally millions of children around the world will go to bed hungry. In fact, <u>thousands of them will die from hunger in the next 24 hours.</u>

It doesn't have to be that way. CARE is at work in the poorest communities around the world, feeding hungry children and helping families find lasting solutions to poverty. In fact, in Afghanistan, we can give a child a warm, nutritious meal for <u>just 17¢.</u>

But we can't do it without <u>caring friends like you.</u> Be one of the special, caring people who join CARE's Atlanta Campaign to help children in the world's poorest countries. Do it for the kids. Because you care.

Will you please send a gift — any amount you can — to help the children?

Your kindness can make all the difference. Please — the children need you!

Sincerely,

Peter D. Bell, President

Source: CARE USA.

"Labels," also focused on hungry children but added a "you can help" message and were considered a marriage of the crisis frame and long-term solutions frame. In the "Meals and More" piece, a cover letter similar to that shown in **Exhibit 15** was accompanied by meal ticket vouchers. (See **Exhibit 16**.) In the "Labels" piece, the letter was accompanied by address labels. The "Pigeon Peas" piece included a package of pigeon peas, and its message was "solutions here today." This piece incorporated many aspects of the new brand. (See **Exhibit 17** for the cover letter.) The "GII" piece (developed in conjunction with the Global Interdependence Initiative of the Aspen Institute) was the piece with the most intellectual articulation of the new brand position, low on the emotion continuum, and the main message was "we have solutions to poverty." "It was also recognized," Hicks added, "that this piece ignored many direct-marketing fundamentals, focusing on solutions versus need and success versus problems." (See **Exhibit 18**.)

One-on-one interviews were held in May 2002 with individuals fitting the skeptical progressives profile. Respondents were exposed to two direct-mail pieces, the "GII" and the "Meals and More" pieces. Researchers found that the "Meals and More" voucher was a very powerful response vehicle, allowing people to know exactly where their donation would go and what results it would achieve. In addition, by managing the value of the vouchers, CARE could influence average donation levels. Researchers also found that having an envelope with more visual punch (in this case, with a larger CARE logo and a picture of two hands holding a globe) increased the percentage of direct-mail letters opened. Finally, researchers found that the photographs in the "GII" piece were positively perceived. On the other hand, many respondents who were unfamiliar with CARE said that they would not even open the letter and that they needed to know an organization before they could feel comfortable donating.

The six direct-mail pieces were sent to a skeptical progressives list drawn from subscribers to magazines such as *Boston*, *The New Yorker*, *Outside*, *Smithsonian* magazine, *Washington Post Weekly*, and similar publications and to donors of organizations such as Project Hope, UNICEF, Freedom from Hunger, Oxfam, Friends of the Earth, and similar nonprofit organizations. (The response rates and average contributions are summarized in **Exhibit 19**.)

The "Pigeon Peas" piece had the highest response rate even though it broke from the traditional crisis frame, and the "GII" piece had the lowest response rate. Some thought the "Pigeon Peas" piece succeeded because the offer was more unusual and used the metaphor to communicate more concisely and powerfully. The envelope carried the stamp "Seeds Enclosed—Keep Dry," which made people curious enough to open the letter. However, the average contribution received for this piece was comparatively low, at $14.79. "Pigeon Peas" had a higher response rate than the "Labels" piece even though people have more use for address labels than seeds. This suggested that the "solution today" message could work if communicated clearly and concisely with emotion and urgency. Even though the "GII" piece had a poor response rate, the average contribution was the highest of all pieces. In addition to the responses to the direct-mail pieces themselves, researchers found that subscribers to news publications recorded higher response rates than subscribers to the other magazines.

Reflecting on the Process and Success of the Brand.

"Looking back," Grist explained, "it was really an education process for the organization and a team effort on behalf of those individuals who believed in the need for

Exhibit 16	Example of Meal-Ticket Vouchers Included in the "Meals and More" Direct-Mail Piece

MEAL TICKET 1

Please join CARE's Atlanta Campaign to help children in the world's poorest countries!

MEAL TICKET TRACKING NO. C150-1272

Mr. Tony Williams
151 Ellis St NE
Atlanta, GA 30303-2420

A gift of **$50** from
Mr. Tony Williams,
when returned with this Meal Ticket,
can help 600 hungry children in the
world's poorest communities.
☐ $ _____ (other amount)

☐ **Charge this gift to my credit card.
See back for instructions.**
Please include this ticket with your check payable to CARE in the enclosed reply envelope. Your gift is tax-deductible to the extent allowed by law. Thank you!

care

010301270SED4 0425060183

MEAL TICKET 2

Please join CARE's Atlanta Campaign to help children in the world's poorest countries!

MEAL TICKET TRACKING NO. C150-1272

Mr. Tony Williams
151 Ellis St NE
Atlanta, GA 30303-2420

A gift of **$15** from
Mr. Tony Williams,
when returned with this Meal Ticket,
can help 180 hungry children in the
world's poorest communities.

☐ **Charge this gift to my credit card.
See back for instructions.**
Please include this ticket with your check payable to CARE in the enclosed reply envelope. Your gift is tax-deductible to the extent allowed by law. Thank you!

care

010301270SED4 0425060183

MEAL TICKET 3

Please join CARE's Atlanta Campaign to help children in the world's poorest countries!

MEAL TICKET TRACKING NO. C150-1272

Mr. Tony Williams
151 Ellis St NE
Atlanta, GA 30303-2420

A gift of **$20** from
Mr. Tony Williams,
when returned with this Meal Ticket,
can help 240 hungry children in the
world's poorest communities.

☐ **Charge this gift to my credit card.
See back for instructions.**
Please include this ticket with your check payable to CARE in the enclosed reply envelope. Your gift is tax-deductible to the extent allowed by law. Thank you!

care

010301270SED4 0425060183

Source: CARE USA.

Exhibit 17   Cover Letter for the "Pigeon Peas" Direct-Mail Piece

care℠

Don't lose the enclosed seeds! They are very, very important!

CARE
151 Ellis Street NE
Atlanta, GA 30303-2440
tel 1-800-422-7385
web www.care.org
e-mail info@care.org

Monday morning

Dear Friend,

Seeds like the ones I've enclosed can make the difference...

Between hunger and plenty.
  Between despair and hope.
    Between life and death.

That's what these seeds -- pigeon peas -- can do. If we can put them to work in the right places.

Since 1945, CARE has offered immediate relief to poor countries all around the globe. We started out delivering CARE Packages, filled with food and other supplies, to help survivors after World War II. Since then, CARE has grown to combat the effects of natural disaster and poverty all over the world.

There are hungry families all over Africa, Asia and Latin America who urgently need pigeon peas -- or other smart solutions. But I need your help to make that happen.

It doesn't take a lot. As little as $1.50 can help buy two pounds of seed, yielding 30 pounds of peas. This can help feed a family of six for five months. Will you send a gift? We'll make sure every dollar you give works smart to fight poverty.

Let me tell you the great news about pigeon peas. They are virtually a miracle poverty-busting crop...

• The peas are a high-protein, high-vitamin food.
• The stalks and pods make great feed for farm animals.
• The plants draw nitrogen from the air and fix it into the soil -- making it more fertile for years to come.
• The deep roots help fight erosion.

Amazing! I want to introduce pigeon peas everywhere! But more than that, I want to put powerful, efficient, long-term solutions to work so poor families can lift themselves out of poverty.

There's a desperate need for meaningful steps against hunger and poverty...

Ask Tesfaye Temesgen, a CARE staff worker in southern Ethiopia. Drought has hit his area hard. "It's very bad," he says. "The cattle are dying."

(over, please)

Source: CARE USA.

Exhibit 18 Example of the GII Direct-Mail Piece

care℠

CARE USA
151 Ellis Street NE
Atlanta, Georgia 30303-2440
USA
tel 1-800-422-7385
web www.care.org

Dear Friend,

The streets of Curacocha, Peru, are busy with activity: children playing a game of soccer; street vendors selling food and wares; farmers coming in from the fields for their noonday meal. It is a thriving village -- a dramatic change from just five years ago.

Building schools

What made the difference? **Teamwork, experience and the support of caring individuals. You can be part of the solution. Won't you join our team of donors today?**

More than 55 years of experience have taught CARE how to address poverty for the long term, and we are doing it every day. There isn't just one simple solution, because every situation is different.

Building farms

It starts by working within communities to find poverty's root causes, and then working alongside local people to tackle those problems together. That may mean teaching new farming techniques in drought-prone regions. Or bringing education to villages that had been without schools. Or working with communities to prevent water-borne diseases with improved water treatment and sanitation. And usually it takes several of these solutions to turn the corner on poverty.

The results are well worth the hard work. We have lots of stories of success from more than 60 countries -- stories of hope that you won't see in the news. Like the micro-credit program that CARE helped to start in

(over, please)

Building futures

Source: CARE USA.

Exhibit 19	Responses to the Direct-Mail Test, September 2002			
Direct-Mail Piece	Message	Frame	Response Rate	Average $ Contribution
Mommy	Starving children	Crisis	.73	$23.03
Children in Crisis	Starving children	Crisis	.54	$24.23
Labels	Starving but you can help	Midway	.53	$15.60
Meals and More	Starving but you can help	Midway	.43	$24.07
Pigeon Peas	They can feed themselves	Solutions	.86	$14.88
GII	We have solutions to poverty	Solutions	.16	$26.33

Source: CARE USA.

a new brand identity. It has been a long and challenging process, and right up until the final vote in June 2001 at the CI annual meeting, I wasn't sure we would be able to reach an agreement on the tagline."

"In retrospect," Louw added,

> [w]e could have done even more internal selling than we did. It was a project conceived internationally but driven out of the USA within a framework that other CARE members saw as distinctly Anglo-Saxon in orientation. We had to stop several times to bring people from different countries and cultures back on board. We were tapping into very different historical, cultural, charitable, and organizational traditions across the CARE world, and getting everyone to attach the same meanings to concepts and proposals was exceptionally demanding.

Louw believed that the branding process had been successful in that CARE, as an organization, had evolved and grown as a result. The mission and vision statements in particular were strongly embraced throughout CARE. He believed that the branding process had been driven by Grist but strongly backed by the CI secretariat and CARE USA executive board and supported by the entire organization. "The organization now has a clear and uniting understanding of itself and its corporate identity," Louw concluded, "but in many countries, the tagline has not been adopted."

In the field, the new logo had been rapidly adopted and accepted by CARE staff. "Everywhere I go," Grist said, "people are incorporating the new logo." She expanded:

> On recent trips I saw that the logo had been hand-woven into material in Malawi and painted onto teacups in Ethiopia. CARE Egypt has just published its annual report, and it is very compatible, in look and style, with the CARE USA Annual Report. Many people have told me that they feel that the logo and tagline reflect what we do in the field, that it feels as if they had grown out of the work we do.

CHALLENGES FACING CARE AND THE NEW BRAND.

Changing International Organizational Structure.

Grist realized that CI was committed to exploring a new organizational structure that would move away from the lead-member model and provide all CARE members with a stronger voice in the management of international operations. She believed that the success of the rebranding process strengthened the movement to implement a new structure. Not only had the rebranding process been launched by a common vision, mission, and consistent identity that all CARE members had adopted, but it had also set a precedent for the way an international working group could operate and the role of the CI board. For the first time in its history, the CI board had, in the case of both the strategic plan and the rebranding effort, taken a constructive and active role in driving decisions throughout the various CAREs.

"In fact," Louw said, "the rebranding strategy started with a recognition of the need to change the international organizational structure." CARE had taken a step back and decided to focus first on developing a common vision and mission for the entire organization, thereby providing a foundation and common ground for exploring new organizational structures.

Shrinking Donor Pool.

During fiscal year 2002, CARE USA saw a significant decline in the number of its core U.S. individual donors. Between 1999 and 2001, the number of active[5] donors declined from 397,000 to 356,000. In 2002, the number of active donors dropped to 277,000. This rapid decline was in part caused by less-than-historical retention rates but more significantly to low rates of new donor acquisitions. (See **Exhibit 20** for details of CARE's active donor pool over time.)

In recent years, CARE had grown revenues by attracting major gifts and through direct marketing's ability to increase average giving among existing small-sum donors. CARE donor retention rates were comparable with peer organization rates, but donor acquisition performance was weaker. A key stated objective of CARE's External Relations Department was to "acquire new donors and turn them into satisfied customers, by learning about them, their communication preferences, and their humanitarian interests." This process was known as the CARE donor loyalty cycle. (See **Exhibit 21**.)

The low awareness of the CARE brand affected new donor acquisition efforts. CARE executives believed that a focused media strategy was required to target the

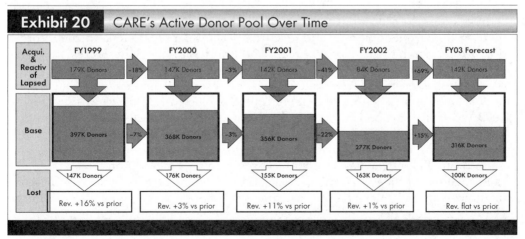

Exhibit 20   CARE's Active Donor Pool Over Time

Source: CARE USA.

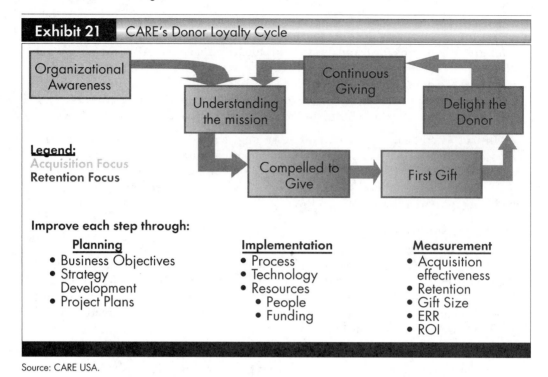

Exhibit 21   CARE's Donor Loyalty Cycle

Legend:
Acquisition Focus
Retention Focus

Improve each step through:

Planning
- Business Objectives
- Strategy Development
- Project Plans

Implementation
- Process
- Technology
- Resources
  - People
  - Funding

Measurement
- Acquisition effectiveness
- Retention
- Gift Size
- ERR
- ROI

Source: CARE USA.

skeptical progressive audience. They suggested media impressions in at least three publications (*Atlantic Monthly, National Geographic,* and *World Press Review*), with each ad running five or six times during fiscal year 2003. The total estimated cost for these impressions was $300,000. They also argued that corporate partnerships should be pursued with companies that had consumer databases compatible with the skeptical progressive profile and multiple distribution channels to reach these consumers. Executives also recommended timing communications efforts to coincide with times of emergencies, when potential donors became more aware of the need for emergency relief assistance and therefore more open to giving.

In addition to acquiring new donors, external relations established plans to increase donor retention rates and reactivate recently lapsed donors. In 2002, core donor retention rates were 66.6 percent and transition donor rates were 37.6 percent. Fiscal year 2003 objectives were to increase these rates to 72 percent and 41 percent, respectively. Reactivation rates for recently lapsed and deeply lapsed donors were established at 20 percent and 4 percent, respectively, in fiscal year 2003, up from 18.8 percent and 2.2 percent in fiscal year 2002. In addition, a slightly reduced average gift size was anticipated in conjunction with higher response rates. (**Exhibit 22** gives details of donor retention and gifts by type of donor.) Strategies to achieve these objectives were largely based on telemarketing calls and direct mailings. In fiscal year 2003, CARE USA planned to spend $8.2 million in direct-mail and telemarketing activities to generate revenues of $25 million. (**Exhibit 23** shows details of CARE USA's projected direct-mail programs for fiscal year 2003 and associated costs.)

Exhibit 22	CARE's Planned Impact in Donor Pool FY 2003

Donor	FY 03 Donor Population	FY 02 Actual Average Gift ($)	Current Gifts/ Donor FY 02	FY 03 Targeted Donor Population	FY 03 Estimated Average Gift ($)	Estimated Gifts/Donor FY 03
Core (continuing multiyear)	193,102	$47.80	1.92			
Objective: Retain 72%				139,034	$45.25	2.58
Transition Donors (second gift)[a]	84,134	$40.42	1.51			
Objective: Retain 41%				34,495	38.42	1.86
Total Active Donors at end of FY 02	277,236					
Lapsed (13–24 months)	157,590	$43.21	1.23			
Objective: Reactivate 20%				31,518	$40.97	1.49
Deeply Lapsed (25+ months)	931,431	$33.47	1.19			
Objective: Reactivate 4%				37,257	$30.45	1.40
New		$27.34	1.2			
Objective: Acquire 61,000				61,000	$25.18	1.49
Total Active Donors at end of FY 03				303,000		

Source: CARE USA External Relations Department.

[a]Transition donors were donors who gave last fiscal year but not the previous fiscal year. They included new donors acquired and lapsed or deeply lapsed donors who had been reactivated in the previous year.

Direct-Mail Strategy.

Over the years, CARE had learned a number of things about direct marketing: first, direct marketing was not an educative medium; second, donors gave in response to urgent human needs rather than to reward an organization's success; third, they gave to things that were easily and immediately understandable; and fourth, giving decisions were made emotionally, not intellectually. "We have a few seconds to grab attention and generate a response," Grist explained. "Shifting an organization's brand image is not easy, but shifting an organization's fund-raising communications is an even greater challenge."

CARE's current base of donors was used to receiving direct-mail offers such as the "Mommy" or "Children in Crisis" pieces, which had a strong emergency relief orientation. Grist was concerned that a change to a long-term solutions message might demotivate a large number of them. On the other hand, she thought it would be difficult to attract a new pool of donors whose interests were aligned with CARE's vision of long-term solutions if the fund-raising message was not changed to be more reflective of the new brand. "One of the challenges we face," Williams added, "is how to bring a sense of urgency to our brand and messages. Emergencies are what get

Exhibit 23	Estimated Cost per Donor Segment and Mail Program, 2003				
Donor Segment/Mail Program	Total Number Mailed/Called	Total Expense	Cost per Mailing/Call	Number of Mailings
Active Donor Renewals	7,190,182	$2,526,473	$0.35	24
Lapsed[a] Donor Reactivation Mailings	2,185,000	$645,095	$0.29	24
Deeply Lapsed Mailings	3,971,384	$622,652	$0.16	12
Monthly Pledge Program	227,925	$203,928	$0.89	12
Gift Receipts	516,375	$330,758	$0.64	N/A
New Donor Acquisition Mailings	8,850,000	$3,009,000	$0.34	12
New Donor 2nd Gift Program	136,290	$132,883	$0.97	N/A
Telemarketing	217,025	$756,338	$3.48	b
TOTALS	23,294,181	$8,227,127	$0.35	

Source: CARE USA External Relations Department.

[a]For lapsed and deeply lapsed donors, CARE maintained a complete file of names and addresses.

[b]Telemarketing plans: Lapsed donor reactivation calls were planned each quarter, a large fall telemarketing campaign was planned for the entire active donors file, a spring campaign was planned for donors previously responsive to telemarketing, and calls to any new donor who had not given a second gift for five months were also planned.

people's attention and bring in the money, and it is sometimes difficult in a direct-mail piece that talks about the root causes of poverty to impart a sense of urgency."

CONCLUSION.

Grist concluded that the new brand was working well with existing donors, staff, and major-gift donors but that it was perhaps more of a struggle making it work for new U.S. individual donor acquisitions. Although she was encouraged that CARE had embraced the new brand, she worried about the consequences of having given up the CARE Package icon, a powerful symbol in both the United States and countries such as Germany and France, where CARE Packages had been so warmly received (although France specifically had been highly positive about the new brand). Without the reference to "CARE Packages," she wondered if CARE was distinctive enough as a brand name.

Looking forward, Grist believed that CARE could leverage what the organization had learned during the branding process to shape the discussions surrounding the international organizational structure, but she was unsure how to most effectively accomplish this.

Rebuilding the donor pool was a top priority for Grist, and she had established a series of goals toward that end. She wondered if these goals were realistic or too timid, and what, in addition to telemarketing and additional direct mailings, she could do to reach and acquire new donors.

The type of direct-mail programs to pursue was another question Grist was grappling with. Should she push for new mailings along the lines of the "GII" piece that closely aligned with the new brand image or should she stick to tried and tested pieces such as "Mommy"? Would a mailing such as the new "GII" piece be effective enough to grow CARE USA's donor pool and meet revenue growth expectations?

Notes to Case

1   CARE Package® is a registered trademark of the Cooperative for Assistance and Relief Everywhere, Inc. (CARE).

2   For example, in 2003, CARE Australia was the lead member for CARE programs in Iraq.

3   Restricted fund were funds earmarked by donors for specific programs or areas. As a general rule, nonprofit organizations preferred unrestricted funds, which gave them greater flexibility in their programs and operations.

4   This direct-mail piece was called "Mommy" because, in its original form several years earlier, it contained a photograph of a child saying, "Mommy, I'm hungry."

5   An active donor was any donor having made a gift in the past twelve months.

CASE 9
The BRAC and Aarong Commercial Brands

BRAC has always operated with a market perspective and an entrepreneurial spirit. We are a flexible nonprofit development organization that responds to the needs of our members and seizes opportunities as they present themselves. Over the last few years BRAC has pursued an increasing number of commercial ventures, many of which are very successful. We plan to continue to profitably support our members and generate income in order to become increasingly self-sufficient in achieving our objectives of alleviating poverty and empowering the poor. There is, however, a potential question about what type of organization BRAC is becoming and where, if at all, we should draw the line in terms of continued diversification into the private sector. There is some concern that too great an expansion into for-profit commercial enterprises might drain our resources and take attention away from our core development programs. We have become a multisector conglomerate operating under two brands: BRAC and Aarong. We are active in commercial areas ranging from banking and education to food processing, from luxury goods retailing to basic agricultural inputs and farming, and from being an Internet service provider company to a printer. We face a challenge organizing these and future enterprises into a coherent structure and need to start thinking about our commercial expansions more strategically, particularly in terms of building up our two brands.

—Dr. Salehuddin Ahmed, BRAC deputy executive director

BRAC OVERVIEW.

In February 2003, BRAC, formerly known as Bangladesh Rural Advance Commission, was a national, private, nonprofit development organization employing 26,000 regular staff members and 34,000 teachers. It worked in 64,000 of the 80,000 villages throughout Bangladesh and operated within a budget of $174 million, 82 percent of which was self-financed. It had a network of more than 1,500 field offices and fourteen training residential centers and was, after the Bangladesh government, the nation's second-largest employer and the world's largest nongovernmental organization (NGO).[1]

Professor John Quelch and Research Associate Nathalie Laidler prepared this case. HBS cases are developed solely as the basis for class discussion. Cases are not intended to serve as endorsements, sources of primary data, or illustrations of effective or ineffective management.

The BRAC philosophy was that "poverty is a complex syndrome that can be overcome only by using a holistic approach and innovative interventions." BRAC provided the landless poor, whom it called members and the vast majority of whom were women, with credit and financial services, training in income-generating activities, and access to consumer markets under the BRAC Development Program (BDP). In 2003, BRAC served more than 3.5 million microfinance clients. Under the BRAC Health, Nutrition, and Population Program, BRAC provided preventive, curative, and rehabilitative health services to an estimated 31 million people, and under the BRAC Education Program, initiated in 1985, BRAC operated 34,000 one-room classrooms, educating more than 1.1 million children in 2002. (See **Exhibit 1** for a summary of quick facts on BRAC and **Exhibit 2** for a statement of income and expenditures.)

Village organizations (VOs) were at the heart of the BRAC system and the channel through which BRAC introduced and delivered services to its members. Made up of thirty-five to fifty women from a single village, VOs met every week with a BRAC program organizer to discuss and carry out credit operations as well as learn about health and other issues that affected their lives. In addition to facilitating weekly repayment of loans, the VOs worked as a peer support group through which members guaranteed one another's loans. In 2003, there were more than 113,000 VOs, up from 56,000 in 1998.

To support these three core areas of development, BRAC had two key internal divisions: the BRAC Training Division, which, through its network of twelve residential training and resource centers and two centers for development management, provided capacity building and professional development for both BRAC staff and members and trained more than 60,000 people in 2002; and the BRAC Research and Evaluation Division, which was world renowned and carried out field research, impact assessments, and program evaluations for both BRAC and external clients. Other support divisions included a monitoring division providing quality control for

Exhibit 1	BRAC Overview—Quick Facts, 2002
• Villages	63,922 (out of 86,000)
• Urban Slums	2,369
• Village Organizations (VOs)	113,756
• Microfinance Clients	3.65 million households
• Loan Disbursement in 2002	US$295 million
• Repayment Rate	99.27%
• Health Services	31 million people with access to services
• Health Centers	90
• Education	1.1 million children currently enrolled (2.4 million graduated)
• Schools	34,000
• Reading Centers	8,000
• Libraries	700
• Handicraft Production Centers	245
• Field Offices	1,500 in all 64 districts
• Training Centers	14 residential
• Employees	26,000 staff members, 34,000 teachers, 33,000 health volunteers, 3,645 community veterinarians, 51,200 poultry workers, 7,226 community nutrition workers
• Budget 2003	$174 million (80% self-financing)

Source: BRAC.

Exhibit 2	Statement of Income and Expenditures		
Millions of Taka	**2000**	**2001**	**2002**
INCOME			
Donor grants	1,721	1,536	1,980
Revenue from commercial projects	1,173	1,135	1,218
Revenue from program support enterprises	1,014	1,569	1,716
Service charge on loans to VO members	1,893	2,195	2,404
Investment income	195	160	138
Other income	131	159	141
Rental income from house property	91	96	89
TOTAL	6,218	6,850	7,688
EXPENDITURES			
Commercial projects	1,101	1,029	1,089
Program support enterprises	916	1,380	1,594
House property-related expenses	52	56	76
Education Program	960	993	1,190
Nutrition Program	189	290	355
Health and Population Program	292	229	134
Microfinance Program	1,823	2,045	2,157
Relief and Rehabilitation Program	22	24	0
Poultry Extension Program	102	100	156
Fisheries Extension Program	64	42	80
Agriculture Extension Program	77	63	88
Sericulture and Silk Development Program	79	28	61
Human Rights and Legal Education Program	72	50	92
Rural Enterprise Development Program	24	24	104
Training, workshops, and seminars	60	56	42
Grant to BRAC University	0	50	
Grant to BRAC Afghanistan			6
Research, monitoring, and evaluation	10	16	24
TOTAL	5,844	6,476	
NET SURPLUS	374	374	
Exchange rates	US$1 = Taka 52	US$1 = Taka 56	US$1 = Taka 58

Source: BRAC annual reports.

the entire organization, a publications department, a public affairs and communication department, and a construction and logistics department. BRAC's audit and accounts department was particularly strong and progressive, possibly because the organization's founder, Fazle Hasan Abed, was a chartered accountant, and it collected and collated detailed financial information every month. There was also an emphasis throughout the organization on programs being self-financing as much as possible, and members were expected to pay (sometimes a nominal sum) for services and products BRAC provided.

Much had already been written about the BRAC culture of innovation, its flexibility and commitment to excellence, and the fact that it was truly a "learning" organization willing to take risks and learn from its mistakes.[2] These strengths had enabled BRAC to consistently achieve impressive growth and continuously diversify its activities and scope of expertise. (See **Exhibit 3** for BRAC expenditures over time.) In 2002, BRAC initiated a new program to target the ultra-poor in Bangladesh and ventured outside Bangladesh for the first time by registering as a foreign NGO

Exhibit 3	BRAC Expenditures: 1980–2002

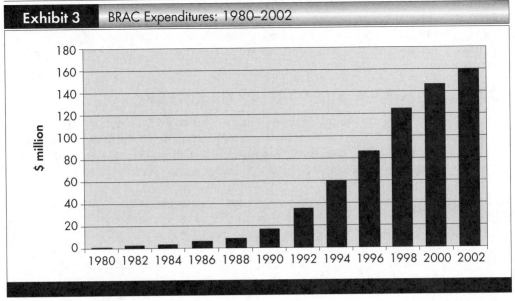

Source: BRAC.

in Afghanistan, providing credit for the poor and primary education for girls and setting up a number of health clinics.

In an effort to link its members with markets and provide them with high-quality inputs, BRAC had established a number of program support enterprises and commercial projects whose profits were plowed back into BRAC's core development activities. Program support enterprises primarily provided inputs to BRAC members and included poultry farms, feed mills, prawn and fish hatcheries, seed-processing centers and seed-production farms, silk-reeling centers and sericulture grainages, plant nurseries, and a bull station. (See **Exhibit 4** for details on the program support enterprises.) Commercial projects and related companies included retail handicraft stores, a dairy plant, a printing press, a cold storage and vegetable export business,

Exhibit 4	Overview of BRAC Program Support Enterprises

Enterprise	Number	Annual Capacity, 2002
Poultry Farms	6	15 million chicks
Feed Mills	3	35,000 MT
Prawn Hatcheries	8	15 million post larvae
Fish Hatcheries	4	4,500 kg fish spawn
Seed Processing Centers	2	6,000 MT
Seed Production Farms	18	4,000 MT
Silk Reeling Centers	2	15 MT
Sericulture Grainages	12	2 million dfl
Nurseries	20	2.1 million
Bull Station	1	120,000 doses

Source: BRAC.

Note: MT = Metric Tonnes/dfl = disease-free laying cocoons/doses = bull semen doses

BRAC University, BRAC Bank, an Internet service provider, information technology (IT) education services, a housing and housing finance company, and a poultry farm. (**Exhibit 5** details BRAC's commercial enterprises and related companies, and **Exhibit 6** summarizes the associated revenues, net income, and return on investment of selected enterprises.)

BRAC PROGRAM SUPPORT ENTERPRISES.

BRAC believed that community development depended on the existence of varied income-generating sectors within that community. By establishing a range of income-generating enterprises for its members, BRAC sought to bring about social and economic change. "The driver behind our entry into commercial and program

Exhibit 5	Overview of BRAC Commercial Projects and Related Companies, 2002

Company	Description
Aarong Shops	Eight luxury handicraft and clothing retail outlets
BRAC Printers	Printing press
BRAC Dairy and Food Project	Milk and milk products processing plant
BRAC University	Tertiary education
BRAC Bank	Small and medium-size enterprise finance and banking
BRAC BD Mail Network	Internet service provider
BRAC Services Ltd.	Hospitality
BRAC Renata Agro Industries Ltd.	Poultry farm
BRAC Industries Ltd.	Cold storage
BRAC Concord Lands Ltd.	Land and housing
Delta BRAC Housing Finance Corp.	Housing finance
BRAC Information Technology Institute (BTI)	IT education

Source: BRAC.

Exhibit 6	Revenues, Net Income, and Return on Investments Generated by Selected BRAC Enterprises

Millions of Taka	Revenues 2001	Net Income 2001	Revenues 2002	Net Income 2002	ROI 2002
Aarong Shops	627	48	651	64	16.2%
BRAC Printers	163	11	182	14	12.5%
BRAC Dairy and Food	309	10	353	19	6.8%
Poultry Enterprises	122	27	128	19	5.1%
Seed Enterprises	373	34	447	23	3.9%
Feed Enterprises	641	29	465	8	1.6%
Fish and Prawn Hatchery	23	5	33	8	12.0%
Nursery	39	11	37	3	4.1%
TOTAL	2,297	175	2,296	158	7.5%
Exchange rates	US$1 = Taka 52		US$1 = Taka 56.5		

Source: BRAC.

support enterprises was the need to provide quality inputs and distribution channels for products generated by our members," Ahmed explained. He continued:

> Because the basic inputs, infrastructure, and markets did not exist, we had to create them for our members, enabling them to work towards economic independence. BRAC has been successful setting up and managing a variety of income-generating activities that not only link our members into the mainstream value chain but also generate profits that can be plowed back into our health and education programs, enabling us to be less dependent on donor contributions.

"We are really a nongovernmental corporation," added Abdul-Muyeed Chowdhury, executive director, "but the majority of our commercial activities are connected either forwards or backwards to our members, who are both consumers, producers, and beneficiaries of BRAC commercial enterprises."

"We run these enterprises commercially," added Mr. Kairy, finance manager, "but they can be thought of as semicommercial entities in that their main objective is to provide our members with quality inputs while covering their costs."

Poultry Farms, and Fish and Prawn Hatcheries.

To provide high-quality inputs to its members, BRAC operated six poultry farms, eight prawn hatcheries, and four fish hatcheries. BRAC provided more than 15 million day-old chicks, 15 million post-larvae prawns, and nearly 5,000 kilograms of fish spawn each year. Although BRAC members were the main customers for these inputs, many non-BRAC farmers also purchased inputs from BRAC, which had a reputation for fair prices and high quality.

Seed-Processing Center.

In 2003, eighteen BRAC seed-production farms fed two BRAC seed-processing centers, where more than 6,000 metric tons of rice and various vegetable seeds were dried, sorted, cleaned, weighed, and packaged. Seeds were sold to small-scale rural farmers through BRAC field offices, and 60 percent of production was sold to non-BRAC members. All BRAC seeds carried the BRAC brand. (See **Exhibit 7** for an example of a spinach seed package.) "We started processing seeds in 1999 and used to have to import all the seed," Ahmed explained. "Now we have our own farms that provide two-thirds of our seed needs. In addition, we have just started a tissue-culture operation for optimal seed production. In this way, we are able to bring the benefits of technology and science to the poor."

Feed Mills.

In 2000, BRAC established its third and largest feed mill. In 2003, total feed production exceeded 40,000 metric tons, representing more than 20 percent of Bangladesh's feed needs and placing BRAC second, behind the government, in feed production. Approximately 10 percent of production was cattle feed and 90 percent chicken feed, and only 30 percent of production was sold through BRAC field offices to BRAC members. The remaining 70 percent was sold through a network of 350 dealers throughout the country. All feed products carried the BRAC brand. In 2003, BRAC had plans to expand feed production by opening a fourth mill in the near future. (See **Exhibit 8** for an example of a feed brochure and **Exhibit 9** for photographs of the recently opened plant.)

Exhibit 7   Example of a BRAC Seed Package

Source: BRAC.

Exhibit 8 | Reproduction of a BRAC Chicken Feed Brochure

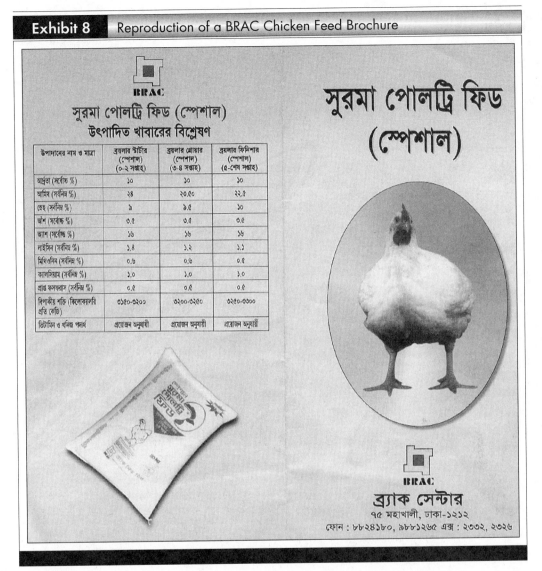

Source: BRAC.

Other Enterprises.

Other BRAC program support enterprises included silk-reeling centers and grainages for sericulture,[3] a bull-husbandry station, and twenty plant nurseries producing high-yield varieties of fruit trees and plants.

In Bangladesh, BRAC was viewed as having something of a Midas touch.[4] When asked if BRAC had experienced any failures, Mohammad Abdur Rahman, senior trainer, explained:

> BRAC has had a number of failed initiatives. For example, we attempted to initiate an irrigation program that would allow the rural poor to extract and sell water, but it was not sustainable. The key, though, is that BRAC is constantly piloting and brainstorming at all levels of the organization. New ideas are tested

Exhibit 9   Photographs of the New BRAC Seed Plant

Source: BRAC.

out all the time, and those that look as if they have strong potential for success are adopted and scaled up quickly. Most of BRAC's initiatives into commercial areas have been driven either by the direct requests or the unmet needs of our members.

BRAC's medium-term strategic plan (2002–2007) called for program support enterprises to provide BRAC members with access to national and international markets, competitive prices, and high-quality inputs as well as to encourage the development of new products.

BRAC COMMERCIAL PROJECTS IN 2003.

BRAC's commercial projects linked BRAC members and the consumers of the products they produced.

Aarong Handicrafts Stores.

"Aarong" was a Bangla word meaning "small village fair," and the 245 handicraft production centers and eight retail stores managed by BRAC were the oldest of BRAC's commercial ventures. It began in 1978 to bring marketing to rural artisans and expand the market for their goods both domestically and internationally. In 2003, more than 30,000 women were involved in the production of pottery, woven baskets, silk and luxury garments, leather, jewelry, and other handicrafts. The department store–like outlets were in the major cities of Dhaka, Chittagong, Sylhet, and Khulna. Over the years the Aarong brand had become known as one of the finest producers of high-quality rural crafts. Aarong also sold and took orders for its products through its Web site. (See **Exhibit 10** for a photograph of the inside of an Aarong store in Dhaka.)

BRAC Dairy.

The dairy project was initiated in response to complaints in 1998 by members who had taken out BRAC loans to purchase milk cows but were unable to make a profit because prices were driven down at the local village level by oversupply and lack of access to wider markets. "As a learning organization," Ahmed said, "we analyzed how

Exhibit 10	Photograph of the Inside of an Aarong Store in Dhaka

Source: BRAC.

the Amul Dairy Cooperative worked in India and how the Bangladesh government ran the MilkVita project and decided to launch our own dairy." In 2003, the BRAC dairy operations comprised a sophisticated and modern milk-processing plant employing 146 people that produced pasteurized milk, fresh milk, and a variety of milk-based products (see **Exhibit 11** for a list of current products and annual production volumes); twenty chilling plants that collected the milk directly from the farmers; and a fleet of tankers that collected the milk from the chilling plants to bring it to the processing plant in Dhaka. In 2003, BRAC accounted for 25 percent of Bangladesh's fresh milk market, behind MilkVita, a government-owned company that held a 65 percent share.

Products. The first product produced at the plant in 1999 was fresh pasteurized milk, but BRAC Dairy quickly launched a full line including UHT (**u**ltra-**h**igh **t**emperature processed) milk, low-fat milk, mango and chocolate milk, yogurt drinks, ghee, cream, and curd in a variety of sizes and packages. (See **Exhibit 12** for examples of product packages.) In 2002, BRAC Dairy won a contract to produce 100,000 cartons of 200-milliliter UHT milk a day for a school-feeding program jointly financed by the U.S. Department of Agriculture (USDA) and the U.S.-based Land O'Lakes Company.[5] To secure the contract, BRAC Dairy had to invest in Tetra Pak packaging equipment and supplies but believed this paid off, given that the Land O'Lakes contract represented 25 percent of the company's sales. In April 2003, BRAC also planned to introduce a variety of fruit drinks and cheese. Syed Rezaul Karim, director of BRAC Dairy and previously managing director of Hoechst Bangladesh, explained the BRAC Dairy product philosophy:

> *Our key goal is to produce high-quality products. This has led us back up the supply chain to expand the number of chilling stations and work more closely with rural BRAC member farmers. We have created incentives for these farmers to pay attention to the quality of the milk they produce by establishing pricing on the basis of fat content. This has reduced the practice of watering down the milk and focused attention on optimal feeding regimes for the cows.*

Customers and competition. The majority of the dairy's customers were the urban populations of Dhaka, Chittigong, and Sylhet. "When we discussed the branding of these products we hesitated between the BRAC and Aarong brands," Ahmed explained. "Some people argued that we should keep the BRAC brand and others argued that, in the city, people were more familiar with the Aarong brand name and

Exhibit 11	BRAC Dairy Products and Volumes		
Annual Sales (Thousand of Liters/Kg)	2000	2001	2002
Pasteurized Fresh Milk	10,453	10,074	10,506
UHT Milk	0	0	741
Chocolate Milk	787	484	439
UHT Chocolate Milk	0	115	151
Mango Milk	57	637	522
UHT Mango Milk	0	0	158
Yogurt	56	121	107
Butter/Ghee	67	65	85

Source: BRAC.

Exhibit 12   Examples of BRAC Dairy Products and Packages

Source: BRAC.

that the latter stood for high quality, which is particularly important in the case of milk." Karim expanded:

> *Recently in Bangladesh, there have been scandals surrounding the use of vegetable fat in condensed milk. In addition, raw milk presents a health risk*

*because of the high bacterial content. Our main competition comes from pow-
dered and condensed milk, which are predominantly used in tea. We want to
position fresh pasteurized milk as a better-tasting, healthier, real milk alternative. We aim to position our milk and yogurt drinks as healthy snack alterna-
tives for children, and we want to expand the UHT milk market because it has
a shelf life of four months and doesn't require refrigeration. This would enable
us to penetrate the rural markets as well. MilkVita is our main competitor in
the urban fresh milk market, but we are confident that we can continue to gain
share, and our goal is to reach 45 percent of the market in two years.*

Production and distribution. The sophisticated production plant had been purchased from Denmark as a turnkey project in 1998. (See **Exhibit 13** for a photograph
of the plant.) "The first year we had a number of teething problems," Karim said,
"but everything is running smoothly now." In 2003, total plant capacity for fresh
milk was 50,000 liters a day, and capacity utilization stood at 70 percent for fresh pasteurized milk, 80 percent for UHT milk, and 50 percent for other products. "We are
hoping to use some of the excess capacity to expand into fruit drinks," Karim said.
In 2003, third-party distributors accounted for 50 percent of BRAC Dairy sales, but
the company planned to integrate forward and distribute 70 percent of production
directly to retail outlets.

"In essence," Karim concluded, "we provide 12,000 farmers with a steady cash business every day by creating a bridge to the formal market, and we provide consumers

Exhibit 13	Photograph of BRAC Dairy Plant

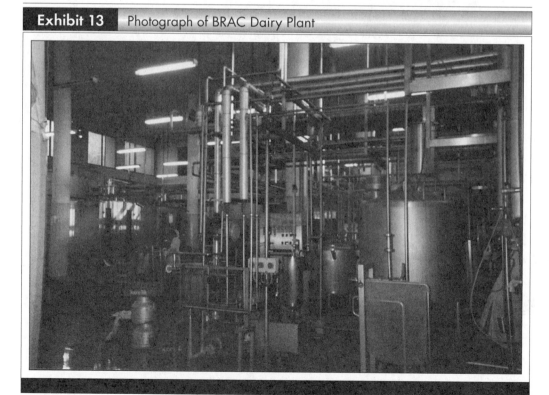

Source: BRAC.

with a healthy, high-quality product that can play a role addressing malnutrition in Bangladesh. The Aarong brand has been successfully extended to milk and dairy products and represents quality."

BRAC Poultry Processing.

In 2003, BRAC was building a large, modern poultry-processing plant in Dhaka that would provide an opportunity for BRAC members to see their production reach urban markets. In much the same way that BRAC Dairy operated, this venture, Ahmed hoped, would market value-added products and ensure steady revenues for BRAC's members. It was expected that this plant would become operational in 2004 and join BRAC's list of commercial projects.

BRAC Printers.

BRAC Printers started out in the early 1980s printing books for BRAC's Functional Education program, a precursor to BRAC's Non-Formal Primary Education program. In 2003, the BRAC printing business moved into new, larger facilities and, in true BRAC fashion, supported both BRAC internal programs and activities on a competitive transfer-price basis and provided printing services to entities outside the BRAC organization. BRAC Printers printed the books and educational materials used by BRAC's 34,000 schools (representing 60 percent of revenues), the health charts and manuals used by BRAC's health programs, the research reports developed by BRAC's Research and Evaluation Division, and BRAC's many internal training documents and newsletters. In 2002, BRAC Printers generated revenues of 182 million taka (1 USD = 60 Bangladesh taka), of which 15 percent came from outside contracts.

BRAC's Vegetable Export Business.

In 1999, BRAC initiated a project to link small rural vegetable farmers to export markets. The vertically integrated operation provided inputs, training, and technical support to members and undertook processing, storage, packaging, and transportation to markets in the United Kingdom, France, Germany, the Netherlands, Belgium, Italy, Bahrain, Abu Dhabi, the United Arab Emirates, Maldives, Singapore, and Hong Kong. In 2003, BRAC worked with close to 2,000 contract farmers and guaranteed them a fixed price at the time of planting that was substantially higher than local market prices. (See **Exhibit 14** for a list of vegetables and export volumes.)

Mallik A-As-Saqui, general manager of the vegetable export business, explained:

> *There is a strong demand from Europe and the Middle East for high-quality fresh vegetables, and we strive to deliver high-quality produce. We currently ship to sixteen countries with an average of twenty-seven plane shipments each week and hope to expand this shortly. We are also building a new cooling and packaging plant near the airport that will have a capacity of ten tons a day, or between ten and fifteen plane shipments daily, and will produce shelf-ready consumer packs carrying the BRAC brand. In addition to the contract farmers, we currently employ over fifty women in the processing plants who sort, grade, and package the vegetables. This is, however, a high-risk business, and we face a spectrum of challenges, including a shortage of cargo space, flight cancellations resulting in damage to the goods, price fluctuations on the international markets, and price adjustments when products arrive in substandard quality. For*

Exhibit 14	BRAC Vegetable Export Business		
Tons	2001	2002	2003 (est.)
French Beans	102	80	95
Potatoes	190	350	1,000
Broccoli	5	5	5
Chili	99	189	225
Bitter Gourd	39	132	160
Long Beans	34	213	255
Teasle Gourd	10	8	9
Okra	1	12	14
Other	40	30	36
TOTAL	520	1,019	1,799

Source: BRAC.

example, a cockroach was once found in a shipment to the U.K., and the whole consignment had to be destroyed. We investigated the incident and found that the shipment had been left outside by the airline.

In 2000, BRAC was approached by the Bangladesh government and asked to attempt to export fresh potatoes to generate foreign currency earnings. "Prior efforts had failed," A-As-Saqui explained, "but in three years we have had tremendous success, growing fresh potato exports from just under 100 tons in 2000 to an estimated 1,000 tons in 2003, with Singapore being our main market."

BRAC's main customers included large retail chains in Europe such as Sainsburys in the United Kingdom and Selection in France. "If you go to Sainsburys," A-As-Saqui said, "you will find our vegetables nicely packaged, with packaging provided by BRAC Printers and stamped with the BRAC brand." BRAC sought to develop long-term relationships with these players, and many had already visited BRAC's farms and processing plants and worked in partnership with BRAC on hygiene, pesticide use, and quality control. BRAC had, however, been unable to enter the U.S. market because, in 2003, the USDA had restricted imports of B produce.

Contract farmers benefited from training in modern farming techniques, a supply of high-yield variety seeds and technical support, and a steady source of income. BRAC benefited financially, as well as furthering its goal of empowering the poor. Revenues in foreign currency benefited the government, and A-As-Saqui believed that BRAC's high-quality products helped provide Bangladesh with a positive image in the minds of consumers in Europe and the Middle East. Future plans included expanding into other vegetables and fruits, growing the business, and entering organic farming and the marketing of organic products.

RELATED COMPANIES AND INSTITUTIONS.

Most of BRAC's related companies and institutions were not directly linked to BRAC members, and these companies and institutions often sought to play a role in building Bangladesh's institutional capability. In addition, they were separate legal entities and did not report through the BRAC organization but had their own boards and governance structures, though top executives from BRAC sat on their boards. It was clear, from the way the BRAC name featured prominently in all of these companies and institutions, that the expectation was for the goodwill and trust afforded the BRAC brand to extend to them.

BRAC University.

BRAC University was inaugurated in 2001 with the mission of providing broad-based, high-quality education for undergraduate and MBA students. In 2003, BRAC University had more than 1,000 full-time, tuition-paying undergraduate students and fifty tuition-paying MBA students, and all classes were in English. That same year, Bangladesh had a total of fifteen universities in operation. In some ways, BRAC University extended BRAC's existing role in primary school education and addressed the increasing objective of nation building that BRAC saw itself taking on. "We must help the future generation think out of the box," Ahmed summarized. "BRAC University can help the future leaders of Bangladesh accomplish three things: be experts in their chosen domain, develop capacities in critical analysis and thinking, and gain a breadth of exposure."

BRAC Bank.

BRAC Bank was formed in 2001 and functioned as a full-fledged commercial bank focusing on providing financial services to small and medium-size enterprises. "The idea," Ahmed expanded, "was to offer microfinance graduates and other small and medium entrepreneurs a bank tailored to their needs. The formal banking sector in Bangladesh does not cater to small and medium enterprises, and so BRAC decided to build the institutional capability of doing so." By the end of 2002, BRAC Bank served more than 2,000 customers.

BRAC BD Mail Network Ltd. was an Internet service provider described as a sister concern of BRAC targeted at both companies and individuals.

BRAC Concord Lands Ltd. was a private joint venture between BRAC and Concord Condominium Ltd., established in 1988, whose vision was to develop modern satellite townships around the city of Dhaka for middle-class communities.

DBH-Delta BRAC Housing Finance Corporation was a public company and financial institution licensed by Bangladesh Bank and the first housing finance institution in the country. The main objectives of the corporation, the shares of which BRAC held 25 percent, were to promote affordable home ownership through financing and contribute to the growth of the housing stock. Loans were offered to both individuals and companies.

BRAC Renata Agro Industries Ltd., BRAC Industries, and BRAC Services Ltd. were three companies that ran a poultry farm, a cold storage facility (mostly for potatoes), and a hotel/restaurant business, respectively. Once again, these businesses were run as separate legal entities but used the BRAC brand.

Other Revenue-Generating Activities.

BRAC's philosophy was to charge members, sometimes a nominal fee, for services and goods provided under the microfinance, health, and education programs. This market approach or perspective permeated all of BRAC's activities and was also evident in BRAC's support activities. The Research and Evaluation Division, for example, covered two-thirds of its expenses through external consultancy fees, and BRAC's training and resource centers recorded revenues of 120 million taka in 2002, including a net profit of 10 million taka.

CHALLENGES.

Financial Independence.

In 2003, program support enterprises were expected to net 85 million taka in profits, Aarong Stores 65 million taka, BRAC Dairy 25 million taka, BRAC Printers 10 million taka, and BRAC Bank and other companies 15 million taka, for a total forecast of 200 million taka in net profits. Although in 2003 the microfinance activities under BDP were self-financing, education programs would cost more than 1,200 million taka to run and health and nutrition programs an additional 500 million taka.

BRAC's stated goal was to become as financially self-reliant as possible. Long-term plans had been developed to attempt to increase charges to BRAC members and gain government funding for both the education and health programs. "Right now," Kairy expanded, "net profits from our commercial ventures only cover about 10 percent of the health and education program costs. We would have to continue to expand into commercial activities at a dramatic rate in order to fill this gap. In addition, we have just started a new five-year program focused on the ultra-poor that will cost us 400 million taka a year."

Organization Structure and Growth.

BRAC had not only experienced tremendous growth in its development programs in the last decade, but within the last five years it had expanded into numerous commercial ventures that fundamentally changed the nature of the organization. As the organization absorbed these changes, two sets of payment structures had started to emerge. Employees working in development activities continued to be paid, as was typical in nonprofit organizations, fairly modest salaries. Those individuals managing commercial areas of the organization, however, were paid market rates. This created a two-tiered structure within the organization that was causing some discontent.

In addition, it was increasingly confusing to many people both outside and within BRAC what BRACs commercial strategy was and how commercial activities were organized within the organization. There seemed to be three main groups of commercial activities:

1. The program support enterprises that provided inputs to BRAC's members.

2. The commercial projects that provided market access for BRAC members. (The exceptions were BRAC's vegetable export business, which did both, although its reporting structure was similar to that of the program support enterprises; and BRAC Printers, which provided inputs to BRAC development programs but was considered a commercial project.)

3. Related companies and institutions that tended to be engaged in nation-building activities, had no direct link to BRAC members, and were connected to BRAC by name and the involvement of top BRAC executives.

All program support enterprises, including BRAC's vegetable export business, reported to a program coordinator at headquarters, who reported to the deputy executive director heading up BDP, who in turn reported to the executive director. The Aarong stores, BRAC Dairy, and BRAC Printers, however, were each managed by individual directors who reported directly to the CEO.

Ahmed wondered if BRAC should continue to pursue commercial activities and, if so, which ones and to what extent. Did it make sense to attempt to become completely financially sustainable through the use of profits generated by commercial ventures? Did this divert too much top management attention and resources from BRAC's development activities? Was BRAC becoming too big, too diverse?

The BRAC Brand.

The BRAC brand was a household name in Bangladesh, particularly in the rural areas where 80 percent of the population lived, and commanded great respect and trust. The Aarong brand was well known in the urban and middle-class community and was synonymous with high-quality products. Given this dual brand structure, Ahmed wondered which brand future BRAC commercial ventures should adopt. The poultry-processing plant, for example, would soon be packaging fresh poultry. Should these products be branded as Aarong or BRAC?

Some BRAC executives were concerned that by extending the use of the BRAC name to a bank, a university, and a variety of other for-profit companies, BRAC would dilute its brand reputation and image. Others argued that BRAC had a reputation that attracted trust and that this enabled these companies and institutions, which were sorely needed in Bangladesh, to be successful, resulting in the long-term aim of alleviating poverty and empowering the poor.

Ahmed wondered if BRAC should continue to build these two brands simultaneously or if one single BRAC brand might not provide more power.

BRAC's Competition—Grameen Bank.

Grameen Bank was the best-known microfinance organization in the world. It employed 11,770 staff members and worked in more than 41,000 villages in Bangladesh, providing US$287 million in loans. Grameen operated in a similar way to BRAC, through village organizations managed by a Grameen employee, but it did not train members and ran no community health or education services. (See **Exhibit 15** for a comparative summary of these enterprises and their activities.) "The major difference between BRAC and Grameen," Ahmed said, " is that Grameen believes that credit is a fundamental right of the people and that market forces will take care of the rest. BRAC believes that, in Bangladesh right now, poor people cannot compete in the market. Basic infrastructure and inputs don't exist—there is no way for poor people to even access the markets, and that's where we come in."

Grameen had expanded the scope of its activities and now operated a family of Grameen enterprises, including a telecom company, a knitwear factory, an Internet service provider, a venture capital fund, and a trust whose mission was to replicate the Grameen model worldwide through a network of partner organizations. In 2002, the Grameen Trust, whose role was to help its microfinance institutions learn about Grameen's lending methodology, had 112 partners in twenty-four countries. Grameen Bank itself was 93-percent owned by its borrowers and did not own any shares in the other Grameen companies. In addition to the companies in the Grameen network, Grameen Bank had created three organizations to spin off donor-funded activities: Grameen Fund, which invested in a variety of enterprises; Grameen Krishi (Agricultural) Foundation; and Grameen Motsho (Fisheries) Foundation. (See **Exhibit 16** for a summary of the Grameen family of enterprises.)

Grameen had been successful in creating multiple partnerships and building its brand name worldwide. Many of its commercial ventures were established as joint ventures, and it had created a network of partner organizations throughout the world. In the early 1990s, Grameen had partnered with Results Educational Fund, a U.S.-based lobbying organization with close to 40,000 volunteers who sought to create the political will to end hunger and used Grameen as a model. Building on its

Exhibit 15	Comparative Table of BRAC and Grameen

	BRAC	Grameen
Members served (microfinance)	3.8 million	2.4 million
Members served (health)	31 million	0
Members served (education)	1.1 million	0
Members trained	600,000	0
Number of villages covered	64,000	41,000
Number of employees	26,000 full-time, 34,000 part-time	11,752
Annual loans disbursed ($ millions)	317	171
Average loan size	$100	$110
% activities funded by donors	20%	0%
Number of countries present in	2	24 (through network)
Revenues generated by commercial activities (taka million)	2,881	150 (est.)

Source: Adapted from BRAC and Grameen Web sites.

Exhibit 16	Summary of Grameen Family of Enterprises, 2002

Company	Activity	Investment by Grameen Fund (million taka)
Grameen Trust	Founded in 1989 to share information about Grameen's model	N/A
Grameen Telecom	For-profit company projecting to bring cellular phone access to 100 million people in Bangladesh by 2005	N/A
Grameen Communications	Not-for-profit IT company that provides complete systems solutions through software products and services	N/A
Grameen Textile Mills Ltd.	Joint-venture composite textile mill producing woven fabrics	N/A
Grameen Shakti/Energy	Not-for-profit rural power company whose objective is to supply renewable energy to unelectrified villages	N/A
Grameen Shikkha/Education	Provides loans and grants for education and education programs	
Grameen Funds	Not-for-profit company providing finance to ventures (listed below)	N/A
Grameen Cybernet Ltd.	Bangladesh's leader in Internet services since 1996	Investment = 6/Equity = 51
Grameen Software Ltd.	Joint venture with private investors, software producer for local and foreign markets	Investment = 6/Equity = 65
Grameen IT Park	Joint venture offering floor space for rent with infrastructure support	Investment = 4/Equity = 29
Grameen Star Education Ltd.	Computer education and training	Investment = 1/ Equity = 65
Grameen Bitek Ltd.	Manufacturing company producing electronic products and electro-medical equipment	Investment = 2/Equity = 51
Tulip Dairy and Food Products	Public limited company producing milk products and fruit drinks	Investment = 4/Equity = 26
GlobeKids Digital Ltd.	Joint venture with New York-based GlobeKids Inc., digital animation production	Investment = 1/ Equity = 35
Rafiq Autovan Manufacturing	Four-stroke tri-wheeler passenger and goods carrier	Investment = 1/Equity = 40
National Soya Food Industry Ltd.	Joint venture to produce soya-fortified wheat flour and soya milk	Investment = 1/Equity = 25
Grameen Knitwear Ltd.	For-profit knitwear company exporting 100% of production with annual revenues of 505 million taka	Investment = 21/Equity = 22
Grameen Capital Management	For-profit merchant bank	Investment = 15/Equity = 75

Source: Adapted from Grameen Bank Web site.

strong brand name, Grameen created in 1999 the Grameen Foundation USA, based in Washington, D.C. This served as Grameen's fund-raising arm in the United States, with the objective of raising money to replicate the Grameen model in other countries.

BRAC, on the other hand, had expanded organically, focusing inward on its members and on meeting their needs. "We are a very shy organization," explained Shabbir A. Chowdhury, program head of microfinance. "We believe our work will speak for itself."

"We have never proactively marketed BRAC," Ahmed added. "Our ethos has been that we focus on the work and that recognition will come by itself."

New Opportunities.

"One area that I think is worth exploring," Ahmed said, "is using the member network we have in the villages throughout Bangladesh to distribute other BRAC and perhaps non-BRAC products to meet the current needs of villagers." Ahmed wondered to what extent BRAC could profitably supply other goods and services, in addition to its current microfinance, training, health, and education services, to its member network. For example, through BRAC's health program, more than 22,000 Shastho Shebikas (health volunteers) provided basic health care and medicines to the rural population, including a series of paramedical products that BRAC had developed. These included saline to combat dehydration; low-cost sanitary napkins; iodized salt; and a hygienic delivery kit that contained a sterile blade, needle and thread, and small piece of soap. BRAC manufactured these products and sold them to the Shastho Shebikas, who in turn sold them to their customers with a small markup. "Not only do we provide much-needed products," Ahmed said, "we help the Shastho Shebikas earn a small stipend." In 2003, these health products carried their own individual product brand names such as "Safe" and "Welfare," but all also carried the BRAC brand on their packaging.

In essence, this approach could change the role of BRAC members from being suppliers providing inputs for products that were then sold either to urban or international markets, to becoming customers for a potentially whole new range of products targeted at the rural population. Given that BRAC worked closely with millions of people through its microfinance and education programs, BRAC had ready access to a vast potential consumer market. Ahmed wondered what the cultural effect on BRAC would be of such an approach and what, if any, resistance it might meet.

CONCLUSION.

Abed, founder and CEO of BRAC, reflected on the evolution of the organization since it was established in 1972:

> Our objectives are not static, and the strategies we deploy to meet our mission have changed with the times and opportunities afforded us. There was no defined strategy behind our entry into the different commercial and program support enterprises; we have simply responded to our members' needs and the opportunities that have surfaced. We continue to be a highly entrepreneurial organization. If something looks like it might work and helps us further our mission, we try it. We are also constantly learning and sharing our learning both within and outside the organization. I find it interesting that BRAC is one

*of the only development nonprofit organizations that has successfully entered
the private sector, and the reasons why this is so might also help us shape our
future strategy.*

Notes to Case

[1] "Helping Hand for Bangladesh's Poor," *The New York Times*, March 25, 2003.

[2] Catherine Lovell, *Breaking the Cycle of Poverty* (Bloomfield, CT: Kumarian Press, 1992).

[3] See HBS Case No. 395-107 for details of BRAC's sericulture business.

[4] In that everything it undertook was successful.

[5] The project enabled the USDA to dispose of surplus soja beans, powdered milk, wheat, and maize, which were sold on the open market and the revenues from which were given to BRAC as a grant to fund free milk for schoolchildren.

PART 4

Brand Value

CASE 10
Habitat for Humanity International: Brand Valuation

We discovered that we have the same brand value as Starbucks, $1.8 billion! This was a shock to us and may change the way we view ourselves as an organization. The question now is how do we leverage brand value to further our mission and goals? Should we change our strategies and operations to increase our brand value?

—Dennis Bender, senior vice president of communications

Habitat for Humanity International (HFHI) was a nonprofit, ecumenical Christian housing ministry that sought to eliminate poverty housing and homelessness from the world. Founded in 1976 by Millard and Linda Fuller, HFHI had, by 2002, built more than 133,000 houses around the world, providing more than 650,000 people in more than 3,000 communities with affordable shelter. In 2002, HFHI comprised 2,285 active affiliates in eighty-seven countries.

Through volunteer labor and donations of money and materials, HFHI built and rehabilitated simple houses with homeowner (partner) families. The houses were sold to partner families at no profit and financed with no-interest loans, and the homeowners' monthly mortgage payments were then used to build still more houses. HFHI positioned itself as an organization "helping people to help themselves" rather than as a "giveaway program." In addition to mortgage payments, partner families were expected to invest hundreds of hours of their own labor (sweat equity) into building their own Habitat house and the houses of others. (See **Exhibit 1** for a fact sheet on HFHI.)

HISTORY.

The HFHI concept was conceived at Koinonia Farm, a small, interracial Christian farming community founded in 1942 outside Americus, Georgia, by farmer and biblical scholar Clarence Jordan. Millard and Linda Fuller had left a successful business and affluent lifestyle in Montgomery, Alabama, to begin a new life of Christian service and, with Jordan, developed the concept of "partnership housing." This model called for those in need of adequate housing to work side by side with volunteers to build simple, decent houses. The houses were built with no profit added and no

Professor John Quelch and Research Associate Nathalie Laidler prepared this case. HBS cases are developed solely as the basis for class discussion. Cases are not intended to serve as endorsements, sources of primary data, or illustrations of effective or ineffective management.

Exhibit 1	HFHI Fact Sheet 2002
WHO	HFHI is a nonprofit ecumenical Christian housing ministry seeking to eliminate poverty housing and homelessness from the world and to make decent housing a matter of conscience and action. An ecumenical board of directors determines policy and guides the mission of HFHI.
	HFHI invites people from all walks of life to work together in partnership to help build houses with families in need.
	Habitat is a grass-roots movement. Concerned citizens from all walks of life come together as volunteers to form an HFHI affiliate in their community which is responsible for fund-raising, house construction, and family selection.
HOW	Through volunteer labor and donations of money and materials, HFHI builds and renovates simple, decent houses with the help of homeowner (partner) families. These houses are sold to partner families at no profit, financed with affordable, no-interest loans. Homeowners' monthly mortgage payments go into a revolving Fund for Humanity that is used to build more houses.
	Habitat carries out its mission at the community level through organized groups called affiliates. Affiliates around the world raise the funds used to construct the houses and some affiliates in developing countries also receive grants from HFHI. All affiliates are asked to "tithe"—to give 10% of their contributions—to fund house-building work in other nations.
WHAT	Habitat is not a giveaway program. In addition to down payments and monthly mortgage payments, homeowners invest hundreds of hours of their own labor—sweat equity—into building their house and the houses of others. In the United States the average Habitat house costs $46,642.
	Families in need of decent shelter apply to their local Habitat affiliate, whose selection committee chooses homeowners on their level of need, willingness to become partners, and ability to repay the no-interest loan. Neither race nor religion is a factor in choosing homeowner families.
VOLUNTEERS/ PARTNERS	Any group of people may apply to form an affiliate, and any person may volunteer their time and or money through their local affiliate.
	HFHI also takes people to serve as International Partners (IPs) to serve with affiliates around the world, who make a three-year commitment.

Source: HFHI.

interest charged, financed by a revolving Fund for Humanity. The fund's money came from new homeowners' mortgage payments, donations, no-interest loans provided by supporters, and fund-raising activities. An open letter to the friends of Koinonia Farm in 1968 read as follows:

> *What the poor need is not charity but capital, not caseworkers but co-workers. And what the rich need is a wise, honorable and just way of divesting themselves of their overabundance. The Fund for Humanity will meet both of these needs. Money for the fund will come from shared gifts by those who feel they have more than they need and from non-interest bearing loans from those who cannot afford to make a gift but who do want to provide working capital for the disinherited. The fund will give away no money. It is not a handout.*

In 1968 Koinonia laid out forty-two half-acre house sites, with four acres reserved as a community park and recreational area. Capital was donated from around the country, and homes were built and sold to families in need at no profit and no interest. The basic model of HFHI was born. In 1973, the Fullers decided to apply the Fund for Humanity concept in developing countries, and the family moved to

Zaire (now the Democratic Republic of Congo). Over the next three years they worked to build adequate shelter for 2,000 people.

After returning to the United States in 1976, the Fullers called together a group of supporters to discuss the future of the fund, and HFHI as an organization was born. In 1984 former President Jimmy Carter and his wife, Rosalynn, took their first work trip, the Jimmy Carter Work Project, to New York City. Their personal involvement brought HFHI national visibility, and the number of new affiliates increased rapidly.

MISSION AND GOALS.

HFHI's stated mission was "To work in partnership with God and people everywhere, from all walks of life, to develop communities with people in need, by building and renovating houses so that there are decent houses in decent communities in which every person can experience God's love and can live and grow into all that God intended." "Habitat is clearly a Christian organization," Bender added. "We are guided by the love God has for all his people. We welcome anyone, and religious conviction does not play a role in the selection of a future homeowner."

HFHI's self-described purpose was "To partner with specific programs in habitat development globally, by constructing modest but adequate housing, and to associate with other organizations functioning with purposes consistent with those of Habitat as stated in the Articles of Incorporation, to witness to the Gospel of Jesus Christ throughout the world:

1. By working in cooperation with God's people in need, to create a better habitat in which to live and work.

2. By working in cooperation with other agencies and groups which have a kindred purpose.

3. By exemplifying the gospel of Jesus Christ through loving acts and the spoken and written word.

4. By enabling an expanding number of persons from all walks of life to participate in this ministry."

"Home ownership is part of the American dream," explained David Williams, executive vice president and chief operating officer. "You work hard, build your house, and pay for it. That's a story that resonates very strongly with people in the United States. We provide partnerships that help people achieve this dream."

According to the HFHI 2002 annual report, HFHI's goal was "To eliminate poverty housing and homelessness from the face of the earth by building adequate and basic housing. Furthermore, all of our words and actions are for the ultimate purpose of putting shelter on the hearts and minds of people in such a powerful way that poverty housing and homelessness become socially, politically, and religiously unacceptable in our nations and world." HFHI's five-year strategic plan, 2000–2005, called for completing 200,000 homes by the end of 2005, housing 1 million people, establishing a presence in 100 countries, and developing the organizational capabilities necessary for future growth. (See **Exhibit 2** for an overview of the strategic plan.)

"We are in the vanguard of an emerging movement," said Millard Fuller, founder and president of HFHI, "to end substandard housing and homelessness. This is akin

Exhibit 2	Overview of HFHI Strategic Plan, 2000–2005

LEADERSHIP	INNOVATION	CAPACITY	ADVOCACY
The commitment: To establish a framework through education and experience that supports leadership development throughout Habitat for Humanity.	**The commitment:** To develop or evolve housing models and forms of governance that achieve community sustainability through flexible strategic alliances, representative governance structures and advancement of the 21st Century Challenge.	**The commitment:** To increase the strength of Habitat for Humanity at all organizational levels to support the 200,000-house and 100-country goals and to put in place an organization of achieving even greater goals beyond 2005.	**The commitment:** To strengthen and expand Habitat's education/ advocacy role in effectively communicating the needs of all persons for safe and decent shelter.
Habitat for Humanity International action steps will include: • Evaluating current leadership development programs and needs. • Identifying programs, including possible creation of a "Habitat University," to meet existing and emerging leadership development needs. • Identifying new sources of funds for leadership development programs.	**Habitat for Humanity International action steps will include:** • Exploring new or existing models that transform communities. • Studying how Habitat for Humanity can impact housing needs in complex urban environments. • Actively promoting the concept of setting a date for eliminating substandard housing globally. • Developing guidelines to ensure the formation of effective strategic alliances.	**Habitat for Humanity International action steps will include:** • Creating country-specific plans for assisting local fund-raising efforts. • Facilitating a land use and acquisition policy that supports house-building goals. • Developing organization-wide communications strategies. • Developing fair and equitable compensation systems. • Developing an HFHI Diversity Initiative.	**Habitat for Humanity International action steps will include:** • Defining and understanding community transformation consistent with Jesus' teachings on peace, reconciliation, and concern for the poor. • Reviewing existing parameters and successes in serving as the "voice" for adequate shelter. • Maximizing use of public and media opportunities to advance the case for decent shelter. • Giving the topic of education/advocacy a prominent place in major HFHI convocations throughout the year.
What does the goal of leadership development mean to you? Here are some questions to help start your discussions: • What is the leadership structure of this (affiliate, national office, department, state organization, etc.)? • How does this leadership influence the success of our work? • What is needed in terms of support or training to make leaders more effective? • What should our leadership structure look like in five years? How will we get there? • How will we measure the strengthening of leadership?	**What does focusing on innovation mean to you?** Here are some questions to help start your discussions: • Are we participating, or preparing to participate, in the 21st Century Challenge? What do we need to do to get ready to set a date for eliminating substandard housing in our service area? Are we actively promoting the concept that substandard housing can be eliminated? • Is our work having the greatest impact possible on transforming this community? How can we expand our impact? • What alliances can be formed with other like-minded groups to further our work? • What can we learn from other affiliates, national organizations or HFHI departments that would increase our effectiveness?	**What does the goal of capacity building mean to you?** Here are some questions to help start your discussions: • What are our building targets? What would the targets be if we really stretched? • How will we raise the money to reach those targets? • How will we acquire the land to achieve our building targets? • Do the numbers and knowledge of our staffing/volunteer base support success in meeting the building targets? Does our staff and volunteer base reflect the diverse demographics of the area we serve? Are staff and volunteers treated appropriately in terms of compensation and/or recognition? • Are we taking full advantage of support offered by Habitat for Humanity International? Are we operating within proven "Best Practices"? • Are we meeting the tithe expectation?	**What does focusing on education/ advocacy mean to you?** Here are some questions to help start your discussions: • Are we recognized as a turn-to "voice" on the issue of adequate shelter in this community, state, region or country? What can we do to increase our visibility as advocates for decent shelter? • Have we developed effective "advocates"—writers, speakers, spokespersons? • Do we have the information to effectively discuss the "state of housing" in this service area? If not, how do we develop that information? • Does our performance as an organization match our words on the topic of adequate shelter? • Are we regular participants in meetings and conferences on the needs of the poor and the need for adequate shelter?

Source: HFHI.

to the movement to end slavery, the civil rights movement, or Gandhi's nonviolent independence movement. We are propelling humanity to find it unacceptable that human beings live in desperation and degradation. We want to make poverty housing socially, politically, and religiously unacceptable."

NEED AND ACTIVITIES.

Global Need.

In 2002, an estimated 1.2 billion people worldwide were experiencing "income poverty," meaning they lived on the equivalent of less than one dollar per day.[1] The United Nations Center for Human Settlements (UNCHS) estimated that 1.1 billion people were living in inadequate housing conditions in urban areas alone, and that some 21 million new housing units would be required each year in developing countries to accommodate growth in the number of households between 2000 and 2010.[2] Some 14 million additional units would be required each year for the next twenty years if the current housing deficit was to be eliminated by 2020.

In Latin America, households needed 5.4 times their annual income to buy a house. In Africa, they needed an average of 12.5 times their annual income. The highest rents were found in the Arab states, where a household spent an average of 45 percent of its monthly income on rent. Real estate costs were highest in Asia and the Pacific. Less than 20 percent of households in Africa were connected to piped water, and only 40 percent had piped water within 200 meters of their homes. In the developing world, 29 percent of cities had areas considered "inaccessible" or "dangerous" to the police. In Latin America and the Caribbean, this figure was 48 percent. In cities of the developing world, one out of every four households lived in poverty. Forty percent of African urban households were living below the locally defined poverty line, and fewer than 35 percent of cities in the developing world had their wastewater treated. In countries with economies in transition, 75 percent of solid wastes were disposed of in open dumps.[3]

Taking Action.

In fiscal year 2002, HFHI built 19,532 homes worldwide, 5,400 of which were in the United States. (See **Exhibit 3** for details of the number of houses built by affiliates worldwide.) In HFHI's 2002 annual report, four focus areas were highlighted: leading in the mission to build decent homes with people in need; developing methods to better accomplish goals; building the capacity to serve; and advocating and educating about the ills of substandard housing and HFHI's solution.

As part of HFHI's twenty-fifth anniversary and in keeping with the objective of leadership, eighty-seven delegates from HFHI affiliates around the world gathered in late 2001 for a global leadership conference. This included structured training sessions, open forums and panel discussions, and the opportunity to share best practices around the world.

The 2002 annual report also highlighted innovative programs that had been initiated in developing countries to increase people's ability to afford decent homes. The first of these was a "Save and Build" program in which prospective Habitat homeowners were organized into groups of twelve families. Each family saved the equivalent of 15 cents per day for six months. At the end of this period, the group's savings were matched by funds from HFHI sufficient to build three houses, each consisting of a single room with an attached kitchen and bathroom area. Within twenty-seven months, all twelve families had completed their houses. The "Save and Build" program was also adapted to a single family that saved up for their home over time and built it in incremental stages. In Eastern Europe, HFHI also began to renovate substandard apartments into decent housing.

Exhibit 3	HFHI Affiliates Worldwide, 2002

Country	Year of Affiliation	Active Affiliates	FY 2002 House Total	Cumulative House Total
AFRICA AND THE MIDDLE EAST				
Botswana	1992	10	161	857
Burundi (partnership)	1987	0	0	988
Cameroon	2001	1	0	0
Central African Rep.	1991	7	19	461
Dem. Rep. of Congo	1975	6	78	2,473
Egypt	1989	12	1,056	3,162
Ethiopia	1990	4	40	172
Ghana	1987	34	512	2,763
Ivory Coast	2000	10	49	49
Jordan	2001	2	21	21
Kenya	1982	35	92	1,186
Lebanon	2001	1	28	28
Lesotho	2001	1	0	0
Liberia	2000	6	18	18
Madagascar	2000	15	74	100
Malawi	1985	5	208	5,176
Mozambique	2000	1	1	1
Nigeria	1989	2	1	1
South Africa	1987	17	300	903
Tanzania	1985	12	109	1,867
Uganda	1982	41	509	3,051
Zambia	1985	12	94	909
Zimbabwe	1996	12	165	630
TOTALS		246	3,535	24,816
ASIA AND THE PACIFIC				
Australia	1988	10	3	36
Bangladesh	1999	2	96	153
East Timor	2001	1	0	0
Fiji	1992	5	14	469
Territory of Guam	1996	1	6	10
India	1982	25	1,210	7,963
Indonesia	1991	3	16	81
Republic of Korea	1995	10	155	242
Malaysia	1998	2	9	15
Mongolia	2000	1	17	19
Nepal	1997	6	182	516
New Zealand	1993	21	31	150
Pakistan	1987	0	0	20
Papua New Guinea	1983	10	41	1,040
Philippines	1986	33	1,087	5,745
Samoa	2000	1	4	4
Solomon Islands	1986	1	9	36
Sri Lanka	1994	9	1,144	2,310
Thailand	1998	4	17	59
Vanatu	2001	1	8	8
Vietnam	2000	1	0	0
TOTALS		147	4,049	18,876
EUROPE AND CENTRAL ASIA				
Armenia	1990	1	13	14
Bulgaria	2001	1	0	0
Great Britain	1995	4	0	9
Hungary	1996	3	16	62
Kyrgyzstan	1999	1	9	9
Northern Ireland	1994	1	0	27

Source: HFHI Annual Report, FY 2002.

Note: U.S. and Canada affiliate house numbers are shown projected for fiscal year 2002.

Exhibit 3 continued

Country	Year of Affiliation	Active Affiliates	FY 2002 House Total	Cumulative House Total
Poland	1992	4	7	23
Portugal	1996	1	0	2
Romania	1996	4	24	54
Tajikistan	2000	1	17	47
TOTALS		21	86	247
LATIN AMERICA AND THE CARIBBEAN				
Antigua and Barbuda	1997	1	2	3
Argentina	1992	2	0	6
Belize	1999	1	4	8
Bolivia	1987	8	582	3,507
Brazil	1987	12	398	2,152
Chile	2000	1	0	0
Colombia	1995	8	89	450
Costa Rica	1987	6	86	298
Dominican Republic	1987	7	154	807
Ecuador	1998	5	97	131
El Salvador	1993	7	604	2,090
Guatemala	1979	17	2,470	11,505
Guyana	1995	4	30	152
Haiti	1981	6	21	425
Honduras	1988	5	571	3,364
Jamaica	1993	8	6	82
Mexico	1987	24	764	12,278
Nicaragua	1984	16	367	2,314
Paraguay	1998	1	83	133
Peru	1982	19	7	4,708
Trinidad and Tobago	1996	3	9	32
Venezuela	2000	1	9	9
TOTALS		162	6,353	44,454
UNITED STATES	–	1,651	5,400	44,617
CANADA	–	58	109	631
GRAND TOTALS	–	2,285	19,532	133,641

Source: HFHI Annual Report, FY 2002.

Note: U.S. and Canada affiliate house numbers are shown projected for fiscal year 2002.

HFHI was taking an increasingly active role in advocacy. The Jimmy Carter Work Projects, initiated in 1984, were annual events at which former U.S. President Carter donated his time to the building of a home. The June 2002 event resulted in the construction of 1,000 homes across Africa, 100 of which were in Durban, South Africa, and drew hundreds of volunteers and the world's attention to HFHI's mission. In August 2002, HFHI also held a six-day "World Leaders Build" event in which twenty-eight heads of state and government from twenty-six countries, including President George W. Bush, along with thousands of volunteers, worked together to build 1,175 houses. This event also drew worldwide attention to the organization.

Operations.

Families in need of housing applied to their local Habitat affiliate, whose selection committee chose homeowners on the basis of their level of need, willingness to become partners, and ability to repay the no-interest loan. Neither race nor religion were factors in this selection process. Throughout the world, average house costs varied widely, running from $800 for a home in some developing countries to $51,219 in the United States. Mortgages varied in length from three to thirty years. "We are a construction company, a bank, and a human services organization all rolled into one," Bender explained, "and, although we are unashamedly Christian, we do not use house-building to evangelize."

Mortgage repayment rates in the United States were very high, with only a 2-percent foreclosure rate. In the case of a foreclosure, the property was made available to the next Habitat homeowner candidate, who in exchange provided sweat equity in the building of another Habitat house. Internationally, however, repayment rates averaged 50 percent in Africa, around 70 percent in Latin America, and 80 percent in Asia. In some countries, particularly in situations of disaster relief, Habitat competed with nongovernmental organizations (NGOs) that built houses and donated them to needy families. "It's difficult," Bender explained, "to implement the Habitat model of sweat equity and mortgages in one village if, in an adjacent village, another organization is giving away a house."

The reasons behind foreclosures varied by country. "In Kenya, for example," added Michael Carscaddon, senior vice president of administration, "many of the foreclosures are complicated by land title issues."

Habitat's business model was easy to communicate, according to Jack Yager, director of marketing and brand strategy:

> We help people build their own homes as economically as possible and provide them with interest-free loans. In exchange, we ask them to participate in the building process itself. People understand the concept of sweat equity and really take ownership of the process and the result. For donors, the brand is highly participatory and practical. Because we are not trying to cure a disease or eliminate world hunger, it's easy for us to demonstrate results. Our supporters and volunteers also become very engaged; not only can they donate their money, but they can donate their time and participate in the construction of a home.

International.

Culturally, the United States was unique in the prevalence of volunteerism, which was generally a less accepted practice in other countries. Bender explained, "In the ex-USSR countries, for example, volunteering has a whole different meaning since it was an activity that was mandated by the state." Habitat marketing objectives in Western Europe were also different from those in the United States. "Substandard housing is less common because of the government involvement in this area," Bender said. "In many European countries, home ownership is not that big of a deal, and HFHI does not necessarily have the same appeal as in the United States. As a result, much of our focus in Europe is geared to raising funds to build homes in the developing world." He continued with a number of examples:

> In Northern Ireland, however, we are developing a project called the Bridge for Reconciliation. This involves teams of Catholic and Protestant volunteers building eight houses in a Protestant neighborhood and eight houses in a Catholic neighborhood. In Central Asia and Eastern Europe, the need for housing is greater, but we have faced many obstacles to attracting volunteers, even with the prospective homeowners. In the U.K., Habitat is a name of a home-furnishing

retailer, and we have experienced a lot of brand confusion there. We are clearly challenged in the Middle East, and we don't talk about our mission in these countries but about our work. In Jordan, Lebanon, and Egypt, it takes a lot of negotiation, explanation, and use of the right words. We don't want to be viewed as using house-building as a disguise for evangelism. One difficulty we face, given our global presence, is to manage our image. What we say on the ground to a specific geographical audience cannot be customized much, given the wide access to the Internet. Ninety-five percent of our resources come from the U.S., but most of our houses are built internationally.

"Africa is the toughest place to work," Carscaddon added, "because of the lack of infrastructure. Asia and Latin America, on the other hand, have excellent community organizations, and self-help initiatives are thriving." Ted Swisher, vice president of U.S. affiliates, expanded:

In the Middle East we have difficulty even registering as an organization, and in Egypt, for example, we work through another existing Christian organization. In many countries, it is illegal to evangelize, and so we have to carefully adapt all our materials and some of our practices. For example, it is Habitat tradition to give the new Habitat homeowner a Bible. Obviously, in Nepal, for example, we don't maintain that tradition. Our strong Christian core means that, in many Muslim countries, we walk on eggshells and have really struggled to establish ourselves. In Latin America, on the other hand, it has been an asset. Asia has a lot of potential, and we are starting to gain a foothold in China and Vietnam through alliances with existing Christian NGOs.

Specific Projects and Campaigns.

The "More Than Houses" fund-raising campaign was launched in 2000 with the objective of raising $500 million, the funds necessary to build 100,000 new homes by the end of 2005. In 2002, this campaign was on track to achieve its goals, with more than 50 percent of donations coming from corporations. (See **Exhibit 4** for a status report of the More Than Houses campaign and **Exhibit 5** for a More Than Houses campaign advertisement.)

Exhibit 4	Status Report of the More Than Houses Campaign (as of November 2002)	
	FY03 Totals	**Cumulative Totals since January 2000**
Overall Goal		$500,000,000
FY 03 Goal	$65,000,000	$305,000,000
Total Raised by November 2002	$28,246,403	$272,279,451
% Goal Raised	43%	54%
Funds Raised through HFHI	$19,541,672	$138,440,072
Funds Raised through Affiliates	$8,704,731	$131,218,260
Timetable Elapsed	33%	60%

Source: HFHI.

Exhibit 5	More Than Houses Campaign Advertisement, January 2003

More Than Houses Campaign
Exceeds Halfway Mark

Habitat for Humanity for Humanity can continue building decent, affordable housing only to the extent that partners throughout the world share our concern for families enduring substandard conditions—and manifest that concern through their support of Habitat's efforts.

We rely on the generosity of individual donors, corporate partners, foundations and church congregations to further our mission through monetary donations and gifts of land and building materials.

Coupled with active hands and compassionate hearts, resource development extends Habitat's capacity to build better housing with those who need it. Launched in January 2000, the More Than Houses: Rebuilding Our Communities fund-raising campaign is one measure of Habitat's commitment to overcoming substandard housing wherever it exists.

Thanks to the involvement from partners at many levels, this initiative recently exceeded the halfway mark to its $500 million objective. As of Nov. 1, campaign donors had contributed $264,450,451.

However, as long as families suffer the hardships of inadequate housing, our work is far from over ... and we need your support to continue.

Countless families around the world depend on it.

To learn more about how you or your company can donate to Habitat for Humanity or its More Than Houses campaign, please contact Tony DiSpigno, HFHI's senior vice president for Development, at (800) 422-4828, ext. 2771, or via e-mail at tdispigno@hfhi.org.

Habitat for Humanity® International

KIM MacDONALD

Habitat for Humanity® International
121 Habitat St.
Americus, GA 31709-3498

NONPROFIT ORG.
U.S. POSTAGE
PAID
HABITAT FOR HUMANITY
INTERNATIONAL

Source: HFHI.

HFHI also ran a Women Build program, a Prison Partnership program, a Campus Chapter and Youth program, and a Habit for Humanity University:

- The Women Build program was established to encourage the involvement of women in the construction of Habitat homes. In the United States, women made up 50 percent of HFHI's volunteer force but accounted for less than 15 percent of the work done on construction sites, and almost 50 percent of Habitat homes were built for women heads of households. By 2002, 350 Habitat homes in the United States had been built by women crews.

- The Prison Partnership program linked HFHI affiliates with volunteers who were incarcerated offenders. These volunteers produced completed housing components, landscaping materials, and other items for house construction and found opportunities to develop marketable job and social skills. In 2002, there were seventy-five prison partnerships throughout the United States, with offenders building or contributing to the building of 250 homes a year.

- The Campus Chapters were unincorporated, student-run organizations that acted in partnership with affiliates to help build, educate, and raise funds for Habitat. In 2002, close to 10,000 students in the United States built houses during their spring breaks for the Collegiate Challenge. In addition, HFHI organized creative opportunities for youth volunteers to become involved in Habitat, ranging from landscaping and drawing greeting cards to constructing and painting window boxes and building picnic tables.

- Habitat for Humanity University was created to foster global knowledge sharing and to identify and nurture the next generation of leaders in the movement to eliminate poverty housing. The intended audience went beyond Habitat staff members and volunteers, and the university sought to serve as a catalyst for other like-minded organizations and individuals, acting as an advocate in raising global awareness of issues and approaches to eliminating substandard housing. It sponsored a lecture series, mentoring, online learning, and scholarly research in partnership with academic institutions, other nonprofits, and corporations.

In 2002, HFHI was building a global village and discovery center near its headquarters in Americus, Georgia. The village would include geographic neighborhoods of Habitat houses throughout the world, a museum simulating the experiences of Habitat homeowners and volunteers, and a marketplace with international crafts and merchandise. Among other activities, visitors would be able to make pressed-earth bricks like those used in Kenya or construct roofing tiles like those used in India. (See **Exhibit 6** for graphic of the HFHI Global Village.)

ORGANIZATIONAL STRUCTURE.[4]

HFHI comprised three organizational layers: local and national affiliates, area and regional offices (U.S. and international), and HFHI headquarters. At the community level, HFHI worked through its affiliates: independent, locally run, nonprofit organizations. In 2002, there were 2,285 affiliates worldwide, of which 1,651

| Exhibit 6 | Graphic Depiction of HFHI Global Village |

Global Village & Discovery Center

Habitat for Humanity® International

Source: HFHI.

were based in the United States. (See **Exhibit 3** for details of affiliates.) Williams expanded:

> *Our organizational structure centers on affiliates. The relationship between affiliates and HFHI is principally governed by a covenant. Internationally, we work through national organizations, for example Habitat Guatemala, which is staffed by local people and which we are currently helping become self-sufficient through local fund-raising. Other than funding, a national organization works in the same way as a U.S. affiliate. We run a very decentralized organization, but this can get us into trouble. In the past, we have had a few badly run or corrupt affiliates, and we've had to bail them out. Obviously, the negative impact of these problems on the brand is important.*

Although Habitat affiliates varied in size and character, they all had to undergo a nine- to twelve-month affiliation process consisting of seventy-seven steps, including establishing committees and a board of directors, fund-raising, and gaining local community support. Each affiliate coordinated all aspects of Habitat home-building in its local area: fund-raising, building-site selection, partner family selection and support, house construction, and mortgage servicing. U.S. affiliates were asked to "tithe"—in other words, give a percentage of their contributions to fund house-building work in other nations where affiliates had difficulty raising funds locally. In 2002, U.S. affiliates donated nearly $9 million to support HFHI's work overseas. Some European affiliates, for example in Germany and the Netherlands, were focused entirely on fund-raising to support home-building in developing countries.

U.S. affiliates also varied in their effectiveness. In Jacksonville, Florida, for example, a partnership had been struck between the local authorities and the Habitat affiliate to provide 20,000 people living in substandard housing with a Habitat home over the next twenty years. In Montgomery, Alabama, however, the local affiliate had built only one house, and in 1993 the Boston affiliate's board had been asked to resign. Fuller commented, "Arson, robbery, lying . . . we have survived it all because the concept is right. When you have good leadership at the affiliate level, it soars."

Within the United States, seven regional offices worked to coordinate the U.S. affiliate program. They ensured that local affiliates were well acquainted with Habitat's vision and methods of operation and ran annual regional conferences, training sessions, and state meetings. HFHI also had four regional offices overseas: the Africa/Middle East office, in South Africa; the Asia/Pacific office, in Thailand; the Europe/Central Asia office, in Hungary; and the Latin America and Caribbean office, in Costa Rica. These regional offices played a similar coordination support and cross-learning role for international affiliates.

HFHI's headquarters, in Americus, Georgia, provided information, training, and support services to Habitat affiliates worldwide. Headquarters comprised 325 paid employees, an additional 600 who worked internationally or in the area and regional offices, and more than 150 long-term volunteers, who typically served for more than a year. "The role of HFHI is fourfold," Williams explained:

> First we provide resources in terms of dollars and volunteers. Outside the United States we are the main provider of funds, and within the United States, the total contributions and services provided to affiliates by HFHI is equal to about 20 percent of the average cost of a Habitat house. Second, we provide best practices, training, and coordination for our affiliates. We are currently creating the Habitat for Humanity University. Third, we are the guardian of the Habitat brand name and have standards of excellence for our affiliates, which we put on probation if we feel there is a problem. Fourth, we are keeper of the torch, the Christian mission.

HFHI permeated the town of Americus, where it was one of the largest employers and numerous volunteer houses had been built. Poverty housing in the town had all but been eliminated. "Americus is a model for what we're proposing," Fuller said. "We have ended poverty housing here." Bender added:

> In the last three or four years, this organization has become increasingly professional in its management, recruiting people from the for-profit world. For example, I was in the automotive industry for a long time; Jack Yager, director of marketing and brand strategy, was in the advertising world; and Michael Carscaddon, senior vice president of administration, used to work for First Union bank. We are open to outsiders who can bring the new disciplines and practices necessary for Habitat to strengthen its organizational capacity. [See *Exhibit 7* for an organizational chart of HFHI.]

Exhibit 7	Organizational Chart for HFHI, 2002

Source: HFHI.

FUNDING AND RESOURCE ALLOCATION.

In fiscal year 2002 (ending June 2002), the headquarters organization of HFHI recorded revenues of $162 million, with some 74 percent of funding coming from individual contributions, up from 63 percent in 2001. U.S. affiliates accounted for 39 percent of expenditures, international affiliates a further 26 percent, fund-raising 25 percent, public relations and awareness programs 7 percent, and general management expenses 3 percent. (See **Exhibit 8** for details of revenues and expenditures.)

This did not, however, reflect the scope of the entire organization. As autonomous nonprofit organizations, HFHI affiliates and national organizations maintained their own revenues and expenditures, which were not included in HFHI's financial statements. Estimated total revenues for the worldwide organization in 2002 were $689 million (including the $162 million), of which $394 million came from cash contributions, $168 million from sales to homeowners, $78 million from gifts in-kind, and $49 million in other support. Roughly 80 percent of funds received were spent on programs, 10 percent on fund-raising, and 10 percent on management and general expenses.

Because of the economic downturn, depreciation of stock values, and tragedy of September 11th, 2001, raising funds had become increasingly difficult. The cancellation of a direct-marketing solicitation scheduled for soon after September 11th was another factor explaining the 5-percent decline in revenues in FY 2002. (See **Exhibit 9** for an example of a direct-mail piece.) "Churches are our strongest support base," Fuller added. "A single church this year gave us $1 million, for example. We receive enormous support from churches—we must remember this."

When asked about the effect of competition on fund-raising, many HFHI executives did not think competition played an important role. "We don't really talk in

Exhibit 8	HFHI Revenues and Expenditures ($ millions)	
$ millions	**FY 2002**	
Revenues		
Contributions	120.4	
Government grants	21.9	
Other income	9.4	
Donations in-kind	10.4	
Transfers to homeowners	0	
TOTAL	162	
Expenses		
Program services		
U.S. affiliates	62.2	
International affiliates	42.5	
Public awareness and education	10.6	
Total	115.3	
Supporting services		
Fund-raising	39.3	
Management and general	4.9	
Total	44.2	
TOTAL	159.6	
Transfers	(4.3)	
Losses on receivables	1.9	
Total	165.8	
Changes in net assets	(3.8)	
Net assets at beginning of year	74.9	
Net assets at end of year	71.1	

Source: HFHI Annual Report 2002.

terms of competitors, but there are organizations that we consider to be comparable to ours," Williams explained. "I suppose organizations such as World Vision or the Enterprise Foundation would be the closest. It's going to take more than one organization to solve the problems of poverty housing in the world, and the more of us there are, the better."

THE HABITAT BRAND.

HFHI's unaided awareness had doubled between 1996 and 2002. Peter D. Hart Research Associates had conducted research in both 1996 and 2002, asking respondents in the United States which were the nonprofit organizations they knew of that focused on helping poor people. In 1996 the unaided brand awareness for HFHI stood at 4 percent; in 2002, it had risen to just over 8 percent.

In June 2002, HFHI retained Peter D. Hart Research Associates to conduct a series of focus groups and surveys to understand how the general public, HFHI partners, potential new partners,[5] and corporate officers viewed the Habitat brand.[6] Specifically, the project sought to probe these audiences for any emerging negative views or concerns, compare the organization's current image with that identified in a 1995 research study, identify which messages helped bond partners most, and explore reactions to the fledgling First Shelter concept of providing emergency housing.

Exhibit 9	Excerpts from an HFHI Direct-Mail Piece Distributed in the United States, 2002

Dear Friend,

Please gently remove the Bless This House keepsake above and hold it in your hand ...

... while I share with you the amazing story of what this keepsake means.

Our story begins in Sarasota, Florida.

That's where Dewey Furr arrived in the late 1970s after serving with the Army. He had nothing more than his work tools and 44 cents in his pocket. And because he had to drop out of school when he was a boy to help support his family, he didn't know how to read and write. At most, he had the equivalent of a fourth or fifth grade education.

But Dewey did know how to work, and he was determined to get a job to support his wife, Tammy, and their three daughters.

One day he spotted a construction crane in the distance and he walked right over to the work site. The foreman hired him on the spot. It was more than he had ever made in his life, but still a very modest wage.

Because money was tight, Tammy and Dewey and their three girls lived in a cramped, squalid apartment infested with termites, frogs and rats.

Dewey wanted so badly to move his family into a safe, decent home of their own. But as hard as he worked, there just wasn't money enough to move them out of their rundown apartment.

But, then Dewey heard about Habitat for Humanity.

Dewey did volunteer construction work on three Habitat houses — "to see if it was real," he says, and to overcome an initial skepticism about Habitat for Humanity's program to help families in need build decent, affordable homes.

Only then, after he had both witnessed and participated in

Habitat for Humanity® International
121 Habitat Street · Americus, GA 31709 · www.habitat.org

may & real from you by December 27th?
Bless you for helping! Millard

For a family in need ...

Yes! *I want to reach out in love to parents and children and help provide them with a modest, affordable home. Please count on me as one of your Habitat friends! Enclosed please find:*

☐ **$20** *to help pay for a 50-lb. box of nails.*
☐ **$35** *to help purchase roofing materials.*
☐ **$50** *to help pay for a kitchen door.*
☐ **$_____** *to help as much as possible.*

Milana McLead
121 Habitat St
Americus GA 31709-3423

262 994 5276   1231 08SED

Your gift is tax-deductible to the fullest extent of the law. Please make your check payable to Habitat for Humanity International and return it with this reply in the envelope enclosed or mail to:

Habitat for Humanity® International · 121 Habitat Street · Americus, GA 31709 · www.habitat.org

3647

Source: HFHI.

The research found that HFHI enjoyed both a high profile and broad popular support, with 69 percent aided recognition and all people knowing the brand having positive or very positive feelings toward HFHI. Only 17 percent of those surveyed said they did not know of the organization. In addition, very few people were found to hold negative views, and the public regarded HFHI as an effective and efficient organization. (See **Exhibit 10** for the market research results.)

However, the researchers also found that current and potential partners had an inaccurate image of Habitat, believing that the organization was a secular and community-based charity rather than a faith-based, global organization. They found that the faith-based nature of the organization was not an issue if it was made clear that faith was not a criterion for becoming a new Habitat homeowner. Although some people had misgivings when they first learned that HFHI did not give homes away, these negative views turned positive once they understood the partnership concept and the idea of "sweat equity." (See **Exhibit 11** for examples of some donor comments.) The market researcher's report suggested that "The Christian faith that is central to the organization's work does not also need to be central to the organization's message." Top management at HFHI disagreed about this issue, and Fuller illustrated the tension with the following example:

> It was Building on Faith Week, an annual fund-raising and awareness-building event. I saw that the banners reading "Proclaiming Christ in Word and Deed" were not up as planned. I inquired and was told that some Jewish and Muslim people were attending and that they might be offended. "They are welcome," I replied, "but we are a Christian organization, and we should not be ashamed of it." There is danger in these types of trade-offs. We don't have to exclude Jesus to include people of other faiths. We must not deny the essence of who we are.

Although partners and prospective partners were both found to be attracted to HFHI's core mission, different aspects of the organization appealed to the two groups. When asked to pick one or two statements that best described their reasons for contributing to HFHI, current partners chose the tangible results of the work (36 percent) and the role of Jimmy Carter (25 percent), whereas volunteered labor and materials (34 percent) and involvement of the recipients (34 percent) were the most appealing for prospective partners. (See **Exhibit 12** for further details.)

Attitudes toward HFHI's international mission were not valued widely in the United States. Many of HFHI's own partners felt strongly that problems within the

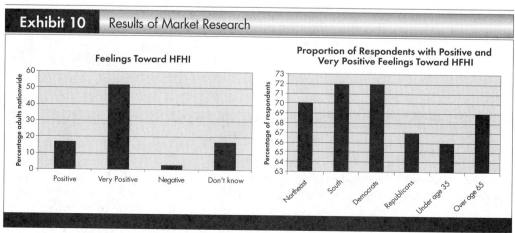

| Exhibit 10 | Results of Market Research |

Feelings Toward HFHI

Proportion of Respondents with Positive and Very Positive Feelings Toward HFHI

Source: Peter D. Hart Research Associates, courtesy of HFHI, 2002.

Exhibit 11	Examples of Donor Comments

"I don't have a problem if that's where they started. I would have a problem if I'm giving money to them and they're promoting . . . oh, you need to be a Christian . . . in whatever form they might do that."
—Sacramento donor

"I didn't pay attention to the fact that it was Christian-based. Plain and simply, the organization leaves something behind. There's a house that a family now has. It's kind of basic to me."
—Baltimore donor

"It's nice to help Third World countries and all that, but we have a lot of problems here. We need to take care of our own first. We have this great nation, and we've got so many poor and homeless here."
—Sacramento donor

"I'm all for helping other countries, but we've got a lot of problems, a lot of people hungry here, and a lot of people that need homes."
—Baltimore prospective donor

Source: Peter D. Hart Research Associates, courtesy of HFHI, 2002.

Exhibit 12	Appeal of HFHI for Partners and Prospective Partners

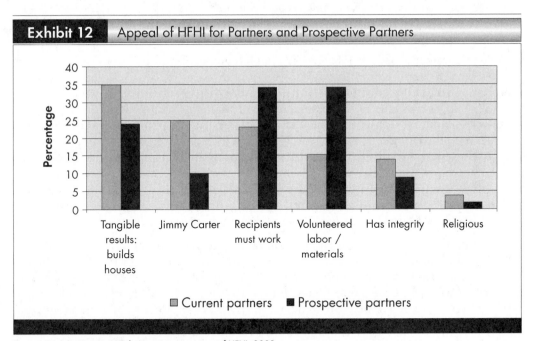

Source: Peter D. Hart Research Associates, courtesy of HFHI, 2002.

United States should be addressed before sending money abroad. (See **Exhibit 11** for examples of donor comments.) With respect to expanding the organization's role into emergency housing, partners offered a cautious "go-ahead," but many voiced concern about mission dilution and redundancy with other organizations. In focus groups, 57 percent of current partners and 53 percent of prospective partners supported the First Shelter concept.

Market research conducted in the United Kingdom in May 2002 showed that HFHI's aided brand awareness stood at just 18 percent. Respondents did not place homelessness or slum housing as a social priority and were more likely to support domestic rather than international issues, with only 9 percent of respondents giving to charities working internationally. In addition, 28 percent of respondents had taken part in some kind of volunteer activity in the past twelve months, 45 percent of which had been in fund-raising activities. Respondents' initial reactions to the aims of HFHI were cautious, with only 17 percent saying they thought HFHI was a good or excellent idea, 9 percent saying they would donate to HFHI, and 14 percent saying they would volunteer for a cause like Habitat.

Corporate Partnerships.

Over the past few years, HFHI had been approached by many corporations and asked to form partnerships. Bender expanded:

> *Corporations keep coming to us because we are the American nonprofit that America loves to hug. Unlike many other nonprofits, we are able to give our supporters the ability to get directly involved in our work. You can literally pick up a hammer and see the results of your efforts. There is a saying that America will contribute to anything people can take a picture of, and that's true of what we do at Habitat. We are builders of both houses and new lives. Everyone can identify and contribute to what we do, and many people have a positive and emotional identification with the Habitat brand.*

The volunteer aspect of HFHI work enabled employees of partner corporations to become directly involved in HFHI, which many corporations viewed as a strong positive aspect of the partnership. "The volunteer opportunities HFHI offers can be used by partners as part of their management training activities," Bender said. "For example, Bain and Co. pay for their new MBA recruits to spend time volunteering for Habitat for Humanity, building a house in a foreign country." In January 2003, Tufts University also offered a ten-day alumni program to participate in a Habitat house build in Costa Rica. "We are trying to develop that aspect of our program and become a competitor of Outward Bound," Bender explained. "I think that many *Fortune* 500 companies would be interested in getting their management teams to build a Habitat house as part of a creative leadership program."

Traditional partners had included companies in the home-building industries, banks, and a number of foundations. Major corporate sponsors of the More Than Houses campaign, for example, included Whirlpool Corporation, Lions Clubs International, The Case Foundation, Bank of America, Dow Chemical Company, Wells Fargo Housing Foundation, and Square D/Schneider Electric. "We have tended to stick to those partners where the reason for the brand linkage is clear," Bender explained. "As attention to corporate social responsibility among *Fortune* 500 companies increases, we expect companies will seek the halo that a partnership with a nonprofit can bring."

Originally, many corporate partnerships had been based on cash donations or in-kind gifts of building materials or products. For example, in 1999, Habitat signed a five-year agreement with Whirlpool, worth $5 million annually, to provide all the refrigerators and stoves for new Habitat homes in North America. "What began as a product relationship has evolved into a broader partnership," Bender said. "New Whirlpool employees are required to donate one day in their first month to helping on a Habitat worksite, and special team-building exercises are held at Habitat worksites to help build esprit de corps." In addition, financial partners such as Wells Fargo and Citigroup partnered with HFHI by investing in bonds secured by Habitat mortgages, thereby freeing up resources for affiliates and facilitating their growth.

Increasingly, corporate partners were looking for deals whereby they could directly link their activities and brand names with Habitat. HFHI was also assessing a potential partnership with Marriott, a hotel management company. The proposal was for each hotel property to ask its guests to contribute $1 to HFHI per night of stay. This had already been successfully implemented in Costa Rica and Indonesia and was being evaluated for broader implementation. "It's hard to estimate the monetary value of this partnership," Bender said. "It really depends how broadly it is implemented, but potentially it could bring in millions of dollars a year."

"We are also currently looking at a partnership with Lafarge that is potentially worth multiple millions a year," Williams added. "Given their leadership in the cement business, they are compatible potential partners." Other partnerships, however, existed with companies where the link was less clear. In 2001, for example, to celebrate its 100th anniversary, Maxwell House spent $8 million on television commercials that promoted Habitat and provided $2 million in house sponsorships.

Bender was unsure if sharing the brand valuation information with corporate partners had increased the average monetary benefits to HFHI, but existing partners were increasingly interested in renewing their relationship with HFHI. Some executives at HFHI believed that funding from corporate sponsorship and partnership represented an important, as yet largely untapped, opportunity for the organization. "Outside the U.S., corporations don't partner as willingly," Williams explained. "Companies donate money but don't see a value in cobranding." Carscaddon added:

> There are also risks to partnering with corporations, and we have not always recognized that. For example, we need to establish minimum payments for the use of our brand name and logo, say $100,000, to avoid dilution of the brand. In addition, we must be aware that potential partner corporations also face a certain risk. We had a recent example where a corporation sponsored a specific house, and the homeowner was a convicted felon. In this case, the corporation's PR has somewhat backfired.

Interbrand's Brand Valuation Study.

In May 2002, Interbrand was retained to conduct a study of HFHI's brand value. Interbrand defined a brand as "a relationship that secures future earnings by retaining customer loyalty" and believed that brand value typically accounted for 30 percent to 70 percent of a public company's market capitalization. Interbrand used financial analysis, market analysis, and brand analysis to establish a specific brand's value. (See **Exhibit 13** for Interbrand's discounted cash flow [DCF] brand value calculation model.) Since nonprofits offered no direct equivalent to economic earnings, Interbrand suggested that a surrogate for the value they created was in the number and economic value of lives saved and/or lives improved. One approach to assessing the value of a nonprofit, it argued, was to treat the total funds and raw materials directed to the cause as the equivalent of a for-profit brand's economic earnings. Although used for HFHI, this approach ignored all the nonfinancial value added by the nonprofit brand, such as volunteer time.

Exhibit 13   Interbrand's Brand Valuation Model

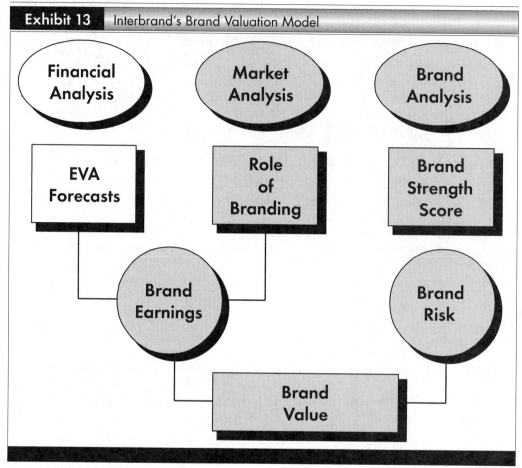

Source: Interbrand, courtesy of HFHI, 2002.

Jeffrey Parkhurst, managing director of brand valuation at Interbrand, directed the Habitat study. He expanded on the rationale for nonprofits to place a value on their brands:

> First, an organization's brand is a valuable asset that can be leveraged in corporate partnerships to open the door for cobranding, licensing, and other partnering opportunities. In addition, by comparing brand values, an organization is able to select appropriate partners and extract the correct value from each partnership. Internally, knowing the value of the brand and communicating it effectively can result in budgeting the funds and human resources necessary to protect and grow the brand asset, as well as achieving buy-in and commitment throughout the organization to adopt practices that protect and enhance brand equity and define the use of the brand in the field.

Interbrand's market analysis looked at the drivers within a brand's industry and assessed the importance of each and the role the brand played in contributing to each driver. For bulk chemicals, for example, the role of the brand overall was estimated at

10 out of 100. In perfumes, however, the contribution was estimated at 90 out of 100. The market analysis helped focus attention on which drivers of the business were most dependent on the brand, as well as which drivers could or should be leveraged. For HFHI, nine drivers were identified by Interbrand through research and interviews with Habitat staff and reviewed by Habitat executives. These weighted drivers included tangible results, being part of the solution, local impact, heritage, spiritual motivation, flexibility for volunteers, inertia, tax benefit, and self-image. The role of the HFHI brand was estimated for each of these at between 25 and 100 percent. The resulting overall branding index (RBI) for HFHI was calculated at 58 out of 100. (See **Exhibit 14** for HFHI brand index chart.)

Interbrand's brand analysis was based on a brand-strength score and brand-risk model that scored a brand relative to a notional "ideal" brand against seven core attributes associated with strong brands: market, stability, leadership, geography, trend, support, and protection. HFHI's resulting brand strength score (BSS) was calculated at 76 out of 100. Based on multiple studies of other brands, Interbrand attached a discount rate to future cash flows based on the BSS. In HFHI's case, the discount rate was 7.5 percent. This was applied to HFHI's RBI-adjusted cash flows over a seven-year period with a conservative assumption of zero revenue growth.

The result was a net present value of future brand earnings—that is, operating income caused by the brand itself—of $1.8 billion. Compared with the values of other major brands, HFHI had the same brand value as Starbucks Coffee but had substantially less than Coca-Cola, at $68 billion; Intel, at $35 billion; and IBM, at $53 billion. However, HFHI's brand value as a percentage of revenue was 270 percent, compared with 350 percent for Coca-Cola, 130 percent for Intel, and 60 percent for IBM.[7]

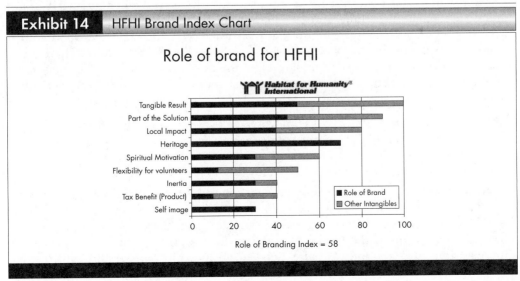

Exhibit 14   HFHI Brand Index Chart

Source: Interbrand, courtesy of HFHI, 2002.

Based on the study, Interbrand recommended partnering with higher-value corporate brands or getting paid accordingly. Interbrand cautioned that HFHI's brand value varied by type of partner or its application but noted that it was unlikely that any HFHI partner was overpaying—otherwise it would not have signed the deal. In addition, Interbrand showed how some of the brand drivers used to calculate the brand index were less unique and defensible versus competition over time. Drivers such as local impact, spiritual motivation, flexibility for volunteers, inertia, tax benefit, and self-image were highlighted as being less unique to HFHI. (See **Exhibit 14** for brand drivers.)

Parkhurst expanded: "Knowing what truly differentiates their brand versus competition, and what brand drivers are strong or need to be protected, gives HFHI a sense of the actions they need to take to maintain and grow the value of their brand." Bender added, "Knowing our brand value has helped us speak the same language as our corporate partners and helps our partners sell potential partnership to their managements and boards. It has also caused us to reevaluate whom we want to partner with in the future. We are setting our sights much higher."

"We knew that the Habitat brand had widespread recognition and that it had a lot of value," Swisher said. "The Interbrand work confirms the fact that it is our greatest asset, and we must do everything we can to protect it. We had a rare opportunity with public figures such as Carter and Fuller that helped establish the brand. The trick is now to maintain brand value." Bender added:

> Given the difficulty in assessing and comparing NGOs, I think that brand value would be a very useful tool for making comparisons. For-profit companies have a set collection of figures and facts that are used to assess success; they have a common language that everyone speaks. This is not the case for nonprofits. The key question for me is how do we promote brand value as an assessment tool to be used by the NGO community.

Future Direction and Challenges.

Maintaining the culture. Several top executives were concerned about HFHI's ability to maintain its culture and Christian heritage. "Our main challenge," Fuller said, "is keeping Jesus at the center of our work as we grow and move ever more into a diverse world. Keeping that strong Christian focus is of great importance. There are many organizations that have floundered because they have forgotten who they are, and there is a danger to HFHI of erosion of our values and vision." Williams agreed:

> Most people come to work at Habitat out of a sense of calling. We don't want to become like a for-profit company. Our main challenge is how to maintain our Christian ministry. How do we continue to grow and go into countries where the population is not Christian and not lose who we are? The more diverse and popular we become, the more difficult it is going to be to hold on to our Christian core."

Achieving the mission through growth. The objective of eliminating poverty housing in the world was very ambitious and, to some, overwhelming, if not impossible. "We only build 20,000 houses a year," Williams said. "As much success as we've had, it's just a drop in the ocean. In order to have a greater impact, we need to increase our advocacy role. We also need to do more in partnership with third parties. We need to adapt our methods so that we can grow more quickly and achieve our goals faster."

"A key challenge," Carscaddon added, "is how to grow given limited resources. We have expanded outside the U.S., gone to Europe to access grants and individual donations, and we want to help affiliates in developing countries to raise more of their own funds. But how do we obtain the resources to make the big leaps necessary to achieve our overall mission of poverty housing elimination?" Swisher expanded, "Growth has slowed. Our pledge and core income growth grew last year by only 5 percent. We have saturated the U.S. market and have mailed enough acquisition letters to have reached every American household at least once already!"

Some senior executives, however, questioned the drive for growth, arguing that the large number of affiliates was already a challenge to manage and proposing that money be put into recruiting more professional staff members to make the organization more effective.

Expanding the mission. One issue that was being evaluated was the possibility of providing temporary housing for people displaced by disasters. "We get calls when there are natural disasters, for example, in Nicaragua, asking us if we are providing relief," Bender said, "and people are obviously supportive of these activities. However, that's not really the core of our business historically, and doing too much in this area might risk mission creep."

Protecting the brand. Bender believed that one of Habitat's key challenges was effectively protecting the brand. "The issue is that we have shared ownership of the brand," he explained. "We are not like a corporation that can dictate the precise terms for use of its brand. We have a large number of affiliates with whom we have a covenant agreement, and we don't control our brand to the degree we would like." Within the United States, Habitat's reputation varied by location, depending on local market conditions and effectiveness of the local affiliate. To address the brand protection issue, Bender had initiated a new corporate identity program to achieve greater standardization of the Habitat brand throughout the organization.

CONCLUSION.

In light of the recent market research results and the brand valuation study, Bender wondered what actions HFHI should take to both protect and leverage brand value. The effect of any such actions on the organization's ability to meet its major challenges of maintaining the culture, achieving the mission through growth, and expanding the mission would also have to be considered.

Notes to Case

1 World Development Report, World Bank, Washington, 2000, Table 1.1.

2 *Basic Facts on Urbanisation*, UNCHS (Habitat), Nairobi, 1999, p. 9.

3 UNCHS (The United Nations Center for Human Settlements) State of the Cities Report, March 2001.

[4] Based on Jerome P. Baggett, *Habitat for Humanity—Building Private Homes, Building Public Religion* (Philadelphia: Temple University Press, 1999).

[5] In this case, the term "partners" includes all supporters and volunteers.

[6] In February 2002, a short national survey among 806 adults was conducted. In March 2002, four focus groups, two among existing partners and two among prospective partners, were held. In April 2002, 502 current HFHI partners and 250 prospective partners were surveyed, and, in May 2002, 125 corporate-giving officers were surveyed.

[7] Best Global Brand Study, *Businessweek*, July 2001.

CASE 11
WWF

The brand is like the tip of the iceberg. In isolation of the mission and product it makes no sense. Your mission determines what your brand stands for, not the other way around.

—Claude Martin, director general, WWF International

Paul Steele, chief operating officer of WWF International, sat at his desk in Gland, Switzerland, on September 23, 2002, and reviewed the details of three potential corporate partnerships. Over the past few years, WWF had entered into a range of partnership and licensing agreements with various businesses, and Steele now had to decide whether WWF should pursue additional corporate partnerships and, if so, with which company or companies.

WORLDWIDE FUND FOR NATURE (WWF).

Founded in 1961, WWF was by 2002 one of the largest independent, nonprofit organizations dedicated to the conservation of nature in the world. It operated in about 100 countries and was supported by nearly 5 million people worldwide. Initially focused mainly on protecting threatened species and spaces, WWF activities had broadened to include tackling pollution and looking for new and sustainable ways of using the planet's natural resources.

In 2002, WWF employed more than 3,800 people, 90 percent of whom were scientists, and invested some $280 million per annum. WWF carried out 700 international projects per annum in addition to the thousands initiated at a local level by WWF's national offices around the world. At the international headquarters in Gland, thirty-five different nationalities were represented. The WWF Web site summarized the scope of the organization as follows: "Our reach is global yet local, combining localized, practical actions and field projects with broader initiatives to influence environmental decision making and industrial practices."

WWF was a factual, science-based organization with clear objectives and goals. In 2002, it focused on six global priorities: forests, fresh water, oceans and coastal

Professor John Quelch and Research Associate Nathalie Laidler prepared this case. HBS cases are developed solely as the basis for class discussion. Certain details have been disguised. Cases are not intended to serve as endorsements, sources of primary data, or illustrations of effective or ineffective management.

ecosystems, threatened species, toxic pollution, and climate change. (See **Exhibit 1** for WWF global conservation targets.) In addition, WWF's approach was one of ecoregional-based conservation, meaning large-scale programs at the biosphere level combining on-the-ground project work with the necessary policy and advocacy frameworks. In 2002, WWF had identified more than 200 regions most representative of the world's biological diversity, called the Global 200, and was working in 77 of these areas.[1] WWF's Living Planet report was an example of the organization's scientific approach and focus on quantifying results. The report used an algorithm called

Exhibit 1	WWF Global Conservation Targets, 2002
Global Issues	**Conservation Targets**
Forests	By 2010, the establishment and maintenance of viable, representative networks of protected areas in the world's threatened and most biologically significant forest regions
	By 2005, 100 million hectares of certified forests, distributed in a balanced manner among regions, forest types, and land tenure regimes
	By 2005, at least 20 forest landscape restoration initiatives under way in the world's threatened deforested or degraded forest regions to enhance ecological integrity and human well-being
Freshwater Ecosystems	By 2010, 250 million hectares of high-priority freshwater ecosystems worldwide protected and/or sustainably managed
	By 2010, ecological processes maintained or restored in at least 50 large catchment areas of high biodiversity importance
	By 2010, private-sector practices and related governmental policies concerning key water-using sectors established and/or changed in order to sustain the integrity of the freshwater ecosystem on which they depend and/or impact
Oceans and Coasts	By 2020, the establishment and implementation of a network of effectively managed, ecologically representative marine protected areas covering at least 10% of the world's seas
	Maintain the status of all fish stocks that are currently exploited sustainably and by 2020 halve the number of fish stocks that are overexploited or depleted as currently categorized by the Food and Agricultural Organization
Species	By 2010, populations of key species of global concern stabilized or increased and their critical habitats safeguarded
	By 2010, at least 10 species of global concern no longer endangered by overexploitation
Toxic Chemicals	By 2007, elimination or reduction of at least 30 of the most hazardous industrial chemicals and pesticides with special emphasis on persistent organic pollutants (POPs) and endocrine-disrupting chemicals
	By 2007, scientific, educational, and regulatory initiatives firmly in place, enabling decision makers (government, industry, consumers) to make informed choices about toxic chemicals and their alternatives
Climate Change	By 2010, a 10% reduction below 1990 emissions in industrialized country carbon dioxide emissions
	By 2010, initiatives under way in 30 developing countries to implement solutions leading to a significant reduction in carbon intensity, in particular from the combustion of fossil fuels
	By 2010, 50 countries implementing adaptation strategies in key ecoregions/biomes and sectors of their economies on the basis of national plans for the reduction of vulnerability to climate change

Source: WWF's Global Conservation Programme 2001/2002.

the ecological footprint to measure humanity's use of renewable natural resources. (See **Exhibit 2** for an excerpt from the Living Planet report.)

WWF's international campaigns and advocacy work spotlighted key issues and influenced national and international policy decisions. In 2002, campaigns included promoting sustainable forestry practices, advocating for a reduction in greenhouse gas emissions, eliminating toxic chemicals, lobbying to halt the depletion of fisheries, and working to ensure that fresh water was available for people and nature. To encourage corporations and governments to act, WWF had developed a tool called the Gift to the Earth, an award to recognize specific actions and commitments. The organization's advocacy successes included the international moratorium on the ivory trade in 1990, the international moratorium on whaling established in 1985, and the introduction of the Forest Stewardship Council.

Partnerships with governments, local communities, international agencies, and business and industry were considered central to WWF, which believed that dialogue was key for long-term success and an important conduit for creating awareness and spreading ideas.

In 2001, WWF's total annual operating income was $329 million, with 49 percent coming directly from individual donations (see **Exhibit 3** for WWF network financial statements).

| Exhibit 2 | Excerpt from the Living Planet Report 2002 |

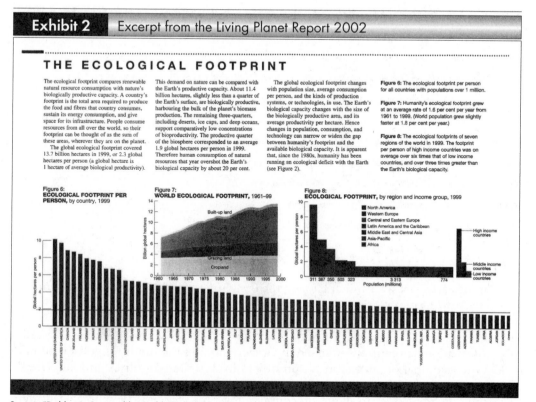

Source: "Building a Sustainable World," A First Report on our Economic, Social and Environmental Performance, 2001, WWF.

Exhibit 3	WWF Network Income and Expenditure, 2000 and 2001		
	2000 (CHF 000)	2001 (CHF 000)	2001 (US$ 000)
Operating Income			
Individuals[a]	251,242	275,742	159,879
Legacies	66,171	68,139	39,508
Corporations[b]	23,688	19,877	11,525
Trusts and Foundations	28,811	32,274	18,713
Government and Aid Agencies	113,483	125,621	72,837
Royalties[c]	34,058	29,652	17,193
Financial Income (net)[d]	44,538	7,762	4,500
Other	8,804	8,090	4,691
TOTAL	**570,795**	**567,157**	**328,846**
Operating Expenditure			
National Conservation			
Conservation[e]	89,723	89,329	51,794
Conservation Policy, Education and Awareness[f]	109,845	120,705	69,987
International Conservation			
Conservation[g]	231,956	237,588	137,757
Conservation Policy, Education and Awareness[h]	23,819	23,771	13,783
Fund-raising	80,223	88,786	51,479
Finance and Administration	42,312	45,104	26,152
TOTAL	**577,878**	**605,283**	**350,952**
Surplus (deficit to support current and future projects)	(7,084)	(38,126)	(22,106)

Source: WWF Annual Report 2001.

Note: Exchange rate, CHF 1.798 = US$1, as of June 30, 2001.

[a]Monies received from WWF individual supporters, including regular dues and fund-raising activities.

[b]Donations from corporations excluding royalties and licensing and sponsoring fees.

[c]Monies received from royalties, licensing, sponsorship fees, and sale of WWF products via WWF catalogs and retail outlets.

[d]Net results of dividends, bank interest, exchange differences, gains/losses on marketable securities.

[e]Costs of conservation activities of WWF national organizations within their own territory.

[f]Thirteen percent = policy, 44% = education, and 43% = awareness.

[g]Costs of the WWF International Conservation Programme.

[h]Sixty-four percent = policy, 3% = education, and 33% = awareness.

History.

In the early 1960s, Sir Julian Huxley, the first director of UNESCO and cofounder of The World Conservation Union (IUCN), raised public awareness in Britain with a series of articles highlighting the destruction of the East African habitat. Max Nicholson, director general of Britain's Nature Conservancy, and others established an international organization, based in Switzerland, to raise funds for conservation. The international organization set up offices in different countries and launched national appeals that would send two-thirds of the funds to WWF International, keeping the remainder to spend on conservation projects of its own choice. During this time, Chi-Chi the panda arrived at the London Zoo from China, creating a wave of international attention, and the new organization decided to make the animal its logo based upon a design drawn by Sir Peter Scott.

The first national appeal, with the Duke of Edinburgh as president, was launched in the United Kingdom in November 1961, followed by appeals in the United States and Switzerland in December of the same year. By 2002, national appeals had become institutionalized as national organizations, twenty-eight of which were affiliated with WWF International and four of which operated under a different name and were associated with WWF.

During the 1960s, the majority of funds raised were from individual donations, but in 1970 His Royal Highness Prince Bernhard of the Netherlands, then president of WWF International, launched an initiative that would provide WWF with a solid, independent financial base. The organization set up a $10 million fund, known as the 1001, to which 1,001 individuals each contributed $10,000. Since then, WWF International had used the interest from the 1001 trust to meet basic administrative costs.

In 1980, WWF collaborated with IUCN and the United Nations Environment Programme (UNEP) on the publication of a joint world conservation strategy that was endorsed by the United Nations secretary general and launched simultaneously in thirty-four world capitals. WWF continued to build its popular base, and in 1981 the organization had more than 1 million regular supporters worldwide. In 1983, in collaboration with Groth AG, WWF worked with postal authorities in more than 200 countries to select threatened species to feature on official postage stamps. By 2002, the Conservation Stamp Collection program had raised more than $13 million.

In 1986, as part of its twenty-fifth anniversary celebrations, WWF invited leaders from the world's five main religions to attend a retreat in Assisi, Italy. After the retreat, the leaders issued declarations that conservation was a fundamental element in their respective faiths, and since then an international network consisting of eight religious groups and WWF has worked to achieve common aims.

The 1990s began with the launch of a revised mission and strategy that reiterated WWF's commitment to nature conservation. In 1991, WWF once again joined forces with IUCN and UNEP to publish "Caring for the Earth—A Strategy for Sustainable Living," which was launched in sixty countries and listed 132 actions that people at all social and political levels could take to safeguard or improve their environment. (See **Exhibit 4** for a description of key WWF projects and achievements over time.)

Initially established to channel funds, WWF quickly established its own field projects and by 1990 started balancing field and advocacy work. In September 2002, Martin summarized WWF's history as follows:

> WWF is part of environmental history and has always had a broad environmental mission, focusing on developing harmony between man and nature. In the 1960s WWF was largely project oriented, and impact was achieved through specific field projects. In the 1970s, organizations like WWF realized that unless they changed the fundamentals, they could not impact sustainable change. The UN Conference on the Human Environment held in Stockholm in 1972 was instrumental in this shift. In the 1980s, several forces led to an environmental globalization, which preceded economic globalization by a decade: global warming, the Chernobyl disaster, concern about the ozone hole, the disappearance of

Exhibit 4	WWF Key Projects and Achievements

Date	Project/Achievement
1964	WWF works to protect the last 25 Javan rhinos in Ujung Kulon, western Java. In 2002 there were about 60 animals in the reserve.
1969	WWF helps establish the Donana nature reserve in Spain—a haven for the last few Iberian lynx.
1970s	WWF is instrumental in setting up CITES to protect plants and animals threatened by international trade.
1971	WWF participates in the creation of the Ramsar Convention to safeguard wetlands worldwide.
1972	WWF launches "Operation Tiger" to raise funds to protect the last 1,800 Bengal tigers left in the wild. In 2002, there were 2,500 to 3,750 tigers in India and 5,000 to 7,000 in the world.
1973	The World Organization of the Scout Movement and WWF launch the "World Conservation Badge," which is adopted by scouts in 30 countries.
1973	WWF and IUCN persuade the five Arctic nations to sign the International Polar Bear Convention to help protect the species.
1975	WWF raises the funds to establish protected areas in Central and West Africa, Southeast Asia, and Latin America.
1976	WWF and IUCN launch TRAFFIC (Trade Records Analysis of Flora and Fauna in Commerce) to monitor trade in wild animals, plants, and wildlife products.
1980	WWF is the first international environmental organization to be invited into China to help save the giant panda.
1980s	WWF pioneers "debt-for-nature" swaps in countries such as Madagascar, Ecuador, the Philippines, and Zambia, where a portion of the nation's debt is converted into funds for conservation.
1982	Ten Arabian oryx are released on the Jiddat plateau in central Oman—the result of the captive-breeding program that WWF helped set up in 1962.
1986	WWF brings together representatives from Buddhism, Christianity, Islam, and Judaism to forge an alliance between religion and conservation.
1987	WWF and IUCN launch the "Botanical Gardens Conservation Strategy," which guides a network of 600 botanic gardens working for plant conservation in 120 countries.
1988	The WWF-supported Communal Area Management Programme for Indigenous Resources (CAMPFIRE) in Zimbabwe helps villagers see wildlife as a source of income rather than as crop-destroying pests.
1990s	Three new species of large mammal are discovered in Vietnam thanks to WWF-sponsored surveys: the Truong Son muntjac, the giant muntjac, and the Sao la.
1992	WWF plays a critical role in establishing the Convention on Biological Diversity (CBD), which sets the basis for long-term biodiversity conservation around the world.
1993	WWF pioneers the Forest Stewardship Council (FSC) to oversee the independent certification of wood and wood products that come from well-managed forests.
1994	WWF's vigorous lobbying culminates in the Southern Ocean being declared a whale sanctuary.
1996	WWF instigates "Gifts to the Earth"—public celebrations of conservation actions by governments, companies, or individuals.
1996	WWF and Unilever launch the Marine Stewardship Council (MSC), setting global ecostandards for certifying and labeling seafood products.
1997	WWF plays a significant role in protecting the Antarctic from mining and drilling by pushing for a stronger Antarctic Treaty.
1997	WWF acts as the key force in the creation and subsequent improvement of the Kyoto Protocol—the international agreement to fight global warming.
1997	WWF and the World Bank join forces to conserve the world's forests.
1999	WWF brings together the governments of six central African countries to sign the "Yaounde Declaration" on forest conservation.
2000	WWF Living Planet report shows that in just 30 years the world has lost one-third of its natural resources.
2000	Black rhinos in Africa increase to 2,700, and the Siberian tiger numbers 500 (up from 30 in the 1940s).
2001	The 1,000th golden lion tamarin is born in the wild, thanks to WWF's captive-breeding programs.
2001	WWF plays a major role in finalizing the Stockholm Convention to eliminate a number of toxic chemicals.

Source: WWF Annual Report 2001.

rain forest. . . . In response, WWF adopted a global mission, which translated into three broad priorities: forests, fresh water, and marine. In the 1990s, following the Earth Summit in Rio, WWF started focusing on specific goals and key targets, and in 1997, WWF played a key role in the creation of the Kyoto protocol. For an NGO [nongovernmental organization], focus is even more important than for a business. Focus requires that you define clearly the few things you want to stand for and want to influence. The impact of this focus, of establishing goals and targets in combination with the strength of the WWF brand, has been formidable. For example, in 2002, through ARPA [Amazon Protection Plan], Brazil established 12 percent of its rain forest under permanent protection, in no small measure thanks to the 10 percent goal established by WWF five years ago.

In 2001, WWF's stated mission was to stop and eventually reverse the degradation of the planet's natural environment, and to build a future in which humans live in harmony with nature.

Organizational Structure.

In 2002, WWF comprised an international secretariat (WWF International), twenty-eight national organizations, twenty-four program offices, including two specialist offices (based in Brussels and Washington, D.C., which worked to influence the policies and activities of the European Union and institutions that dealt with global economic issues), and four associate organizations. Each national organization was a separate legal entity, responsible to its own board and accountable to its donors and bound to WWF International by a contract that covered the WWF name and mission. WWF International was accountable to the national organizations, donors, and the Swiss authorities. Most of the members of WWF International's board were drawn from the boards and CEOs of the national organizations. The twenty-four program offices were linked directly to WWF International as subsidiaries and were responsible for field program implementation and management.

WWF International's role was to identify and monitor emerging conservation concerns and guide the development of WWF's position on international issues as well as coordinate campaign, communications, and fund-raising activities. In addition, WWF International managed the international conservation programs and policy work and built global partnerships.

One of the national organizations' main roles was fund-raising. Additional activities ranged from practical field projects and scientific research to advising on environmental policy, promoting environmental education, and raising public awareness and understanding. WWF International applied a levy to the national organizations to cover common activities such as communications, trademark protection, and marketing and to ensure funds to the program offices for the implementation of field programs. National organizations could not start their own field projects abroad and had to operate within the international programs. In 2002, the expectation was that national organizations would spend the majority (two-thirds) of their funds on these international programs, although this depended on the size and maturity of each national organization. (See **Exhibit 5** for details on national organization income and expenditures for fiscal year 2002.) "The field programs," Martin explained, "need to excite the national organizations so that they will give a large amount of the funds they raise for field programs." Overall, relationships between WWF International and the national organizations were based on consensus building and influence.

Throughout the 1980s the number of national organizations remained steady. However, in the 1990s WWF added six additional national organizations (including in Brazil, the Philippines, Turkey, and Indonesia) and a number of program offices. Over the next few years, WWF planned to add at least two additional national organizations, in Hungary and Russia.

Exhibit 5	National Organization Income and Expenditure Details, FY 2002 (CHF 000)			
National Organizations	Gross Income	National Programs as a % of Expenditures	Administration and Fund-raising as a % of Expenditures	International Conservation as a % of Expenditures
Australia	9,331	42%	39%	19%
Austria	10,085	16%	51%	33%
Belgium	7,251	12%	44%	44%
Brazil	7,643	0%	24%	76%
Canada	16,070	52%	26%	22%
Denmark	8,602	4%	32%	64%
Finland	3,437	31%	40%	29%
France	7,820	55%	40%	5%
Germany	30,097	23%	39%	37%
Greece	3,014	59%	34%	7%
Hong Kong	4,228	6%	48%	45%
India	5,762	64%	24%	13%
Indonesia	8,163	77%	23%	0%
Italy	28,416	52%	42%	6%
Japan	7,523	24%	63%	13%
Malaysia	4,472	32%	17%	51%
Netherlands	69,902	3%	37%	60%
New Zealand	1,395	37%	57%	7%
Norway	2,403	15%	25%	60%
Pakistan	3,245	5%	32%	63%
Philippines	3,130	51%	11%	39%
South Africa	9,719	47%	32%	21%
Spain	5,289	38%	39%	23%
Sweden	19,113	22%	31%	46%
Turkey	321	0%	73%	27%
Switzerland	39,964	14%	64%	22%
United Kingdom	74,049	9%	47%	44%
Unites States	146,767	3%	37%	60%
TOTAL National Organizations	**537,211**	**16%**	**40%**	**44%**
International	104,109	0%	15%	85%
Nonconsolidated Program offices	21,300	0%	10%	91%
Other adjustments	(117,487)	0%	2%	98%
TOTAL NETWORK	**545,133**	**16%**	**40%**	**44%**

Source: WWF.

Fund-raising and Membership.

In 2002, nearly 5 million supporters contributed to WWF on an annual basis. In comparison, Greenpeace had 2.5 million members (although the organization had had 5 million in 1990) and the Red Cross had 50 million members. Typical WWF members gave to six or seven different NGOs and were quite ready to shift loyalties. Mario Fetz, director of fund-raising and marketing, expanded on this willingness to shift: "In previous years, WWF would publish a members' newsletter that gave members a sense of exclusivity, but with the advent of the Internet, information is readily available and people tend to move in and out of causes. They no longer want to belong to a club." According to an International Research Associates (INRA) survey conducted in Europe in 2000, 11 percent of Europeans supported WWF because WWF protects nature (44.7 percent), saves animals (43 percent), is a good cause (19.9 percent), saves the rain forests (13.6 percent), fights pollution (13.4 percent), improves industry's behavior (5.2 percent), and influences governments (4.7 percent).

WWF's total membership levels had been fairly constant since 1990 but varied considerably by country; in the Netherlands it was as high as 6 percent of the total population because of the heavy use of TV advertising and the association with Prince Bernhard. In Switzerland it was also very high (around 4 percent of the total population) and was built on strong youth programs and teachers' use of WWF materials. (See **Exhibit 6** for membership levels by major national organization.) Annual attrition rates of members throughout the WWF network averaged 25 percent but also varied quite widely by country. In Italy, for example, they were higher, and in the United Kingdom and the United States they were much lower in part because of a direct debit system for collecting membership dues.

Membership income had been declining for many organizations, and the fund-raising environment had become increasingly difficult. As Fetz put it, "In the 1980s you could raise money and get away with a thank-you letter. Today donors want to know what WWF is doing with the funds we raise. In the 1980s a cold mailing would result in about a 3 percent response rate; in 2002 a response rate of 0.5 percent is considered good." (See **Exhibit 7** for details on revenues by national organization.) In addition, the total number of NGOs had increased dramatically over the previous few decades and was estimated at more than 2,500 in the Northern Hemisphere alone.[2] These NGOs could be broadly divided into two main groups: large global organizations and fragmented, single-issue groups, the latter often struggling just to survive. The term "NGO" was increasingly being applied, sometimes to the detriment of established NGOs, to any activist organization, including some extremist groups. "This clutter and confusion makes having a strong brand even more important," Fetz declared.

In 2001, the number of WWF members declined slightly, but overall membership revenues had increased because WWF had been successful in "upgrading" some

Exhibit 6	WWF Membership Levels: Rank Order of National Organizations

National Organizations

United States	Canada
Netherlands	Denmark
Germany	Spain
Switzerland	South Africa
United Kingdom	Japan
Italy	Australia
Austria	Hong Kong
Sweden	Greece
France	Brazil
India	New Zealand
Pakistan	Malaysia
Finland	Norway
Belgium	Indonesia

Source: WWF.

Note: The five countries with the most members—the United States, the Netherlands, Germany, Switzerland, and the United Kingdom—accounted for 71% of WWF's 4.6 million members worldwide and 45% of WWF's 8,630 corporate supporters.

Exhibit 7	2002 Revenues by National Organization (CHF 000)

National Organizations	Individuals % Gross Income	Corporations % Gross Income	Trusts and Foundations % Gross Income	Government and Aid Agencies % Gross Income	WWF Network % Gross Income	Earned % Gross Income	Gross Income Total
Australia	26	0	3	34	16	19	9,331
Austria	61	0	0	11	14	13	10,085
Belgium	42	0	0	48	0	10	7,251
Brazil	2	2	3	12	69	10	7,643
Canada	54	7	18	9	3	10	16,070
Denmark	32	0	5	52	1	10	8,602
Finland	37	2	2	25	6	29	3,437
France	67	12	0	16	4	0	7,820
Germany	62	7	2	14	2	7	30,097
Greece	13	0	86	2	0	(1)	3,014
Hong Kong	43	21	6	24	0	3	4,228
India	1	0	0	71	13	10	5,762
Indonesia	1	1	8	45	44	(0)	8,163
Italy	36	0	1	53	0	6	28,416
Japan	48	12	2	5	3	29	7,523
Malaysia	2	4	2	29	57	5	4,472
Netherlands	97	1	0	0	0	1	69,902
New Zealand	57	17	2	2	11	6	1,395
Norway	12	16	11	48	11	2	2,403
Pakistan	10	2	0	34	38	6	3,245
Philippines	1	18	14	14	47	5	3,130
South Africa	9	26	8	4	6	42	9,719
Spain	12	0	11	11	19	24	5,289
Sweden	45	21	4	24	1	5	19,113
Turkey	9	25	14	0	26	20	321
Switzerland	88	1	2	1	0	8	39,964
United Kingdom	77	6	2	10	0	3	74,049
United States	60	4	9	21	10	(3)	146,767
Total NOs	60	5	5	17	7	4	537,208
International	3	3	6	18	64	5	104,109
Nonconsolidated Program Offices		0	0	29	64	0	21,300
Adjustments[a]		0	0	0	100	0	(117,487)
TOTAL NETWORK	60	5	6	22	0	5	545,130

Source: WWF.

[a]Adjustments = to avoid double counting, income has been adjusted to exclude income transfers among WWF entities.

members to higher membership dues levels. However, the tougher fund-raising environment for WWF in 2002 had raised the pressure to look at other areas for sources of funding.

In 2002, it was also becoming more difficult to raise unrestricted funds that were not earmarked for specific projects. In 2001, 24 percent of external funds raised were restricted, and in recent years WWF had also experienced a growth in restricted funds from aid agencies. This was in part because certain projects had a particular emotional appeal, particularly those that focused on saving a species such as the Siberian tigers. (See **Exhibit 8** for an example of a fund-raising mailer.) "Our membership gets attached to particular species or issues," Fetz remarked, "and this has worked well in the past from a fund-raising perspective." However, species conservation accounted for only a fraction of WWF projects in 2002, and there was some concern that the use of a species conservation message for fund-raising purposes did not reflect the organization's broader range of activities.

In September 2002, the WWF International Web site was receiving 300,000 hits a week, and the organization was just starting to build a base of international members at a rate of ten per week for a total of 1,600 international members. During the fiscal year 2002, WWF International members donated an average of about 309 Swiss

| Exhibit 8 | Examples of the Fund-raising Mailer, 2000 |

From World Wildlife Fund
Exciting news about how you can help us...

SAVE THE TIGER!

Dear Friend:

Please let me quickly explain why I'm sending you the enclosed set of Tiger Post Cards:

You see, they are yours, as a small introductory gift, because quite frankly, I hope they will encourage you...

...to help us save the tiger — and other endangered large cats.

Perhaps you can use one of these Tiger Post Cards to send a quick message to a loved one or a special friend.

Please notice that one post card features the awesome Siberian tiger — the largest of all living cats. This is the only tiger that makes its home in temperate forests.

Regrettably, only about 400-500 Siberian tigers may survive in the wild today, most of them in the Russian Far East...

...where a poacher can earn as much as $10,000 for the fur, head, bones, claws, and teeth of one single tiger!

The second post card features the Bengal Tiger, and even though perhaps 4,000 of these tigers still exist — poaching and habitat loss threaten to thin their numbers.

And so — in plain English: We must save the tigers!

And here at World Wildlife Fund, we urgently need new friends like you to join with us in this endeavor. Will you?

Time is running out!

For example, today scientists are warning us that fewer

(over, please)

WWF
World Wildlife Fund
1250 Twenty-Fourth Street, NW   Washington, DC 20037-7787
www.worldwildlife.org

BENGAL TIGER
(Panthera tigris tigris).
Once roamed widely
across India and
Southeast Asia. Now
threatened by poachers.
Needs protection.

To learn more about endangered wildlife like the Bengal Tiger, go to www.worldwildlife.org

SIBERIAN TIGER
(Panthera tigris altaica)
Largest of all living cats.
Only about 200 still
survive in the wild.
Poachers sell fur, bones,
claws, teeth and other
body parts. Urgently
needs protection.

To learn more about endangered wildlife like the Siberian Tiger, go to www.worldwildlife.org

Source: WWF.

francs ($172) per gift. This included special appeals, unsolicited donations, and membership dues. In addition, WWF had an online tool called the Panda Passport, with 30,000 registered passport holders, that encouraged individuals to participate in WWF's advocacy work through online campaigning.

Competition.

Competition for funds from all sectors, private and public, was increasing, and by 2002, the search for funding had never been more difficult for WWF. Steele noted, "The environment is becoming increasingly competitive, with many more NGOs competing for money in a world economy where people are less willing to give funds. We compete against all NGOs for funding, but there is so much NGO clutter you really need to push your brand. We have no idea how to calculate market share, and frankly we're not sure how meaningful it would be."

WWF differed from the other main nature conservation NGOs in that it was active in both field programs and advocacy work. (See **Exhibit 9** for an overview of the major environmental NGOs.) "Our competitive advantage is that we maintain the difficult balance between advocacy and field work," Martin explained. "Size is also a competitive factor since we are global and have the organizational capacity to deliver on target." Steele expanded, "WWF also has unique experience in establishing partnerships with the private sector. We have the same language as the private sector and focus on establishing shared vocabulary when we start a partnership." By comparison,

| Exhibit 9 | Overview of the Major Environmental Organizations in 2002 |

Organization	2001 Operating Budget (US$ million)	Number of Members	Focus
Worldwide Fund for Nature (WWF)	$329	5 million	Global conservation through field projects and advocacy work
Nature Conservancy	$546		Land conservation through land purchase
Greenpeace	103 (euros)	2.8 million	Focused on advocacy work
BirdLife International	$263	2.6 million	Field projects with focus on bird life and their habitats
Conservation International	$56		"Heavily funded but without a clear idea of priorities," field focus
Sierra Club		700,000	Advocacy organization
World Resources Institute (WRI)			Research and think tank
Friends of the Earth	$1.1		Federation of national environmental organizations focused on advocacy
Earthwatch			
Botanic Gardens Conservation International (BGCI)			

Source: Annual reports.

Greenpeace had a policy of not accepting any funding from companies, and its approach was to "force" a company to sign an agreement. For example, in the 1990s, Greenpeace had publicly criticized Coca-Cola's use of refrigeration systems that emitted chlorofluorocarbons and had managed to get Coca-Cola to replace these systems through public pressure rather than through dialogue and partnership.

BUILDING THE WWF BRAND.

By 1986, WWF realized that its original name, World Wildlife Fund, no longer reflected the scope of its activities, and the organization commissioned its first branding exercise. To publicize its expanded mandate, the organization's name was changed to the Worldwide Fund for Nature (with the exception of the United States and Canada, which both retained the old name), and the panda logo was modified to look a little fiercer (see **Exhibit 10** for an evolution of the logo over time). In 2002, the organization's brand consisted of the acronym WWF and the famous panda logo.

In March 2000, WWF commissioned a study by INRA to evaluate the WWF brand across Europe and test the general public's attitude toward business partnerships. The poll, based on 9,000 face-to-face interviews conducted in nine countries, found that the WWF logo was "well liked and trusted by the large majority of people interviewed." Major findings included the following:

1. Europeans' greatest concerns, in order of importance, were violence, unemployment, health problems, poverty, and environmental disasters/damage

Exhibit 10   Evolution of the Panda Logo Over Time

Evolution of a symbol

When some of the world's scientists and conservationists met in 1961 to plan how to publicise the threat to wildlife and wild places and to raise funds to support conservation projects, they decided to launch the World Wildlife Fund (WWF), known outside Canada and the United States today as the World Wide Fund For Nature. They needed a symbol, and at the time Chi Chi, the only giant panda in the Western world, had won the hearts of all that saw her at the London Zoo in the United Kingdom. She was a rare animal, like her wild panda cousins in China, and her form and colour were the ideal basis for an attractive symbol. Scottish naturalist Gerald Watterson made some preliminary sketches, from which Sir Peter Scott, world-renowned wildlife conservationist and painter, designed the WWF's giant panda logo. The design of the logo has evolved over the past four decades, but the giant panda's distinctive features remain an integral part of WWF's treasured and unmistakable symbol. For years, the giant panda has been thought of by many Chinese as an unofficial national symbol, too. Today, WWF's trademark is recognized not only in China but also in most countries as a universal symbol for the conservation movement itself.

This recognition stems from the understanding that protecting a "flagship" species such as the giant panda benefits more than the single species itself. Conservation of this animal and its habitat provides protection for the whole community of wildlife that coexists with pandas, thus maintaining their entire ecosystem. The mountain forests where the last giant pandas survive shelter over a hundred other mammal species, including the endangered golden monkey, more than 200 bird species, such as the endangered crested ibis, and dozens of reptiles and amphibians. The habitat also contains a rich diversity of endemic species – plants and animals found nowhere else in the world. All these species endure under the protective umbrella provided by giant panda conservation efforts. Panda habitat also encompasses important watershed areas. Keeping the forests healthy maintains the river systems that flow through them, ensuring the livelihoods of millions of humans downstream.

 1961
 1978
 1986

Sketches by naturalist George Watterson (in left column) which Sir Peter Scott used as the basis for his design of WWF's famous logo, which has evolved over the years.

Source: WWF.

to nature. There was a faint decline in people's perceptions of environmental quality, and views for the future were pessimistic.

2. Two-thirds of respondents could, unaided, name at least one environmental organization.

3. WWF's share of voice was about half that of Greenpeace (77 percent of respondents spontaneously named Greenpeace and 46 percent spontaneously named WWF). Friends of the Earth and other organizations were rated at 16 percent or below. (The only notable exception to this ranking was in Italy, where recognition was 84 percent for WWF and 31 percent for Greenpeace.)

4. Prompted awareness of the WWF logo ("Have you seen this logo before?") was at 68 percent, and 67.3 percent knew that the logo stood for WWF. Country variations, however, were considerable.

5. Sixty-four percent of respondents agreed that WWF should be partly supported by private companies, and 62 percent agreed that the WWF logo added value to a consumer product.

6. Sixty-three percent agreed that an association with WWF added value to a company and provided the competitive advantage of "more commitment to the environment (61 percent), more responsible (43.5 percent), and more credible/trustworthy (39.1 percent and 37.9 percent, respectively)."

7. The majority of respondents thought that it was acceptable for WWF to form a partnership in the following sectors: food industry, energy sector, household goods, telecoms and electronics, and banking. The oil companies and car industry were thought to be unacceptable sectors by the majority (43 percent to 36 percent).

(Other INRA findings relating to WWF's image versus that of competitors and reactions to the panda logo are detailed in **Exhibits 11** and **12**.)

In general, top executives were very happy with recognition of the WWF brand and logo. A study conducted by Edelman Public Relations in 2001 described WWF

Exhibit 11	WWF Image versus that of Competitors		
Image[a]	WWF	Greenpeace	Friends of the Earth
Will be a key player in 10 years	7.98	8.18	7.35
Has a good reputation	7.94	7.34	7.11
Is committed	7.84	8.29	7.34
Is the leader worldwide	7.72	7.62	6.46
Is honest	7.65	7.35	6.98
Is competent	7.61	7.66	6.99
Keeps its promises	7.57	7.65	7.07
Is independent	7.28	7.47	5.89
Is dynamic	7.21	7.94	6.84
Is aggressive	4.51	7.35	5.50

Source: INRA 2000.

[a]Scale of 1 to 10 where 1 = strongly disagree and 10 = strongly agree.

Exhibit 12	Perception of the Panda Logo

The Panda Logo is...	% of Respondents Who Agree
Likeable	79
Represents WWF well	71
Trustworthy	70
Successful	62
Gives a feeling of commitment	62
Modern	62
Dynamic	55

Source: INRA 2000.

as a "superbrand" in both Europe and the United States, where WWF came in as the highest-ranked NGO and in fourth place overall, just behind Nike.[3]

However, the organization had a spectrum of constituents, including the general public, the media, WWF membership, staff, business and corporate partners, foundations, government agencies, other NGOs, and the communities affected by the organization's work. These constituents all had different informational needs and perceptions, and WWF's message, image, and positioning might be slightly different for each. In addition, the WWF brand stood for different objectives in the minds of the general public in different countries. In some countries, particularly where WWF was less well known, the brand stood for species conservation. In countries where WWF was very well known, people recognized that the organization stood for the environment. (In Switzerland in the 1970s, for example, the panda logo was also recognized as a symbol for the antinuclear movement.)

Traditionally the brand had been focused on WWF's membership audience and stood for species conservation, but this stakeholder group might have been fading in relative importance. The difficulty in communicating the brand revolved around species conservation versus broader environmental conservation. Children in particular latched on to animal emblems such as the panda, but WWF's activities focused also on global warming and the reduction of carbon dioxide emissions. The key challenge was communicating the link between the two. Martin concluded, "Our focus and perceived focus on wildlife is both a strength and a challenge because many donors, including government agencies, think that we do not address broader issues. However, species conservation is like an icon, closely linked to environmental conservation, that provides identity when fund-raising."

CORPORATE PARTNERSHIPS.

The Role of Business.

In 2002, WWF believed that, in the future, business would play an increasingly key role in environmental issues and that partnerships with major corporations would be essential both to further conservation goals and to generate funds to support conservation.

Of the world's 100 largest economies in 1999, forty-nine were nations and fifty-one were corporations,[4] and influences on corporations were becoming increasingly complex. As demonstrated by the increase in the popularity of ecofunds, particularly in Japan, Eastern Europe, and South America, and the increasing recognition of the Dow Jones Sustainability Index, many investors were looking to invest in corporations that demonstrated a commitment to environmental and social development. In 1995, the World Business Council for Sustainable Development (WBCSD) was formed, and by 2002 it included 160 international companies in thirty countries, representing twenty major industrial sectors. The WBCSD's mission was to "provide business leadership as a catalyst for change towards sustainable development, and to promote the role of eco-efficiency, innovation and corporate social responsibility."

In September 2000, *The Financial Times* published interviews with the CEOs of BP, Coca-Cola, Ikea, and Ford. All emphasized their companies' environmental commitment.[5] For BP, this was reflected in its "Beyond Petroleum" marketing campaigns, and for Coke this implied "becoming more deeply involved in issues of water availability and purity." Ikea worked with both Greenpeace and WWF to address problems of deforestation, and Ford had developed close relationships with environmental groups to work on emission levels and recycling.

Many global companies were recognizing stakeholder groups beyond shareholders and were attempting to become more socially and environmentally responsible. "We really noticed it at the World Summit on Sustainable Development in Johannesburg this year," Steele concluded. "Global corporations are gaining power and becoming increasingly involved. However, these corporations are not always clear on what they want to achieve." In August 2002, an online survey of 212 business leaders across fifty countries on the issue of sustainable development (SD) was conducted by Environics International. Key findings were as follows:

- Nine in ten business leaders said that SD is accepted as a desirable goal in their companies.

- Six in ten business leaders strongly agreed that the benefits of being proactive around SD outweighed the costs.

- Three in four business leaders strongly agreed that there needs to be better cooperation between government aid and private investment to ensure that SD takes place in developing countries.

- One in two business leaders strongly agreed that the benefits of environmental and social reporting outweighed the costs.

WWF's Existing Partnerships.

In September 2002, WWF's corporate partnerships ranged from in-depth conservation partnerships, to purely fund-raising initiatives, to licensing of the panda logo, to corporate clubs (see **Exhibit 13** for a list of corporate partnerships). Steele summarized the benefits that WWF derived from these partnerships in terms of the three currencies (or three Cs): conservation, cash, and communications. The conservation component referred to actions taken by partner companies in support of WWF's conservation goals. These included sustainable use of natural resources, reductions in emissions and toxic chemical use, and recycling efforts. The cash component referred to the donations received from corporations that covered WWF's project and management costs associated with the relationship as well as donations to help fund WWF's different projects. The communications component related to the degree to which the company would go to communicate about the

Exhibit 13	WWF's Corporate Partnerships in 2002

Company	Description of Partnership
HSBC	Major funding of freshwater projects and some discussion of environmental policies
Lafarge	Partnership to help reinforce environmental policies and practices and establish quantitative targets for waste reduction, recycling, energy consumption, environmental audits, and CO2 emissions. Financial support for WWF's "Forest Reborn" program.
Canon	Three-year partnership to raise environmental awareness through joint promotional and marketing activities targeted at young people
Delverde Pasta	Partnership where the association with WWF reinforces the product message of natural ingredients while WWF benefits from in-store promotions of WWF's work
Ogilvy & Mather	Free advertisements and placements worth $5 million

Source: Company interviews.

Note: Value of relationships ranked between $250,000 per annum to $12 million per annum.

relationship with WWF and, importantly, how the WWF logo would be used in such communications. "No two deals are the same, because the balance of the three currencies will vary depending on the company," Steele explained. "Sometimes no money ever changes hands and the effort is purely one of conservation. In other cases the relationship is one that only furthers the communication and cash components. The value to WWF of our five main corporate partnerships ranges from $12 million to $250,000 per year."

WWF also widely licensed the panda logo. In 2001, royalties from licensing accounted for $16.5 million, or 4 percent of total 2001 operating income. In 2002, licensing agreements existed with affinity credit cards, a soft-toy manufacturer, clothing companies, and even a fresh-bread manufacturer, complete with an edible WWF logo. Generally, WWF received a percentage of the wholesale price of the product carrying the panda logo, and these licensing agreements provided both a cash and communication component. Although some executives worried that the breadth of these licensing agreements might dilute the WWF brand and logo, others argued that the revenues generated were important and that the use of the panda logo on licensed products helped WWF maintain its right to the logo in certain countries. The majority of licensing agreements were negotiated at the national organization level.

Lafarge. In September 2002, WWF's most important partnership was with Lafarge, the world's leading cement producer, with sales of $13.7 billion in 2001. Initial discussions had started in 1998 when WWF France representatives had contacted the company expressing concern about a river valley in France from which Lafarge was removing gravel. Discussions extended to forest restoration around quarries, and a partnership evolved to address this issue. In March 2000, a five-year partnership was established with three objectives: restoration of Lafarge's quarries, reinforcement of Lafarge's environmental policy, and financial support of WWF's "Forest Reborn" program. Since 2000, these objectives had been expanded to include agreements on energy use, a reduction in CO_2 emissions of 10 percent below 1990 levels by 2010, and discussions about the reduction of toxic chemical use. In 2001, Lafarge published a sustainability report to be used with the investment community (see **Exhibit 14** for an excerpt of Lafarge's sustainability report). In 2001, the WBCSD published its "cement report," largely based on WWF's work with Lafarge.

Delverde. From initial discussions between WWF Italy and Delverde, centered on the use of water by one of Delverde's pasta plants within a national park, a communication partnership evolved, with Delverde using the WWF brand in point-of-sale advertising and developing an organic pasta product line.

HSBC. In March 2002, HSBC created a five-year, $50 million ecopartnership called Investing in Nature to fund conservation projects around the world and made donations to three NGOs: WWF, Botanic Gardens Conservation International, and Earthwatch. In addition, WWF committed to work with HSBC on environmental policies. "HSBC originally just wanted to donate to support freshwater conservation," Steele explained, "but we've developed a dialogue and relationship where we not only receive funding for our work but get to influence their environmental policies, too."

Other WWF partnerships involved Canon, which maximized the communication component of a partnership with the shared use of photography and the digitization of all wildlife photographs (followed up by recent discussions concerning recycling of photocopiers and use of solar panels), and Ogilvy & Mather, which contributed free advertisements and placements. In both of these cases, initial discussions had been initiated with WWF International. "These were global partnerships that led to local activities, both within the WWF network and within the partners' network, and presented some challenges for both HQs," Steele commented. "We were surprised to find out that other organizations faced the same sorts of local versus HQ office issues that we face."

In 2002, national organizations could make partnership deals at the national level, but any that had global scope had to be referred to WWF International, which played a role both in taking local initiatives global and global initiatives local. Steele summarized:

> We try to assess the impact of a specific partnership on the whole network, and it's up to the international group to demonstrate value added to our national organizations. The difficulty is that no two deals are the same in terms of what they bring to WWF in the way of conservation, cash, and communication. In Europe, though, most prospective corporate partners are operating in more than one country, so, by default, many of the local partnerships become international.

It was the corporate fund-raising team's role to shape the global strategy for corporate partnerships and identify future partner candidates. The team provided leadership and support to the national organizations and helped take some partnerships from local to global. Account managers within the group were responsible for developing partnership opportunities both within specific geographic areas and with targeted large accounts. They managed the partnerships internally, throughout the WWF network, and externally by being the key contact people within WWF. Steele explained:

> It is key to have one person on each side of any partnership who coordinates internally and communicates externally. It is important to have a clear understanding of where, within each organization, the first port of call is. At Lafarge and HSBC, for example, the owner of the relationship is the vice president of

Exhibit 14   Excerpt from Lafarge Annual Report

Message from Bertrand Collomb

In the report entitled "Our Common Future", submitted to the United Nations in 1987 by the Brundtland Commission, sustainable development was defined as "development that meets the needs of the present without compromising the ability of future generations to meet their own needs".

When applied to an industrial group like ours, this concept translates into the need to measure the value created by the company according to a "triple bottom line" which aims to combine economic prosperity, environmental quality and social responsibility. Only if we can succeed in all three aspects will we ensure the company's prosperity and that of the world in which it is developing.

For more than 160 years, Lafarge has been producing construction materials that are vital for the development of human society, and therefore extracting non-renewable, abundant natural resources from the Earth's crust. The very nature of this activity, which necessitated the establishment of a firm local foothold, means that Lafarge has historically worked at integrating all three dimensions of sustainable development into its strategy and corporate culture. For example, our *Principles of Action*, published for the first time in 1977, highlight the central role of individuals, inside and outside the company, as well as the importance of cultural diversity, transparency and respect for the public interest. By the same token, *Lafarge's Environmental Policy* adopted in 1995 formalized the commitments to enable us to turn the environment into a competitive advantage and a source of fresh opportunities instead of a mere constraint.

Lafarge is proud of its achievements regarding sustainability as well as of its corporate culture that has contributed so much in this respect. Our progress is recognized by many, including the financial sector - Lafarge is for example a constituent of the Dow Jones Sustainability Index. Nevertheless, we want to take this approach further; on the one hand by pressing ahead with our analysis of what sustainability really means to our businesses, and on the other hand by committing ourselves more strongly than before to a progressive approach.

While it is key to Lafarge's continued prosperity, our current international development also confronts us with fresh challenges, linked to the difficult socio-economic situation in the countries of the Third World and to our responsibility as a global company to face up to world-wide problems like global warming. These heightened responsibilities are just some of the growing expectations of us from our stakeholders. We must meet these expectations.

Therefore, we intend to make headway by engaging in dialogue and exchanging ideas with all our stake-

external affairs. However, in other more decentralized organizations such as Shell or Unilever, the person with this title sitting in corporate headquarters may not have enough clout.

In 2002, WWF International employed five full-time account managers. Many major partnerships, particularly those involving an intensive communication component, required a full-time account manager. The Lafarge partnership, for example, was managed by a single account manager, based at WWF International, and paid for out of the partnership funds. In the case of the HSBC relationship, which had originated in the United Kingdom and focused primarily on the United Kingdom, the United States, China, and Brazil, a total of four account managers, working out of the U.K.'s WWF office, managed the relationship and were once again paid for out of the partnership funds.

Risks and Benefits.

Partnering with global companies can help us advance our conservation aims and obtain new sources of funding. However, we need some up-front rules of engagement and need to establish safeguards and standards in approaching industry. We want to further our conservation goals and assist companies in sustainability programs, but we need to adhere to the right to criticize them as well.

—Paul Steele

One of the main objectives of establishing corporate partnerships was to further WWF's conservation goals by developing relationships that would bring about change in the way companies operated. "By changing the internal practices of these companies, we can move towards our goals," Steele explained. "The danger, of course, is that we risk being accused of greenwashing." Steele believed that although the environment was not on the agenda for most companies ten years ago, many were keen to address sustainable development by 2002 but did not know how. He expanded, "There are real dangers in our partnering with corporations, and we need to demonstrate concrete results whilst maintaining our right to criticize the companies we are working with." Although WWF had been working closely with Lafarge since 2000, WWF strongly criticized a specific Lafarge project in Scotland. "I think Lafarge works with us because we don't pull any stunts," Steele said, "but we still maintain our right to criticize them." Some NGOs sneered at WWF as the "corporate NGO," but few of them made the same demands for internal change with the companies with which they partnered.

Steele was also determined to continue to not use the WWF brand as a certification or validation tool. WWF had been instrumental in the 1990s in establishing both the Forest Stewardship Council and the Marine Stewardship Council, independent bodies with certification standards and a labeling scheme for sustainable forestry and seafood products, respectively. In addition, Steele was reluctant to place the panda logo on consumer products and was concerned about the possible dilution of the WWF brand. "There are a lot of abuses of the WWF logo around the world," he explained, "but we want to put our money into conservation projects rather than policing efforts."

Moving Forward.

From the INRA study, Steele knew that Europeans seemed to be generally in favor of the relationships that WWF was developing with business (60 percent of consumers polled said they thought association with WWF would add value to a company, and two in three thought WWF should be partly supported by private companies). However, he was concerned that, until now, WWF had pursued a reactive, opportunistic approach to developing corporate partnerships, and he believed that such a piece-meal approach could jeopardize WWF's reputation. Each national organization had had, until 2002, the independence to implement its own local country partnerships. Steele wondered if this policy should continue and how best to manage any change that might be necessary. In addition, given WWF's brand value, Steele wondered if it made sense for any WWF organization to partner with these smaller national and local companies.

"We need three or four more Lafarges under our belt," Steele said, "and we need to make the case that a partnership with WWF can result in financial benefits as well as competitive advantages. We need to make sure that we are also adding value to the partner." In 2002, for example, the global availability of freshwater resources was an emerging issue. Major food companies were starting to realize that freshwater resources were finite and threatened, and that continued access could not be taken for granted. Steele explained, "Companies can see that they benefit, that there is an economic rationale for doing something about fresh water, and as a result, we can progress the agendas of both WWF and the company." In addition, WWF wanted to avoid industry or category exclusivity agreements; for example, WWF wanted to lever-age its experience with Lafarge to partnerships with other cement manufacturers.

Steele had developed a proactive, coordinated approach to assessing future corpo-rate partnerships within the business and industry unit and had engaged WWF exec-utives to identify target-industry sectors and corporations within these sectors (see **Exhibit 15** for an overview of WWF's business and industry approach). This process had identified three major corporations from three different industry sectors. Steele set out to assess the pros and cons of each potential corporate partnership:

Company A was a British multinational consumer products group offering a potential partnership package worth $50 million. The partnership consisted of three components:

1. Changes in the group's internal operating practices around raw materials utilization and decreases in energy consumption and CO_2 emissions, with measurable milestones for each and accounting for 25 percent of the partnership package

2. A contribution to a WWF global conservation program, in this case, a freshwater conservation project, representing 40 percent of the package

3. A communications program with promotions involving the use of the WWF logo, representing 25 percent of the package but to be implemented only after the company proved its ability to meet targets specified in the first component

Exhibit 15	WWF Business and Industry Approach

Essential Elements of B&I Relationships

- Pro-Active, Co-ordinated Approach

- Clear Objectives
  - Conservation and/or Funding?

- Clear Rules of Engagement
  - What's Expected of Both Parties
  - Contract / MOU in Place
    - WWF Right to Publicly Criticise
    - Use of "Panda" Logo etc.
    - Communications Plan

- Clear "Ownership" of the Relationship
  - TDP, NO, PO, International?

- Sound "Account Management" in Place
  - How to "Maximise" the Relationship

What The B&I Unit Will Do

- Assist in the Sector Identification & Targetting Process

- Identify "Non-Critical" Sectors to Programme Objectives
  - Fertile for Fundraising

- Maintain a B&I Database - Links to Existing Knowledge

- Facilitate Setting Integrated Objectives

- Facilitate the Network Screening Process

- Carry Out or Facilitate the Due Diligence Process

- Assist or Facilitiate Direct Engagement With Companies

- Manage "Accounts" Where This Makes Sense For The Network

Source: WWF.

Note: MOU = Memorandum of Understanding, TDP = Target Driven Program, NO = National organization,
        PO = Program Office.

The remaining 10 percent of funds were reserved for managing the relationship, including salaries and benefits, for a WWF-dedicated account team. Benefits of this potential partnership included the group's broad consumer reach and global stature, the access to substantial funds for conservation projects, and the ability to change the group's operating practices and effect on sustainable development. Possible downsides, on the other hand, included the risk of "greenwash," with the group paying lip service to sustainable development rather than being truly committed to it, and the potential for misuse of the WWF brand and logo (for example, the use of the panda logo on a detergent product). "The agreement has to be totally transparent," Steele explained. "WWF has to be able to explain convincingly the benefits of the relationship and prove that we're not just being bought off."

Company B was an American financial services company. The potential partnership centered on a direct financial investment by the company and would be similar in structure and magnitude to the existing partnership with HSBC. The relationship would also include agreed-upon restrictions on lending policies, precluding loans for projects such as forest exploitation, oil exploration, and dam building. "One of the goals we would like to see in this type of partnership," Steele said, "is the development, in collaboration with the partner, of written guidelines for lending procedures. We want to ensure that the right questions are being asked by the company of its prospective loan recipients and the right criteria are being used to assess them."

The benefits of this potential partnership included the fairly straightforward nature of the potential agreement and the relatively low risk to the WWF brand and reputation. The drawbacks included the risk of "greenwash" and the challenge of ensuring that any changes in guidelines were actually implemented.

Company C was a South African mining corporation that had contacted WWF with a proposal to provide funding of $5 million per year over the next five years for a species conservation program. Although the funding was attractive, Steele wondered how he could structure an agreement that would make WWF comfortable. One option would be to accept a donation from the corporation's charitable foundation arm rather than directly from the corporation; in the past, WWF had accepted donations from the Ford Foundation and the Shell Foundation.

Another option would be to structure an agreement that required the corporation to make a major commitment not to go into protected areas. The International Union for Conservancy had categorized protected areas into six categories, and Steele was tempted to ask the corporation not to develop any activities in the first four categories. Such a request, if accepted, would have a substantially positive effect on WWF conservation goals, in addition to the financial contribution. However, the risk of associating the WWF brand with what many considered traditionally to be the "enemy" was considerable.

All three potential partnerships would be constructed as three- to five-year agreements with quarterly or biannual reviews. In each case, Steele believed that CEO buy-in was key to achieving commitment throughout the corporate partner's organization.

CONCLUSION.

In assessing the potential partnership options before him, Steele weighed the pros and cons in each case and wondered which would provide WWF with the greatest benefits for the least risks. Although he was sure that building strong global corporate partnerships was the best way forward for WWF, not least from a sustainable development perspective as highlighted at the World Summit on Sustainable Development in Johannesburg, he had recently seen a letter that a member had written to Martin, complaining that WWF was "selling out" and becoming the "NGO of the corporate establishment." Steele was also aware that some WWF employees and members shared this sentiment at times but was convinced that these concerns could be effectively addressed.

Notes to Case

1 WWF's Global Conservation Programme 2001/2002.

2 Marc Lindenberg and Coralie Bryant, *Going Global: Transforming Relief and Development NGOs* (Bloomfield, CT: Kumarian Press, 2001).

3 Edelman Public Relations presentations.

4 Institute for Policy Studies, 1999.

5 *The Financial Times* business enterprises article, September 2000.

CASE 12
Médecins Sans Frontières

In October 2002, the communications directors of the five operational Médecins Sans Frontières (MSF, known in the United States as Doctors without Borders) sections met to discuss, among other things, the organization's international branding strategy. Since 1998, the organization had been working toward establishing a common international brand that would reduce media and donor confusion, and enable MSF to build a cohesive brand image for the future. This effort was hindered by the high turnover rate of the communications directors. In September 2002, only one of the current communications directors had been involved in the original international brand discussions of 1998.

MSF.

MSF was a private, nonprofit international organization that delivered emergency medical aid to victims of armed conflict, epidemics, and natural and manmade disasters, and the socially marginalized. MSF was a movement, comprising an international network of eighteen country sections. In 2001, MSF assigned more than 2,800 volunteer doctors, nurses, other medical professionals, logistics experts, water and sanitation engineers, and administrators to join 15,000 locally hired staff to provide medical aid in more than eighty countries.

In emergencies and their aftermath, MSF personnel provided primary health care, performed surgeries, rehabilitated hospitals and clinics, ran nutrition and sanitation programs, and trained local medical personnel. Through longer-term programs, MSF treated infectious diseases; assisted with the medical and psychological problems of marginalized populations, including street children and ethnic minorities; and brought health care to remote, isolated areas where resources were limited. In addition to emergency medical assistance, MSF played a key role in publicly bearing witness and speaking out in the event of human rights violations.

In 2002, the organization was supported by more than 2.5 million private and individual donors around the world. MSF derived more than 80 percent of its 2001 income of 340 million euros from private sources, enabling it to maintain its independence to act and speak out. MSF managers considered this level of private funding an important guarantee of the organization's independence.

This case was written by Nathalie Laidler and John Quelch and is reproduced by permission.

Socio-Political and Economic Context.

The 1971 creation of MSF sparked a revolution in the world of humanitarianism, captured the hearts and minds of millions of people, and heightened the increasing importance of NGOs (nongovernmental organizations) in Europe over the last three decades of the twentieth century. Throughout the 1970s in France, both the growing number of disturbing television images of the effects of disasters and conflicts and a feeling of responsibility toward de-colonized countries fueled public opinion and created the context for the growth of emergency assistance by independent NGOs.

During the 1960s and 1970s, the French job market was flooded by doctors from the baby boom generation, who did not need to repay student loans and often had experience in developing countries during their military service. Many general practitioners of this generation were experiencing an identity crisis. Faced in their daily practice with benign pathologies that did not interest them and unsolvable problems that they could only refer to specialists, many of them were tempted to practice what they saw as a more authentic form of medicine in the developing world.

History.[1]

MSF arose from the merger of two groups of international relief doctors. The first group had worked in Biafra, a region of Nigeria torn apart by a brutal civil war, between 1968 and 1970, on behalf of the French Red Cross. Among them was Bernard Kouchner, cofounder of MSF, who later became France's first minister of humanitarian affairs. Back in France in 1970, the Biafra veterans organized the Groupe d'Intervention Medical et Chirurgical d'Urgence (Emergency Medical and Surgical Intervention Group) in the hope of setting up an independent association specializing in providing emergency medical assistance, free from the administrative and legal constraints facing the Red Cross. The second group of doctors had been active in treating the victims of a tidal wave in eastern Pakistan (now Bangladesh) in 1970. Under the leadership of Raymond Borel, editor of the medical journal *Tonus*, who spoke on television about the distress of the Bangladeshi tidal wave victims and the lack of French doctors at the site of the disaster, the group established an organization called Secours Medical Francais (French Medical Relief).

The two groups were frustrated by the shortcomings of international aid at the time, which they viewed as providing too little medical assistance, and as too deferential to international law to be effective in crisis situations. On December 20, 1971, the two groups decided to merge and Philippe Bernier, one of the journalists at *Tonus*, suggested that the resulting organization change its name to Médecins Sans Frontières. "It's interesting," said Stephan Oberreit, director of communications for MSF France, "that journalists have always been involved in the organization and in fact created the brand." MSF was the first nongovernmental organization to both provide emergency medical assistance and bear witness publicly in the event of human rights violations. From 1971 to 1976, MSF acted essentially as a pool of volunteer doctors, at the disposal of large development aid organizations. Its budget was limited and its missions, with a few exceptions (Nicaragua after the 1972 earthquake and Honduras after the 1974 hurricane), were not independent. Oberreit explained, "MSF was, at first, a virtual organization, had no offices, and worked through other organizations."

MSF started to gain momentum in 1976 with its war mission in Lebanon, and in 1977, a major advertising agency, Publicis, created MSF's public identity as an organization that dealt with dangerous emergencies. Oberreit recalled the initial advertising campaign: "I think it ran something like, 'MSF, 2 million people in their waiting room.'" During the same time, the American press reported on the courage of the French doctors in Lebanon. In 1978, despite its strong presence in the media and growing reputation and recognition, MSF was a more symbolic than operational organization, sending out only a few dozen doctors per year.

MSF's formidable growth came after 1978, fueled by the increase in the number of refugee camps. The global refugee population doubled between 1976 and 1979, from 2.7 million to 5.7 million, and doubled once again between 1979 and 1982, settling at 11 million people. From 1976 to 1979, MSF came to the aid of Angolan refugees in the former Zaire; Somali refugees in Djibouti; Saharan refugees in Algeria and Eritrea; and, above all, Vietnamese, Cambodian, and Laotian refugees in Thailand. Initially, MSF offered modest help to the American medical humanitarian organizations that had already been on the scene for more than a year (particularly the International Rescue Committee and World Vision). Yet the French doctors sometimes questioned the purpose of these organizations, suspecting them of being motivated by politics (anticommunism) or religion (proselytizing). During this period, MSF expanded its operations in Thailand, slowly replacing the American organizations, which began to withdraw from the refugee camps as the memory of the Vietnam War began to fade. In December 1979 MSF sent more than 100 doctors and nurses to the Cambodian border.

In the early 1980s, MSF embarked on a course of internationalization. In 1981, volunteers from Belgium and Switzerland established operational sections in their countries. In 1983, a Dutch operational section was added, and in 1985, additional operational sections were established in Spain and Luxembourg. Each operational section operated autonomously, focusing on its own field activities and operations. Between 1986 and 1995, supporting sections were established in Australia, Austria, Canada, Denmark, Germany, Greece, Hong Kong, Italy, Japan, Norway, Sweden, the United States, and the United Kingdom. Partner sections were established with the express objective of recruiting volunteers and raising funds. In the second half of the 1980s, tensions arose between the different operational sections that were competing in the field, and MSF recognized the need for greater cooperation and coordination. In 1991, an international council and international secretariat, based in Belgium, was created to play this coordinating role.

During the 1990s, much of MSF's growing recognition stemmed from its missions in Afghanistan, Ethiopia, Iraqi Kurdistan, the former Yugoslavia, Somalia, Rwanda, and the Republic of Congo (formerly Zaire), which were widely reported by the media. In addition, MSF's field volunteers increasingly spoke out against the injustices and abuses they witnessed. With the collapse of communism in Eastern Europe, MSF also began to participate in the effort to restore the public health systems in Romania, Bulgaria, and a number of republics of the former USSR. In 1999, MSF was awarded the Nobel Peace Prize. By the turn of the century, it was widely known throughout Europe and within the humanitarian aid community.

Mission and Objectives.

Independent humanitarian medical action was at the core of the MSF mission. The organization was often the first relief agency to arrive at the scene of an emergency, and the last to leave. Volunteers worked in the most remote and dangerous parts of the world, and teams arrived at a project site with prepackaged medical kits so that they could start their work immediately. Wherever MSF operated, its volunteers trained and worked closely with local staff and other NGOs, thereby ensuring the sustainability of its programs.

MSF combined medical care with a commitment to speaking out against the underlying causes of suffering. Its volunteers protested violations of humanitarian law on behalf of populations in crisis and brought the concerns of their patients to public forums such as the United Nations, governments, and the media. Raising public awareness of the plight of populations at risk was considered part of MSF's mission.

Beginning in the 1990s, MSF expanded its advocacy role and focused on individual issues with universal themes. The most prominent was the Access to Essential Medicines Campaign, which highlighted the lack of research and development for a variety of neglected diseases. (See **Exhibit 1** for excerpts from a description of the Access to Essential Medicines Campaign.) Nicolas de Torrenté, was the executive director of MSF USA. "The Access to Essential Medicines Campaign is a further step in this area," he said. "It proposes a solution to a huge problem and attempts to involve the public. We have a truck going around the United States that gets people to sign a petition to support what we are trying to achieve."

MSF's members and volunteers adhered to a charter, which specified that MSF was independent from all political, economic, and religious powers, and offered assistance without discrimination and irrespective of race, religion, creed, or political affiliation. (See **Exhibit 2** for MSF's charter.) De Torrenté commented on the importance of providing assistance without discrimination: "Currently, there is a movement to limit humanitarian aid to certain populations or areas of the world and this, we believe, dilutes the true meaning of humanitarian assistance. It is not a political statement to help the populations who are under the control of certain political groups. The war on terrorism has resulted in a categorization of victims, with certain lives being more important than others. MSF believes that all victims should have the same rights and access to medical humanitarian assistance, irrespective of race, religion, creed, or where they happen to live."

Operations.[2]

In 2002, MSF worked in areas of Africa, the Americas, Asia, and Europe where services were inadequate to meet the population's medical needs. Four scenarios could warrant MSF's involvement:

Wars and conflicts. When conflicts erupted, MSF sent teams of surgeons, anesthetists, operating room nurses, and logisticians into the field, with the necessary equipment to establish operating rooms and clinics, provide basic public hygiene assistance, and begin training local medical and support staff. In cases of prolonged conflict, teams provided primary care, nutrition services, and epidemic control to the local population and those displaced by the fighting.

Exhibit 1	Excerpts from Access to Essential Medicines Campaign

KILLER DISEASES: Infectious diseases remain the most common cause of death worldwide. They kill around 14 million people each year and account for more than 25 percent of all deaths globally. Old diseases are reappearing and drug resistance is spreading, rendering useless medicines that were once effective.

AFFECTING THE POOR: An estimated 97 percent of deaths from communicable disease—such as AIDS, tuberculosis, and malaria—occur in developing countries, and people living in poverty are affected disproportionately.

NO EQUITY IN PRICING: For many people today it is the cost of an essential medicine that determines whether they live or die. A capsule of fluconazole, a drug used to treat AIDS-related meningitis, costs less than 30 cents in Thailand but more than $10.50 in Kenya. This is because the drug is not patented in Thailand and can therefore be produced by local generic manufacturers, whereas the lack of such competition in some other countries has led to unaffordable drug prices. Since the global market is failing the poor, it is the responsibility of governments and intergovernmental agencies to bridge the gap between the price of a drug and a patient's ability to pay.

LIFESAVING DRUGS—OLD OR OUT OF PRODUCTION: Leishmaniasis is a parasitic disease endemic in eighty-eight countries in various forms. According to a rough estimate, the most severe variant, Kala Azar, affects up to 500,000 people each year and is usually fatal if not treated. The most commonly used drug to treat the disease was discovered more than half a century ago, and in certain regions, the parasite is becoming resistant to it. The production of a new promising drug, the antibiotic aminosidine, has been abandoned because no company has found sufficient marketing potential.

DISEASE DOESN'T DISCRIMINATE, PEOPLE DO: Research into tropical disease has ground to a halt. For disease such as tuberculosis and sleeping sickness, there are almost no new medicines in the research pipeline. In contrast, drug laboratories are busy developing innovative and profitable cures for non-life-threatening ailments such as baldness. Political leaders have failed to allocate public funding to promote research and to help make existing essential medicines affordable.

MSF's GOAL: MAKING TREATMENT AVAILABLE: MSF is determined to increase access to lifesaving drugs in developing countries. The organization is campaigning internationally to make this happen. To deal with epidemics today, MSF is bringing about tangible case-by-case solutions in its field projects. But the campaign is also mobilizing public opinion and applying political pressure to make those responsible for public health take action.

- MSF is working to get lifesaving antibiotics, AIDS medicines, and drugs to patients in developing countries. MSF negotiates directly with governments, producers, and international agencies to achieve affordable prices. MSF is also pushing manufacturers to re-start the production of certain effective drugs that have been withdrawn from the market.

- MSF supports developing countries in their efforts to improve access to essential drugs. In particular this involves ensuring that protecting lives takes priority over protecting patents. MSF encourages the production or importation of cheaper, quality generic drugs when possible and urges patent holders to offer affordable prices in the developing world.

Source: Based on the "Access to Medicines Denied" pamphlet produced by MSF USA 2002.

Refugees and displaced people. The previous thirty years had seen an explosion in the world's refugee population, rising from 2 million in the early 1970s to more than 39 million refugees and displaced people in 2001. MSF worked with other non-governmental organizations, local health authorities, and the United Nations High Commissioner for Refugees in refugee camps to provide primary health care, epidemic control, immunizations, nutrition, clean water, and effective sanitation systems.

Natural or man-made disasters. Speed was critical to successful intervention after a natural disaster. MSF had tested and stored prepackaged medical and technical

Exhibit 2	MSF's Charter 2002

Médecins Sans Frontières offers assistance to populations in distress, to victims of natural or man-made disasters and to victims of armed conflict, without discrimination and irrespective of race, religion, creed or political affiliation.

Médecins Sans Frontières observes neutrality and impartiality in the name of universal medical ethics and the right to medical humanitarian assistance and demands full and unhindered freedom in the exercise of its functions.

Médecins Sans Frontières' volunteers undertake to respect their professional code of ethics and to maintain complete independence from all political, economic and religious powers.

As volunteers, members are aware of the risks and dangers of the mission they undertake and have no right to compensation for themselves or their beneficiaries other than that which Médecins Sans Frontières is able to afford them.

kits in its warehouses and was able to dispatch them immediately to devastated areas. At the disaster sites, MSF treated and distributed clean drinking water and provided medicine and medical supplies.

Long-term assistance. In countries with collapsed or insufficient health care systems, MSF worked with the local authorities, generally through the Ministry of Health, to rehabilitate hospitals and dispensaries; establish rural clinics, vaccination, and drug management programs; and train local staff. In these situations, MSF's goals were to help build a stable and self-sufficient local health care structure.

MSF started a project when it identified the existence of a medical humanitarian crisis as described above, or when it was invited by a national government or a UN agency. Initially, an exploratory team of experienced MSF personnel visited a site and evaluated the medical, nutritional, and sanitary needs, the political environment, the security situation, transportation facilities, and local capabilities. The team reported its findings and recommendations to one of the five operational offices, which then made the final decision whether or not to intervene. A project could comprise any number of the following key activities: massive vaccination campaigns, training and supervision of medical personnel, water and sanitation improvement, data collection, feeding, patient care, maternal and pediatric care, distribution of drugs and medical supplies, mental health care, rehabilitation of hospitals and clinics, and AIDS care and prevention. (See **Exhibit 3** for details on each of these key activities.)

Once the acute emergency phase of a health project was over and the local health care infrastructure had been restored to an acceptable level, MSF began to phase out its presence. Often an entire program was handed over to another organization, such as an international or local NGO, which concentrated on reconstruction and long-term aid, or the national or local government health services. In addition, MSF sometimes terminated a project if risks in an area became too great to ensure the safety of its staff.

Logistical expertise. MSF's speed and efficiency was based on its strong logistical capability of transporting prepackaged medical kits that had been developed and custom-designed for specific situations and geographical conditions. One kit, for example, comprised a complete operating theater; a second kit included all the

Exhibit 3	MSF Key Activities

- **MASSIVE VACCINATION CAMPAIGNS:** Epidemics often developed in acute emergency situations, where a large number of weakened people lived in close proximity to each other and in poor sanitary conditions. Yellow fever, cholera, measles, and meningitis were liable to spread in such conditions unless a massive vaccination campaign was launched.

- **TRAINING AND SUPERVISION OF MEDICAL PERSONNEL:** MSF was unable to function without local medical personnel. Sometimes, this personnel was not adequately trained, or the well-trained doctors and nurses had fled the crisis area. MSF provided additional training and supervision on subjects ranging from primary health care to drug prescription, diagnosis, and psycho-social care. All training was subject to fixed guidelines to ensure that the same standards were used in all programs.

- **WATER AND SANITATION IMPROVEMENT:** Clean drinking water and sanitary facilities were essential to preventing the outbreak of epidemics. MSF employed specialists who constructed sanitary facilities using existing water sources, newly dug wells, piping, plastic water tanks, tank trucks, and supplies for the construction of toilets.

- **DATA COLLECTION:** To keep track of the health of civilians living in a crisis area, MSF considered it important to register medical data, such as mortality figures, the number of patients suffering from certain diseases, and the degree of malnutrition. These data were generally registered during consultations given at hospitals or outpatient clinics, or during house calls. Sometimes, special surveys were carried out to catalogue specific medical facts.

- **FEEDING:** Lack of adequate food sources or agriculture often caused malnutrition among refugees or war victims. MSF regularly monitored the food situation in the areas where it worked. Seriously malnourished children were administered food under medical supervision, and for this purpose, MSF set up therapeutic feeding centers (TFCs), where children could stay with their mothers. Children whose condition was less critical, pregnant women, and breast-feeding mothers visited MSF-run supplementary feeding centers (SFCs) a few times a day to receive vitamin- and mineral-fortified food.

- **PATIENT CARE:** Diagnosing and treating ill people was mostly carried out by local medical personnel, recruited by MSF, and international volunteers. Experienced staff coordinated the work, provided support and training where necessary, and ensured that there was a sufficient supply of drugs and medical materials. When necessary, MSF had set up special programs to address particular diseases, such as kala azar, tuberculosis, sleeping sickness, and malaria. If fighting produced casualties that exceeded the capacity of local hospitals, MSF would offer surgical assistance.

- **MATERNAL AND PEDIATRIC CARE:** Women and children were often the most vulnerable groups in emergency situations. Pregnancy check-ups, neonatal care, special feeding programs, vaccination campaigns, birth control, treatment of venereal diseases, and health education were therefore important parts of the MSF's work.

- **DISTRIBUTION OF DRUGS AND MEDICAL SUPPLIES:** The supply of drugs and medical materials could be cut off by fighting, dangerous conditions, road destruction, lack of transport vehicles, or lack of funds. When that happened, MSF would take over the supply until local supply lines were reestablished.

- **MENTAL HEALTH CARE:** The death of loved ones, terror, witnessing massacres, and suffering from hunger, thirst, and cold were just a few of the traumatic events that could give rise to serious mental and physical difficulties in victims of conflicts and emergency situations. If help was not forthcoming, trauma victims could suffer protracted insomnia, aggression, headaches, listlessness, and other physiological and psychosocial symptoms. MSF had started its first mental health program in 1991, and psychosocial care had become a component of many MSF emergency and long-term projects.

- **REHABILITATION OF HOSPITALS AND CLINICS:** In acute and chronic conflict situations, hospitals and clinics were often devastated. Where necessary, MSF assumed the task of rehabilitating and re-equipping these buildings.

- **AIDS CARE TREATMENT AND PREVENTION:** Providing general health information was part of nearly all MSF programs. In many countries, this meant addressing the HIV/AIDS epidemic. Poverty, tourism, prostitution, ignorance, lack of money, and unwillingness to use condoms had led to an explosive increase in the number of HIV infections. Providing adequate information to dispel local prejudices, pride, and fears, and explaining the use of condoms were challenges that MSF was facing in many of its projects. In addition, MSF had launched pilot HIV/AIDS treatment programs in several countries to care for HIV positive patients with anti-retrovirals and to prevent mother-to-child transmission of HIV.

Source: From MSF USA Web site, 2002.

supplies needed to treat hundreds of cholera patients. MSF kits were so well designed that they had been replicated by relief organizations worldwide. To maximize its responsiveness to emergency situations, MSF also maintained four logistical centers based in Europe and East Africa, and stocks of emergency materials were kept in storage in Central America and East Asia. The logistical centers purchased, tested, and stored nutritional supplements and equipment, including vehicles, communications material, power supplies, and water-processing facilities. The logistical centers were organized to ensure that, within twenty-four hours, planes could be loaded with essential equipment and flown into any crisis area.

MSF had developed handbooks for use in the field that covered many aspects of relief work, from essential drugs to water and sanitation. Specialized training of field volunteers was essential to MSF's effectiveness, and in 2002, MSF trained more than 1,000 of them. Training sessions ranged from a three-day introductory session for first-time volunteers to two-week programs on how to establish nutrition centers.

In accordance with universal medical ethics and the right to medical humanitarian assistance, MSF observed strict neutrality and impartiality, and demanded full and unhindered freedom in performing its work. Because medical assistance could not save all lives, MSF also spoke out against human rights abuses that its teams witnessed while providing medical relief. To increase awareness of medical humanitarian issues, MSF carried out media and public awareness projects and published *Populations in Danger*, a report on the world's most acute medical humanitarian crises.

Organizational Structure.

MSF acted as a movement, consisting of sections in eighteen countries. Five of these—Belgium, France, Holland, Spain, and Switzerland—were considered operational and directly controlled field projects, deciding when, where, and what medical relief was necessary and when to terminate aid. The remaining thirteen MSF sections were partner sections; their primary function was to recruit volunteers, raise funds for field projects, raise awareness, and carry out advocacy and public outreach on behalf of populations in danger. Nonoperational sections were in Australia, Austria, Canada, Denmark, Germany, Hong Kong, Italy, Japan, Luxembourg, Norway, Sweden, the United Kingdom, and the United States. Each partner section fed into an operational section as shown on the organizational chart in **Exhibit 4**. For example, Australia, Japan, and the United States reported to MSF France. De Torrenté explained further:

> Our organizational structure is a product of history rather than design, and it has not been a smooth road. In the 1980s the French and Belgian sections had such different philosophies and field approaches that they went to court, and the French section attempted to remove the Belgians' right to use the Médecins Sans Frontières name. It is paradoxical that the international, without borders, nature of our organization should be taken up by people who want to add their country name to the brand and act independently. The U.S. section used to be totally controlled by the French section because it invested $5 million to set up

Exhibit 4 MSF Organizational Chart 2002

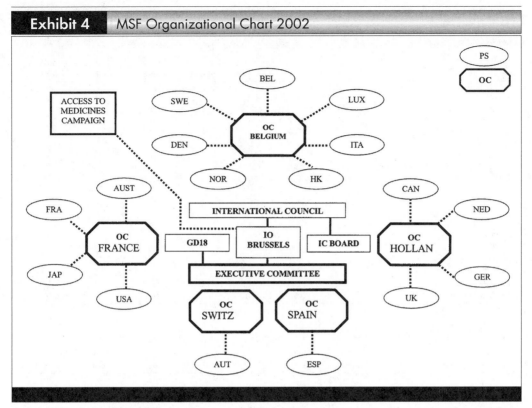

Source: MSF International internal documents.

*the office and fund-raising capabilities. As time has passed, the U.S. section has grown considerably, and our annual income is now greater than that of the French section. [See **Exhibit 5** for a financial overview of the individual MSF sections.] The internationalization of MSF has been a good thing, but we need to connect the partner sections more directly with field programs.*

MSF had four other offices: an international office in Brussels, UN liaison offices in Geneva and New York City, and an office in United Arab Emirates. The international office in Brussels played a coordinating role and was supported by both an international council, made up of the presidents of each of the sections, and an executive committee made up of the directors of the five operating centers.

Marc Schakal, EU liaison coordinator and trademark policy adviser at the international office, explained its function: "The international office has no hierarchical power; it plays a coordination role attempting to ensure that MSF's strategy, policies, and practices are coherent." Five international coordinators reporting to the general secretary played key roles as listed below: (See **Exhibit 6** for the organizational structure of the international office.)

Exhibit 5	MSF Financial Statements 2001—Income and Expenses for Operating Sections and International Office

Millions of Euros	Total	France	Belgium	Switzerland	Holland	Spain	Intern'l Office
Individuals	108	32.1	18.0	18.3	25.2	14.1	0.0
Private institutions	19	1.4	0.9	0.9	15.0	1.1	0.0
Exchange gains (losses)	2	1.7	0.5	0.1	(0.6)	0.2	0.0
Interest/investment income	2	0.9	0.3	0.3	0.4	0.3	0.0
Other income	4	1.5	0.4	1.7	0.0	0.3	0.1
PRIVATE INCOME	135	37.6	20.1	21.3	40.0	16.0	0.2
PUBLIC INSTITUTIONAL INCOME	42	4.6	24.0	1.6	9.0	2.3	0.0
TOTAL INCOME	177	42.2	44.2	22.9	49.0	18.3	0.2
Direct project costs	218	53.6	78.0	16.6	54.5	15.7	0.0
Indirect project costs	26	6.7	4.9	2.9	9.2	2.6	0.1
Bearing witness	12	3.3	2.5	1.6	3.1	1.0	0.4
SOCIAL MISSION	256	63.5	85.4	21.1	66.7	19.2	0.5
Fund-raising expenses	17	6.2	2.5	2.9	2.8	2.3	0.1
Administrative costs	14	2.7	4.6	1.5	2.9	2.2	0.5
Other costs	31	8.9	7.1	4.4	5.7	4.5	0.6
Total expenses	288	72.4	92.5	25.5	72.4	23.7	1.1
Surplus/(deficit)	(111.3)	(30.2)	(48.8)	(2.6)	(23.4)	(5.4)	(0.9)

Major Partner Sections:

Millions of Euros	Total	United States	Italy	Germany	Japan	Sweden	Hong Kong
Individuals	106.8	47.5	19.6	17.1	8.6	7.0	7.0
Private institutions	4.3	3.3	0.8	0.0	0.2	0.0	0.0
Exchange gains (losses)	−0.4	(0.2)	(0.0)	(0.0)	(0.1)	(0.1)	(0.0)
Interest/investment income	1.2	0.8	0.1	0.3	0.0	0.0	0.0
Other income	0.1	0.0	0.0	0.0	0.1	0.0	0.0
PRIVATE INCOME	111.9	51.4	20.4	17.3	8.8	7.0	7.0
PUBLIC INSTITUTIONAL INCOME	5.8	2.3	0.1	0.0	0.0	3.1	0.3
TOTAL INCOME	117.7	53.7	20.5	17.3	8.8	10.1	7.3
Direct project costs	1.3	0.7	0.1	0.0	0.5	0.0	0.0
Indirect project costs	3.1	1.8	0.1	0.7	0.2	0.2	0.1
Bearing witness	3.4	1.4	0.2	0.3	1.0	0.4	0.1
SOCIAL MISSION	8	3.9	0.4	1.1	1.8	0.6	0.2
Fund-raising expenses	13.8	6.0	2.3	1.6	2.0	1.1	0.8
Administrative costs	3.9	0.9	0.7	1.2	0.4	0.4	0.3
Other costs	17.6	6.9	2.9	2.8	2.4	1.5	1.1
Total expenses	25.8	10.9	3.3	3.9	4.2	2.1	1.4
Surplus/(deficit)	91.9	42.8	17.2	13.4	4.6	7.9	6.0

Source: Internal MSF accounting documents.

- An international information coordinator worked closely with the communications directors of the different sections to ensure consistent messages in press releases. An international Web site editor coordinated all the section Web sites and reported to the information coordinator.

Exhibit 5	continued

Other Partner Sections:

Millions of Euros	Total	Canada	Austria	United Kingdom	Australia	Luxembourg	Norway	Denmark
Individuals	18.5	6.1	5.7	5.4	2.8	2.2	1.3	1.1
Private institutions	2.9	0.0	0.1	1.8	0	0.0	0.3	0.7
Exchange gains (losses)	–0.2	(0.1)	(0.0)	(0.1)	–0.1	0.1	(0.1)	(0.0)
Interest/investment income	0.3	0.1	0.0	0.1	0	0.2	0.0	0.0
Other income	0.2	0.1	0.0	0.0	0	0.1	0.0	0.1
PRIVATE INCOME	21.8	6.3	5.9	7.2	2.7	2.6	1.5	1.9
PUBLIC INSTITUTIONAL INCOME	16.1	1.9	0.2	4.3	1.5	5.6	3.4	1.1
TOTAL INCOME	38.0	8.2	6.1	11.5	4.2	8.2	4.9	3.1
Direct project costs	7.8	0.2	0.0	0.3	0.5	7.0	0.0	0.0
Indirect project costs	1.5	0.8	0.2	0.4	0.2	0.6	0.0	0.1
Bearing witness	1.1	1.1	0.1	0.4	0.2	0.2	0.1	0.1
SOCIAL MISSION	10.4	2.2	0.4	1.0	0.9	7.7	0.2	0.2
Fund-raising expenses	4.9	1.3	1.0	2.1	0.6	0.1	0.7	0.4
Administrative costs	1.3	0.3	0.2	0.4	0.2	0.1	0.2	0.2
Other costs	6.5	1.6	1.2	2.5	0.8	0.3	1.0	0.7
Total expenses	16.6	3.8	1.5	3.5	1.7	8.0	1.1	0.8
Surplus/(deficit)	25.5	4.4	4.5	8.0	2.5	0.2	3.7	2.2

Source: Internal MSF accounting documents.

- The international medical coordinator had three roles. The first was to follow up on certain field projects in conjunction with each section's medical directors. The second was to work with the World Health Organization to establish a list of essential drugs (part of the Access to Essential Medicines Campaign). The third was to help coordinate the update of medical guidelines used in the field.

- A financial coordinator consolidated accounts, and an information technology (IT) coordinator ensured IT consistency and integration across the sections.

Oberreit commented on the organization, "Although there is some coordination of activities at the international office, each section is autonomous and a separate legal entity with its own board of directors. The operational sections are highly autonomous. They collect their own funds, manage their own field programs, and make their own decisions on pretty much everything."

Three specialized public health centers—Epicentre, Aedes, and HealthNet—also worked with MSF to further expand the organization's expertise in practical epidemiology and the management of health care programs. Epicentre, originally established by MSF France, was by 2002 largely independently funded and managed, offering both training and consulting services. Epicentre's studies and findings were published in journals such as the *Journal of the American Medical Association*

Exhibit 6   Organizational Structure of MSF's International Office

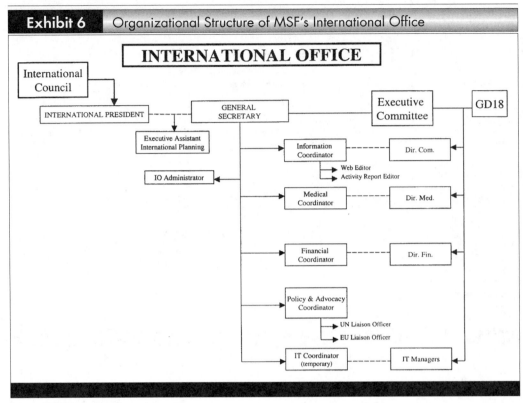

and *The Lancet*, and most of the World Health Organization's disaster training was conducted at Epicentre.

Each of MSF's field missions was initiated and coordinated by one of the organization's five operational sections. Field operations were typically managed by a country coordinator and a coordination team that included a medical coordinator, a logistical coordinator, and a financial coordinator. Typically located in the capital city of each country where MSF worked, the coordination teams oversaw the execution of the projects and acted as liaisons between MSF, local authorities, partners, and other NGOs. In countries where there were several field projects, each project team was also led by a field coordinator. An average field project team comprised four to twelve expatriate volunteers working in collaboration with up to 200 local staff members, paid by MSF. Local staff members assisted expatriate volunteers by helping them better understand the needs of the patients and the overall social and cultural context. Country managers in the field reported directly to operating section headquarters staff, which supported the field with regular visits and advice about program planning and management.

Funding and Planning.

Once a year, the coordination teams in the field submitted project plans and funding requests to the planning departments of their operating sections. In

January, these funding needs were summarized in a budget to which was added a reserve to meet unexpected program emergencies.

Ongoing field projects were mapped against specific institutional funding requests, which were, by definition, earmarked funds, and represented 19 percent of MSF's total income in 2001. Private donations represented 80 percent of income, and the majority of these funds were not earmarked. In cases when individual donors requested that their funds be used for specific programs, MSF complied if possible. "This year," Oberreit said, "we received a number of checks for the victims of 9/11 in New York. Since we did not have a program there, we had to ask these donors if they would prefer to have their checks returned, or consider funding another MSF program. Obviously, we prefer people to make unrestricted donations and trust us to allocate their funds in the best way possible."

In certain cases, MSF launched fund-raising programs for specific countries and programs. In 2001, for example, MSF France established a fund-raising program focused specifically on Angola and raised more than 1 million euros. In cases of major, well-publicized crises, when all eighteen sections wished to raise funds to respond to a specific challenge, such as Afghanistan, MSF would estimate the total financial needs and place a cap on the funds to be raised by the organization as a whole. In this way, MSF would avoid receiving an excess of earmarked funds for a specific program while not having sufficient funds for other, equally deserving programs.

MSF's Evolving Culture.

During the 1970s, MSF remained a very small organization consisting exclusively of young, highly motivated volunteers, each of whom was employed outside MSF. The fledgling organization refused to ask for charity from the public or to "sell" medical humanitarian services, and in the circles of established international organizations, MSF volunteers were considered amateurs, and often labeled as "medical hippies."

Toward the end of the 1970s, the growing number of field missions required MSF to adopt a more professional approach, including paying stipends to local staff members and volunteers. This trend, far from being welcomed by every MSF member, began to divide the organization. On one hand, the veterans of Biafra longed for the days of purely voluntary emergency medicine, and on the other, a new generation of doctors wanted to serve for longer terms and provide more sophisticated medical services. Until 1977, Bernard Kouchner had been the organization's undisputed leader. But his power was challenged in 1978 by the new generation of refugee camp doctors headed by Claude Malhuret. The two groups disagreed on several issues. First, Malhuret's group was concerned with delivering optimal medical care, which required strengthening logistical and communications capabilities. Kouchner's group advocated short, independent, voluntary missions, and feared that MSF would turn into a bureaucracy if it built up its support capabilities at headquarters. The two groups also disagreed on MSF's media posture. In 1978, Kouchner chartered a ship to rescue Vietnamese refugees in the South China Sea. This initiative generated substantial media interest. However, Malhuret's group considered a single ship insufficient to receive the host of refugees, especially given that its very presence encouraged refugees to flee Vietnam.

In 1979, Kouchner left MSF to found Médecins du Monde, or Doctors of the World (MdM) and in 2002, the two groups continued to be competitors. Oberreit reflected on MSF's cultural characteristics: "MSF has always been very 'anti-star.' No single person can represent MSF and we don't like individuals that try to promote themselves. It was actually a real problem when we were awarded the Nobel Peace Prize in 1999. Some people within MSF didn't want to accept the award. We eventually sent two people, the president of the International Council and a young field doctor."

After Kouchner's departure, MSF initiated a number of structural changes, including the development of logistics, marketing, and medical departments, and a salaried administrative system. Until 1980 MSF depended on ad-hoc donations from institutions or private individuals, prompted by media coverage of various disasters. In 1982, MSF began to introduce direct-mail fund-raising (previously unknown in France), providing the organization with regular income and ensuring independence from any single donor or government. In 2002, more than 80 percent of funds still came from private sources, although this varied by section. (Belgium, for example, derived more than 50 percent of its income from public and institutional sources.) Throughout the 1980s, MSF continued to become an increasingly professional organization: standardizing its procedures and protocols, drafting guidelines to be used in the most common emergency relief situations, building specialized expertise in nutrition and vaccination, and building strong logistics capabilities.

Throughout the 1990s, MSF was considered highly professional, effective, and efficient, but also somewhat renegade and unpredictable. MSF continued to speak out against violations and to conduct clandestine missions when its presence was not officially welcomed. In Afghanistan, for example, MSF's stance set it apart from other relief organizations, and over a ten-year period, it was the only foreign humanitarian organization assisting populations that sided with the Afghan resistance fighters.

In 2002, MSF was still an organization composed of young idealistic volunteers. The average tenure of both field volunteers and section staff was 2.5 years, and this enormous turnover made organizational continuity a challenge. Anne Fouchard, communications director for MSF France, explained its effect on the organization. "The amount of turnover means that, at MSF, change is a permanent thing. The organization is fluid and dynamic. What holds the organization together is our values, mission, and charter—in other words, our brand."

Current Challenges.

"Unhealthy growth". Morten Rostrup, president of the International Council, conducted an internal evaluation in 2002 that suggested that MSF was becoming increasingly bureaucratic and less focused on the field. The evaluation concluded that MSF had fewer medical volunteers and was perceived to be spending more time and resources on lobbying and fund-raising. "We are growing older, fatter, and more bureaucratic," Rostrup said. "We are increasingly uncoordinated, and each section plans according to its national interests and priorities rather than with any common international vision. Many partner sections have staffs that outnumber the operational sections in the 1980s, and yet they have no operational activities."

The growth in office positions, particularly in partner sections, was not balanced by a corresponding growth in field activities. From 1999 to 2001, office staff increased by 21 percent (and 53 percent in partner sections), operational costs increased by 19 percent, the number of field positions increased by only 5 percent, and the number of volunteer departures decreased by 9 percent. (See **Exhibit 7** for trends in staff and volunteer departures.) Although the activity of "bearing witness" was part of MSF's core mission, some questioned whether MSF was turning into a lobbying organization, and others believed it needed to define the difference between lobbying activities and bearing witness.

MSF was also seeing an increase in the number of coordination positions in the field relative to the number of medical and project volunteers. The results of this trend were that the humanitarian medical work was increasingly being performed by local staff members, whereas two-thirds of the international volunteers were in coordination roles, and distanced from MSF's beneficiaries in the field. In addition, Rostrup noted that, over the previous five years, the proportion of doctors working within MSF had decreased dramatically, to the extent that the medical identity of MSF was threatened. By 2002, only an estimated 17 percent of international volunteers going to the field were medical doctors.

Many of the larger partner sections wished to play a more significant role in field operations, although it was unclear whether this would increase operational capacity or further exacerbate the growth in the number of section staff. There was also controversy about the opening up of new partner sections. Since 1997, MSF had established a moratorium on new sections, and many believed this should be maintained until the organization had clarified a common strategy, brand, and international governance structure. De Torrenté shared that view. "We already have five MSF field operations in Angola and don't want to add any more," he said. "At the same time we need to enable the partner sections to play a more significant role in managing field projects."

Rostrup believed that in the coming decade, new sections would emerge in countries throughout South America, bringing a new dimension to the organization. At the same time, he thought it possible that certain sections could be merged in Europe; for example, MSF Sweden, MSF Denmark, and MSF Norway could be combined into MSF

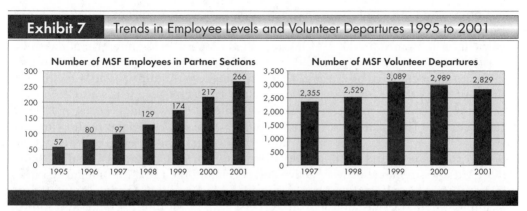

Exhibit 7   Trends in Employee Levels and Volunteer Departures 1995 to 2001

Source: Internal MSF documents.

Scandinavia. In addition, in 2002, all operating centers were in Europe, and many believed this needed to change. MSF was looking into new potential organizational structures that would permit it to grow while maintaining its culture and field focus. Oberreit added, "We need to find a way to share operational activities in a new and unconventional way. What we don't want is to centralize decision making."

In his September 26, 2002, memo, Rostrup urged the section boards to consider the following issues:

- a plan to leverage synergies among sections

- how to integrate or prioritize the concepts of social mission, bearing witness, and advocacy

- an office staff hiring freeze

- how operational sections could share operational activities with large partner sections

- how to increase international volunteers in core field positions (noncoordinator roles)

- how to "re-medicalize" the organization

New areas of medical need. Although refugees remained an important focus for MSF in 2002, the organization increasingly faced additional challenges, including the reemergence of sleeping sickness and tuberculosis, the ongoing challenge of AIDS, the lack of access to health care for excluded populations, and failing health systems in countries of the former Soviet Union. In addition, MSF and other aid organizations were facing increasing threats to the safety of their volunteers in the face of warring parties that neither recognized the neutrality of nor protected humanitarian aid workers. De Torrenté expanded on the problem: "The upsurge in these infectious diseases is actually linked to the breakdown of public health systems in countries thanks to civil war and other conflicts. Our programs have adapted accordingly and we stay in the field longer to address baseline problems. The question now is, How can we have the biggest impact moving forward?"

Competition. In 1979, Kouchner left MSF to found Médecins du Monde, or Doctors of the World (MdM), which grew to become MSF's most direct competition, particularly in France. In 2002, MdM described themselves as an international solidarity organization providing health care and bearing witness with the following mission statement: "Fighting against all illnesses—even injustice." MdM was composed of twelve delegations worldwide, and sent 1,200 field volunteers into 297 projects in eighty-eight countries, supported by a budget of 80 million euros in 1999[3]. (See **Exhibit 8** for a comparison of MSF and MdM.) MdM provided health care to victims of natural disasters, warfare, and political repression; refugees; street children; drug addicts; and those excluded from health care. Although smaller than MSF, MdM was nonetheless very active and vocal, and the use of the similar names, in both French and English, caused considerable brand confusion. In 1999, for example, when MSF was awarded the Nobel Peace Prize, funds flowing into MdM increased substantially.

Exhibit 8	Comparison of MSF and MdM	
	Médecins Sans Frontières	**Médecins du Monde**
2001 budget (millions of euros)	340	80 (1999)
% Private funding	80%	68%
Number of countries in network	18	12
Countries of operation	80+	88
Number of international volunteers	2,800	1,200
Logo	Running person on red and white background	Blue circle with a white bird holding a leaf and the organization's brand name (both in French and English)
Mission statement	Providing medical aid wherever needed regardless of race, religion, politics or sex, and raising the awareness of the plight of the people we help.	Fighting against all illnesses even injustice
Focus in 2002	Access to Essential Medicines Campaign	AIDS/ HIV and medical assistance for illegal immigrants

Source: Web sites and interviews.

INTERNATIONAL BRANDING.

Brand History.

Until 1992, MSF France had used the brand name Médecins Sans Frontières and had adopted, as its logo, the symbol of a white cross on a jagged red background. (See **Exhibit 8** for the original MSF logo.) As other sections came on board, they generally adopted the same logo but often translated the brand name into their local language, sometimes using a combination of the Médecins Sans Frontières brand and the local translation. (See **Exhibit 9** for a summary of different MSF brands and logos.) In addition, the Médecins Sans Frontières brand was often translated into the languages of the countries in which MSF operated, resulting in a proliferation of brand names. Staff members and volunteers worldwide referred to the organization by its three-letter initialism, MSF (as did many supporters), but the initialism was not part of the logo or the brand.

In 1992, the Red Cross threatened MSF with legal action, charging that the use of the white cross on a red background was too similar to its logo of a red cross on a white background, thus causing confusion. "In addition," Oberreit commented, "the cross was not a particularly appreciated symbol in many Islamic countries, and we were quite willing to look for a new one." MSF set about creating a new logo, and took the opportunity to define some broad guidelines for the entire organization about logo and brand name usage. (See **Exhibit 10** for the 1994 logotype field rules.) Selected as the new logo was a running figure on a jagged red background. Translations of the

Exhibit 9   Summary of Different MSF Brands and Logos in 1992

Médecins Sans Frontières

- Médecins Sans Frontières
- Doctors Without Borders
- Ärzte Ohne Grenzen
- Artsen Zonder Grenzen
- Læger Uden Grænser
- Medici Senza Frontiere
- Leger Uten Grenser
- Medicos Sin Frontieras
- Läkare Utan Gränser

- (France, Belgium, Switzerland)
- (USA, Australia, Canada, UK)
- (Austria, Germany, Switzerland)
- (Belgium, Holland)
- (Denmark)
- (Italy)
- (Norway)
- (Spain)
- (Sweden)

MEDECINS
SANS FRONTIERES

Affiliation in 1985

Affiliation in 1989

Affiliation in 1990

Source: MSF France.

brand name, however, continued to be accepted as long as they were used alongside the internationally accepted name Médecins Sans Frontières—MSF.

By 1998, MSF used several different local names in different section countries and many different working titles in the field. International NGOs and the UN knew the organization as Médecins Sans Frontières, and volunteers and staff members referred to the organization as MSF. With the increase in cross-border and global media, such as CNN, and the rise in direct transmissions from disaster zones, which made editing of subtitle local names or reediting commentaries impossible, the range of names MSF used was leading to brand confusion among media, donors, and recipients. In

Exhibit 10 | 1994 Logotype Field and Section Rules

RÈGLES POUR LE TERRAIN

Le Conseil International a décidé, en avril 1994, de saisir l'opportunité d'un nouveau logotype pour promouvoir au maximum le nom de l'organisation «MÉDECINS SANS FRONTIÈRES».

In April 1994, the International Council decided to take the opportunity of promoting the name of "MÉDECINS SANS FRONTIÈRES" to a maximum when introducing the new logotype.

FIELD RULES

1 - Pour toutes les sections exceptée MSF Espagne, le sigle avec MÉDECINS SANS FRONTIÈRES (en français), pour les stickers, les tee-shirts, le papier entête, etc.

1 - For all sections except MSF Spain, the logotype with the text "MÉDECINS SANS FRONTIÈRES" (in French) for stickers, T-shirts, headed notepaper, etc.

2 - Pour MSF Espagne, le sigle avec MEDICOS SIN FRONTERAS.

2 - For MSF Spain the text should read "MEDICOS SIN FRONTERAS".

EXCEPTIONS
EXCEPTIONS

3 - EXCEPTIONS aux points 1 et 2 Sigle + MÉDECINS SANS FRONTIÈRES et la traduction locale (si possible dans le même caractère) pour des raisons de reconnaissance et compréhension.

3 - Exceptions to points 1 and 2 Graphic element + MÉDECINS SANS FRONTIÈRES and the local translation (if possible in the same font) for reasons of recognition and comprehension.

Source: MSF France.

Exhibit 10   continued

RÈGLES POUR LES DELEGATE OFFICES

Le Conseil International a décidé, en avril 1994, de saisir l'opportunité d'un nouveau logotype pour promouvoir au maximum le nom de l'organisation «MÉDECINS SANS FRONTIÈRES».

In April 1994, the International Council decided to take the opportunity of promoting the name of "MÉDECINS SANS FRONTIÈRES" to a maximum when introducing the new logotype.

DELEGATE OFFICE RULES

1 - USAGE COURANT
Le sigle avec :
- MÉDECINS SANS FRONTIÈRES
en français + en dessous,
- MÉDECINS SANS FRONTIÈRES
dans la langue locale et de la même
taille (idem exemples ci-contre).

1 - Normal usage
The text reads :
-"MÉDECINS SANS FRONTIÈRES"
in French + underneath
- "MÉDECINS SANS FRONTIÈRES"
in the local language in the same size
characters (see example on the right).

2 - Mailings grand public :
soit idem usage courant (cf. point n°1),
soit le nom dans la langue locale
seule.

2 - Mailings to the general public :
either the same as usual (cf. point1),
or the name in the local language only.

Source: MSF France.

addition, MSF competed in an increasingly tough environment for scarce resources, because of the proliferation of NGOs vying for funds. Leveraging a single international brand name would greatly increase MSF's ability to build awareness and reputation among the donors and access those funds.

Developing an International Brand.

Oberreit believed a strong brand was critical to MSF for four reasons: First, it enabled the organization to be a credible witness for human rights abuses; second, it enhanced the organization's ability to raise funds for its work; third, it ensured the safety of volunteers in the field; and fourth, it provided a backbone for organizational continuity and culture in an organization where most people stayed only a few years.

MSF started working in early 1999 with Bill Marlow, an international brand-name consultant who worked pro bono, to define the parameters of the international branding challenge and propose solutions. The initial analysis concluded the following:

- The key message the brand needed to deliver included the medical nature of the work, the focus on crisis situations, the fact that MSF bore witness and spoke out, and the fact that MSF was independent of politics and religion and was international.

- Major audience groups were defined as donors in the eighteen section countries, potential medical volunteers, international NGO and UN partners, and current staff and volunteers in both section countries and the field.

- The role of communications was seen as (1) speaking out against inhumanity, to bear witness—to name and shame; (2) recruiting more donors and volunteers; and (3) providing donors with evidence of effective work in the field.

- Three media conduits were identified: electronic and print media in individual countries; regional cross-border electronic and print media; and international electronic and print media, which reported and placed material worldwide.

Marlow recommended including the MSF initialism as a central component of the new international brand and developing a logo that would "not just be a running figure, but a figure working for relief crisis victims and speaking out against inhumanity." He suggested maintaining a full brand, for concept and fieldwork, and an international brand when time and space permitted only the essence to be communicated. The full brand would have three components: the MSF initialism, the new logo, and the words "Médecins Sans Frontières." The international brand, however, would have only two components: the MSF initialism and the new logo.

In January 1999, Erwin Van't Land, director of communications for MSF Australia, commented on his brand challenge as follows:

> The French and English names of Médecins Sans Frontières and Doctors Without Borders are known at equal levels in Australia. This can be quite confusing, and since we are in the process of rapidly broadening our audience, we

have to actively promote only one brand name. Last year we campaigned with our French name in a TV ad titled "MSF—what does it stand for?" This year we will step up our efforts to make MSF/Médecins Sans Frontières a household brand. I don't think we need to work with the English translation of the brand, and I anticipate that over a two- to three-year period, we can introduce MSF to most Australians and convey what we are about. The full meaning of "Médecins Sans Frontières" gets lost in translation anyway.

In February 1999, an MSF international working party, made up of representatives from the United States, Germany, Spain, France, and the United Kingdom met to discuss the issue of international branding and concluded that "A single international identity is essential. The problem is shared, serious and ongoing, but ... the solution must be flexible in application." The representatives from Germany, the United States, Spain, and the United Kingdom all agreed that the "double naming" of the organization led to confusion and that it was particularly confusing in the United States and the United Kingdom, where the international media were strong. In addition, for multilanguage countries such as Switzerland and Belgium, different language groups recognized the organization under different names. For example, a brand awareness study in Austria in January 2001 found that 49 percent of the 1,000 people interviewed recognized the brand name Arzte Ohne Grenzen, 18 percent recognized the brand Médecins Sans Frontières, and only 5 percent recognized the initialism MSF. Of those who recognized the Arzte Ohne Grenzen brand, 25 percent also knew that the organization was called Médecins Sans Frontières and 8 percent also knew the organization as MSF.

Although the group concluded that the MSF initialism was the core to a solution, and that the initialism could be used as a prefix to local country names, a large number of issues were still outstanding. The group was particularly concerned that the full identity Médecins Sans Frontières might be diminished by the strength of the initialism and that the initialism might not work in countries where Latin script was not used (China and Russia, for example). Oberreit explained his resistance to the use of the initialism: "The name Médecins Sans Frontières captures two essential elements of the organization: first, the medical nature of our activity; and second, the lack of borders and lack of discrimination in conducting our work. The acronym cannot capture the essence of the organization in the same way."

Over the next year, the group met several times to refine the international brand and propose recommendations. Some at MSF believed that the initialism should never stand on its own and should always be accompanied by the Médecins Sans Frontières name, with or without local language translations. Others believed that the U.S. market would never accept a French brand name and that the organization should be known as MSF Doctors Without Borders. Still others believed that use of the initialism alone was the best way forward. "Part of the problem," Oberreit explained, "is that, in France, the brand is a household name and we are the leading NGO. As early as 1990, we found that in France we had 93 percent spontaneous recognition of the Médecins Sans Frontières brand. In other countries, such as the United States and Japan, the brand is still being built and establishing a foothold."

In November 1999, the International Council, based on Marlow's input and a presentation by the international working party, ruled on the international brand name as follows:

- The brand name is "Médecins Sans Frontières—MSF." Translations are not brand names and cannot appear without the brand name.

- The visual logo will remain the running person with the letters "MSF" written slightly below the left foot. Below this "Médecins Sans Frontières" will always appear. If, and only if, translation is required, it will appear below a line that underlines the written "Médecins Sans Frontières." (See **Exhibit 11** for an illustration of the proposed new logo.)

- In press releases we will use "Médecins Sans Frontières/MSF" and "MSF" may be used in the text. If a translation is required in press releases, we will use "Médecins Sans Frontières/local translation/MSF" with the organization being referred to as MSF in the text.

- No other initialism may be used and the "MSF" initialism may not be used alone but only with the full name.

During 2000, an international brand guidebook was developed, and internal communications managers worked internally to achieve buy-in for the above branding guidelines. It was agreed that a two-year maximum adaptation period was necessary to persuade all sections and field operations to come on board.

In 2002, de Torrenté expanded on the situation in the United States: "When we first established MSF in the United States, we used the Doctors Without Borders name because it was felt that the French name would never be accepted. Now we use Médecins Sans Frontières, Doctors Without Borders, and MSF. In the NGO world we are known as Médecins Sans Frontières, but the general public still really only knows us as Doctors Without Borders." Kris Torgeson, director of communications for MSF

Exhibit 11 Illustration of Proposed New Logo, 1999

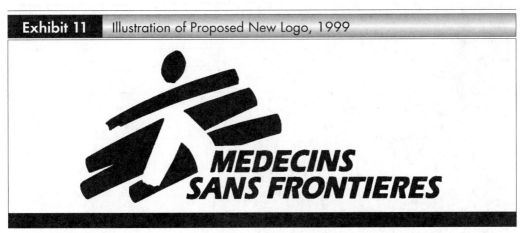

Source: MSF France.

USA, said, "Médecins Sans Frontières is an international brand in a world in which most people don't speak French. For most of us, the local translation of the name has become a brand in our countries, and an increasing number of people in the United States have identified with Doctors Without Borders." (See **Exhibit 12** for a copy of part of an MSF USA direct mail piece.)

Exhibit 12	Excerpts from MSF USA and MSF France Direct Mail Fliers, 2002

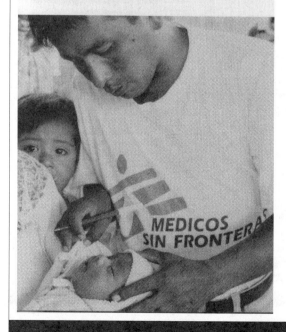

YOUR SUPPORT
SAVES LIVES

**I WANT TO HELP
DOCTORS WITHOUT BORDERS
BRING MEDICAL AND
HUMANITARIAN RELIEF
AROUND THE WORLD:**

NAME

TITLE

COMPANY

ADDRESS

CITY   STATE   ZIP

TELEPHONE

EMAIL

I AM MAKING A TAX-DEDUCTIBLE CONTRIBUTION OF:

○ $35   ○ $75   ○ $100
○ $250   ○ $500   ○ Other

PLEASE BILL MY:

○ Amex   ○ Visa   ○ MC

ACCOUNT #

EXP. DATE

NAME (as it appears on card)

SIGNATURE   DATE

To make a secure online donation:
www.doctorswithoutborders.org

○ Please add my name to the Doctors Without Borders
   mailing list.
○ Please inform me of public education activities
   in my area.
○ Please send me information about volunteering with
   Doctors Without Borders. I am a:
         ○ PHYSICIAN
         ○ NURSE / MIDWIFE
         ○ PUBLIC HEALTH SPECIALIST
         ○ LOGISTICIAN / ENGINEER
         ○ FINANCIAL CONTROLLER
         ○ OTHER _____

Source: MSF USA and MSF France.

Exhibit 12   continued

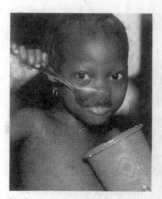

AVEC 1 FRANC PAR JOUR...

Un franc, ce n'est rien. Pour un enfant qui souffre de la faim, c'est le prix de la vie. L'exemple de nos programmes de nutrition est particulièrement éloquent : Un franc, c'est le prix d'un repas dans un centre de nutrition médicalisée. Un franc, c'est aussi le prix d'un vaccin qui protègera un enfant pendant trois ans d'une maladie mortelle, la méningite. En participant à l'Opération «1 Franc par Jour», vous nous permettez d'agir au quotidien, mais aussi d'anticiper les catastrophes majeures grâce à un apport de fonds régulier. Au-delà de la première phase d'intervention, votre soutien nous permet en outre de poursuivre notre aide aussi longtemps qu'elle est nécessaire.

LE PLUS PETIT DES DONS, LE PLUS PRECIEUX DES SECOURS

Donner un franc par jour à Médecins Sans Frontières, c'est à la fois simple, peu contraignant et très efficace : il vous suffit de remplir le formulaire ci-dessous. Chaque mois, le versement direct de votre soutien se fera automatiquement, ce qui réduit considérablement les frais de gestion et nous permet de consacrer une part encore plus grande de nos ressources aux actions de terrain. Enfin, vous pouvez suspendre cet engagement à tout moment : il vous suffit de nous le signaler par simple courrier. N'attendez pas ! Dès aujourd'hui, rejoignez tous ceux qui sont jour après jour engagés contre la souffrance et la maladie. Sur le terrain, votre franc quotidien fait la différence ! ∎

A retourner à Médecins Sans Frontières - 60644 Chantilly Cedex

❏ oui, je veux faire un geste quotidien et je donne **1 franc par jour** à Médecins Sans Frontières (30 F par mois) je préfère donner :   ❏ 2 francs par jour (60 F par mois)   ❏ 3 francs par jour (90 F par mois)
❏ .... francs par mois (autre montant à votre convenance)

❏ je participe déjà à l'opération **"1 Franc par Jour"**, et je souhaite augmenter mon soutien en donnant .... F par mois

Accord de don direct en faveur de Médecins Sans Frontières

Association reconnue d'utilité publique - 8, rue St Sabin - 75544 Paris cedex 11 - Numéro national d'émetteur : 193 046

Nom/ Prénom :	Nom et adresse de l'établissement teneur de votre compte
N° : .... Rue	Nom :
	N° : .... Rue
Code Postal :	
Ville :	Code Postal : .... Ville :

J'autorise l'établissement teneur de mon compte à prélever, directement à partir de ce dernier, mon don mensuel à MÉDECINS SANS FRONTIERES.
Je pourrai suspendre cet accord à tout moment.

N'OUBLIEZ, SURTOUT PAS DE NOUS ADRESSER AVEC CE DOCUMENT UN RELEVÉ D'IDENTITÉ BANCAIRE (RIB) QUE VOUS TROUVEREZ DANS VOTRE CHÉQUIER OU SUR VOS RELEVÉS DE COMPTE.

Désignation de votre compte

Code établissement	Code guichet	N° de compte	Clé RIB

Fait à : ....
le : ....

Signature :
(obligatoire)

Source: MSF USA and MSF France.

In MSF Switzerland in October 2002, Kurt Tonini, head of communications, confessed that he thought the international branding process was still ongoing. "I didn't realize there were any guidelines," he said. "We use both the French and German names, but we never use the acronym. We believe it would be impossible to remove the German translation even though we know that some people think they represent two different organizations."

Martyn Broughton, communications director in the United Kingdom, was one of the few people at MSF who had been involved in the original international branding effort. He commented on the progress made between 2000 and 2002:

> *Everything came to a halt. There was an attempt to implement the decisions made by the International Council in 2000, but this never happened. The international organization is just not strong enough, and there is no will to establish central governance on these kinds of issues. There is also a broader context to this situation. In the late nineties, there was an attempt by the organization to build shared field coordination teams and shared logistics, but many of these attempts failed, resulting in some bad blood among the different country sections. Even today, the effects of the turf battles, severe personality clashes, and political and cultural differences among sections in the late 1990s continue to divide our organization. Because the individual country sections are so strong and have an antagonistic history toward one another, any international decision that is even slightly controversial is impossible to implement. The USA is probably the only section that has made a serious effort to implement the recommendations. Although some progress has been made to limit brand confusion in the press, we still see media articles in which Médecins Sans Frontières and Doctors Without Borders are both mentioned as if they were separate organizations. In the U.K., we are moving towards using the acronym MSF (which we were unable to do until recently, following the merger and renaming of a trade union, which used the MSF acronym).*

Trademark Protection.

The phenomenal success of the Médecins Sans Frontières brand had sparked the development of scores of organizations that included the term "Sans Frontières" (Without Borders) in their names. A telephone survey found that 34 percent of people interviewed in France confused Médecins Sans Frontières to be affiliated with at least one other Sans Frontières organization. (See **Exhibit 13** for a summary of the study on brand confusion.) Those organizations with a medical and/or humanitarian mission were particularly likely to be mistaken for Médecins Sans Frontières. In addition, a majority of people interviewed believed that these organizations were in some way connected to or affiliated with MSF, which was not the case. For example, 51 percent of those surveyed believed Pharmaciens (pharmacists) Sans Frontières was connected to Médecins Sans Frontières, 46 percent thought Dentistes (dentists) Sans Frontières was, and 41 percent thought Enfants (children) Sans Frontières was connected to Médecins Sans Frontières. The same study showed that brand confusion was greater among younger people, lower-income groups, and those with less formal education. "Our problem," Oberreit said, "is the hyper-success of our brand!"

In 2002, trademark protection activities were centralized at the International Office, where alerting systems were in place to supervise the registration of new organizations whose activities were related to MSF, and that carried in their name

Exhibit 13	Summary of 2001 French Study on Brand Confusion

Do you think that the following organizations are part of Médecins Sans Frontières?

	YES	NO	UNSURE
Pharmaciens (pharmacists) Sans Frontières	51%	32%	17%
Dentistes (dentists) Sans Frontières	46%	36%	18%
Enfants (children) Sans Frontières	41%	40%	19%
Pompiers (firemen) Sans Frontières	34%	51%	15%
Reporters (reporters) Sans Frontières	31%	55%	14%
Vétérinaires (vets) Sans Frontières	27%	54%	19%
Avocats (lawyers) Sans Frontières	21%	60%	19%
Banques (banks) Sans Frontières	17%	65%	18%
Average Brand Confusion	**34%**	**49%**	**17%**

Source: Telephone survey conducted in France with more than 1,000 people on MSF brand confusion.

Note: The organizations in the table all exist but are not part of MSF in any way.

Sans Frontières, MSF, Without Borders, Ohne Grenzen, Zonder Grenzen, and so on. The policy was to challenge all "MSF" registrations and all "Sans Frontières" organizations that were involved in activities similar to those of MSF (development, health, and humanitarian aid).

MSF was somewhat cautious in its approach because it did not want to be seen as "attacking" other charities and risk earning a bad reputation among other NGOs, particularly in France and the United States. However, MSF also realized the importance of protecting the brand consistently around the world. In most cases, it chose to send the "Sans Frontières" organization a "cease and desist" letter with the message that the case could go to litigation if the organization was uncooperative. Many organizations also agreed to sign an agreement in which MSF authorized the use of "Sans Frontières" for specified purposes, although this did not reduce brand confusion. Another approach was to ask "Sans Frontières" organizations to include a disclaimer in all their communications. In 2001, twenty-eight lawsuits were filed against organizations on this basis, twenty-five of which were in France. Schakal, the EU liaison coordinator and trademark policy adviser at the international office, explained that MSF divided its challenges into three categories:

1. For an organization starting with "M" Sans Frontières (musique sans frontières or musulmans sans frontières, for example), immediate action was initiated against the registration of the brand because of the confusion surrounding a potentially shared initialism.

2. For an organization active in the medical arena, MSF attempted to negotiate agreements to limit their activities.

3. For other "Sans Frontières" organizations, the extent of opposition depended on the role and presence of these organizations in the countries where MSF had active field projects.

In early March 2002, MSF launched an opposition against Pompiers Sans Frontières—PoSF (Firemen Without Borders). The INPI (French National Institute for Intellectual Property) recognized MSF's rights over the term "SF," given the medical humanitarian assistance that PoSF wished to provide worldwide (ambulance and medical assistance, fire help and prevention, primary health care, medical and first aid training, and donation of medical kits). PoSF refused, however, to withdraw its name and appealed the INPI decision, arguing that

- Sans Frontières was not a distinctive name and had in fact become generic,

- the services they provided were different from MSF's and they did not focus on emergencies, and

- other SF organizations already existed whose activities included medical assistance.

Schakal believed the results of this case would be critical for the future of the MSF brand. "If PoSF wins," he explained, "it will compromise the rights we have on 'Sans Frontières.' If we win, however, no one can deny the rights we have on the term 'Sans Frontières' within the scope of our activities."

CONCLUSION.

As the communications directors gathered to review the international branding recommendations the International Council had made nearly two years previously, many believed that brand confusion continued to be a key issue. Many countries continued to use local translations of the brand, and although the initialism MSF was now being used by some sections, many of the communications directors wondered if it was not an additional element of confusion for the brand.

Rostrup believed that the difficulty in gaining closure on the branding issue was reflective of deeper tensions and struggles within the organization. He wondered if addressing these might pave the way for a resolution on branding.

Notes to Case

[1] This section is based on "The Médecins Sans Frontières Experience" by Rony Brauman and Joelle Tanguy, 1998.

[2] This section is based on the MSF USA Web site, 2002.

[3] Based on MdM Web site.